IN CAMP AND BATTLE WITH THE
WASHINGTON ARTILLERY
OF NEW ORLEANS

IN CAMP AND BATTLE WITH THE WASHINGTON ARTILLERY OF NEW ORLEANS

WILLIAM MILLER OWEN

With a New Introduction by
Nathaniel Cheairs Hughes, Jr.

LOUISIANA STATE UNIVERSITY PRESS

Baton Rouge

Originally published in 1885 by Ticknor and Company, Boston
New material copyright © 1999 by Louisiana State University Press
All rights reserved
Manufactured in the United States of America

Louisiana Paperback Edition, 1999
08 07 06 05 04 03 02 01 00 99
5 4 3 2 1

Library of Congress Cataloging-in-Publication Data

Owen, William Miller, 1832–1893.
    In camp and battle with the Washington artillery of New Orleans /
William Miller Owen ; with a new introduction by Nathaniel Cheairs
Hughes, Jr. — Louisiana pbk. ed.
        p. cm.
    Originally published : Boston : Ticknor, 1885.
    Includes bibliographical references and index.
    ISBN 0-8071-2385-4 (pbk . : alk. paper)
    1. Confederate States of America. Army. Washington Artillery
Battalion (New Orleans, La.) 2. New Orleans (La.) History—Civil
War, 1861–1865—Regimental histories. 3. United States—History—
Civil War, 1861–1865—Regimental histories. 4. New Orleans (La.)—
History—Civil War, 1861–1865—Artillery operations. 5. United
States—History—Civil War, 1861–1865—Artillery operations,
Confederate. 6. Owen, William Miller, 1832–1893. 7. New Orleans
(La.)—History—Civil War, 1861–1865—Personal narratives.
8. United States—History—Civil War, 1861–1865—Personal
narratives, Confederate. 9. Soldiers—Louisiana—New Orleans—
Biography. I. Title.
E565.7 W2 1999
973.7'463—dc21   98-55142
                                                                 CIP

The paper in this book meets the guidelines for permanence and durability of
the Committee on Production Guidelines for Book Longevity of the Council on
Library Resources. ∞

To

MY COMRADES

OF THE

"BATTALION WASHINGTON ARTILLERY"
OF NEW ORLEANS,

IN ADMIRATION OF THEIR
GALLANTRY AND DEVOTION TO PRINCIPLE,
AS EXHIBITED UPON SO MANY BATTLE-FIELDS IN THE LATE

CIVIL WAR,

THIS VOLUME IS DEDICATED.

CONTENTS.

INTRODUCTION BY NATHANIEL CHEAIRS HUGHES, JR. xv

PREFACE xxi

CHAPTER I.

EARLY HISTORY OF THE WASHINGTON ARTILLERY.

The Washington Artillery before the War. — Its Organization. — War
Clouds, 1861. — Expedition to Baton Rouge. — Seizure of U.S. Ar-
senal. — Services of Battalion Offered to Confederate Government.
— Accepted for the War. — Mustering in. — Ordered to Virginia. —
Departure from New Orleans. — Lynchburg. — Richmond. — Camp
Beauregard. — Manassas. — Camp Louisiana. — Head-quarters. —
Personelle. — Our French Cooks, and Cooks in general   1

CHAPTER II.

ADDRESS TO THE ARMY.

Enemy on the March. — Camp Broken Up. — McLean's Ford. —
Union Mills. — Rebel Girl. — Engagement at Blackburn's Ford,
July 18. — Our Armament. — Battle of Manassas. — Bee, Bartow,
Hampton, and Bob Wheat. — "Stonewall Jackson." — Hard Tack
and Sherry. — Beauregard and Johnston. — Griffin's and Rickett's
Batteries. — Defeat of the Enemy. — President Davis. — Appearance
of a Battle-field. — Official Reports 24

CHAPTER III.

BACK IN CAMP.

Back in Camp. — Retrospection. — Bountiful Larder. — New Friends.
— Appointments and Promotions. — Our Camps. — Camp Ben-
jamin. — President Davis Reviews the Army. — Centreville. —
Quaker Guns. — New Tents. — New Battle-flags Distributed. —

Battle at Ball's Bluff. — " Chasseurs-à-pied." — " Here's Your Mule." — " Bolivar Ward." — Col. P. T. Moore. — Major Bob Wheat. — Col. Harry Hays. — " Noctes Ambrosia." — " Little White House on Salisbury Plains." — Winter Quarters. — Waltonville . . .·. . . .   48

CHAPTER IV.

JANUARY, 1862.

Contributions to Charleston Sufferers. — Mardi Gras in Camp. — Dixie Artillery and Chasseurs-à-pied. — The " Waltonville War Cry." — Snow-balling. — Beauregard Ordered South. — Attached to Long-street's Division. — Winter Quarters Abandoned. — On the March. — Orange Court-house. — Dancing Club. — Richmond. — Peninsula. — Williamsburg. — Yorktown. — Richmond. — Camp at Blakey's Mill-pond. — McClellan Investing the City   70

CHAPTER V.

FIGHTING NEAR RICHMOND.

Seven Pines. — Fair Oaks. — Dr. Garnett's. — Gen. R. E. Lee. — Gen. Johnston Wounded. — Seven Days' Battle around Richmond. — Siege of Richmond Raised. — " Change of Base." — McClellan at Harrison's Landing. — Flag of Truce. — Exchange of Prisoners at Aiken's Landing   82

CHAPTER VI.

RAPPAHANNOCK STATION AND MANASSAS.

Gordonsville. — Gen. John Pope. — March from Gordonsville. — Distribution of Batteries. — Spy Hanged. — Engagement at Rappa-hannock Station. — Enemy Moving. — Jackson in Rear of Pope. — Salem. — White Plains. — Narrow Escape of Gen. Lee. — Thorough-fare Gap. — Enemy in Possession. — Gen. Longstreet. — Advance of Longstreet's Corps to Haymarket. — Gen. J. E. B. Stuart. — Jackson Fighting. — Artillery in Position. — Second Battle at Manassas. — Chantilly. — Gen. Phil Kearney Killed. — On to Maryland. — Ford the Potomac   99

CHAPTER VII.

"MARYLAND, MY MARYLAND."

Explosion of Ammunition. — Boonesboro'. — Hagerstown. — Dr. Maguire. — Jackson to Harper's Ferry. — D. H. Hill at Boonesboro'. — Sharpsburg. — Lost Order of Gen. Lee. — Washington Artillery again in Battle. — Longstreet and Staff as Gunners 130

CHAPTER VIII.

ANTIETAM.

Left Attack. — Burnside's Bridge. — A Ride for Gen. Lee. — Attack of Enemy. — Squires, Richardson, and Eshleman Engaged. — D. R. Jones's Division Pressed Back. — Arrival of A. P. Hill. — Gardon's and Riley's Batteries Engaged. — Defeat of Enemy. — Meeting of Generals. — Lee Dubs Longstreet his "Old War-Horse." — Quiet Day after the Battle. — Army Crosses the Potomac. — Enemy Follows. — Is Beaten Back. — March to Martinsburg. — Forces Engaged. — Address of Lee to the Army 150

CHAPTER IX.

FREDERICKSBURG.

Martinsburg. — Culpeper. — March to Fredericksburg. — Alarm Guns. — Boots and Saddles. — City Bombarded. — Enemy Crosses the Rappahannock. — Attack on Marye's Hill. — Great Battle Fought. — Enemy Beaten. — He Recrosses the River. — Winter Quarters 168

CHAPTER X.

CHANCELLORSVILLE.

Contribution to Fredericksburg. — On Recruiting Service. — "Battle House," Mobile. — Manassas Club. — Admiral Buchanan's Ball. — Confederate Guards. — New Orleans Refugees. — Lieutenant E. Owen. — Montgomery. — News from Camp. — Theatricals. — Back to Old Virginia. — Enemy Moving. — Chancellorsville. — General

Jo. Hooker. — Sedgwick at Fredericksburg. — Barksdale's Brigade. — Early's Division. — Hays's Brigade. — Washington Artillery on Marye's Hill. — Flag of Truce. — Enemy Attack. — Guns Lost. — Hooker Defeated. — Diary of a Captured Officer 200

CHAPTER XI.

ĠETTYSBURG.

Army in Motion. — Culpeper. — Stuart's Cavalry Review. — Death of Pelham. — Chester Gap. — Ewell in Winchester. — Defeat of Milroy. — Fording the Potomac. — Lee's Orders. — Chambersburg. — Gettysburg. — Gen. Reynolds Killed. — Lee on Seminary Hill. — Col. Fremantle. — Capt. Ross. — Gen. Barksdale Killed. — Hood Wounded. — Grand Cannonade. — Pickett's Charge. — Retreat. — Williamsport. — Pettigrew Killed. — Crossing the Potomac 231

CHAPTER XII.

CHICKAMAUGA. — INDIAN, A "STREAM OF DEATH."

Wm. Preston Johnston. — General Longstreet. — Richmond. — Promotion. — S. W. Virginia. — Abingdon. — Gen. William Preston. — Knoxville. — March through Georgia. — McLemore's Cove. — Dug Gap. — Gen. Bragg. — Gen. Breckenridge. — Fifth Company Washington Artillery. — Gen. Gracie. — Gen. Polk. — Battle of Chickamauga. — Gen. Wm. H. Lytle Killed. — Preston's Charge up Missionary Ridge. — Rosecrans in Chattanooga. — President Davis 263

CHAPTER XIII.

EAST TENNESSEE AND DREWRY'S BLUFF.

Charleston. — Wilmington. — Richmond. — *En Route* to East Tennessee. — Lynchburg. — Longstreet at Knoxville. — Dublin. — Gen. Sam Jones. — My Birthday duly Celebrated. — Richmond. — Dinner at the Oriental. — East Tennessee again. — Report to Gen. Longstreet. — Assigned to Command a Battalion of Artillery. — Winter Campaign. — Return to Virginia. — Assigned to Duty with Washington Artillery at Petersburg. — Battle of Drewry's Bluff. — Butler Bottled. — President Davis on the Field. — Gen. Beauregard in Command. — Gen. Heckman Captured. — Belger's Battery Captured. — Flag of Truce. — Col. Otis, Tenth Connecticut. — Petersburg 294

CHAPTER XIV.

GRANT IN FRONT OF RICHMOND.

Washington Artillery on the Chickahominy. — Assault at Cold Harbor. — Grant Marches to James River. — Petersburg. — The Siege. — Forts Hell and Damnation. — Shelling the City. — Citizens in Bomb-proofs. — Capt. Dunn. — "*Dum vivimus, vivamus.*" — Gen. Alexander. — — Fourth of July. — Col. Walton's Resignation. — Explosion of the Mine. — Negro Troops. — Gibbs's Battalion of Artillery. — Flag of Truce 327

CHAPTER XV.

IN THE TRENCHES AT PETERSBURG.

Enemy on a Raid. — On the March. — Ice and Snow. — Christmas Dinner. — Virginia Hospitality. — Gen. Pegram Killed. — Gen. J. B. Gordon — Louisiana Brigade. — Winter Quarters. — Hatcher's Run. — Short Rations. — Fasting and Prayer. — Sherman in Charleston. — Promotion. — Pickett at Five Forks. — Lines Broken. — Defence of Battery Gregg. — Petersburg Evacuated. — Gen. A. P. Hill Killed 358

CHAPTER XVI.

SURRENDER OF THE ARMY OF NORTHERN VIRGINIA.

On the Last Retreat. — Amelia Court-House. — Forty Hours without Food. — Pursued by Cavalry. — Wagons Burned. — Army Demoralized. — Fighting, Marching, Starving. — Organization giving Way. — Marching without Orders. — Appomattox. — Gordon Fighting. — Artillery Captured — Custer, Sheridan, and Longstreet. — A Game of "Brag" 374

CHAPTER XVII.

DISBANDMENT, AND HOME AGAIN.

Less than 8,000 Veterans with Lee. — Terms of Surrender. — Paroles. — Turning in our Batteries. — On to Mexico. — Lee's Farewell Address. — Dispersion of the Confederates. — On to Richmond. — General Halleck. — Sherman's Army. — Fortress Monroe and Baltimore. — "Barnum's Hotel." — "Maryland Club." — "New York Hotel." — Steamship "Monterey." — Bound for Home. — "Pelicans" Returning. — New Orleans. — Home Again 388

CHAPTER XVIII.

The Fifth Company Battalion Washington Artillery 399

CHAPTER XIX.

CONCLUSION.

The Washington Artillery after the War 425

ADDENDA.

Popular Camp Songs of the Washington Artillery. — Muster-Roll of the Washington Artillery from 1861 to 1865. — Memories of "Try Us." — Roll of Honor 433

INDEX 469

ILLUSTRATIONS.

                                                    Facing Page

CAMP LOUISIANA 50

THE ARTILLERY DUEL 104

FORMING LINE OF BATTLE; ARTILLERY AND SKIRMISHERS

    ENGAGED 276

TOUT PERDU 392

MAPS.

FIRST BATTLE OF MANASSAS, JULY 21, 1861 . . . 40

SECOND BATTLE OF MANASSAS, AUG. 29 AND 30, 1862 . 116

BATTLE OF ANTIETAM, SEPT. 17, 1862 142

BATTLE OF FREDERICKSBURG, DEC. 13, 1862 . . . 180

FEDERAL ATTACK ON MARYE'S HEIGHTS AT FREDERICKS-

    BURG, MAY 3, 1863 212

BATTLE OF GETTYSBURG, JULY 3, 1863 250

BATTLE OF DREWRY'S BLUFF, MAY 16, 1864 . . . 316

ENTRENCHED LINES AT PETERSBURG 330

INTRODUCTION.

NATHANIEL CHEAIRS HUGHES, JR.

WILLIAM MILLER OWEN was adjutant of the Battalion Washington Artillery of New Orleans. What an excellent vantage point he had for an author of unit history. He received the orders from superior authorities; he drafted the orders for the individual batteries; and he stayed close by the side of Major J. B. Walton, the battalion commander. Owen chatted with General Longstreet, he took rides with General Lee, and he dined with President Davis. He knew the officer corps of the Army of Northern Virginia.

In time Owen would command a battery himself; he would serve as chief of artillery and later as chief of staff for General William Preston in southwest Virginia and east Tennessee. He would move on to become chief of staff for Bushrod Johnson at Drewry's Bluff and, in the closing months of the war, would lead a battalion of Virginia artillery.

Owen and his beloved Washington Artillery fought with distinction from the beginning to the end. He was on the field at First Manassas, and he awaited Lee's return from the meeting with Grant at the McLean house, April 9, 1865, listening to the commander in chief explain, "I have done the best I could for you. My heart is too full to say more."[1] At Gettysburg, Owen heard Longstreet order Walton, his chief of artillery, to arrange the signal for the Confederate batteries to fire on the line of the First and Third Corps— 137 guns. Upon Walton's command they were to open simultaneously, preparing the way for the attack of Pickett's Division. At Antietam, Owen watched the Third Company's gunners being shot down until only enough men remained to serve one section. Longstreet and his staff appeared at this critical point. As Moxley Sorrel and his comrades worked the guns, Longstreet directed their fire in person, "and by example animated the soldiers near him"(157). The following day, in an open field back of Sharpsburg, Owen observed Longstreet ride up to a group including Lee, Jackson, Early, and the Hills. As Longstreet dismounted, Lee went to meet him, and "grasping him by the hand, said, 'Ah! here is Longstreet; here's my old *war-horse!*'"(157).

Thus major figures and major battles of the Army of Northern Virginia come alive, but Owen also allows the reader to experience the depressing, interminable

---

1. The quotation is on page 387, within. Subsequent references will be given in text by page number. Owen's account was first published in 1885 by Ticknor and Company, Boston. Subsequent reprintings came in 1964 by Pelican Publishing Company, New Orleans, which provided an introduction by Kenneth T. Urquhart, and in 1985 by R. Van Sickle, Gaitherburg.

months of the Petersburg siege, and the lesser known but sharp actions at Rappahannock Station and Drewry's Bluff.

Equally valuable are Owen's insights into secondary Confederate figures. Battery comrades Tom Rosser and James Dearing rise to become general officers in the cavalry. Owen fights beside William Barksdale and his Mississippians, he is in frequent contact with General David R. Jones, and he is drawn into close association with Generals William Preston and Archibald Gracie. Indeed, the death of his friend Gracie leaves Owen distraught.

Although Owen writes with balance and seriousness befitting his subject, his narrative is devoid of the bitter partisanship that so often mars reminiscences. As noted by Richard B. Harwell, the pages are "filled with local color, pertinent comments and observations," which explains why it has remained for over a century the "most read, most quoted account of Louisiana Confederate soldiers."[2] Douglas Southall Freeman in *Lee's Lieutenants* and *R. E. Lee* cited Owen's *In Camp and Battle* as "a standard authority. Includes documents not found elsewhere." It is "often quoted."[3] Allan Nevins, James I. Robertson, and Bell

---

2. Richard B. Harwell, *In Tall Cotton: The 200 Most Important Confederate Books for the Reader, Researcher, and Collector* (Austin: Jenkins Publishing Co. and Frontier America Corp., 1978), 48.

3. Douglas Southall Freeman, *Lee Lieutenants: A Study in Command*, 3 vols. (New York: Charles Scribner's Sons, 1942–1944), 3:824; D. S. Freeman, *R. E. Lee: A Biography*, 4 vols. (New York: Charles Scribner's Sons, 1934–1935), 4:561.

I. Wiley, in their indispensable critique of Civil War literature, consider Owen's work "the unchallenged champion of Louisiana soldiers' narratives; packed with color, drama, personal incidents, and battle descriptions, this volume is a Confederate classic."[4] More recently, in his valuable study *The Civil War in Books*, David Eicher has noted the vividness of Owen's narrative and revealing detail. He stresses that this unit history, although published in 1885, is based on Owen's diary.[5] This not only enhances its reliability but often gives the work a sense of immediacy, indeed intimacy. In all it makes for pleasurable reading. One shares Owen's despondency as his girlfriend in Richmond spurns him for a general officer. "I was miserable now," he confides to his diary, "thoroughly, and determined to throw my life away in battle with the Yank"(303). He does not. Instead, dinner at the Oriental Restaurant in Richmond with his English friends of the Coldstream Guards and the *Illustrated London News* revives his spirits and prompts him to record for posterity the bill of fare.

Owen also introduces the reader to humble peanut coffee; "starvation parties"; the songs, performers and performances of the Washington Artillery's Literary and Dramatic Association; and the "Waltonville War-

4. Allan Nevins, James I. Robertson, Jr., and Bell I. Wiley, eds., *Civil War Books: A Critical Bibliography*, 2 vols. (Baton Rouge: Louisiana State University Press, 1967–1969), 2:140.

5. David J. Eicher, *The Civil War in Books: An Analytical Bibliography* (Urbana: University of Illinios Press, 1997), 336.

Cry," affording the reader a splendid picture of soldier and civilian life behind the lines. Many readers also will be pleasantly surprised by the account of Owen's trip west to join the Army of Tennessee at Chickamauga. His insights on the debacle at McLemore's Cove are particularly noteworthy.

Over the years scholars and general readers have observed with regret that Owen failed to provide an index. This has been remedied and should make the richly detailed study more useable. Limitations of space, however, still necessitated the omission in the index of the long rosters on pages 9–11, 403–405, and 436–467. Also absent from the index is the "Organization of the Artillery, Army Northern Virginia, August 31, 1864," pages 351–353. Some readers will be disappointed at the small proportion of the work (twenty-five pages) allotted the Fifth Company (Slocomb's Battery), and, for that matter, the Sixth Company is not even mentioned. Owen's account, therefore, should not be considered the history of the Battalion Washington Artillery but of the four companies that fought with the Army of Northern Virginia.

For an appreciation of the role of artillery in that army, for insight into the functioning of Longstreet's Corps and his style of command, and for a stirring account of one of the most colorful and effective Confederate units, one cannot wish for better than William Miller Owen's *In Camp and Battle with the Washington Artillery of New Orleans*.

PREFACE.

A FEW days prior to the battles of Bull Run and Manassas, in July, 1861, an order was issued from the head-quarters of Gen. Beauregard in reference to the posting, at the several fords over Bull Run, the different brigades and batteries of the Confederate forces under his command, to meet the advance of the army of invasion, under Gen. McDowell, then on its march towards Richmond from Washington.

I remember the last sentence of the order; it read as follows: "In the event of the defeat of the enemy he is to be pursued with cavalry and artillery until he is driven across the Potomac."

After the affair of the 18th July, McDowell's advance having arrived at Centreville, orders were issued, on the night of the 20th, or the morning of the 21st, July, to Generals Ewell, D. R. Jones, and Longstreet, to cross their commands at their respective fords, and taking the different roads in their front, concentrating at Centreville, to attack

McDowell in flank as he continued his march down the Warrenton turnpike southward.

One or more of these orders miscarried, and a great dispute arose as to the exact hour of the receipt of others by the commanding officers to whom they were addressed.

Meanwhile McDowell chose his crossing-place at Sudley Ford, on Bull Run, completely flanking the left of the Confederate army, causing the battle to be fought on entirely other ground from what was anticipated.

After the battle it was readily seen how important it was for officers (commanding and staff) to keep an exact record of date, time, and place of all incidents by " flood and field," to assist in stating, in official reports, facts which could not be controverted.

Being at that time First Lieutenant and Adjutant of the Battalion Washington Artillery of New Orleans, and realizing the importance of this method, I resolved henceforth to be specially careful in my record of events. I adhered rigidly to this determination until the surrender of General Lee at Appomattox Court-House, and upon these records our official reports were made as long as I remained Adjutant of the Battalion.

These records, and many important original orders, are still in my possession, and, at the urgent request of General Fitz Lee and others, I have endeavored to prepare them in this form for the use of the future historian, should they prove of sufficient importance.

I do not pretend to write a history of the Civil War, nor any romance, nor will I set down aught in malice, but

> " Will a round, unvarnished tale deliver
> . . . .
> Of the battles, sieges, fortune, that I have pass'd,"

which made up our experience and life during four years' service in the armies of the Confederate States.

WM. MILLER OWEN,

First Lieut. and Adj. Battalion Washington Artillery, 1861,

A. N. Va.

NOTE.—For the illustrations of this volume I am under obligations to Capt. Fred M. Colston, of Baltimore, Md., formerly Ordnance Officer of Col. Alexander's Battalion Artillery, A.N.V., for his kindness in having photographic copies taken, from original drawings in his possession, of War Scenes by the eminent American artists, Allen C. Redwood, W. L. Sheppard, and John A. Elder.

For the accurate and finely executed Maps I have to thank Mr. W. J. Hardee, Civil Engineer, New Orleans, La.

LETTER FROM WM. PRESTON JOHNSON.

136 GRAVIER STREET,

NEW ORLEANS, April 12, 1884.

COL. W. MILLER OWEN, *New Orleans, La.:—*

MY DEAR SIR,—I have read with great interest the MSS. of your proposed volume, and can congratulate you on the success with which you have carried out your plan.

The book is remarkably entertaining, and full of incident, as is quite natural, since it was hardly possible for any officer to have a more eventful experience than you had in the army.

You won deserved distinction on many fields, and it is a source of satisfaction to me that I perceived your merit early in the war; and to be distinguished in a corps of such especial renown as the "Washington Artillery," won in such an army as Lee's, is a record of which any man may be proud. You had the good fortune, too, to gain the special commendation of some of our best Generals.

The narrative of your personal experience has, therefore, a peculiar value to all students of warfare.

I have not verified the historical accuracy of your book, but I may say that in the points which came under my observation from September, 1861, till the close of the war, and they are very numerous, your account is marked by that veracity in purpose and detail of fact without which such a narrative has no historical value. I am sure your intention is always to be just, and the magnanimity and cheerfulness of your temper make it generally easy for you.

I regard your book as a valuable contribution to the history of the war, and, indeed, to the history of warfare, from the side-lights it lets in on the life of the soldier. Wishing you much success,

I am, very sincerely, your friend,

(Signed),   WM. PRESTON JOHNSTON.

LETTER FROM COL. J. B. WALTON.

NEW ORLEANS, May 31, 1884.

COL. W. MILLER OWEN, *New Orleans, La.:* —

MY DEAR SIR,—Having carefully read your very interesting narrative, compiled from your Diary, kept while Adjutant of the Battalion Washington Artillery, and from a mass of authentic documents, it affords me peculiar satisfaction to congratulate you upon having written a book upon the war, at once entertaining and accurate in all the statements and incidents you so happily and graphically describe.

My position during the war as Colonel of the Battalion Washington Artillery of New Orleans, and Chief of Artillery of the First Corps, Army of Northern Virginia, enables me to give the fullest endorsement to the historical accuracy of your interesting volume. You have succeeded in presenting a book upon the war, at once entertaining and so replete with fact and incident that it deserves, as it will be, to be universally read and appreciated.

The advantage you possess of having been a prominent and distinguished actor in the scenes and events you describe, shows itself unmistakably all through the pages of your veracious and modest narrative. I heartily commend it as a notable and most worthy production.

I am, very truly, yours,

(Signed),   J. B. WALTON.

IN CAMP AND BATTLE

WITH THE

WASHINGTON ARTILLERY

OF

NEW ORLEANS

A NARRATIVE

OF EVENTS DURING THE LATE CIVIL WAR FROM BULL RUN
TO APPOMATTOX AND SPANISH FORT

*Compiled by the Adjutant from his Diary and from Authentic
Documents and Orders*

ILLUSTRATED WITH MAPS AND ENGRAVINGS

"When a historian would be deemed oracular,
He must preserve date, time, and place in his vernacular."

BY

WM. MILLER OWEN

FIRST LIEUTENANT AND ADJUTANT B.W.A.

BOSTON
TICKNOR AND COMPANY
1885

Facsimile of original title page.

IN CAMP AND BATTLE

WITH

THE WASHINGTON ARTILLERY.

CHAPTER I.

EARLY HISTORY OF THE WASHINGTON ARTILLERY.

The Washington Artillery before the War. — Its Organization. — War
Clouds, 1861. — Expedition to Baton Rouge. — Seizure of U.S. Ar-
senal. — Services of Battalion offered to Confederate Government.
— Accepted for the War. — Mustering in. — Ordered to Virginia. —
Departure from New Orleans. — Lynchburg. — Richmond. — Camp
Beauregard. — Manassas. — Camp Louisiana. — Head-quarters. —
Personelle. — Our French Cooks, and Cooks in general.

THE Washington Artillery of New Orleans is distinguished as being the oldest military organization in
the State of Louisiana.

In the year 1840 the Washington Regiment, commanded by Col. Persifer F. Smith, was the only military organization in the American quarter of the city. It
was composed of cavalry, infantry, and artillery, partaking
of the character of a legion.

The Washington Artillery, then just reorganized (February 22, 1840), was the right-flank company of the regiment.

Thus composed, the regiment became the crack corps of the State.

Upon the breaking out of the war with Mexico, in 1846, the Washington Artillery, under a requisition from Gen. Zachary Taylor, volunteered, and with its battery of six 6-pounder bronze guns, proceeded to Corpus Christi, Texas, where Gen. Taylor and his army were then encamped, and remained there three months in the service of the United States, without incident.

At the expiration of that time the battery returned to New Orleans, and was mustered out of service.

In May, 1846, another requisition was made upon the State of Louisiana for a brigade of four regiments of infantry.

The Washington Regiment was the first to offer its services, and was the first in the field.

The Washington Artillery, acting as infantry, was Company A of the regiment, and served with it, under Gen. Taylor, until all the volunteers on the Rio Grande line were, by orders of the Secretary of War, sent home and discharged.

From that period the company, in face of all adverse circumstances, constantly maintained its organization in a state of efficiency and readiness for service, at the individual expense of the members.

In 1852 another reorganization took place, and Gen. E. L. Tracy was elected captain. He was succeeded by Soria, who lost his life by the premature discharge of a gun while the battery was firing a salute.

After this sad event the company languished until but

thirteen members answered to roll-call. But on the 19th of March, 1857, the command was offered to, and accepted by, Col. J. B. Walton.

From that date the command began to build up, and in 1860 a full company had been organized, splendidly uniformed and equipped.

It was perfectly drilled in infantry as well as artillery tactics, and was possessed of both rifles and cannon in its arsenal. For efficiency, drill, and discipline it was not surpassed by any organization of citizen soldiery in the Southern States.

On the 6th of December, 1860, I was elected a private in the command.

Early in January, 1861, the city of New Orleans was in a great state of excitement, and rumors were current that the State authorities intended to take steps hostile to the United States authorities, and orders were issued to the various militia organizations in the city to prepare for service. The Artillery received the following order : —

HEAD-QUARTERS FIRST BRIGADE,
FIRST DIVISION L.S.M.,
NEW ORLEANS, January 9, 1861.

To CAPT. WALTON, *Washington Artillery :* —

You will repair immediately to the foot of Canal street, in conformity to orders from head-quarters, to receive the reports and assume command of the following-named companies : —

WASHINGTON ARTILLERY,
LOUISIANA GRAYS,
LOUISIANA GUARDS,
CHASSEURS À PIED,
SARSFIELD RIFLES,
ORLEANS CADETS.
CRESCENT RIFLES.

You will report the command when formed to the Adjutant-General for further orders. Strict order and discipline will be enforced by you, in accordance with the rules and regulations of war now in force in the army of the United States.

By order of Brig.-Gen. E. L. Tracy,
T. F. WALKER,
Brigade Inspector.

At a late hour in the evening of the 9th of January, 1861, the company assembled at the arsenal, completely equipped for service as infantry, and embarked on board the steamer "National," with the other city companies, and then it was made known that the purpose of the expedition was to seize the United States Arsenal at Baton Rouge.

Upon arriving at that place ball cartridges for our muskets were issued, and it began to look serious. Some of the young soldiers, who had come on a frolic, commenced to look a little blue. After breakfast, on the 11th, we were all marched ashore, where we met some country companies, not uniformed, to whom the commanding officer of the barracks had refused to surrender his post.

With a 12-pound musket on my shoulder and a heavy knapsack on my back I tramped around in the rear rank through the deep dust of the streets of the city. At last we were halted, stacked arms, and rested, and while doing so a few of us went out in the direction of the United States Arsenal, the acting adjutant, Lieut. H. M. Isaacson, accompanying us. On the way we met an ordnance sergeant of the U.S.A., who told us he was of our way of thinking, and intended to desert. By and by we marched to the arsenal, and, Major Haskins surrendering, we took possession in the name of the State of Louisiana. The casualties were few. Sergeant Buck Miller fell down a cellar when performing a "backward dress," and two privates, who were overcome by the excitement, were brought in under arrest. At night I was detailed for guard-duty, and my post was the gangway plank, where I paced my "two hours on and four off," all night. It began to rain, and I got wet, and when I lay down to rest during my "four hours off," using a coil of rope for a bed, with my legs hanging over one side, and head on the other, I felt cramped and miserable, but, with my then developing soldier spirit, I thought it was all right. My sergeant was my friend Eshleman, and we divided the coil of rope between us. The expedition returned to New Orleans on the 12th of January.

A few days after our return from Baton Rouge I was appointed by Major Walton, adjutant, with the rank of first lieutenant, in which position my duties were more confining and numerous, but pleasant.

By the surrender of the arsenal at Baton Rouge the State came into possession of a large number of small arms and some old-fashioned cannon.[1]

---

[1] NEW ORLEANS, April 27, 1861.

MAJOR J. B. WALTON,
Commanding Battalion Washington Artillery: —

SIR, — Having, in conformity to orders from you under date of 25th inst., visited Baton Rouge for the purpose of "ascertaining, through Capt. Booth, at the Ordnance Department, what there may be there subject to requisition which may be used to place our battery in complete order for active service," I beg leave to report as follows : —

This was regarded as a proceeding of the gravest importance, in view of the fact that it constituted the first serious act of hostility to Federal authority.

The harsh voice of war, with all its attendant horrors, was even then heard resounding throughout the Southern States.

The bombardment and fall of Sumter, and the universal rush to arms North and South had not then occurred.

On the 22d of February the ladies of New Orleans presented to the Artillery a magnificent stand of colors, and the presentation speech was delivered by the Hon. J. P. Benjamin, then the distinguished senator from Louisiana,

---

Through the kind assistance of Capt. Booth and Mr. Lambert, military store-keeper, I discovered the following-named arms, etc., subject to requisition of the military commander of this district, viz.: —

350 Artillery sabres.
350 Artillery sabre-belts, and sword-knots.
220 Hall's patent carbines.
 48 Colt's patent carbines.
An abundance of old-fashioned pistols and holsters, altered from flint-locks.
An abundance of Colt's army revolvers.
A large quantity of fixed ammunition for 6-pounders.
200 fixed shells for 12-pounder howitzers.

I found one battery-wagon that can be spared. Capt. Booth is now fitting up a battery of six 6-pounders, for which he will require the only forge and caissons he has on hand. He has no extra carriages or wheels.

I found an abundance of the following articles, viz.: —
Cannon locks, and percussion caps for same.
Fuse gouges, hammers, shears, spikes, pouches, etc.

There is no camp or garrison equipage of any description stored at this post.

I regret I am unable to make a more satisfactory report. Capt. Booth informed me that the numerous requisitions made upon him within the last few weeks have almost stripped the arsenal. I noticed in the workshops a large number of hands employed in making rammers, fuses, port-fires, and filling shells for columbiads, moulding bullets, etc.

I have the honor to be
Very respectfully, your obedient servant,
WM. MILLER OWEN,
First Lieutenant and Adjutant, B.W.A.

and later the late eminent Queen's Counsel of London, who made the startling announcement that war was inevitable between the States, North and South, and told his audience to prepare for the great struggle, the end of which no one could foretell.

On May 3, 1861, the command was increased, by the election of new members, to four full companies, fully equipped. Authority was given to their Major, J. B. Walton, to offer their services to the Confederate States government at Montgomery, Alabama, which was done in a communication of that date to the Hon. J. P. Benjamin.

On the 13th May the following telegram was sent to Hon. L. Pope Walker, Secretary of War, by Major Walton : —

The Battalion Washington Artillery under my command, numbering upon its rolls over three hundred men, two hundred and fifty for service, and divided into four companies, with a battery, complete in all respects, of six 6-pounder bronze guns, two 12-pounder howitzers, one 8-pounder rifle gun, is ready and desirous to take the field.

The Battalion can take the field within a very few days after being notified and provided with horses, camp, and garrison equipage, etc., for which, of course, I will be obliged to make requisition upon the Confederate States.

A delegation was sent — consisting of E. A. Palfrey, who had been elected captain of the second company, and private David Urquhart — to Montgomery to make the necessary arrangements for receiving the command directly into the service of the regular Confederate army.

They were instructed to offer its services " for the war."

On the same date Secretary of War Walker sent the following telegram : —

MAJOR J. B. WALTON, — Your Battalion of Artillery is accepted for the war. You are ordered to Lynċhburg, Virginia.

L. POPE WALKER,
Secretary of War.

Immediate preparations were made. Contributions were received from ladies and citizens generally, in great profusion. Large amounts of money were contributed by members and friends to fill the military chest to overflowing. Each member furnished his own uniform and equipment, officers their own horses. The whole command was put upon a war footing without expense to the State or general government.

In organization and equipment the Washington Artillery was not excelled by any command North or South, and the finest material in the State of Louisiana filled its ranks.

On the 26th day of May, 1861, — a bright Sabbath morning, — the four batteries, in their showy uniforms, bearing aloft the silken colors, the gift of the ladies, marched and formed in double file in Lafayette square.

They were then formally mustered into the service of the Confederate States by Lieut. Phifer, C.S.A. It was an impressive scene ; the square was densely packed with the friends and families of the young soldiers. After the ceremony of being mustered in was concluded, the command was marched through the streets to Christ Church, which ancient and sacred edifice was filled to its utmost capacity by the immediate families and friends of the departing soldiers, and by the Battalion. Their colors were distinguished by being placed against the chancel rail. The venerable Dr. Leacock, Rector of Christ Church, delivered a most eloquent address, which impressed profoundly all who were present. Suppressed sobs of mothers, sisters, wives, and sweethearts were audible throughout the church. He enjoined all to remember that they were educated to be gentlemen, and it behooved them to bring back their characters as soldiers and gentlemen unblemished with their arms. He concluded by saying: "Our hearts will follow you, our ears will be open for tidings of your condition, and our prayers will ascend for your safety and return."

After the discourse the colors were held aloft before the altar, and the benediction was pronounced, the entire assembly rising to their feet, roused to the highest pitch of hope, patriotism, and enthusiasm.[1]

---

[1] The following are the names of the officers and men who, on Sunday morning, May 26, 1861, answered to Lieut. Phifer's roll-call, and who thus became mustered into the Confederate service: —

Staff.—Major, J. B. Walton; Adjutant, Lieut. W. M. Owen; Surgeon, Dr. E. S. Drew; Quarter-master, Lieut. C. H. Slocomb.

Non-commissioned Staff. — Sergt.-Major, C. L. C. Dupuy; Quarter-master Sergeant, Stringer Kennedy; Color-Sergeant, Louis M. Montgomery.

Color Guard. — Corporals, George W. Wood, E. L. Jewell, A. H. Peale, J. H. Dearie.

Buglers. — F. de P. Villasana, Jo. Kingslow.

Roll of First Company. — Captain, H. M. Isaacson; First Lieutenant, C. W. Squires; First Lieutenant, J. B. Richardson; Second Lieutenant, H. G. Geiger; First Sergeant, Edward Owen; Second Sergeant, J. M. Galbraith; Third Sergeant, C. H. C. Brown, Jr.; First Corporal, F. D. Ruggles; Second Corporal, E. C. Payne; Third Corporal, W. Fellows; Fourth Corporal, F. F. Case.

Privates. — Thomas S. Turner, G. M. Judd, E. I. Kursheedt, J. W. Kearney, C. Rossiter, W. Chambers, W. F. Perry, J. E. Rodd, M. E. Jarreau, J. A. Tarlton, T. Y. Aby, C. Chambers, G. W. Muse, L. Labarre, M. Mount, P. A. J. Michel, J. M. Payne, R. McK. Spearing, A. F. Coste, J. R. McGaughy, E. A.

At an early hour on the 27th of May, 1861, the crowds of citizens assembling upon the streets gave token of excitement in the public mind. From every tongue came the remark, " The Washington Artillery is going to the war." Then men in the familiar uniform of the corps could be seen flitting about, completing preparations for the journey. At the arsenal all was commotion, — wagons being loaded, knapsacks packed, and blankets rolled. The

---

Cowen, F. A. St. Amand, W. T. Hardie, H. Chambers, E. V. Wiltz, J. P. Manico, L. E. Zebal, H. L. Zebal, W. R. Falconer, G. B. DeRussy, F. Lobrano, C. A. Everett.

Artificers. — S. G. Stewart, W. D. Holmes, Israel Scott.

Drivers. — George Bernard, Sergeant; Michael Hock, Charles Rush, Jno. E. Scheman, Jno. O'Neil, W. K. Dirke, John Wilson, Pat. Mooney, H. Meyer, Jno. Jacobs, Thos. Kerwin, David Nolan, Wm. Forrest, J. L. Hoch, Fred. Lester, R. Nicholas, Jno. Charlesworth, Jno. Anderson, Matthew Burns, Jas. Heflogh.

Roll of Second Company. — First Lieutenant, C. C. Lewis, commanding; First Lieutenant, Samuel J. McPherson; Second Lieutenant, C. H. Slocomb; First Sergeant, J. H. DeGrange; Second Sergeant, Gustave Aime; Third Sergeant, H. C. Wood; Fourth Sergeant, C. Huchez; First Corporal, J. D. Edwards; Second Corporal, C. E. Leverich; Third Corporal, Jules Freret; Fourth Corporal, B. V. L. Hutton.

Privates. — H. N. Payne, J. S. Meyers, Tracey Twichell, T. J. Land, J. W. Emmett, J. A. Hall, G. Humphrey, W. C. Giffen, J. C. Woodville, A. A. Brinsmade, E. L. Hall, R. Axson, Wm. Roth, E. D. Patton, A. G. Knight, J. D. Britton, W. A. Randolph, W. F. Florence, J. W. Parsons, J. Howard Goodin, Thomas H. Suter, F. Alewelt, F. P. Buckner, G. E. Strawbridge, A. R. Blakely, R. Bannister, Jr., R. C. Lewis, H. B. Berthelot, W. J. Hare, J. H. Randolph, W. H. Wilkins, Samuel Hawes.

Artificers. — John Montgomery, Leonard Craig.

Drivers. — John Weber, Toney Hulby, John Fagan, George Barr, Wm. Carey, B. B. F. McKesson, William Little, James Crilly, John Cannon, Jas. Leyden, Ed. Loftus, Edwin Lake, James Brown, W. F. Lynch, Louis Roach, William Oliver, Corn'l McGregor, Alex. Bucher.

Roll of Third Company. — Captain, M. B. Miller; First Lieutenant, J. B. Whittington; Second Lieutenant, L. A. Adam; First Sergeant, Frank McElroy; Second Sergeant, A. Hero, Jr.; Third Sergeant, L. Prados; Fourth Sergeant, J. T. Handy; First Corporal, E. L. Jewell; Second Corporal, A. H. Peale; Third Corporal, W. H. Ellis; Fourth Corporal, W. A. Collins.

Privates. — Napier Bartlett, H. D. Summers, J. H. Moore, W. Mills, Robert Bruce, John Holmes, T. H. Fuqua, O. N. DeBlanc, E. W. Morgan, P. W. Pettis, E. Riviere, F. Kremelberg, Chas. Hart, Samuel C. Boush, George

day was fearfully hot, the thermometer ranging over 90°. The march to the railroad station, escorted by all the city troops, was a perfect ovation. All places of business on Canal street were closed, and ladies filled the galleries, waving their handkerchiefs.

At the City Hall the Rev. Mr. Palmer delivered an address, and wished the Battalion " God speed."

After what was to the young soldiers, under the intense heat, a fearful march, the station was reached, but not, however, without the loss of two privates, — Lane and Carl, —

McNeil, J. H. Collis, Frank Shaw, Jr., E. Toledano, W. S. Toledano, P. O. Fazende, Fred. L. Hubbard, Jos. H. DeMeza, L. E. Guyot, J. F. Randolph, S. Chalaron, J. T. Brenford, C. W. Deacon, Stringer Kennedy, Howard Tully, Wm. Leefe, I. W. Brewer, C. H. Stocker, J. R. Porter, S. G. Sanders, B. L. Braselman, R. P. Many, F. A. Carl, C. E. Fortier, R. Maxwell, E. Avril, E. Charpiaux, T. M. McFall, M. W. Cloney, Ed. Duncan, C. A. Falconer, H. J. Phelps, T. Ballantine, E. W. Noyes, M. W. Chapman, W. P. Noble, W. G. Coyle, L. P. Forshee, George H. Meek, J. C. Bloomfield, A. B. Martin, R. Turnell.

Artificers. — Jos. Blanchard, Jas. Keating.

Roll of Fourth Company. — Captain, B. F. Eshleman; First Lieutenant, Jos. Norcom; Second Lieutenant, Harry A. Battles; Second Sergeant, W. J. Behan; Third Sergeant, G. E. Apps; Fourth Sergeant, J. D. Reynolds; First Corporal, Geo. Wood; Second Corporal, J. W. Dearie.

Privates. — A. D. Augustus, B. F. Widler, J. R. McGowan, J. M. Rohbock, H. F. Wilson, C. C. Bier, J. C. Wood, Jno. S. Fish, F. A. Brodie, E. Lauer, G. Beck, R. F. F. Moore, H. H. Baker, J. W. Burke, Jno. Meux, J. B. Valentine, Phil. Von Coln, T. B. White, Bernard Hufft, G. L. Crutcher, J. F. Lilly, T. J. Stewart, Samuel A. Knox, Wm. Palfrey, L. C. Lewis, J. H. Smith, G. Montgomery, Isaac Jessup, A. F. Vass, W. W. Jones, P. C. Lane, T. Carey, W. P. S. Crecy, W. C. Morrell, W. T. O'Neill, A. Banksmith, Frank Williams, H. N. White, Jno. B. Chastant, W. Snead, H. D. Seaman, Eugene M. Bee, C. W. Marston, C. A. Deval, E. A. Mellard, J. W. Wilcox, V. D. Terrebonne, E. F. Reichart, Thos. H. Cummings, R. H. Gray, S. T. Hale, J. W. Lesene, Chas. Hardenburg, J. C. Purdy, E. Jaubert.

Artificers. — Levy Callahan, Jno. McDonnell.

Band. — J. V. Gessner, Leader; T. Gutzler, Ch. W. Struve, J. Arnold, Jno. Deutsch, Jno. Geches, Peter Trum, Jno. Lorbs, Thos. Kostmel, J. H. Sporer, Charles Meir.[1]

---

[1] The Battalion, when in Virginia, was several times recruited to fill the places of the killed, wounded, and disabled, who averaged about one hundred to each company.

both sunstruck. *En route*, my old friend, Mr. John Connelly, threw around my neck a little amulet, saying : " Wear that, my boy, and your life will be saved." It was of the class of medals that were blessed by the Pope and sent to the French soldiers in the Crimean war.

The train moved out of the station amidst the firing of artillery and the strains of brass bands. The boys cheered, the engine whistled an adieu, and the Battalion Washington Artillery was off " for the war."

On June 2 the Battalion reached Lynchburg, Virginia, after an uneventful trip. There we found preparations on a grand scale for our reception.

A large building had previously been engaged for our use, and a capital lunch served.

In fact, at almost every stopping-place along the route reception committees waited upon us, and a free lunch was extended.

The Battalion paraded the principal streets of Lynchburg in the afternoon, just " to take the wrinkles out," as was said, and, as we were to remain there until the following morning, the citizens carried off the boys for the night to their hospitable homes.

The Colonel, importuned by so many to go and spend the night, and unwilling to show a preference, concluded to go to the hotel, whither he went, with the adjutant and the chief bugler. The command was dismissed, with orders to report in the morning at *réveille*.

At daybreak, June 3, the bugles rang out the *ré-veille* at all the corners of the streets, and effectually awakened the whole town, and soon the boys, singly and in squads, were seen rushing to roll-call, like college students a little late at chapel.

The companies were formed briskly at the rendezvous agreed upon, and, to the credit of the discipline of the command be it said, not a single man failed to answer "Here" at the call of his name.

The boys were then allowed to breakfast with their hospitable hosts, with orders to report at 10 A.M. at the station for departure.

At that hour an immense crowd assembled to see them off, and with the band playing "Dixie" we moved out of the station *en route* for Richmond, followed by the enthusiastic cheers and waving of handkerchiefs of the throng. Many a heart was left behind with the fair maidens of dear old Lynchburg.

During our whole trip from New Orleans to Richmond we had a special train, — passenger cars for officers and men, box cars for private horses, and open platform cars for our cannon, — twenty-one cars in all. When passing through East Tennessee, Brownlow's country, we experienced some delay at Morristown by the desertion of an engineer, who was too "loyal" to pull us through; and another, truly "loyal," abstracted Capt. Eshleman's trunk from one of the open cars, much to the disgust of its owner. This was the first practical application of the term "heavy baggage to the rear."

Just before daybreak, on the 4th of June, we arrived at Richmond, and noticed with some interest the sentinels on post about the large warehouses near the station, containing, we supposed, quarter-master's stores. This began to look like business.

At 8 A.M. the command fell in for breakfast, and, with the band playing, marched, without sabres, to the Exchange Hotel. This concluded, and the score settled, amounting to two hundred and fifty dollars in "gold coin of the realm" from our military chest, we were ordered to prepare to march to the location selected for our camp. About noon we were marched to Union Hill, a bald spot, — not a tree or a shrub upon it. There tents were furnished us, and by dark our canvas city was pitched, and by common consent dubbed "Camp Beauregard."

As ordered, we reported our presence to Gen. R. E. Lee, commanding the Virginia forces. Here we expected to remain for some time, to be supplied with horses and harness, and some changes to be made in our armament, and numerous things to be done needful for service in the field.

Our camp was thronged daily at dress-parade with the *élite* of Richmond, — scores of ladies in their carriages being always present. President Davis frequently rode through the camp. One day he rode up to the sentinel on the flank of the camp, and as he was passing through he was halted by the man on post (Von Coln). "Don't you know the President?" asked Gen. Wigfall, who accompanied him. "No," said Von, "I know no one. I only know my orders. Go round by the guard tent: you can't pass here." The President, who was an old soldier, was rather pleased at this display of discipline in the command.

Of course, our Colonel, being a fine-looking soldier, and

commanding such a splendid contribution óf the best of young Louisianians to the Virginia army, was feasted and fêted ; and the adjutant shared the hospitalities extended to his chief, and sipped 1798 Madeira at the hospitable board of Mr. Macf——d, breakfasted with the charming Mrs. S——d, and supped with ponderous statesmen and brigadiers, who had yet to win their spurs.[1]

On June 24 the first and second companies, having completed their equipment, were ordered off to Manassas, with orders to report to Gen. Beauregard. Headquarters accompanied this detachment, and the third and fourth companies were left under command of the senior officer, Capt. H. M. Isaacson, to complete equipping and to follow after.

On the 25th of June the two batteries reported to Gen. Beaureguard at Manassas, and by his orders pitched their tents on the banks of Bull Run, at Mitchell's ford. Here a beautiful camp was laid out, — plenty of

---

[1] The Richmond (Va.) " Dispatch " of the 20th of June, 1861, says : —

"On Tuesday evening the commissioned and non-commissioned staff of the Battalion Washington Artillery, with Major Walton, came from camp to this city, accompanied with their excellent brass band of twelve pieces, and serenaded President Davis at the Spottswood House. After discoursing several appropriate airs to the admiration of a large audience, Major Walton and staff were invited to the reception-room of the President, where Mrs. Davis did the hospitable attentions, aided by a large number of ladies, in her wonted generous style. An hour was agreeably passed, both Mr. and Mrs. Davis paying the Battalion high compliments. The Battalion band also serenaded some of our distinguished citizens, and after three or four hours of festive entertainment, the staff returned to ' Camp Beauregard ' toward the ' sma' wee hours.'

" This Battalion is now being supplied with an additional battery by the Confederate government, composed of 6-pounders, 12-pound howitzers, and rifled cannon, and are now in a very superior state of artillery drill, ready for action. In the course of six or eight days they will get marching orders for the seat of war."

fresh green grass and shade trees, and fine bathing in the clear mountain stream. This was called "Camp Louisiana."

Before leaving Richmond there had been assigned to the Battalion, Lieuts. T. L. Rosser, James Dearing, and J. J. Garnett. These young officers had been at West Point Academy when hostilities broke out, resigned, and came home to Virginia before graduating. They were assigned to the artillery as instructors and for general service, and assisted very materially in battery drills upon the Manassas plains.

In due time the glorious Fourth of July came, and was duly celebrated, as of yore.

Information was received that it would not be long before we should smell " villanous saltpetre." The enemy was reported very active between Fairfax Court-House — our outpost — and Washington. The two companies which were left behind at Richmond joined us on the 8th, and the family was again united.[1] We were drilling

[1] MORNING REPORTS BATTALION WASHINGTON ARTILLERY.

July 13, 1861.	Officers.	N. C. Officers.	Private.	Total.	Absent on leave.	Absent sick.	Aggregate.
Field and Staff	4	4	. .	8	. .	. .	8
First Company	4	8	58	70	1	. .	71
Second Company	3	7	59	69	. .	. .	69
Third Company	4	8	50	62	. .	1	63
Fourth Company	4	8	51	63	. .	. .	63
	19	35	218	272	1	1	274

constantly, and had perfected ourselves in light-artillery manœuvres, having been provided with excellent horses and equipment.

The first section of the first company had been off on an expedition to Occoquan creek, and the boys were in hopes of paying a few compliments to the enemy, but were disappointed. The following is a list of the detachments that afterwards made themselves famous : —

Rifle Piece.

Lieut. Squires commanding.
First Sergeant Edward Owen.[1]
First Corporal F. D. Ruggles.[1]
Private G. M. Judd.[1]
     "   W. F. Perry.[1]
     "   C. Rossiter.[1]
     "   E. I. Kursheedt.[1]
     "   T. S. Turner.[1]
     "   J. Watts Kearney.
     "   W. Chambers.[1]
     "   John E. Rodd.[1]

12-pd. Howitzer.

Lieut. Slocomb [1] commanding.
Sergeant J. M. Galbraith.[1]
Corporal J. N. Payne.[1]
Private J. R. McGaughy.
     "   W. L. Norment.

---

[1] Killed or wounded in battle.

Private R. McK. Spearing.[1]
"   W. T. Hardie.[1]
"   A. F. Coste.[1]
"   E. Riviere.
"   P. O. Fazende.[1]
"   H. Chambers.[1]

And now a word about the *personnel* of our field and staff. *Imprimis*, our Colonel, and for a description of him I quote from a special correspondent, who has written (after enumerating all the officers of the command) : " These are all men of marked character, and gentlemen in every sense of the word. Col. Walton is a man of powerful frame, straight and soldierly, and looks very much like the portraits of Napoleon III. He has a heavy mustache and *barbe d'Afrique*, now tinged with gray. His dress, like all the officers of this corps, is always neat and becoming, giving the wearer an appearance of elegance seldom seen among army officers in the field."

Second Lieut. C. H. Slocomb, Second company, acting. quarter-master, was a young man of twenty-eight years, and an efficient officer. By his personal magnetism he endeared himself to the whole command.

Dr. E. S. Drew, surgeon, or, as he was called by the boys, "Drugs," was an experienced " sawbones," and was looking forward to the time when his beautiful case of instruments would come into requisition.

Sergeant-Major C. L. C. Dupuy was a most careful, conscientious, and methodical officer. He kept his roster care-

---

[1] Killed or wounded in battle.

fully preserved in folds of cotton cloth, as voluminous as the
wrappings of an Egyptian mummy, and after the unrolling
process was completed he could inform the adjutant just
how many men or fractions of men could be drawn for
daily guard-detail. The irreverent ones dubbed him
" Sergeant Detail." He was not only a walking encyclo-
pædia, but had compiled a perpetual calendar, and, if one
had any desire to know on what day of the week the
Fourth of July would fall one hundred years hence, he
could furnish the information in a style " equalled by few
and excelled by none."

Ordnance-Officer B. L. Brazelman was also a conscientious and faithful adjunct to the staff, always busy about
the guns, overhauling the ammunition chests, replacing
implements, careful as to fuses and primers. No gunner
lacked any essential for instant action.

Color-Sergeant L. M. Montgomery, or " Bliffkins," as
the boys called him, was a decided character. Why he was
called " Bliffkins," or " Bliff" for short, no one knows.
" Bliff" was a Bohemian, in New Orleans, connected with
the press. In full-dress uniform he was immense ; and to
see him with his red kepi cocked upon three hairs, with his
Dundreary whiskers, one would be apt to mistake him for
a major-general at least. " Bliff" had a charger assigned
him by the Colonel, and when he was off duty, which was
about three hundred and sixty-four days out of the year,
he was allowed to roam over the country, and would return
with long yarns of what he had seen and heard. We could
believe as much as we chose of it all ; but, from all accounts,
the commander-in-chief had no grave secrets he did not

impart to "Bliff." Everybody knew him, and he was always welcome. He was our perambulating news-reporter. During a battle he was all in all to us, for he would bring the news from the right and from the left, how this or that command had gone in, who had been hurt, how things were going, and the like. Late in the war "Bliff" was commissioned in the adjutant-general's department, and while on his way to the trans-Mississippi was intercepted by gun-boats; so he reported to Gen. Pemberton, at Vicksburg, and was the only officer with that general when the famous interview was held with Gen. Grant to arrange the terms for the surrender of the city.

And now for our immediate *ménage* at the Colonel's tent. First, John Bahr, a plethoric, full-breasted, and bow-windowed native of Germany, who, filled with patriotic ardor, volunteered with the command as hospital steward. The Colonel appointed him his major-domo. John looked after the "flesh-pots," so to speak, and would ride miles and miles for provender for the mess; but woe unto him, if, when returning from a raid, laden with chickens, eggs, butter, and buttermilk, he passed near the drill-grounds of the batteries. As soon as he was descried an immediate cessation of drill was ordered, and the mounted officers would charge down upon him and make the lightning flash before his eyes with their sabres, and demand "toll," which they generally got by a fair divide; and he was paroled with the injunction, that, if he told the Colonel, they would chop him up into sausage-meat; but stolid John would only say, "All recht; vait dil dot paymaster koms. I get you even on der leetle game of boker."

"Mistress John," his *frau*, whom Slocomb had uniformed as a *vivandière* before leaving home, accompanied us, and bore the fatigue of the campaigns as well as any. She made herself indispensable in many ways. The little woman was a heroine in her way, as true as steel; and many a sick or wounded fellow has felt her motherly hand as she bathed his hurts or made for him a good broth or a cup of creole coffee. The boys, always ready for *sobriquets*, dubbed the worthy couple, more from affection than from any disrespect, the "he-bear and the she-bear;" and so they were known for the term of the war.

But the all-important personage was our French cook, Edouard, from Victor's restaurant, in New Orleans. Ah! he was *magnifique*. A Frenchman of great resources, his dishes were superb, and the objects of admiration of all visitors who did not enjoy the luxury of French *cuisine* in their own camps. But Edouard soon tired of camp-life, and after a while, when, with the curtailed transportation, his utensils used to be pitched into the ditches by the roadside, his reputation was at stake, and he finally returned to his dear New Orleans, with his sole companion, his pet fox.

François, a splendid specimen of a creole darky, speaking better French than English, succeeded. It was said he had a lady-love in every section of the Old Virginia State we travelled over. A French darky was a curiosity.

The negro cooks in the Battalion were an institution unto themselves. When the command left New Orleans for Virginia every mess had its two or three servants, or "boys," as they were universally called. These "boys" would take charge of the mess, and, in very many cases, were the slaves of the officers and men. They were expected to black the shoes, forage for provisions at times, rub down private horses, etc. Many were accomplished body-servants, good barbers, and the like. Quite a number served faithfully until the end of the war; some deserted to the enemy when it was bruited amongst them that the war had set them free, and appeared in the Northern papers as "intelligent contrabands." Of the latter were Jim Ingraham and Dick Kenner, who served the fourth company officers' mess. They both, in reconstruction times, became prominent politicians, and served in the legislature of Louisiana, but always leaned kindly towards the interests of their old masters. In the field and in the trenches the "boys" would prepare the meals for the officers and men at the front, and carry them to them during quiet times; but let the guns open, and they would make tracks to the rear in a hurry.

They were not without humor, as, for instance, old François, the Colonel's French servant, who, upon one occasion, while unloading the head-quarters wagon, drew forth a small stove, of which one leg of the four was missing. The Colonel, very wroth, demanded to know where the missing leg had gone. François, with a grimace and shrug of the shoulders peculiar to his class, said: "Muschoo Col-o-nel, I do not know, but I dink it must be lost on de battlefield."

At the first battle of Manassas the enemy fired some

very large shells, that made a peculiar humming noise; they were dubbed " bird-cage shot." The darkies declared they said in their flight, " Whar is yer? Whar is yer?" and would take to their heels to hide from them.

The flight or passage of a minie bullet was translated into "Zip! I've got yer!"

But let justice be done these faithful servants, for surely many were devoted and faithful to the bitter end of the war, in camp and in the far-away homes of wives and children of the men who were in the armies; and then, too, their class is extinct: they are now politicians and office-holders.

CHAPTER II.

ADDRESS TO THE ARMY.

Enemy on the March. — Camp Broken Up. — McLean's Ford. — Union Mills. — Rebel Girl. — Engagement at Blackburn's Ford, July 21. — Our Armament. — Battle of Manassas. — Bee, Bartow, Hampton, and Bob Wheat. — "Stonewall Jackson." — Hard Tack and Sherry. — Beauregard and Johnston. — Griffin's and Rickett's Batteries. — Defeat of the Enemy. — President Davis. — Appearance of a Battlefield. — Official Reports.

JULY 17th, 1861. — The enemy is on the move. We can hear his guns at Fairfax Court-House. Our advanced forces all falling back steadily to cross to the south side of Bull Run. We will watch and hold the fords.

Camp broken up, and tents and baggage sent to Manassas, under charge of the quarter-master.

Until this business is concluded we will rough it in the open air.

The morning report of the Battalion shows two hundred and eighty-four officers and men for duty, and an armament of thirteen field-pieces, say : —

> Six smooth brass 6-pounders.
> Four 12-pounder howitzers.
> Three 6-pounder rifles.

The whole command was marched to McLean's ford, and bivouacked for the night under the shelter of the pine thickets. Our first night out. Some wounded men from the outpost passed by this afternoon, one fellow with his ear shot completely off, — a close scratch.

On the 18th we were up and stirring at the peep of dawn, and, after a hasty breakfast of fried bacon and crackers, mount, and with the four howitzers, under Lieut. Rosser, moved in the direction of Union Mills ford, further down the Run, where it is crossed by a railroad bridge. The other guns of the command were left at Blackburn's and McLean's fords, under Lieut. Squires and Capt. Miller. Union Mills ford was the extreme right of our line, which extended for eight miles up the stream to the stone bridge at the Warrenton turnpike, where our left rested. From our elevated position at the Mills we could see the enemy's Zouaves coming out of the patch of woods opposite, drawing water from the tank beside the railroad. They were evidently there in force, and Rosser wants to shell them out; but Gen. Ewell said, "Wait awhile."

While lounging under the trees we were surprised to see riding towards us a little lady, with the rebel colors pinned upon her dress.

We sprang to our feet, and, with our kepis doffed, greeted her. What a strange sight! — so young and gentle a girl here, among a thousand soldiers and frowning cannon awaiting battle.

To our inquiries where she was from, and how she came, she replied, "Oh, I'm from Fairfax Court-House. I came around the Yankees, and have information for your commander; who is he?" We told her Gen. Ewell was in command, and, at her request, escorted her to his head-quarters. What news she brought we never knew;

but we all thought she was a brave little woman anyhow.

About noon, away on the left, we heard the boom of a
big gun, and then another ; soon the rattle of a volley of
musketry, and, as the sounds increased in volume, we knew
the enemy was attacking one of the fords, but which one
we could not tell.   At any rate, some of our boys were
engaged, we knew.

The bugle sounded the assembly, and the cannoneers
took their posts at the guns, ready for action if the Zouaves
opposite proved troublesome ; but they made no move.   The
heavy firing on the left kept us on the anxious seat until it
ceased, about 4 o'clock P.M., when "Bliffkins," "whip
and spur," was seen coming towards us up the road, his
horse covered with foam.   A general rush was made for
him, and an avalanche of questions hurled at him:
"What's the news, 'Bliff,' old boy?   Give us the news !"
"Any of our fellows been in ? "   "Anybody hurt ? "   "Have
we licked 'em ? "   Poor "Bliff," all out of breath, tried to
speak, but could only get out : "All right — Blackburn's
ford — Been in — Whipped enemy's artillery — George
Muse killed — Eshleman, Zebal, Tarleton, Tully, Harry
Baker wounded — Rest all right — Gim'me a drink, somebody ! "

This was good news indeed, and we danced and shouted
ourselves hoarse over it.

We bivouacked that night at the Mills, and the boys,
around the camp-fires, discussed the chances of "getting a
show" on the morrow.   The Colonel and I slept in a cabin,
in which were also quartered Col. Siebal and his ad-

jutant, Lieut. John B. Gordon[1] of the Sixth Alabama, and Col. Seymour of the Sixth Louisiana.

On July 19th I visited the battlefield at Blackburn's ford, and that portion of the command that had been engaged, saw Lieut. Squires, who had been the senior officer in command of the guns, and he reported as follows : —

" Early yesterday morning the three rifle pieces of artillery under my command were ordered to move in the direction of Blackburn's ford, with Col. Early's brigade. Upon arriving at McLean's farm-house we were joined by two more guns of our Battalion, under Lieuts. J. B. Whittington and L. A. Adam, and were ordered to act together as one battery. The enemy very shortly opened fire upon a barn of McLean's that was occupied by the medical department as a hospital. Musketry fire soon opened along the banks of Bull Run, and our infantry became engaged with the enemy. A section of our battery was soon ordered to follow the Seventh Louisiana regiment, which was moving into position, and two of the rifle guns, under command of Lieut. J. B. Richardson, assisted by Capt. Eshleman, did so. One rifle and two 6-pounders remained with Col. Kemper's Seventh Virginia regiment. Lieut. Garnett then came up with two more of our guns (6-pounders), that had been attached to Gen. Longstreet's command. Presently the rifles under Richardson opened fire, — the first shots fired at the enemy by the Washington

---

[1] Lieut. Gordon afterwards went through the grades of major, colonel, brigadier, major, and lieutenant-general, and was wounded a number of times. His wife accompanied him in his marches, riding by his side on horseback. He has, since the war, served as U.S. Senator from Georgia.

Artillery. These rifles were soon joined by the five other guns, — making seven in all, — and at it we went. We had a lively time of it ; but the boys behaved splendidly. Richardson, Garnett, and Whittington deserve special mention for coolness. The former had his horse shot under him. Sergts. Edward Owen, John Galbraith, and Ike Brewer, together with Corporals Ruggles, Fellowes, Payne, and Ellis, and, in short, all the cannoneers and drivers, deserve thanks for coolness and perfect obedience to orders."

"Sergts. Edward Owen and Galbraith I shall recommend highly for promotion. They behaved most gallantly throughout the whole of the engagement, reporting at every moment the different positions of their guns, the ammunition they were using, and every little detail connected therewith."

" The enemy's shells bursting in the midst of the guns killed George Muse, and wounded, while doing their whole duty, Capt. Eshleman and privates H. L. Zebal and J. A. Tarleton of first company, and H. Tully of the third company, and H. H. Baker of fourth company. We fired away three hundred and ten rounds in the engagement, and lost six horses, killed and wounded."

I had the pleasure of congratulating upon their " fiery baptism " Watts Kearney, Rossiter, McGaughy, Hardie, L. E. Zebal, and others. They had all donned the high black army-hats of the enemy, found on the field, and were about as fierce a looking set of brigands in appearance as one could wish to see. They were all in high spirits and chock-full of confidence in themselves and their capacity to whip anything and anybody.

On my way back to Union Mills I met Gen. Beauregard, who said to me, "Tell Col. Walton I want to see him, to tell him how like veterans his boys behaved." I felt quite mortified that I had been so unfortunate as not to have been in the engagement myself.

On the night of the 18th, the company of American Rifles, under Capt. W. D. Rickarby and Lieut. Sam Flower, 7th Louisiana regiment, crossed Bull Run and hastened the falling back of the enemy by a sharp and unexpected fusilade upon his flank.

In Gen. Beauregard's official report of the engagement of the 18th July, he says : —

"Our artillery was manned and officered by those who, but yesterday, were called from the civil avocations of a busy city."

"They were matched with the picked artillery of the Federal regular army, — Company E, Third Artillery, under Capt. Ayres, with an armament, as their own chief of artillery admits, of two 10-pounder rifle Parrott guns, two 12-pounder howitzers, and two 6-pounder pieces, aided by two 20-pounder Parrott rifle-guns of Company G, Fifth Artillery, under Lieut. Benjamin."

"Thus matched, they drove their veteran adversaries from the field, giving confidence in and promise of the coming efficiency of this brilliant arm of our service."

.   .   .   .

"The skill, the conduct, and the soldierly qualities of

the Washington Artillery engaged were all that could be desired."

"The officers and men attached to the seven pieces already specified won for their Battalion a distinction which, I feel assured, will never be tarnished, and which will ever serve to urge them and their corps to high endeavor."

After sundown I accompanied Col. Walton to the headquarters of Gen. Beauregard, at McLean's farm-house. While there quite a number of general officers rode up and dismounted. There were Longstreet, Ewell, Bonham, Early, D. R. Jones, and Kershaw.

As they sat under the trees it was a subject for a painter, — their grave faces plainly showing the seriousness of the occasion. A battle had been fought, but a greater was to follow to-morrow, or the next day. The deliberations were carried on in a low tone, and we youngsters and staff officers smoked our pipes as we lay upon the grass at a respectful distance.

All was so calm and still that it was difficult to realize the fact that within a radius of probably ten miles many thousands of soldiers were encamped awaiting the dreadful work before them. And the homes of these men far away! Alas, how many were houses of mourning before three suns had set!

At last, when each commanding officer had received his definite instructions as to the part he was to play in the approaching drama, they arose to go. Beauregard then said to them, in a tone loud enough for us to hear, "Now, gentlemen, let to-morrow be their Waterloo."

We all sought our different bivouacs, and in an uneasy sleep I dreamed of the story I had once heard of the old guide upon the field of Waterloo, who, in describing the battle, said, "About this period of the action a most tremenjos shower-r-r-r of musket-balls was heard, and the Duke of Wellington was heard to exclaim, 'Up, black-guards, and at 'em !' "

A little incident occurred at the close of the fight on the 18th that the boys tell with gusto. They were right well used up, working the guns this hot July day, when Sergt. Dearie happened to espy, at the foot of the only tree on the plain, a demijohn. It was quickly seized, and upon examination proved to be, as it was labelled, *spiritus frumenti*, which was translated into "throat wash."

There was an immediate rush for the tin cups that had enclosed the cartridges, and which lay in profusion all around the spot where the guns had been worked, and each tired cannoneer took a hearty pull with a feeling of profound thankfulness for the unknown giver of such a welcome stimulant.

It turned out afterwards that the demijohn had been sent from the hospital to Col. Moore, of the First Virginia regiment, by its surgeon, Dr. Cullen. The negro servant, in whose care it was placed, was "stung by a bung," and, dropping the demijohn under the tree, where he had taken refuge, decamped, and without ceremony "extended his rear."

We had a laugh at the expense of the colonel and the surgeon of the First Virginia when, in after army life, we knew them better.

The total casualties of all our forces engaged on the
18th were as follows : —

Killed   15
Wounded 53

Of the enemy we buried about 64, found a few
wounded, and took 20 prisoners, 175 stands of arms, a
large number of accoutrements and blankets, and quite
150 hats.[1]

---

[1] "His (Longstreet's) battery was the 'Washington Artillery' of New Orleans, and it fired superbly.

"After four years' fighting, in half a hundred battles, it attained no greater
skill than it displayed in this its first action." — *Extract from J. Esten Cooke's
novel, " Hammer and Rapier."*

Nicolay, in his " Outbreak of the Rebellion," says of this same affair : —

" About noon, on the 18th, they (Tyler's division) were within a mile of Blackburn's ford. Then followed the ever-recurring experience in such affairs.
First, an experimental cannonade from a couple of field-pieces, before which the
enemy's guns retired. Next, the advance of a skirmish line, before which the
enemy's skirmishers retired. Then, the advance of some of the field-pieces and
the planting of a stronger battery, the posting of a regiment to support the skirmishers, and soon after the posting of the entire brigade to support the regiment, followed by calling up a reserve brigade to support the first.

" Thus the afternoon's work drifted quickly from a reconnoissance to a skirmish,
and from a skirmish to a preliminary battle. It was not until sixty men had fallen,
until the two exposed field-pieces were with difficulty extricated, until one regiment (Twelfth New York) had retreated in confusion and the other three were
deployed in line of battle to make a new charge, that Tyler heeded his instructions, and withdrew his reluctant officers and men from the fight, partly demoralized and generally exasperated, and returned to Centreville."

Swinton, in his "Army of the Potomac," says: "From Centreville Gen.
McDowell proceeded to push out reconnoissances with a view to a projected
movement by his left, but examination soon proved the impracticability of the
ground for the purpose.

" Moreover, the character of Gen. McDowell's move was revealed to Beauregard by an affair which the silly ambition of a division commander brought on
that afternoon at Blackburn's ford on Bull Run.

" Gen. Tyler had been ordered to occupy Centreville with his division, and
thence observe the roads to Bull Run, but was cautioned not to bring on an
engagement. In obedience to this he pushed a brigade forward to Blackburn's
ford, which proved to be about the centre of Beauregard's true defensive line
along Bull Run.

" Reaching the heights on the north side of the stream, he opened an artillery

On the 20th of July Gen. Jo Johnston arrived at Manassas from the " Valley," with the brigades of Gens. T. J. Jackson and Bee, the advance of his army. These troops were posted near Bull Run, at Mitchell's and Blackburn's fords.

On the 21st of July we were up and stirring at daylight, and rode over to Beauregard's head-quarters. The enemy, throwing an occasional shell over us from a big gun on the high ground between Blackburn's ford and Centreville, were evidently feeling for our lines.

To-day the guns of our battalion were assigned for duty as follows : —

Four 12-pounder howitzers, under Lieut. T. L. Rosser, commanding; Lieuts. C. C. Lewis, C. H. Slocomb, and H. A. Battles, with Gen. Ewell, at Union Mills ford.

Two 6-pounder smooth bores, under Capt. M. B. Miller and Lieut. Joe Norcom, with Gen. D. R. Jones's Third Brigade, at McLean's ford.

One rifle 6-pounder and one smooth 6-pounder, under command of Lieut. J. J. Garnett and Lieut. L. A. Adam, with Gen. Longstreet's Fourth Brigade at Blackburn's ford.

---

fire of two 20-pounder Parrott's, which had the effect of first developing, and afterwards silencing, the enemy's batteries near the ford.

" Thus far he had not exceeded his instructions : but he got it into his head that the enemy would run whenever seriously menaced, and he declared that ' the great man of the war would be the man that got to Manassas first, and he was going through that night.' His notion as to the method of executing his project was to file his brigade down to the stream, draw it up parallel to the other shore, and open an unmeaning fusilade. While engaged in this fooling, a force crossed the stream from the other side, and, striking his left flank (the Twelfth New York), disrupted it completely. This admonished Gen. Tyler to defer his intended visit to Manassas that night, and he withdrew."

Three 6-pounder smooth bores, and two rifle 6-pounders, under command of Lieut. C. W. Squires and Lieuts. J. B. Richardson and Whittington, with Col. Early's brigade, bivouacking near McLean's farm-house, — thirteen guns in all.

At 7 o'clock A.M. orders were received to send the five guns under Squires to Stone bridge, following Gen. Jackson, who, with his and Bee's brigades, had been ordered to that point, as the enemy had crossed Bull Run on the extreme left of our line, where there was but a small force of ours under Gen. Evans. Col. Walton and myself, Lieut. Dearing, and the buglers accompanied the five guns, and, upon arriving at the Lewis House, we found the situation about as follows : The enemy had crossed to our side of the Run, above the Stone bridge, where Evans, with a demi-brigade, and Latham's battery of four guns, were posted. Evans, becoming convinced that the enemy was only making a feint at the bridge, left two of Latham's guns and some of his infantry there, and had hastened to put himself in the way of the advancing Federals, who were marching against our left flank. Major Bob Wheat's battalion of Louisiana Tigers were with him, and Bee had just gone to help him with his brigade and two regiments of Bartow's. They were fighting hard against superior numbers. Besides the two guns of Latham's, with Evans, Imboden's battery was in position and firing. This was about 10 o'clock. The firing grew heavier as new troops were put in by the enemy, and they had two or three batteries at work. Lieut. Richardson, with our two rifle-guns, was ordered to a position on a plateau near the

Henry farm-house, not far from Imboden's guns. The conflict was raging in full view, and Richardson did some excellent firing, dismounting one of the enemy's guns. Between our position and the hill where Evans and Bee were engaged is a valley, through which runs Young's Branch, a small stream that crosses the Warrenton turnpike and empties into Bull Run below the Stone bridge. But it was useless to try and hold in check the enemy, with the small force under Evans, and our men fell back, down the hill, across the Warrenton turnpike and Young's branch, and ascended the hill upon which is the Henry House, situated upon a plateau skirted with dwarf pines. Richardson held his position as long as possible, and then fell back after the retreating infantry. The direct road to Manassas junction passes over the Henry Hill, and many of Evans's men kept straight on to that place, spreading the report " that all was lost," "they were cut to pieces," etc. Bee and Bartow's men appeared in great confusion, and not much disposed to rally and form promptly. Two of Richardson's boys were wounded, — E. C. Payne and Crutcher, — and all hands were furious and fighting mad that they had fallen back. They expected everything to go as easily as on the 18th. Sergt. Edward Owen was making things sulphurous with his damns. "D— 'em! We'll beat 'em yet — d— 'em! — before the day is out; " and he expressed the feeling of all hands. But affairs looked squally indeed. Lieut. Leftwich, of Latham's battery, with one gun, came up at a run, and desired Col. Walton to allow him to attach himself to our battery; but the colonel said he had better go in on his own hook. Capt.

Atkins, a tall Englishman commanding the Wheat Life-Guard of the Tigers, came up with tears in his eyes and a bayonet in his hand, and said his men had all scattered, and he feared Wheat had been killed. But now came Jackson's brigade and Hampton's Legion, and a line was quickly formed in the woods skirting the plateau. Bee, being informed of Jackson's arrival, rode over to him and said, excitedly, " General, they are driving us back." " Sir," replied Jackson, "we must give them the bayonet." Bee, riding rapidly back to his disordered troops, shouted to his men to rally and form, and, pointing with his sword to Jackson's brigade, said, " See! there's Jackson standing like a stone wall."

It was now about noon. Squires, who had been sent to Gen. Cocke with his 6-pounders to engage a battery across Bull Run, where a demonstration had been made by the enemy to cross, checked it. His guns were then joined with Richardson's Rifles at the Lewis House.

Just at this time Gens. Johnston and Beauregard dashed at full speed upon the field, and rallied the troops, and restored order. They had concluded that here was to be the fight, and, ordering to our assistance the brigades of Holmes, Bonham, and Early from their positions on the right, along Bull Run, had ridden rapidly up to look into the condition of things. As they passed our guns Gen. Johnston inquired whose they were, and we told him, and he ordered them to follow him. After us came the batteries of Pendleton (little 4-pounders, from the Virginia Military Institute) and Alburtis, which gave us thirteen guns in all. We were put in position between the newly formed line of Jackson and Bee, reinforced by Hampton, who had just arrived at Manassas and hurried to the field.   Our line was well concealed by the pines skirting the plateau over which the enemy had to cross.   As our guns went into position I could not but admire the coolness of our officers and men.   They went "into battery" as coolly as upon drill.   I must confess I was in rather a nervous condition in this my first experience under fire of the enemy's guns, which had opened again, and a little uncertain how I would stand the plunge ; but the un-uneasiness soon passed off, and, as we came up the hill, I espied two remarkably fine-looking hard crackers lying in the grass, probably dropped by some soldier.   Dismounting and picking them up, I placed them in my saddle-pocket, intimating to Col. Walton that "perchance we would be glad to have them for dinner, and that I had a flask of sherry in my off-pocket."   The Colonel laughed, and replied, "You are a cool one."   I was all right after that, and my confidence in myself was somewhat assured.

After our guns commenced firing we could see but little of our surroundings, owing to the thicket, through which we fired, and the smoke.   Two of the enemy's batteries were in front of us, near the Henry House, at short range, but aiming high, sending their shells over our heads and away off into the valley beyond.   The Colonel, Lieut. Dearing, and I dismounted, and went in amongst the guns, and the gunners of the Rifles allowed us to try a few shots, and we were inclined to think we made some good hits.   The infantry of Jackson and Bee were banging away on our right and left at the enemy, who was standing and delivering volleys around the Henry House, sometimes attempting to advance, but each time falling back, showing gaps in their ranks.   A shell burst over our heads, — aimed better than the others, — and a fragment struck Sergeant Reynolds in the head, entering the brain.   The grass around the guns now took fire; but we stamped it out and cut it down with our sabres.   While the firing was at the hottest Gen. Beauregard and staff rode up, coming down the lines on our left.   He called out, "Col. Walton, do you see the enemy?"— "Yes," was the reply.   "Then hold this position, and the day is ours.   Three cheers for Louisiana!" The "boys" cheered wildly and with a will, and worked their guns the faster.   The cheer was taken up all along the line of battle, and gave much encouragement.   Just as the General turned to ride away, a shell burst under his horse, disembowelling him, but not injuring the General. Sergt. Owen's clay-bank mare was quietly nibbling grass about the caissons when she was appropriated by Capt. Chisholm of the staff, and the General mounted her and rode away.   When the sergeant, after a while, discovered his loss, the fact that his bag containing all his toilet articles, etc., had gone too, was too much, and his temper, expressed a short time before, was eclipsed by the very sulphurous expletives in regard to this transaction.

It was but a short time after the General had gone down the line that the enemy's guns ceased firing, and, as the smoke lifted, they could be seen, abandoned upon the field. They then became the object of charge and counter-charge, and to secure them was the aim of each combatant. At 2.45 P.M. a general forward movement caused the enemy to retire beyond the plateau, and our guns were withdrawn to refill the ammunition chests, followed by the batteries that had been firing on our right.

Troops that had been ordered up by Johnston and Beauregard (Kershaw and Cash's regiments, S.C. troops) now began to arrive, and as fast as they came up were sent to the left of our line to confront the enemy, whose right was being extended to outflank our left. At about 3.30 P.M. Gen. Kirby Smith arrived from Winchester, with Gen. Elzey's brigade, and was formed also on the left. Gen. Smith was wounded, and the command devolved upon Gen. Elzey, who immediately assailed the enemy, and Beauregard gave orders for the whole line to advance. The enemy was driven from the hill, and fell back upon his reserves on the Warrenton turnpike, and rallied for another and stronger attack.

In the meanwhile, at about 4 P.M., Col. Early came upon the field with his splendid brigade, composed of Kemper's Seventh Virginia, Early's Twenty-fourth regiment Virginia Volunteers, and Hays's Seventh Louisiana regiment, and was ordered to move around the left of our line and attack the enemy's right, just re-forming and apparently about to resume the offensive. This was done, our own Seventh bearing aloft the colors of Louisiana in the van, yelling and firing as they advanced. They were joined by a section of artillery under Lieut. Beckham, and a squadron of cavalry under Col. J. E. B. Stuart.

The enemy's right was thrown into confusion, and, a general charge being immediately ordered by Gen. Beauregard, a panic ensued, and the whole Federal army fled in wild confusion from the field.

The artillery captured in front of the Henry house was turned upon its late owners by Capts. Chisholm, Ferguson, and others of the staff, and a number of rounds fired.

Eleven guns were taken here from the enemy.

At 4.30 P.M. I rode over the field, near the Henry house, where we had been fighting, and saw the effects of battle for the first time. Dead and wounded men lay about on every side; broken muskets, pieces of clothing, dead horses, disabled cannon were scattered about. We found men in the uniform of the New York Fire Zouaves, the Marines, the Seventy-ninth Highlanders, and the Fourteenth New York regiment.

To the wounded we gave water, and had some of them sent to the hospitals.

The Fire Zouaves thanked us for our attention, but frankly said they were "after us" especially, and would not have given us quarter.

The batteries we had been fighting were those of Griffin and Ricketts.

A large proportion of their men and horses were killed or wounded. Some of the men got away on the battery horses, cutting them loose from the traces with knives. Capt. Ricketts was left behind wounded, and fell into our hands. Any damage our guns failed to inflict upon them was completed by the Thirty-third Virginia regiment, of Jackson's brigade, who approached so near the guns as to wipe out the cannoneers with one volley.

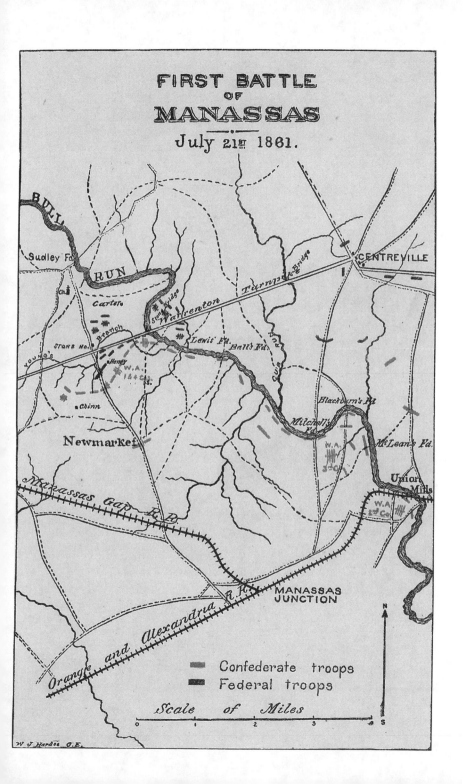

FIRST BATTLE OF MANASSAS

July 21ST 1861.

Confederate troops
Federal troops

Scale of Miles

Close by an exploded caisson, near the Henry house, was the body of a handsome lieutenant of artillery. He was noticed particularly for his splendid apparel. He wore the finest of linen, and silk stockings. His mustache was waxed to a nicety. He was dressed with evident care, as though going to a ball.

He was recognized by an old acquaintance, a Virginian, as Douglas Ramsey, a well-known member of Washington society.

I met Gen. Jackson riding about the field, and spoke to him of the events of the day. He had been slightly wounded in the hand, and had it bound up in his handkerchief. He was a very quiet, plain-looking man, dressed in a blue military coat, and wore the shoulder-straps of a colonel in the United States army. His cap was of the old army pattern, in vogue during the Mexican war, — blue cloth, flat on top.

Lieut. Dearing and I secured the colors of the Second Wisconsin regiment, and took them to Gen. Beauregard.

At about 5 P.M., President Davis came upon the field; as he passed the spot where our guns were halted, the boys cheered him, and, turning to his Aid, he said, as he raised his hat, "Don't they look like little game-cocks?"

While the enemy was rushing off towards Bull Run, in a panic, we could see them quite distinctly from the Lewis-house hill, and opened fire upon them with our rifles, just to "help them along," but soon received an order from Gen. Johnston to cease firing, and "save our ammunition for the pursuit."

Our day's work being done, the Colonel and I sat down under a spreading oak-tree, and lunched upon the two hard crackers and the sherry, verifying to the full my remark, that " we would be glad to get them."

We heard a good many reports from the field from Bliffkins. Bob Wheat had been desperately wounded, and might die. His " Tigers" had scattered.

The Seventh Louisiana received much praise. They double-quicked five miles to get into the fight, and some of the men were overcome by the heat. They say Capt. Dan Wilson, commanding the "Blues," although a large man, made as good time as any one, and called out to his men, when they showed fatigue, " Come on, Blue-birds, light on me !" The soubriquet of "Blue-bird Wilson" had already been applied to him in the regiment.

During the day (21st) Gen. D. R. Jones moved his command across Bull Run at McLean's ford, — in conformity to the original orders of Gen. Beauregard, — and advanced along the road towards Centreville, but soon encountered a heavy force of infantry and artillery strongly posted behind an *abatis* of felled trees. He was met by a furious fire of infantry and artillery at short range, and withdrew his troops to his former position. While doing so one of Capt. Miller's 6-pounders got fast against a tree, and there was some little delay in moving it on. An irate staff-officer rode up, and began finding fault with the men at the piece. This annoyed the sergeant, and he called out, "Who are you, anyhow?" To which the officer replied, "I am *Capt. A. Coward*, of Gen. Jones's staff. Who are you?" "I am *Sergt. A. Hero*, of the Washington Artillery." The singularity of names and meeting put all hands in a good-humor.

The Howitzer Battery, under Lieut. Rosser, was on the march from 2 P.M. with Ewell's brigade in the direction of Fairfax C.H., and, returning to Union Mills, arrived at our position, with the reserves, unfortunately too late to take part in the battle.

The guns under Lieut. Garnett, with Gen. Longstreet, were not engaged.

All the officers and men of our battalion were uniformed in blue, as were many other commands, and resembled the Federal troops. A lot of red-flannel strips were distributed to us to be tied upon the left arm above the elbow. And we so wore them.

The commissary wagon coming up, all hands enjoyed a supper of bacon and hard-tack, and bivouacked under the trees.

On the 22d we were awakened by the rain beating upon our faces; and it was wet, muddy, and disagreeable. After breakfast I rode out with Rosser along the Warrenton turnpike, following the route taken by the enemy on the previous afternoon. We came across evidences of great demoralization; the road was strewn with muskets, clothing, haversacks, all abandoned in the flight.

At Cub Run, a small stream crossing the turnpike near Centreville, there was a narrow suspension bridge. In the headlong flight this bridge became blocked by wagons, ambulances, and cannon, those following in rear jammed against those in front, and the result was confusion and death. The barricade was complete. Here a battery of artillery was found and a small boat howitzer. Dead men were in the abandoned ambulances, and, altogether, it was a dreadful and sickening sight. A canvas-covered trunk lay wide open in the middle of the road, marked " Col. Berry, Fourth Maine Regiment." The contents had evidently been already overhauled, so my conscience permitted me to examine the remainder. I found a new uniform coat, of blue cloth, — judging from its size, the colonel of the Fourth Maine must have been a large man, — a bag of tea, some warm under-clothing, which I appropriated as " spoils of war."

We had heard from prisoners that at Centreville there had been quite a large party of excursionists, Congressmen, and others from Washington, who had come out with their women to " see the fun."

We saw evidences of their presence in the shape of baskets of champagne, etc., and several carriages of different kinds were being carried to the rear. One of these Rosser secured, and accredited its ownership to the Hon. John P. Hale, of New Hampshire.

We gathered up as many red blankets, overcoats, and other " loot," as we could carry upon our horses, and started back to the battery. *En route* we saw in a fence corner a full set of brass-band instruments ; but the musicians had beaten them all out of shape. The big drum, however, was in good order, and I took it up behind me after the manner of a travelling circus, and sent it to our band leader, who was at Manassas Junction, attending our wounded. Upon our return to our bivouac we distributed the blankets and overcoats to the boys, and they gladly received them, as it was raining hard. Col. Berry's uniform fitted our Colonel exactly, and so he appropriated it. Col. Tom Taylor afterwards wore it into Washington on flag-of-truce duty.

During the 22d and 23d of July there was a general clearing up of the battle-field. Details were burying the dead, ordnance officers collecting arms and equipments, ambulances, wagons, etc. A new bridge was brought by the Federals to replace the stone bridge, in case we had blown it up. It was reported that a large lot of handcuffs had been found in a wagon, — several thousands of them; we presume, if the enemy had defeated us, all the prisoners would have been furnished with bracelets free of cost, and we would have marched into Washington as the animals went into Noah's ark, two by two.

The sorriest sights upon a battle-field are in those dreadful field-hospitals, established in barns, under large tents, and in out-houses. The screams and groans of the poor fellows undergoing amputation are sometimes dreadful, — and then the sight of arms and legs surrounding these places, as they are thrown into great piles, is something one that has seen the results of battle can never forget. No longer do the rush, roar and boom of shot and shell, and the volleys of musketry bring the fire to the soldier's eye and make his blood tingle through his veins in glorious excitement; but now the saw and the knife prove that all is not glory when grim-visaged War shows his wrinkled front, and strikes down so many thousands of brave fellows, who, but yesterday, boldly marched in scrried ranks.

On the 24th of July we were allowed to return to our old camping-ground, and our tents were pitched as before.   We were glad to get where we could rest.   We *had* experienced a lively time of it since we struck tents a week ago, and no mistake.

Since the afternoon of the 21st — when we were told to " save our ammunition for the pursuit " — we had heard nothing in reference to the intention then to pursue. We had seen some printed placards from Washington calling upon stragglers to rejoin their regiments, and people who came through the lines reported great demoralization and fright prevailing.

We presumed the President and our generals had good reasons for our inactivity.

During the battle of the 21st our army numbered, all told, 32,070 men ; but we had only 13,000 engaged, the remainder being stationed at the several fords along Bull Run, — so far away they could not get into action.

Our loss was put down at : 378 killed, 1,489 wounded, 30 missing.

We captured : 28 pieces of artillery, 4,500 muskets, 500,000 cartridges, a garrison flag, 10 regimental colors, besides 64 artillery horses with their harnesses.[1]

---

[1] Extract from Johnston's Narrative, p. 55 : —

The retreat was marked by great disorder, all semblance of military organization being lost.   Many did not even stop on reaching the camps on the south of the Potomac but fled by the bridges and ferries to Washington.

.   .   .   .

The Union loss must have been above 2,000 (2,952 ?), for the prisoners, well and wounded, left in Beauregard's hands, numbered 1,460. — *Swinton, p. 57.*

ADDRESS TO THE ARMY.

HEAD-QUARTERS ARMY OF THE POTOMAC,
MANASSAS, July 25, 1861.

SOLDIERS OF THE CONFEDERATE STATES : — One week ago a countless host of men, organized into an army, with all the appointments which modern art and practical skill could devise, invaded the soil of Virginia.

Their people sounded their approach with triumphant displays of anticipated victory.

Their generals came in almost royal state ; their great ministers, senators, and women came to witness the immolation of our army, and the subjugation of our people, and to celebrate them with wild revelry.

It is with the profoundest emotion of gratitude to an over-ruling God, whose hand is manifest in protecting our homes and our liberties, that we, your generals commanding, are enabled, in the name of our whole country, to thank you for that patriotic courage, that heroic gallantry, that devoted daring, exhibited by you in the actions of the 18th and 21st of July, by which the hosts of the enemy were scattered and a signal and glorious victory obtained.

The two affairs of the 18th and 21st were but the sustained and continued efforts of your patriotism against the constantly recurring columns of an enemy fully treble your number, and this effort was crowned on the evening of the 21st with a victory so complete that the invaders were driven disgracefully from the field, and made to fly in disorderly rout back to their entrenchments, a distance of over thirty miles.

They left upon the field nearly every piece of artillery, a large portion of their arms, equipments, baggage, stores, etc., and almost every one of their wounded and dead, amounting, together with prisoners, to many thousands. And thus the northern hosts were driven by you from the soil of Virginia.

Soldiers, we congratulate you on an event which insures the liberty of our country.

We congratulate every man of you whose glorious privilege it was to participate in this triumph of courage and truth, — to fight in the battle of Manassas. You have created an epoch in the history of liberty, and unborn nations will rise up and call you blessed.

Continue this noble devotion, looking always to the protection of a just God, and, before time grows much older, we will be hailed as the deliverers of a nation of ten millions of people.

Comrades, our brothers who have fallen have earned undying renown on earth, and their blood, shed in our holy cause, is a precious and acceptable sacrifice to the Father of truth and right.

Their graves are beside the tomb of Washington, their spirits have joined his in eternal communion. We will hold the soil in which the dust of Washington is mingled with the dust of our brothers. We will transmit this land free to our children, or we will fall into the fresh graves of our brothers. We will drop one tear on their laurels and move forward to avenge them.

Soldiers, we congratulate you on a glorious triumph and complete victory.

We thank you for doing your *whole duty* in the service of your country.

(Signed)   J. E. JOHNSTON,
General, C.S.A.

(Signed)   G. T. BEAUREGARD,
General, C.S.A.

CHAPTER III.

BACK IN CAMP.

Back in Camp. — Retrospection. — Bountiful Larder. — New Friends. — Appointments and Promotions. — Our Camps. — Camp Benjamin. — President Davis Reviews the Army. — Centreville. — Quaker Guns. — New Tents. — New Battle-flags Distributed. — Battle at Ball's Bluff. — "Chasseurs-à-pied." — "Here's Your Mule." — "Bolivar Ward." — Col. P. T. Moore. — Major Bob Wheat. — Col. Harry Hays. — "Noctes Ambrosia." — "Little White House on Salisbury Plains." — Winter Quarters. — Waltonville.

HOW delightful it is to stretch one's self upon the clean straw on the tent floor and have a good, long rest, taking time to recall the events of the past week! No enemy to bother you, no sudden orders to be up and doing, no bugle sounding "Boots and saddles," or "Column forwar-r-r-d!" Nothing to do but eat and sleep and drink! Happy soldier, to feel that he has been through the fiery furnace and has come out with his escutcheon bright and his body whole.

What a physical change has come over us! We are bronzed by exposure and seasoned thoroughly. We have given our dead a soldier's burial and our wounded are lionizing it in Richmond. Lucky fellows, with their hurts! Of course they will hurry back to us less fortunate ones. Oh, yes! of course, if the charming girls will let them.

We can just imagine the full charges of "Pizzini's" ice-cream they will be loaded with, the nice Virginia rolls the dear matrons will provide, and the sweet flowers and fruit they will receive from the maidens, and all that, filling the sick-room with delightful and fragrant odors.

Then the time when the crutch comes to the front. Good gracious ! — two of them ! — two crutches ! A double charge of " Pizzini " — then the box from home, and — the imagination fails — we roll over and fill a pipe with "Lone Jack," and try to think what kind of rations our cook will serve to-day.

How we have reduced our equipment since active service began ! Knapsacks have been voted a bore, and have been or will be thrown aside. On leaving home each man had his revolver for "close quarters," and the sabre was part of the regulation uniform. Both are in disgrace. The revolver will be traded off, sold, or sent home, and the sabres (all that are left, for many have disappeared during the past week) will be turned over to the cavalry.[1]

Even the officers will hereafter strap theirs to their saddles, or, better still, hang them up in the company wagons.

---

[1] HEAD–QUARTERS DEPT. NOR. VIRGINIA,
RAPIDAN, March 23, 1862.

GENERAL ORDERS, No. 34.

I. Commissioned officers are forbidden to carry fire-arms except pistols. Non-commissioned officers and privates are prohibited from carrying pistols.

II. On the march, captains of batteries will not allow the cannoneers to ride on the limbers or caissons, nor allow any baggage to be carried thereon.

III. Brigadier-generals and colonels are especially charged with a rigid enforcement of this order.

IV. The chief of ordnance is directed to purchase, at a fair price, all pistols or carbines of which their owners may wish to dispose.

By command of Gen. Johnston.
THOS. G. RHETT,
A. A. Genl.

A blanket snugly rolled inside of a rubber cloth, the ends tied together and thrown over one shoulder, will hold all the necessary change of clothing; the haversack will carry the crackers and bacon, the comb, the soap, and the towel, and the tooth-brush will decorate the button-hole of the jacket, together with tobacco-bag. We still retain our white gaiters and red kepis, but they are bound eventually to go. The blue cloth dress uniforms have been shipped to Richmond, and will there remain for swell occasions.

We were called "Band-box Soldiers" by the commands which came to Richmond direct from Pensacola, and saw us there before we took the field. We are now fast approaching an appearance that would have met their entire approbation, only, as Bull Run flows just back of our camp, we could claim to be somewhat cleaner than the average; and let it be of record, that, all through the war, the Washington Artillery-man, though he might wear a ragged jacket and torn shoes, was clean and presentable. Indeed, this condition of things was necessary, as the command had, or claimed to have, cousins and aunts in every city or hamlet in the whole of the eastern part of the Old Dominion. The best rooms everywhere were opened to them, and the land flowed with eggs, chickens, milk, and "wild honey."

August 1 we were still in camp, and were visited by numerous sight-seers, who came to look at the battle-field. There was an exploded caisson near Mrs. Henry's house, and the boys had so constantly informed the curious that it belonged to Sherman's battery that they began to believe it themselves, and chips of it were sent far and wide as souvenirs. The Henry house was also being

CAMP LOUISIANA, JULY 25, 1861.

chopped down, with a prospect that, in a little while, only the stone foundation would be left.

Thanks to kind friends in New Orleans, our larder was bountifully supplied with claret, *pâtés*, sardines, etc., and our caterer, Capt. Johnson, or " Captain Shabrack," as the boys called him, on account of his handsome saddle-cloth, in conjunction with the major-domo, procured for the mess, from the surrounding country, milk and butter, eggs, chickens, and ice.

Our military chest was the " Aladdin's lamp." Our circle of acquaintance was gradually extending among the Virginia regiments encamped near us, and especially in the First Virginia. The surgeons of the latter, Drs. Cullen and Maury, afterwards on Gen. Longstreet's staff, we saw much of, and became greatly attached to.

The Hon. John Slidell and Judge Alexander Walker of Louisiana were often in our camp. Mr. Slidell was a guest of Gen. Beauregard, whose head-quarters, removed to Weir's house, were not far from our camp on Bull Run. We often rode over after dress-parade, in the evening. In the yard a number of tents were pitched for the general and his staff. The office of Col. Jordan, his adjutant-general, was in the house. Capt. Gray Latham, with his red flannel shirt, was the hero of the hour, his battery having fought well with Evans on the 21st of July. Capt. H. E. Peyton also loomed up as a hero. On the 21st he was a private in the cavalry, but stuck so tight and so gallantly to Beauregard, as a volunteer aid, that the General had him promoted to a staff position with the rank of captain.

The General's staff was composed mostly of young South Carolinians of good family, such as Capts. Heyward, Chisholm, Ferguson, and others. He had also a number of volunteer aids, all men of distinction. Ex-Governor James Chesnut, William Porcher Miles, Col. John S. Preston, and ex-Governor Manning, a most charming gentleman. His juleps, made of his own dark Cognac, and served in a large bucket, with huge lumps of ice, and plenty of straws protruding from the fragrant mint, were simply marvellous. We shall never forget them.

Drs. Chopin and Beard, of New Orleans, were also on Gen. Beauregard's staff as surgeons.

It appears that we were now booked as the " famous Washington Artillery" for our services on the 18th and 21st of July, and, in truth, a finer set of fellows never " drew sword or poised a lance." They enjoyed every hour with a gusto that is always catching ; — sometimes, but not often, under roof, sometimes, in the drenching rain, they slept without a murmur, and woke in the morning with the same cheerful faces and happy hearts. When they had food all ate and grew fat, and when they had none they smoked cigarettes and fought just as well.

The camp of the artillery is always picturesque, but especially so when on outpost. The guns are parked in order, the caissons in rear, and the horses near by ; four streets of tents, when in regular camp, run back in straight lines to the line of officers' quarters, at right angles, in the rear. In front of the camp is the guard-tent, and on the rear line are the Colonel's head-quarters, and the flag-staff and bulletin board for posting the orders of the day. The camp-flag is hoisted every day at *reveille* and lowered when the bugles sound retreat at sunset. The men, when not on fatigue duty, lounge about, smoking, playing euchre, cribbage, or chess; some are reading or writing letters. The arrival of the mail from home is a moment of great excitement. As the package is opened by the adjutant and distributed, what joy it brings to some, what probable distress to others! Who knows?

On the 1st of September camp was moved to Centreville, and called Camp Orleans. This camp was laid out with great regularity, and the company streets were covered over with arbors of green boughs. Close by, the Seventh Louisiana regiment was encamped, and there was much social intercourse between us. We often met Col. Harry Hays, Lieut.-Col. Penn, Major Rickarby, Capts. Sam Flower, Morgan, and the adjutant, Lieut. John New.

A frolicsome humor came over a party of officers one evening, and a raid was planned, led by " gallant old Rickarby," — " officer of the day," — who, returning with some of us to our camp, convinced the sentinel over our guns that it was " all right," and we removed all the " fifth wheels " from the caissons and rolled them noiselessly through the main street of the camp, and piled them up in front of head-quarters. At guard-mounting next morning, *our* " officer of the day" got a raking from the Colonel[1] and pined away in arrest for a week.

---

[1] After the first battle of Manassas Major Walton was recommended by Gens. Johnston and Beauregard for promotion to the rank of " *colonel* of artillery." No such grade being possible at the time in artillery, — major being the highest rank in that branch of the service, — a law was passed by the Confederate Congress to meet the case, and, on receiving his commission, Col. Walton was at

While at Centreville the battalion received a new fatigue outfit for the men, — jackets and pants, "made to order" by Ira Smith & Co. Each man was measured for his suit, and they came, properly labelled, to their owners, — another good thing from the military chest. The material was what is known as the Crenshaw Mills stuff, a bluish-gray in color, and gave the command a neat and distinctive appearance. Thus far we had no use for government money.

Messieurs Lanier, Wood, and Cammack arrived from New Orleans as commissioners for the State of Louisiana to furnish clothing to the troops. It was doubtful whether we should be included in the distribution, as we were not really "State troops" but entered directly the regular Confederate army.

They had expressed a desire to visit the outposts, and we proposed to take them out and get up a little skirmish for them, so they could astonish the people at home with their experiences.

The enemy crossed the Potomac river September 11 in force, accompanied by Griffin's battery of eight guns. They were met by a regiment of infantry and two of our guns from Munson's Hill, under Lieut. Rosser.[1] The affair occurred at Lewinsville, five miles from Munson's Hill. The enemy retired.

once appointed by Gen. Beauregard Chief of Artillery of the "Army of the Potomac" (as the Confederate army in Virginia was then called), remaining, however, in command of the Washington Artillery.

[1] HEAD–QUARTERS THIRD BATTERY, WASHINGTON ARTILLERY,
MUNSON'S HILL, September 14, 1861.

COLONEL : — In obedience to an order received from Col. J. E. B. Stuart, on the 11th inst., about 12 o'clock, I immediately proceeded with one section of my Battery (one 3-inch rifle gun and one 12-pound howitzer) in rear of the regi-

We had a report that night that the enemy had crossed on our left flank, and a battle was looked for in a day or two. Gen. McClellan was in command of the Federals. Gen. Beauregard had moved his head-quarters to Fairfax C.H. His son, René Beauregard, pitched his tent in our camp as a cadet. He came to perfect himself in artillery.

We had but two companies now in camp, the Third and Fourth; the first, under Lieut. Squires, was at Germantown, and four of our guns were under Rosser, at Munson's Hill, overlooking Washington. The dome of the capitol could be distinctly seen, and the flags waving over large fortifications. The enemy was apparently in large force. Our skirmishers were engaged daily.

---

ment of infantry (which I found at Taylor's cross-roads), in the direction of Lewinsville, until we reached, in the vicinity of the enemy, and considerably in his rear, a narrow lane, where the column halted.

I then rode forward, to observe the position of the enemy. I ascertained that his right had discovered our approach, and was moving rapidly to the rear and left to join the main body of his forces.

But, before the alarm had been communicated to the left, I moved my section of artillery forward, and surprised, by a shot from the rifle, a large body of infantry which was occupying an inclosure and house about six hundred yards off.

This evidently was their first notification of our presence, and threw them into great confusion.

This shot was followed quickly by a spherical case from the howitzer, whose effect was to scatter the enemy and put him in retreat.

The road over which the enemy retired is, in this locality, nearly parallel to the lane in which my pieces were planted, and, from the rapidity of my fire, and the confusion of the enemy consequent upon every discharge, I can but believe that he suffered terribly.

After he had been driven from the field I rode over this ground and found two killed, one mortally wounded, and captured one prisoner.

The road here was ploughed by my projectiles and thick with fragments of shell, and strewn with the canteens, haversacks, and a few guns (muskets) of the enemy.

Upon a slight eminence was a house, a few paces from the road, and to the right of my position were posted two field-pieces, a rifle and a howitzer, which returned our fire warmly until their retreating column had passed, then, rein-forced by six more pieces, kept up the fire for a short time from this position, then fired retiring, evidently supposing themselves pursued, for, as I rode along

A few days previously the enemy sent up a large balloon, and our boys fired at it with a rifle-gun. The ball must have passed unpleasantly close, as the balloon was immediately drawn down.

Our first company under Squires returned from an expedition to Little Falls, on the Potomac, where they fired into a large Federal camp, inflicting some loss. The enemy struck tents and moved away.

The following order was issued : —

HEAD-QUARTERS WASHINGTON ARTILLERY,

CAMP ORLEANS, CENTREVILLE, VA.

ORDER No. 34 : —   September 29, 1861.

The attorney-general and acting secretary of war having decided finally that the 11th section of the Act of Congress of the 6th of March,

---

in their rear, I observed their projectiles falling far in advance of me and fully a mile in advance of my battery.

It affords me great pleasure to say that the conduct of my men was admirable. Though in position, when the enemy's greatly superior force could be clearly seen, and opposed by great superiority in numbers of cannon, every man performed his whole duty coolly and cheerfully.

My attention was called particularly to Lieut. Slocomb, for whose gallant service I am truly grateful. He was engaged all the time, assisting the cannoneers in pointing and ranging the pieces, by pointing out the enemy and observing the effect of each fire.

One of the gunners being sick, I assigned private John D. Britton to the important post of gunner of the howitzer, and the accuracy of his fire, his coolness and energy entitle him to the greatest praise.

The inefficiency of the case and shell projectiles furnished me a few days since for the service of the rifled guns was again exemplified in this engagement, not one of them (owing to the want of sufficient windage for the time fuze) exploding.

The "Boarman" fuze, with which the spherical case and shell for the howitzer were served, showed, in their manufacture, great deficiency. There was no uniformity whatever in their burning. Some cut at five seconds did not burn, in many cases. Two others cut at two, burnt as long as four or five seconds.

Very respectfully, your obedient servant,

T. L. ROSSER, *C.S.A.,*

Commanding Battery 2, W.A.

COL. J. B. WALTON,

Commanding Washington Artillery,

Centreville, Va.

NOTE. In this engagement, sixty-six (66) rifle and forty-one (41) spherical cases were fired.

1861, entitled "An Act for the establishment and organization of the Army of the Confederate States of America," is the law which governs this battalion in the filling of vacancies in the commissioned officers, the president has made the following appointments, to wit: —

First Lieutenant C. W. Squires to be a captain *vice* Capt. H. M. Isaacson, resigned.

Second Lieutenant H. A. Battles to be a first lieutenant *vice* Lieut. C. C. Lewis, resigned.

Second Lieutenant H. G. Gieger to be a first lieutenant *vice* Lieut. J. B. Whittington, resigned.

Second Lieutenant C. H. Slocomb to be a first lieutenant *vice* Lieut. S. J. McPherson, resigned.

First Sergeant Edward Owen to be a first lieutenant to fill an original vacancy.

First Lieutenant T. L. Rosser has been appointed to temporary rank of captain for service with volunteer troops, under Act No. 155 of 2d section of Congress, approved May 21, 1861, and ordered to report to these head-quarters for duty.

Second Lieut. J. J. Garnett is in like manner appointed to temporary rank of first lieutenant, and ordered to report to these head-quarters.

Capt. Rosser will assume command of the second company, to which he has heretofore been attached as lieutenant commanding.

Lieut. Battles is assigned to the fourth company.

Lieut. Gieger is assigned to the second company.

Lieut. Edward Owen is assigned to the first company.

The vacancies of second lieutenants will be filled at an early day by the president.

The following comprise the officers of this Battalion: —

Captains. — M. B. Miller, B. F. Eshleman, C. W. Squires, and T. L. Rosser.

First Lieutenants. — Joe Norcom, J. B. Richardson, W. M. Owen, H. A. Battles, J. J. Garnett, H. G. Gieger, C. H. Slocomb, Edward Owen.

Second Lieutenants. — All vacant.

By order of

J. B. WALTON,
Colonel Commanding.

W. M. OWEN, *Adjutant.*

The vacancies were afterwards filled by the appointment of meritorious non-commissioned officers.

The Battalion sustained during its first year a severe loss in the resignation of some of its best officers, among whom were Capt. Isaacson and Lieuts. Lewis, Slocomb, Whittington, and Adam, whose talents had greatly contributed to the successful organization of the Battalion in its infancy, and most of whom afterwards did good service in other companies.

On the 14th of October our batteries were moved forward to Fairfax Court House, and we called our tenting-place " Camp Benjamin," after the distinguished secretary of war.

The Second company remained on outpost duty under Capt. Rosser, with Gen. J. E. B. Stuart, near Washington city. While at "Camp Benjamin" we received three 24-pounder howitzers, which gave us a complement of four guns to each battery — making a total of sixteen (16) guns.

The battalion of " *Chasseurs-à-pied*," Major St. Paul, of New Orleans, were here assigned to our Battalion as sharp-shooters. They were all creoles, and splendid fellows.

During our stay at "Camp Benjamin" we experienced one of the severest thunder-storms conceivable, and sad havoc was made with our canvas coverings.

Lieut. Garnett shared my tent, and, as the wind rose and the thunder rolled, we sprang from our blankets, and each seized a tent-pole, and steadied our frail habitation as best we could; but it soon became evident that we must succumb to the elements. Just as Garnett cried out " that it was glorious to die for one's country!" down went the whole structure prone upon the ground, with the rain pattering upon our backs. I could hear Garnett ripping and tearing about "patriotism!" "love of country!" "It's glorious so to live, — yes, very, in mud and water," "Whose war is this, anyhow?" etc., etc. I asked him what we had better do about it, and he replied, "Do about it? Why I'm going to stay right here, just to be revenged upon the whole Southern Confederacy!" So we did, — upon wet blankets in the mud, — and the tent-cloth flapping like a wet sail over us.

At daylight we discovered the whole camp in about the same condition, and the Colonel had fared no better. The wind had actually carried his loose articles, including his watch, to a neighboring fence corner, and it puzzled the "major-domo" not a little to get them all together again. The army was reviewed here by President Davis.

On October 19 the enemy made a strong demonstration upon Fairfax Court House, and our army was withdrawn to Centreville for a better position, there to encamp and fortify. In most of the works "Quaker guns" (logs of wood mounted on wagon wheels, and covered partially with brush) were placed. They made a formidable appearance, and "intelligent contrabands" could report them to MacClellan.

The Battalion received from New Orleans a full set of new tents, and our camp was pitched close by Gen. Beauregard's head-quarters, and called "Camp Hollins."

The tents were of excellent material, and presented a most comfortable appearance.

An inspection being ordered, everything was found in "apple-pie order." Passing along the line of tents one could see a hundred evidences of the character of the men. Everything was as neat as a parlor, and in perfect order. Many of the tents had been floored, others filled with straw, over which rubber cloths had been spread. Knapsacks (a few still remaining) and blankets had been carefully packed and rolled, and arrayed along the back wall, in the centre of which was a rack for clothes and small arms. Every tent looked really comfortable, and gave evidence of the remarkable ingenuity of the men.

The *Chasseurs* destroyed their baggage upon leaving Fairfax. They had a lot of *trunks*, and, having no wagon to bring them off, set fire to them, thinking the emergency greater than it really was.

While here the army received the new battle-flags, — a blue St. Andrew cross upon a field of red. This was the particular flag of the army, wholly different from the " Confederate flag," and is not to be confounded with that.

The new flag was from a design furnished Congress by our Col. J. B. Walton and E. C. Hancock, of New Orleans, and the first ones made were fashioned by the Misses Carey, of Baltimore, out of their own silk dresses. They sent three to Centreville, — one for Gen. Beauregard,[1] another for Gen. Johnston, and a third for Gen. Van Dorn.

Every regiment had now its own flag.

---

[1] Gen. Beauregard's flag was sent to New Orleans, and when the city fell into the hands of the Federals it was sent to Havana. It now (1883) rests among the archives of the " Washington Artillery," in its new Arsenal in New Orleans, having been presented to the command for safe-keeping by the General.

On the day of presentation the whole army was massed upon the heights of Centreville and received their colors with great enthusiasm.

Gov. Letcher, of Virginia, presented each Virginia regiment with a stand of State colors, — blue ground with the coat of arms in the centre.

After the ceremony of presentation was over, a large number of officers were by invitation assembled at the head-quarters of Gen. Van Dorn, where a collation was spread, and as Capt. Fairfax, of Gen. Longstreet's staff, had sent to his ancient manor-house, in Loudon county, for South-down mutton and rare old wines, we had a royal time.

On the afternoon of October 21 a courier galloped to Gen. Beauregard's head-quarters with information that an engagement had been fought at Leesburg.

Evans's brigade had been attacked by Federal troops under command of Col. Baker. It was reported that the odds were greatly against our forces. Four Federal regiments crossed the Potomac at Edwards's ferry and were met and checked by Barksdale's Thirteenth Mississippi regiment. Five other regiments crossed at Ball's Bluff, and were met by Hunton's Eighth Virginia, Featherstone's Seventeenth Mississippi, and Burt's Eighteenth Mississippi regiments, and after a furious fight were driven over the Bluff in a panic equal to Bull Run. Many rushed into the river and were drowned. Col. Baker was killed on the field.

This affair waked us up considerably and increased confidence in the powers of our army, already so well and securely established. We heard that Col. Jenifer was very active and came in for a large share of credit for the success of our troops.

On the 22d it was deemed necessary, in view of further movements of the enemy at Leesburg, to send some troops to Evans, and among the forces ordered out for the march we received orders to send the "*Chasseurs*" and a battery.

It was the "Third company's" turn, as they didn't have much of a show on the 21st of July, and so the men rolled their blankets and received three days' rations.

The other companies that were to remain behind were satisfied, however, not to leave their comfortable tents for a long march through mud and rain.

The "*Chasseurs*" filed out of camp about 8 A.M.; the Third company's bugle sounded, "Boots and Saddles," and the boys marched away, followed by the cheers and good wishes of their comrades.

The parting of Major St. Paul and his cook (female Irish) was affecting in the extreme. "Adieu, Louise! *ma chère!* Adieu, I may never more the *plaisir* to see you again. Adieu!" and with tears in his eyes he gave her a French hug, throwing his arms around her two hundred pounds avoirdupois. "Good luck to ye, ye ould divil!" Louise murmured, and returned to her camp-fire.

In the evening news came of another affair at Leesburg, our troops again driving the enemy.

On the 29th the "*Chasseurs*" and the "Third company" returned to camp, tired out and disgusted that they had "marched up the hill, and then marched down again," and didn't get a shot. They stood the quizzing of the boys with resignation and philosophy, and settled down again to camp-life.

That mythical personage, "Bolivar Ward," seemed to have arrived to-day, for he was much inquired after. It was a camp joke to send some credulous fellow off on a wild-goose chase to find a letter or a package from home, or something imaginary, said to be in the possession of "Bolivar Ward." The information would probably emanate from the guard-house, and the victim would be sent to the extreme end of the camp for "Bolivar," only to be sent to the other extreme, all the while asking every one he met, "Have any of you fellows seen Bolivar Ward?"—"Oh, yes! I saw him at the picket rope," one would reply. At the "picket rope" he had been seen at the Colonel's quarters, and back he would go; after wasting his precious time for a few hours, he would discover the "sell" and "acknowledge the corn." This afforded great amusement, and it became a standard reply to all inquiries such as "Where's the skillet?"—"Bolivar Ward has it."—"Where's the water-bucket?"—"Bolivar Ward has it."

The expression of "Here's your mule" seems to have come into vogue in this camp. It seems to have originated when an old farmer visited the camp in search of a lost mule. When it became known in camp that some one was in search of a stray hybrid, from all quarters would be heard, "Here's your mule;" and the searcher was trotted about as was the anxious inquirer after "Bolivar."

At this time our forces had dwindled down to about 40,000 men, and it was reported by scouts that MacClellan was organizing in front of Washington an army of 100,000 men.

We had an immense number of absentees; in fact, it looked as though the authorities had been thinking that " Manassas" ended the war, and that everybody could go home and have a good time; that they had come on to Virginia for the summer months, and to have a " day's shooting."

The weather was now so bad and the roads so deep in mud that it was not believed possible to move an army or begin a campaign until early spring.

During the month of November Col. P. T. Moore, of the First Virginia regiment, returned from sick leave, having been wounded on the 18th of July. We had many social gatherings at our respective head-quarters, his regiment being encamped alongside. He had an excellent band, better, I think, than ours, and each gave excellent music at guard-mounting and dress-parade. " Listen to the Mocking-bird" was the favorite air of the Virginians.

We became intimate with " the Surgeons," and we had Capt. Willie Allan, the quartermaster of the First Virginia, and Major Bob Wheat (who had recovered from his wound), of the "Louisiana Tigers," besides other kindred spirits, for our *coteries*.

We had a frame house transported from the outposts and fitted up for head-quarters, with a right royal fire-place of the old baronial hall fashion whereon one might roast an ox whole; and many very delightful evenings did we pass in the " little white house on Salisbury Plains," as we called it. The sparkling wit, the song, the anecdote, — accompanied by hot punch, that drove dull care away, and brought oblivion of the snow, the mud, and rain outside, — can we forget them? Never! Allan, with his song of "Sally in our Alley," and the "Prisoner's Lament," — who was always "cussing his eyes," and going "up Tyburn hill in a cart;" Rosser, with his "Dragoon bold," and Garnett, with "The Captain with his Whiskers," accompanied by a sly glance at the imaginary pretty girl behind the blinds, and the "Soldier's Dream;" Brewer, with his "Maryland, my Maryland!" — their voices rang out, awakening the echoes of the Blue Ridge. Moore was full of Irish song and story; his "Mr. McShane" and "Jacob and Esau" were inimitable; while "Old Bob Wheat" would contribute a roaring chorus, and would at intervals prognosticate the future life, — "when, on the high battlements of Heaven, George Washington would be officer of the day, and Bob Wheat officer of the guard."

One day, when the snow was on the ground half a foot deep, we received a visit from Wheat and Major Cabell, chief quartermaster of the army. As they dismounted from their horses we observed a pair of new boots tied together at the tops, and flung over Wheat's saddle after the fashion of hostlers. They were made welcome before a roaring fire of hickory logs. After a little while, when they were thawed out, Wheat said, "Walton, I have a treat for you: please ask your servant to bring in those boots that hang on my horse." Was he going to present the Colonel with boots? In came the boots; they were remarkably heavy. "Now," said Wheat, "have you any glasses? If so, have them filled with snow." We *had* glasses,

and they were, as requested, filled with snow; then, to
our surprise, he pulled out of each boot a bottle of champagne.   It *was* a surprise.   Pop went the corks, and
the sparkling fluid was poured into the snow-filled glasses.
It was delicious, — the best champagne, we thought then,
we had ever tasted.

Almost daily we mounted, and made visits to different
head-quarters; and it is safe to say there never was such a
sociable and agreeable set of officers and men assembled
together as those of the army that fought at Manassas.

We often welcomed to our fireside Gens. Longstreet,
Sam Jones, Fitz Lee, J. E. B. Stuart, Capt. John Pelham, Col. Tom Rhett, and a host of others.   At Gen.
Johnston's head-quarters, in Centreville, where Rhett presided as adjutant-general, we had some excellent suppers,
after the "green cloth" had been removed, which was
usually about the "witching hour of night."

Upon one occasion quite a number of officers made a
long ride to visit Col. Julian Harrison, of the cavalry, and
spent a delightful evening.   "The shades of night were
falling fast" when we mounted and started for Centreville.
The snow had fallen and the paths through the woods were
obliterated; but Gen. Sam Jones, who was supposed to be
a good woodsman, took the lead.   He was mounted on a
gray steed and directed us to "follow the gray," which we
did, in Indian file; but after proceeding a mile or so, he
halted, and confessed himself at fault: he had evidently
gone astray.   Just then a light was seen, and we rode towards it "following the gray."   It was a camp-fire of the
Eighth Georgia regiment.

The General inquired the way; the sentinel gave the direction. "All right!" cried the General, "follow the gray;" and away we went. After a while we saw a light again, and a lone sentinel. "What camp is this?" said the General. The answer came: "The Eighth Georgia."

"The mischief it is," quoth the now puzzled General. "Which way to Centreville?" "I told you before," replied the sentinel; and again he gave the direction, and away we went, the General saying, "All right, now; just follow the gray."

We probably rode for more than an hour through the thick woods, the branches sometimes scraping our faces, — and, besides, the cold was not pleasant, — when we approached what seemed to be another firelight; but, again, in answer to the General's question, came back the same reply, — "Eighth Georgia." We began to think this was becoming monotonous; but just then an officer appeared and said, "Gentlemen, you are evidently lost. You have already stopped at this fire three or four times. I am the adjutant of this regiment, and the Colonel sends his compliments and invites you to alight, and come into his tent and warm up."

We did not wait for a second invitation, but dismounted at once, and Col. "Dignity Smith" gave us a hearty welcome and hot punch, after having a laugh at our mishaps. It was in the small hours of the night when we again started for our objective point, Centreville, with a guide furnished by the Colonel, and we sent the gray in disgrace to the rear. But Gen. Jones for a long time after was sure to be reminded of "following the gray."

On the 21st of December Stuart had a brisk fight at

Drainsville with a body of the enemy. He and they were both out with foraging parties and met. Stuart engaged the enemy until his trains were safe, and then fell back with his escort.

We were ordered to begin building winter quarters, and selected Blackburn's ford, on the ground which the enemy occupied on the 18th July, 1861.

The year ended sadly for the Battalion, for we were called upon to record the death of Hubert Chambers, one of the three brothers of the First company, who died of typhoid fever in camp. He was much beloved for his quiet and genial nature, and had gained the admiration and esteem of his comrades for his behavior on the fields of the 18th and 21st of July. On the 31st of December these comrades and brothers bore him to a young patriot's grave. We buried him with all military honors, and his body rested one day in a temporary grave on the battle-field of Bull Run, and was then forwarded to his relations in the far South.

All hands were now hard at work building winter quarters, and the ring of the axes and falling of trees was heard the livelong day.

The winter camp was laid out with great regularity, each company having its street, only, instead of canvas tents, log huts are substituted. The " Sunday soldiers " had learned to handle the axe with skill, as well as their cannon.

Through the kindness of the depot quartermaster, Col. Fisher, we were supplied with planks for roofing, window sash and glass, and a lock and door knobs for each hut. Each mess had its habitation, and over the doors its appellation, — the " Growlers," the " Howlers," the " Pilgrims,"

" Buzzard Roost," " Sans Souci," " No. 4 Carondelet," etc.,
etc.

The officers had double cabins at right angles with the
streets. In front of the camp were the stables for our horses,
a double line running across the whole front of the camp.
These had plank roofs, and the sides were filled in with
brush, to temper the wind to the animals. In front of all,
our guns were parked, and snugly stored under tarpaulins
to protect them from snow and rain.

Near by we had the " *Chasseurs-à-pied* " and the " Dixie "
battery of artillery, also in huts.

We were now settled down for an almost Arctic winter, and,
with big fires roaring all the time in the big mud fireplaces,
killed time as best we could with snowballing, chess,
euchre, and a little poker.

We have named our camp " Waltonville," out of compliment to the Colonel of the Battalion.

CHAPTER IV.

JANUARY, 1862.

Contributions to Charleston Sufferers. — Mardi Gras in Camp. — Dixie Artillery and Chasseurs-à-pied. — The " Waltonville War Cry." — Snow-balling. — Beauregard Ordered South. — Attached to Longstreet's Division. — Winter Quarters Abandoned. — On the March. — Orange Court-house. — Dancing Club. — Richmond Peninsula. — Williamsburg. — Yorktown. — Richmond. — Camp at Blakey's Mill-pond. — McClellan Investing the City.

THE Battalion learned with regret of the great fire at Charleston, S.C., and the distress of the people caused thereby, and subscribed for the relief fund the following amounts, to be deducted from the forthcoming pay-rolls.

A general order was issued to the army, asking aid, and this was our reply : —

HEAD–QUARTERS WASHINGTON ARTILLERY,

Jan. 4, 1862.

MAJOR W. L. CABELL,

Chief Quartermaster, Department of Northern Virginia : —

MAJOR, — Responding to the suggestion contained in the circular of Maj. Thos. G. Rhett, A.A.G., A.P., that a collection be made for the relief of the sufferers by the late fire in Charleston, S.C., I have the honor to report to you, as recommended, the following amounts contributed by the Battalion Washington Artillery : —

Field and staff	$40 00
First Company	328 50
Second "	600 00

Third Company	$151 16
Fourth "	379 50
	$1,499 16
Col. Thos. Jordan, A.A.G.	20 00
	$1,519 16

Of which amount I hand you, enclosed, $75 in cash and $1,444.16 subscribed, to be deducted from next pay-roll by the quarter-master, who has been furnished with a list of the subscribers.

I am, Major,

Your obedient servant,

J. B. WALTON,

Colonel Commanding.

Col. Walton and some of the company officers, having obtained leave of absence, left us for New Orleans, Capt. Eshleman, of the Fourth company, being in command of the Battalion and camp.

Before moving from " Camp Hollins " to " Waltonville " we obtained from the quartermaster's department, Richmond, overcoats for the men, and received a great bale of blankets from the ladies of New Orleans. From their variety and quality it was easily seen that the ladies had stripped their own beds that the boys should be comfortable. All praise and honor to these noble women !

Now all were talking about how we should celebrate " Mardi Gras," for we did not mean to let the carnival go by without paying it due respect; it would remind us of home, if such reminder were necessary.

It was determined that we should give a grand fancy and masked ball, a grand supper, and such other " divertisements " as the occasion demanded.

The "*Chasseurs*"[1] and the Dixie Artillery, now our neighbors, the latter commanded by Lieut. W. H. Crisp, our histrionic friend of yore, were to participate.

The day at last came, and, in spite of short rations and of cold, the ball was given, and never did more gayety prevail in any assembly, whether under the "gilded panels of a palace" or the "green foliage of a kingly park." Ladies, personated by our youngest fellows, and showing right pretty arms and necks, were there with their girlish chat and their coquettish flirtations ; and under improvised masks and dominos one might believe they were the genuine article from our celebrated "St. Louis" and "Odd Fellows' balls."

The most ludicrous and outlandish costumes were there in all the variety that the most splendid costumer, during the carnival, could have supplied.

---

[1] LIST OF OFFICERS BATTALION "CHASSEURS-À-PIED."

Major, Henry St. Paul.
Adjutant, J. W. Sanders.

Co. A. — "*Chasseurs-à-pied.*

Lieutenant Commanding, Edgard Macoin.
Second Lieutenant, Charles M. René.
     "   "   D. P. White.

Co. B. — "*Catahoula Guerillas.*"

Captain, I. W. Buhoup.
First Lieutenant, S. W. Spencer.
Second Lieutenant, W. Guss.
     "   "   I. H. Dales.

Co. C. — "*Crescent Blues.*"

Captain, I. McG. Goodwyn.
First Lieutenant, G. W. Crump.
Second Lieutenant, V. G. De l'Isle.

Corporal Bob Many was so pretty and girlish with his plump neck and rounded arms that he was voted the "belle of the ball," and had a train of admirers following him the whole evening. The boys actually wanted to hug him, but the floor committee wouldn't permit such infractions.

The band, led by Gessner, was discoursing, now the sweetest, now the most warlike, music, during the supper. Capt. Eshleman presided. And the supper! — a genuine Virginia shoulder, flanked by ponderous corn-meal cakes. And the party! There was Rosser and Dearing, Miller, Squires, McG. Goodwyn, Edgar Macoin, Spencer, and Adjt. Sanders of St. Paul's Battalion, whose commander, the major, sat at Eshleman's right.

And as we sat chatting of the monotony of camp-life, citing the methods of the French in the Crimea, who managed to amuse themselves with their theatres, almost every corps having its own daily bulletin, to which all could contribute, Montgomery ("Bliffkins") proposed that we should start a paper. The idea was hailed with enthusiasm, and Major St. Paul was elected "editor-in-chief," and a solemn pledge was given that the first number should be issued on the following Saturday.

A bottle of whiskey was passed around and all drank to its success. In honor of Colonel Walton it was to be called the "Waltonville War-cry,—a national paper issued occasionally."

In due time the "War Cry" appeared. It was written on foolscap, the sheets being fastened together top and bottom, and rolled on a stick. It was spicy in the extreme, and was passed around, causing much amusement.

But alas for the plans of men! On the 3d of March the first paper appeared, but, before the next Saturday, marching orders came, and the second number was never issued. Gen. McClellan was responsible for this loss and the destruction of the printing materials, namely, half a bottle of ink and one steel pen.

Meanwhile Gen. Beauregard had been ordered south and Gen. Joe Johnston was left in command, and the Washington Artillery was by his order attached to Gen. Longstreet's division.

At this time the army near Manassas numbered only about 25,000 men, and it was said McClellan was massing 100,000 men near Washington.

On March 6 preparations were begun to take leave of winter quarters and "seek pastures new." We were not sorry to go, for the country had been completely eaten up. We were ordered not to set fire to the huts, because McClellan, perceiving the smoke, might come on to see what was the matter, and Gen. Johnston rather preferred to take "French leave" and glide away modestly.

Our guns were brought from under cover and put in order for the march. Quartermasters' stores were selected to fill the wagons and the remainder were destroyed. It was great fun to start a barrel of flour from the top of the steep banks of Bull Run and see it bounce to the bottom, covering the surrounding rocks and trees with snow-like whiteness.

When the enemy came into possession of "Waltonville" they found the cabins so well constructed that it was dignified by being converted into a large commissary depot.

McClellan fell heir to a good many of our valuables that we were compelled to leave behind, especially the batteries of " Quaker guns " in the forts of Centreville. Much good may they do him !

At last the garrison flag was lowered for the last time, and a sanguinary black flag run up in its place, and we hauled out on the Warrenton turnpike to join the column of march *en route* to the Rapidan. Stuart brought up the rear, and McClellan followed a few miles, cautiously, to see that Johnston was surely off.

After an uneventful march of one hundred miles the Battalion reached Orange Court-house, and pitched tents on Terrill's farm, in a charming grove of pines. But in lack of incident the daily march and bivouac were inspiriting. The rumbling of the guns on the smooth macadam road, the rattling of the harness, the laughter and jokes of the boys as they tramped along were decidedly pleasant after a winter in log huts and over smoky fires. And then we had again the " square meals," which the boys picked up in this new and undiscovered country, where the straggler hath not been " heard in the land," with his plaintive " Please, mam, can't you give a poor soldier a little snack,—I'm so hungry,—I don't know where I'm going to sleep to-night." The Battalion contained at least one skilful " pirooter " (forager), who never wanted a dinner, but only a " snack." Upon one occasion, when he had made a *détour* of a few miles to head off the Battalion, he came to a farm-house, upon the gallery of which he sighted a party of officers. He flanked them and made for the kitchen, where he found the " lady of the house " up to her elbows cooking dinner for the *officers.* "Oh, my!" said M——, "I don't want a dinner, madam, not a bit of it. Just a little 'snack' will do, — half a chicken, a 'pone' of corn-bread, some ham, and a hard-boiled egg, if you have one, that's all — '*only a snack.*'" He got it, and, passing the officers on the gallery, he pulled away at his half-chicken and half a foot of ham, and, being observed, M——'s "snack" was after that day a by-word in the command, — "only a snack, madam!"

While at Orange Court-house we discovered that the town was plethoric with pretty girls, so we organized a dancing club at the tavern, and our band and that of the First Virginia furnished the music. The dancing men were as follows: Gen. A. P. Hill (just promoted from Colonel), Col. P. T. Moore, Capt. Allan, Dr. Maury and Adjt. Palmer of the First Virginia; Col. Williams of the Seventh Virginia, Maj. Sam Mitchell, Capts. G. M. Sorrel, Manning, Fairfax, and Goree of Gen. Longstreet's staff, Dr. J. S. D. Cullen, also of the staff; Capts. Eshleman, and Rosser, Lieuts. Owen, Garnett, Dearing, Brewer, Battles, Capt. Miller and Dr. Drew, of the Washington Artillery. Our little hops at the old-time tavern were decidedly delightful, and again hearts were thrown around loosely and vows and hair exchanged, the latter done up in blue ribbon.

But all things have an end somewhere; so marching orders came one bright Sunday morning, the 6th April, when all were in church, and we galloped away, bidding the dear girls an affectionate "adieu."

We moved out of camp at 8 P.M., and marched down

the plank road, and it was 3 A.M. before we were instructed to go into bivouac. It was rumored that McClellan was transferring his army to Fredericksburg, and we were heading in that direction. On the 7th April we were halted all day in the road, and it was snowing and sleeting ; we had no wood for fires, and no shelter, and, to cap the climax, no rations ; so we had anything but a pleasant time of it. On the 8th and 9th, having retraced our steps, we were put on mud roads *en route* for Louisa Court-house, the snow and sleet still falling, and the mud axle deep. Men and horses suffered terribly. Miller's heavy 24-pounders were almost out of sight in the snow and mud, and Lieut. Apps, with one gun, stuck fast. Finally they gave up, and took possession of a huge tobacco barn, and built immense fires to warm up. The First, Second, and part of the Fourth companies, pressed on and bivouacked in a church at Thorn Hill.

This had been a regular " Valley Forge " day, and we could realize what our " Rebel " forefathers may have suffered in the first Revolution.

On the 10th the Battalion reached Louisa Court-house, where we found Col. Walton and Lieut. Norcom at the tavern, having just arrived from New Orleans. The army was being transferred to Richmond, and on the 13th we again pitched our tents near that city. McClellan had gone to Yorktown to try and get in by the " back door " as it were.

On the 20th the guns and horses were embarked on transports on the James river, bound for the peninsula. The wharf at which we embarked was just opposite the rear of the Libby prison, and the Federal officers watched our movements with interest, saying, " Well, never mind ; McClellan will be here in two weeks, and take Richmond, and let us all out." On the 21st we arrived at King's wharf and disembarked the command, and before a camp could be pitched we were treated to a heavy rain-storm, that drenched all hands completely. On the 23d the Battalion was reported to Gen. Longstreet at Lee's farm-house.

McClellan had laid siege to Yorktown, and, now that our whole army was concentrated, the question seemed to be, "What shall be done with it?" Gen. Magruder had been deceiving the enemy here for some time ; having but a small force, he had, by marching and countermarching from point to point, so bewildered the enemy as to his strength that they had magnified it fourfold.

On the 25th the Battalion marched from Blow's mills to Williamsburg, leaving the Second company, under Capt. Rosser, in front of Yorktown, and on the 2d of May, while in bivouac at Burnt Ordinary, we received news of the fall of New Orleans and its occupation by Gen. Butler. Thus we were cut off from friends and home, and left here in Virginia, a band of orphans, as it were.

On the 4th of May our troops evacuated Yorktown, on account of some evidences of McClellan's getting on our flank, by the way of York river, and placing himself between our army and Richmond.

The enemy shelled Yorktown for more than an hour after our people left, and then marched in and took possession. The army fell back towards Richmond, the enemy following.

On the 5th the enemy attacked our rear-guard, under Longstreet, and was defeated, losing a battery of artillery, and the march was resumed.

On the 6th the enemy renewed the pursuit, and some of our infantry of Gen. D. R. Jones's command were ordered back; but, on account of the bad condition of roads, the artillery remained in bivouac, in a beautiful pine grove, where there was a spring of cool, clear water, and we had a good rest.

On May 7 we received an order from Gen. Jones to "move forward," crossing the Chickahominy at Long Bridge.

This order was rather indefinite as to the distance to be marched; but, in the absence of further instruction, we continued on until the 8th, when, after a march of twenty-three miles, made in six hours, we went into camp at Blakey's mill-pond, two miles from Richmond, leaving the army away in the rear. This was a rapid march, but the boys made it without much evidence of fatigue.

We reported our arrival in Richmond to Gen. R. E. Lee, who was surprised to see us, as our coming was unlooked for. We had presumed too much upon the indefinite order of Gen. Jones, and perhaps a slight desire to get to Richmond had its influence upon our interpretation of it. However, here we were, and Gen. Lee instructed us to be ready to march again at any moment.

Blakey's mill-pond was a delightful camping-ground, and bordered by a grove of large fine trees. It was only a short ride to Richmond, and we visited the city frequently to see the friends whose acquaintance we made when we halted there in June of last year.

We enjoyed promenading the Main street, gazing into the shop-windows, and lounging about the "Spottswood Hotel," rigged in our swell uniforms, and forgetting Bull Run and Manassas.

On the 13th May the enemy's gun-boats were reported coming up the James river, and this created quite an alarm among the good people of the city. Gen. Lee sent for a battery to go to Drewry's Bluff to aid in repelling an attack, and Capt. Miller, Third company, with his 24-pounder howitzers, was sent off upon this duty.[1]

On the 14th Gen. Lee ordered the Battalion to report to Gen. Jo Johnston on the Chickahominy, which order was immediately obeyed. Capt. Miller joined us upon the road with his battery, the iron-clads of the enemy having been beaten off by the guns at Drewry's Bluff.

The Battalion returned on the 17th May to Blakey's mill-pond, and went into camp again.

The entire army was now concentrated about Richmond, and McClellan had invested the city.

Our camp was delightfully pitched, and we received many visitors. Among them were our friends "the surgeons." Dr. Cullen had become medical director of

---

[1] RICHMOND, May 13, 1862.

COL. WALTON, *Washington Artillery* :—

If you have a light battery that you think will be efficient on the banks of the river, I wish you to send it on the left bank, either to Chapin's Bluff or opposite the obstructions at Warwick's Bar, to retard the ascent of the enemy's gun-boats said to have arrived at City Point.

The battery must select concealed positions, not near residences, and endeavor to cripple and destroy the wooden boats, and drive from deck the men on the iron boats.

Very respectfully,

R. E. LEE.

Longstreet's corps, and Drs. Maury and Barksdale were associated with him. Col. P. T. Moore, of the First Virginia, also rode out often, and we enjoyed their hospitality at their homes in Richmond. McClellan had begun a regular siege, and " spades were trumps ; " meanwhile the Battalion had nothing to do but refit and enjoy itself.

CHAPTER V.

FIGHTING NEAR RICHMOND.

Seven Pines. — Fair Oaks. — Dr. Garnett's. — Gen. R. E. Lee. — Gen.
Johnston wounded. — Seven Days' Battle around Richmond. —
Siege of Richmond raised. — " Change of Base." — McClellan at
Harrison's Landing. — Flag of Truce. — Exchange of Prisoners at
Aiken's Landing.

ON May 31 McClellan placed two corps of his army
on the Richmond bank of the Chickahominy, and
heavy rains having swollen that river until it had over-
flowed its banks and cut off these troops from other por-
tions of his army, Gen. Johnston determined to attack him
at Seven Pines or Fair Oaks.   Gen. Longstreet commanded the Confederate right, and attacked on the
Williamsburg road.   The fighting was fierce and desperate, and we could hear from our camp the furious fusillade.
We mounted our horses and rode out to see what was
going on.   Of course all sorts of rumors were afloat.
That the affair was a very serious one we could see from
the number of wounded that were coming in and the long
lines of prisoners being escorted to the rear under guard.
We learned that at Seven Pines the enemy, under Gen.
Casey, were attacked and routed.   In front of his position
large trees had been cut down to form an *abatis*, through
which our men had to climb and crawl.

We met " Bliffkins," who reported that our old friends, the
Chasseurs-à-pied, had been engaged and had been roughly

handled, McGoodwyn wounded and Edgar Macoin killed. We met Col. Coppens, of the New Orleans Zouave Battalion, coming out in an ambulance, badly wounded, and his red breeches rather the worse for the mud he had fallen into. Dearing, who had lately been put in command of a battery, had been in and lost very heavily in men and horses.

There was a battery of four Napoleons lately belonging to the enemy stuck in the mud and abandoned on the field. "Bliffkins" was sent to bring up Capt. Buck Miller and his horses to haul off the prizes. Miller soon accomplished the task, and was allowed to keep them for his battery, turning in to the ordnance department his clumsy 24-pounder howitzers.

By a singular coincidence the captured battery had been commanded in the Federal service by a Capt. Miller. The "boys" declared the Federal was a brother of our Miller, and the leaving of the guns behind was only an evidence of a "brotherly esteem and regard."

At about 7 o'clock in the evening the army had the misfortune to lose its chief, Gen. Johnston being stricken down by a severe wound, and the command devolved upon Gen. G. W. Smith, the next in rank.[1]

Early on the 1st of June Gen. Pickett engaged a body of the enemy and drove him from the field, and our army

---

[1] . . . The Union army (lost) upwards of 5,000. But a severer loss befell the Confederates . . . for the able chief of the army of Northern Virginia was stricken down with a severe hurt.

. . . .

Preparations for withdrawal were actively pushed forward during the night, but, through some accidental circumstance a portion of Sumner's line having become engaged on the morning of the 1st of June, there ensued an encounter of some severity, which lasted two or three hours." — *Army of the Potomac.* SWINTON.

held the ground all day not molested by the enemy. Gen. Lee was assigned to the command of the army on the same day, and by his order the troops were withdrawn to their camps near Richmond.

When Gen. Casey's troops were driven in on the 31st ult., a fine head-quarters ambulance was captured, — a two-seated, covered vehicle, with outside seat for the driver. It was marked upon the sides in gilt letters, "*Second Rhode Island Regiment.*" It was appropriated by "the surgeons," and by them presented to Col. Walton. It accompanied the Battalion upon all of its marches during the war, and was of great service.

On June 6 Capt. Squires, with the First company at Dr. Garnett's farm, on the Chickahominy, together with the Maryland Battery, Capt. Snowden Andrews, and some guns of Col. Stephen D. Lee's artillery battalion, engaged the enemy's batteries across the river at New bridge.

The cannonading continued two hours, and the enemy withdrew his batteries, losing one caisson (exploded) and several horses and men killed. Our loss was two men in Andrews's battery wounded, and two horses killed.

In the evening Squires shelled a regiment of the enemy, who were engaged in building a pontoon bridge across the river below Dr. Garnett's, scattering them. The battery then took position near Dr. Garnett's residence, and opened fire upon a house occupied by Federal sharp-shooters, distance about six hundred yards. The shells drove the enemy out, but failed to set fire to the house. Lieut. E. Owen volunteered to head a party to burn the house. A dozen of the Eighteenth Mississippi regiment volunteered to accompany him, and they started at a double-quick. Lieut. Owen crept through a window and fired the staircase, and the building was soon reduced to ashes, nothing remaining except the chimneys. The adventurous party returned safely, not having been fired upon, although in close proximity to the enemy's lines.

For three weeks the Battalion spent the time pleasantly enough in camp, — in the city and riding about the lines. Gen. Jeb. Stuart, with his cavalry, took an extended ride around McClellan's army, and returned safely, and Gen. Lee was watching the enemy closely. One day Gen. Longstreet visited our camp, accompanied by his staff, and announced to Col. Walton that he had appointed him "chief of artillery" of his right wing of the army, and that the "Washington Artillery" would be his reserve artillery, reporting directly to him and receiving its orders from him. We were pleased with this arrangement.[1] Col. Walton was, however, to retain command of the Battalion. Meanwhile Gen. McClellan made but a slow advance upon Richmond, seemingly satisfied with throwing up dirt.

Capt. Rosser, with the Second company, had been out with Stuart, and had been wounded in the arm during a skirmish at Mechanicsville across the Chickahominy. Upon

---

[1] HEAD–QUARTERS RIGHT WING, NEAR RICHMOND,
June 20, 1862.

GENERAL ORDERS, NO. 28 : —

Col. J. B. Walton, of the Battalion Washington Artillery, having reported for duty with this command, is announced as chief of artillery.

He will be obeyed and respected accordingly.

By command of Major-Gen. Longstreet.

G. M. SORREL,
A.A. G.

his recovery he was promoted to a majority in the artillery service at large, and soon afterwards transferred to the cavalry and to the command of the Fifth Virginia cavalry regiment. Before the war closed he reached the rank of major-general and was greatly distinguished.

On the 26th of June orders were received for the Battalion to move out of its camp and halt upon the Mechanicsville road,[1] and, everything being in readiness for action, we marched, and halted at a farm-house directly upon the turnpike. Lee was about to pounce upon McClellan. Gen. A. P. Hill's division rested, stretched along the Meadow Bridge road. Longstreet's division was on the Mechanicsville road. At a dwelling on the right of the road the general officers and their staffs were congregated, their horses tied to the trees and fences.

A big movement was evidently on foot, and all were awaiting the word from Gen. Lee to begin. Some said they were waiting to hear from Jackson, who was expected from the valley to strike the enemy's right when Hill and Longstreet attack.

At 3 P.M. there was a great stir, and Hill and Longstreet mounted their horses, and staff officers dashed along the lines of the divisions, up and down the roads, carrying orders to

---

[1] HEAD-QUARTERS LONGSTREET'S CORPS,
June 26, 1862.

COLONEL: — The commanding general directs me to write you to move out until the head of your column reaches the Mechanicsville turnpike.

I am, Colonel, with great respect, your most obedient

JOHN W. FAIRFAX,
A.A. and Insp. General.

COL. WALTON,
Chief of Artillery, Right Wing, A.N. Va.

the brigade commanders. The loud voices of the officers could be heard calling, "'tention! 'tention! Fall in, men, fall in!"

The columns were quickly formed and moved forward, the canteens rattling and the company officers crying, "Close up! close up!"

Across the Meadow Bridge Hill's men went at a swinging pace, and into the woods on the other shore. Almost instantly the crack of the rifles of the skirmishers was heard, and the gallant fellows, who but a few minutes ago were resting by the roadside, were engaged in deadly conflict. A. P. Hill having crossed and unmasked the Mechanicsville Bridge, Longstreet and D. H. Hill followed with their fine divisions over the bridge. Longstreet turned to the right and followed along the banks of the stream. D. H. Hill went to the support of A. P. Hill, and now the artillery opened its brazen tongues and the battle had begun.

Lee had "let slip the dogs of war" upon McClellan's right, and we had it "*à l'outrance.*"

All day long the Battalion remained in the road in reserve. The boys were impatient to go ahead, but must await orders. The roar of battle continued unceasingly. Wounded men were carried by in ambulances, and many prisoners passed under guard; among the latter a goodly delegation of the Pennsylvania "Buck-tail Rangers."

The battle continued long into the night; our men said to be doing well. The Battalion bivouacked on the roadside.

The roar of battle began at early dawn on the 27th, with

artillery and musketry. We were still in reserve. The sound of the conflict was moving away from us. Old "Stonewall" was up, and was pounding away upon the enemy's right. We bivouacked another night upon the road.

At 9.30, on the morning of the 28th, orders were received from Gen. Longstreet to move the Battalion to the Mechanicsville Bridge.[1] "Boots and saddles" were sounded, and we were off, all in fine spirits, glad to be in motion. The First and Third companies were ordered to cross the Chickahominy to report to Gen. Longstreet upon the field.

The Second and Fourth companies bivouacked near the bridge. Desperate fighting yesterday, and the enemy driven beyond the Chickahominy near New Bridge.

At 9 A.M., on the 29th, the Second and Fourth com-

---

[1] HEAD–QUARTERS, June 28, 1862, 8 A.M.

COLONEL : — Please move two of your batteries by the Mechanicsville Bridge and road, to report to me on this road.

Very respectfully,

J. LONGSTREET,

Major-General Commanding.

COLONEL WALTON, *Commander Artillery :* —

I sent a message to put your command on the New Bridge road. You had better keep it on the Mechanicsville road near the bridge, and on the Richmond side of the Chickahominy.

HEAD–QUARTERS, June 28, 1862.

COLONEL : — You will please send your extra horses and some cannoneers to take off the Yankee guns captured.

By order of the commanding General.

With great respect, your obedient servant,

JNO. W. FAIRFAX,

A.A. and Insp. Gen.

COL. WALTON, *Chief of Artillery.*

panies were ordered to the Williamsburg road.[1]   The First
and Third companies joined them.   McClellan was falling
rapidly back to the James river, our forces pressing closely
after him.   At 5 P.M. the Battalion marched down the
Darbytown road, following closely the rear of Longstreet's
division.

That night we bivouacked in the dark and in a pelting
rain.   On the 30th we marched at 6 A.M., and, passing
Longstreet's troops, halted by the roadside and awaited
orders.   "By particular request" we outraged military
etiquette, and requested Longstreet to "put us in somewhere."   He said "he would try to do so."   The boys
did not fancy being in reserve.   In the afternoon Longstreet, with his own and Magruder's division, passed by us
going to the front.   I saw my old friend, Lieut. Eugene
Janin, marching with his company (C, Tenth Louisiana
regiment).   The troops that passed us fought the battle
of "Frazier's farm" that evening.

All day long on the 1st of July, we remained in bivouac,
listening to the roar of battle at "Malvern Hill."   "Will
Longstreet send for us to-day?" is asked on all sides.

---

[1] The following orders were received during to-day : —

HEAD–QUARTERS, June 29, 1862.
COLONEL : — The General directs that you move your two batteries back
towards Richmond in front of redoubt No. 3. Your other two will be sent in
this morning.   Very respectfully,
P. T. MANNING, *A.D.C.*
COL. WALTON, *Chief of Artillery.*

LONGSTREET'S HEAD–QUARTERS, June 29, 1862.
COLONEL : — The Major-general commanding directs that you park your
artillery where it is now and be ready to move early in the morning.
Very respectfully,
G. M. SORREL, *A.A. General.*
COL. WALTON, *Chief of Artillery.*

The guns are "in park," and in perfect order. The horses are partially harnessed, and the boys, without exception, have their traps ready for a quick move; but the day wears on; the roar and pounding at Malvern continue; we are three or four miles away. We are becoming indifferent, from inaction, and the meal termed dinner is despatched, and we spread our blankets upon the ground, just to take "forty winks." But at 5 P.M. a courier comes galloping down the road. Is he looking for us? He turns into the field; he has a despatch in his hand. The boys are on their feet in an instant. "Orders! orders!" they call to one another. The courier draws rein. "Is this the Washington Artillery?" he asks. "Yes! yes!" cry a hundred voices. "Where is Col. Walton?" asks the courier. "Over there, by that ambulance," is the reply. He puts spurs to his steed, and draws up at head-quarters. "Col. Walton, despatch from Gen. Longstreet," and hands him a small scrap of paper without envelope, and is off like a flash. Frank, the bugler, has lifted his bugle almost to his lips. The boys look at the group at head-quarters anxiously; drivers are quietly arranging their harness upon their teams. It is but a moment of suspense; it seems an age. The despatch reads : —

HEAD–QUARTERS, BATTLE–FIELD,

July 1st, 1862.

COLONEL : — The general directs that you move the "Washington Artillery" down as soon as possible.

Yours, etc.,

P. T. MANNING,

Major and Ordnance Officer.

To COL. WALTON, *Chief of Artillery.*

Instantly comes the order for " Boots and Saddles," and
the welcome notes from the bugle are given tongue. The
boys yell with delight; the quiet bivouac is changed as
if by a magician's touch; all is hurrying to and fro. But
few moments pass, and the Colonel's loud-voiced order
comes : " 'Tention ! Drivers, prepare to mount. Mount ! "
" Cannoneers, mount ! " " Column, forwa-r-r-rd ! ". And
the Battalion moves out into the road towards the battle-
field.

This is a supreme moment in the history of the Washington Artillery, — the first time it ever moved in full
armament, with its four batteries, to the battle-field. As
we stretch out upon the road the Colonel orders, " Battalion, trot, march ! " The drivers sling their strong whips
and the teams break into a brisk trot, and away we go, with
the carriages rumbling, the harness rattling, and the iron
hoofs of the horses striking fire from the flinty road.

What a glorious sight it is ! See the sixteen guns !
What beauties ! the finest in the world, — rifles and Napoleons taken from the enemy at Manassas and Seven Pines.
Sixteen caissons, — thirty-two carriages in all, — nearly
three hundred men and two hundred horses. What a sight
to gladden a soldier's eye ! In front of all rides the Colonel,
on his black stallion, " Rebel ; " a pace behind rides the
adjutant ; then the chief bugler, and the guidon-bearer,
carrying the little scarlet banner with its blue cross, the
gift of Constance Carey, fashioned from her own gown.
Just behind come the batteries, the captains riding in
front of each, — Squires with the First, Richardson with
the Second, Miller with the Third, and Eshleman with the

Fourth, the lieutenants on the flanks, the sergeants beside their teams. The officers are in full rig, with sabre and pistol.

The " Washington Artillery " has at last given proof of perfection, and evinces the discipline imparted by the commander. It is complete; it is perfect in all its parts. Now could be realized its terrible power for battle, its capability of meeting its like in the armies of the world.

The dust is fearful, and the boys are covered with it, as we trot along uphill and downhill; no drawing of rein, but straining our eyes in the direction of the smoke curling above the pines, while our ears take in the sounds of battle. As we reach the level ground the bugler sounds the "Gallop." We are approaching the outskirts of the field; the customary sights greet our eyes : the dead, wounded, and the dying, the field-hospitals, the ambulances, and the ordnance-wagons.

We pass a battery at the side of the road; it is our old friends, the " Dixies," of Waltonville; they have been in the fight and are crippled; they recognize us, and three cheers are given for the " Washington Artillery," with a yell. The Colonel touches his cap. We rattle past a brigade of Texans, and again we are cheered. It makes our hearts leap to hear them. " Here's the ' Washington Artillery !' Bully for the ' Washington Artillery !' Go in, boys ! Hurrah for Longstreet's reserve ! Now we'll have hell ! " The boys take it all in, and their nerves are strung to the utmost, lips compressed, and eyes flashing bright and fierce as those of the " Tiger," the noble emblem of the corps, about to spring upon its prey.

There on the left of the road is our surgeon friend, Cullen, in a group of officers. *He* must know where Longstreet is. The column is halted. Cullen, in his cheery voice cries out, " How are you, Walton? How are you, Adjutant? How magnificent the Battalion is to-day! You're grand." " Where's Longstreet? " the Colonel asks. " On the hill to the left," is the reply. " Adjutant, go forward and report; we will wait here ! "

It is now almost dark, — when I find the General, it is quite so. He says, " We have done all we can to-day; will need you to-morrow. Park your guns in the field alongside of the road."

It was a great disappointment to us all, but no fault of ours that we were not " put in."

A few shells whistled over our heads after we had parked, so we were under fire ; and that was some consolation, although the boys hardly thought so, and growled outrageously.

July 2d. — Slept in a fence-corner last night. A field-hospital was near by, and the groans and cries of the wounded kept us from sleeping much, although tired out.

As usual, after heavy cannonading, it rained. The little camp-fire, where our "major-domo" (who had come up with the " Second Rhode Island ") was cooking the breakfast, had a hard struggle for life.

The Battalion was ordered to march, and to follow Longstreet's division. We passed over the battle-field of yesterday. The dead were lying thickly around.

The enemy had the crest of Malvern Hill covered with two tiers of guns, and the gun-boats in the James river protected his flanks with heavy pieces. We saw several of his big shells unexploded; the boys called them "lamp-posts," for they were apparently as large. Our troops had been expected to drive him from the crest, but, by some mischance, regiments were put in to do the work of brigades, and consequently were cut to pieces in detail. The Tenth Louisiana regiment, under Col. Eugene Waggaman, made a most gallant charge, fought their way into the batteries, and fell, or were captured among the guns. Col. Waggaman was taken prisoner, after he had defended himself like a hero. His sword had been wielded by his father at the battle of New Orleans, and was returned to the Colonel by its gallant captor after the war ended. The Third Alabama was also much cut up amongst the enemy's guns.

The pine thicket we marched through to reach the field was cut up into "toothpicks" by solid shot, and at the edge of the field we saw a battery of ours knocked out of shape, and were informed it was done in two minutes.

We would have had a hot time of it had we been put in yesterday; and one is made to reflect upon the fact that, after all, it is a good thing to wait for orders, — *patiently*.

McClellan had continued his flight to the James river. Lee was again pursuing. On the road we passed the "Louisiana brigade," and saw many old friends in the Seventh Louisiana, — Harper, Flower, and others. Old "Stonewall" passed, and recognized our cheers by lifting his old, faded cap. We bivouacked in the rain near the Poindexter House, where Lee had his head-quarters. President Davis rode by us to-day, and was loudly cheered

by the troops.   He wore a Mexican " serape," to keep off
the rain, which was falling.   He was constantly with the
troops, and getting himself under fire more than he ought.

On July 3d McClellan found shelter under cover of his
gun-boats in James river.   Unfortunately for us, but
fortunately for the enemy, Stuart pushed his cavalry too
far in pursuit, opening Pelham's guns from elevated
ground which commanded the whole position of the enemy
where his troops were massed.   McClellan at once detected
the importance of getting possession of the ground occupied
by Stuart, and attacked him in large force, driving him off
and fortifying the position.   Our infantry was too far
away to take advantage of Stuart's movement.   We bivouacked on Waterloo farm.

On the 6th of July Capt. Squires, with the First company, accompanied Col. S. D. Lee below McClellan's
position, and fired into the enemy's transports, doing considerable damage.   As it was now impossible to inflict more
damage upon the enemy the bulk of the army was withdrawn to Richmond.

On the 12th of July we were all in camp again on
Almond creek, near Richmond, and all the artillery of the
First corps was there massed.   We called it "Camp Long-
street."

We again enjoyed the gay society of Richmond.   Our
camp was visited daily by ladies and their escorts.

A large number of wounded officers captured during the
seven days' battles were to be exchanged, under the direction
of our friends, "the surgeons," and a member of Gen.
Longstreet's staff.   Dr. Cullen invited us to join the

party, and with him we visited the "Libby prison." While passing through one of the wards I was hailed by a wounded officer, and, going to his cot, I failed to recognize him. He said, "Why, don't you know your old secretary of the 'Prairie Shooting Club' (an old-time institution in the West), Stanhope?" Of course I did, and was glad to meet my old friend even under these peculiar circumstances. I told him my mission, and, at his solicitation, had him put on Cullen's list for exchange. He was made happy at the prospect of seeing his home again.

A long line of ambulances and wagons was drawn up before the Libby, and in these the wounded were carefully placed, and we rode with them to Aikin's landing on the James river, where we found the fine steam-boat "New York," flying an immense white flag, awaiting the arrival of the exchange train. We were introduced to a number of Federal officers, and I had the pleasure of meeting Col. N. B. Sweitzer, of Gen. McClellan's staff, an old schoolmate. We "fraternized" at once.

The cabin of the boat was filled with cots, all beautifully clean and fresh, and under charge of the "Sanitary Commission."

The arrangements for the comfort of the wounded were wonderfully complete, and surprised us poor "Confeds." not a little, so accustomed were we to getting along with the merest necessaries of life, and sometimes not even those. The officers treated us most hospitably, and in the after-cabin a lunch was served, and the blue and the gray harmonized beautifully, and had a good time.

Some surgeons on board made a loud "hullabaloo" about

the way they had been treated in Richmond, cursing every-body generally, and Gen. Winder in particular. Col. Clitz, whose cot was at the end of the row in the after-cabin, became incensed at their conduct and language, and suddenly raised himself on his elbow, and shouted, " Here, you d— doctors ! don't you know you are under a flag of truce ? " Just then Col. Sweitzer came in, and, being informed of what had happened, turned the whole lot of " medicos " out of the cabin, and up to the hurricane roof, and made them " mark time " until we went ashore.

After concluding the business of the exchange we bade Stanhope, Clitz, and Sweitzer good-by, and rode back to Richmond, much pleased with the excursion.

Ex-Lieut. L. A. Adam, who resigned his commission last fall, has rejoined the Battalion Washington Artillery as a private, in the Third company. He says he " didn't feel at home except with his battery."

On the 5th of August Gen. McClellan made a demonstration against Gen. Evans's troops at Malvern Hill, but being repulsed, fell back again to the river, and troubled us no more.

The siege of Richmond was raised. More than 10,000 prisoners, including officers of rank, 52 pieces of artillery, and upwards of 35,000 stand of small arms, were captured. The stores and supplies of every description which fell into our hands were great in amount and value, but small in comparison with those destroyed by the enemy.[1]

On the 20th of June, McClellan reported present for

---

[1] Rise and Fall of the Confederate States. Jefferson Davis, p. 153.

duty in front of Richmond 105,825 men.   He reached the James river with between 85,000 and 90,000 men.[1]

The effective strength of Gen. Lee's army in the seven days' battles around Richmond was 80,762.[2]

Granting that the losses in Lee's army were 19,000,[3] it would then appear that when McClellan reached James river with "85,000 or 90,000 men," he was being pursued by Lee with but 62,000.[4]

"Thus the campaign which had been prosecuted after months of preparation, at an enormous expenditure of men and money, was completely frustrated."[5]

---

[1] Swinton, Army of the Potomac.
[2] Four Years with Lee.   Taylor, p. 53.
[3] Swinton, Army of the Potomac.
[4] Four Years with Lee.   Taylor, p. 56.
[5] Rise and Fall of the Confederate States.   Davis, 153.

CHAPTER VI.

RAPPAHANNOCK STATION AND MANASSAS.

Gordonsville. — Gen. John Pope. — March from Gordonsville. — Distribution of Batteries. — Spy hanged. — Engagement at Rappahannock Station. — Enemy moving. — Jackson in Rear of Pope. — Salem. —White Plains.—Narrow Escape of Gen. Lee.—Thoroughfare Gap. — Enemy in Possession. — Gen. Longstreet. — Advance of Longstreet's Corps to Haymarket. — Gen. J. E. B. Stuart. —Jackson fighting. — Artillery in Position. — Second Battle at Manassas. — Chantilly. — Gen. Phil Kearney killed. — On to Maryland. — Ford the Potomac.

ON the 9th of August, 1862, we were put under marching orders. We were to assume the offensive. McClellan was powerless, and Lee proposed to draw him away from Richmond. On the 10th we marched from " Camp Longstreet," and took the turnpike towards Gordonsville, where the whole army was concentrating, and where Jackson's corps was already encamped.

On the 13th, by order of Gen. Longstreet, we pitched our tents at Gordonsville. Jackson had already marched northward. The Federal army, under Gen. John Pope, was in our front, and on the 16th we heard that Jackson had encountered him at Cedar Mountain and worsted him.

Pope had been issuing all sorts of brutal orders, threatening to burn farm-houses and lay waste the country.

We marched from Gordonsville at 3.30 P.M. on the 16th of August, and pushed on until 1.30 A.M., encamping within a mile of Orange Court-House. *En route* we

had the pleasure of seeing some of our fair dancing-
club friends, and some of us took supper with them.

Early on the 17th we were on the move again, closing
up on the enemy. On the 18th we moved out of camp
at 12 M., and reaching the neighborhood of Raccoon Ford,
over the Rapidan river, bivouacked for the night at 11
o'clock.

On the same day orders were issued by the chief of
artillery to the different batteries of Longstreet's corps, to
be assigned for duty as follows : —

Capt. Rogers's battery to Gen. Kemper's brigade.
    "   Stribling's "   "   "   Jenkins's   "
    "   Anderson's "   "   "   Wilcox's   "
    "   Maurin's   "   "   "   Pryor's   "
    "   Chapman's "   "   "   Featherstone's "
    "   Brown's   "   "   "   Anderson's   "
    "   Boyce's   "   "   "   Evans's   "
    "   Leake's   "   "   "   Drayton's   "
    "   Eshleman's battery (4th Co. Washington Artillery)
        to Gen. Pickett's brigade.
    "   Richardson's battery (2d Co. Washington Artil-
        lery) to Gen. Toombs's brigade.
    "   Squires (1st Co. Washington
        Artillery),
                        } held in reserve.
    "   Miller (3d Co. Washington
        Artillery),

The several captains were ordered to report immediately
to the brigade commanders for duty during the present
campaign.

On the morning of August 21, as the troops were marching towards Stevensburg, a mounted man, clad in gray uniform, rode up to Gen. D. R. Jones, commanding division, and told him that Gen. Jackson had sent him to say that he was to halt his column where it then was. As Jones was under the orders of Gen. Longstreet he couldn't understand why Jackson should send him orders of any kind, especially as it was known that Jackson was a long distance in advance. Suspicion being aroused, the man was ordered to dismount, his person examined, and a memorandum-book found containing an account of all of our movements since we had advanced beyond Gordonsville. A cipher alphabet was also found. One barrel of his pistol was empty. The night before, one of Gen. Longstreet's couriers, while carrying despatches, was joined on the road by a mounted man whose description corresponded with this man. After riding a short distance with the courier, the stranger dropped a little to the rear, and shot the courier through the back. He fell from his horse apparently dead, and was then robbed of his despatches. He was discovered in the morning still alive, and then told his story.

Further examination of the man's clothing showed the uniform not to be of the Confederate regulation, the cuffs and collar of his jacket being black instead of yellow. His under-clothing, boots, and spurs were unmistakably those furnished the enlisted men of the United States army. A drum-head court-martial was convened, circumstantial evidence was against him, and he was condemned to be hung as a spy. He took his sentence quite coolly, and gave his name as Charles Mason, of Terrysville, Pennsylvania.

Longstreet's couriers requested permission to carry out the sentence of the court, to avenge their fallen comrade, murdered in cold blood by this spy. He was marched into the woods, placed on a mule, a rope looped around his neck and its end thrown over a limb of a tree, when a stalwart courier, with a heavy stick, by striking the mule upon the rump, caused him to surge ahead, and Charles Mason, "spy" and murderer, was left swinging. When dead, a grave by the roadside was dug, and he disappeared from the face of the earth.

This affair, of but little moment in the history of an army, detained the division nearly three hours.

We had now come close upon the enemy near Brandy station, and our batteries were engaging some of his just ahead. We were ordered to move along briskly.

One of Fitz Lee's aids informed us that he had captured Gen. Pope's head-quarters ambulance, with papers and his full-dress uniform. The uniform was sent to Richmond for the curious to feast their eyes upon. Pope's orders were dated " Head-quarters in the saddle," and he seemed to have a very poor opinion of his army, as, in his address, he wrote as follows : " I have come to you from the West, where we have always seen the backs of our enemies ; from an army whose business it has been to seek the adversary, and to beat him when found, — whose policy has been attack, and not defence. I presume I have been sent here to pursue the same system."

We " presume " he expects to see the " backs " of the army of Northern Virginia. He will probably be astonished before long.

On the afternoon of the 22d August the two batteries

(reserve) arrived in the vicinity of Rappahannock station and Beverly Ford, across the Rappahannock river, and Col. Walton, accompanied by Major Garnett and Capt. Squires, was ordered to make a reconnoissance of the enemy's position, who, with considerable artillery, held the opposite bank, also the railroad bridge and a "*tête de pont*" on the south bank. Under orders from Gen. Longstreet the enemy was to be driven from his positions on both sides of the river with artillery. The reconnoissance completed and positions selected for the different batteries to occupy in the morning, the party was returning, when, approaching the woods in which lay the brigade of Gen. Drayton, they were suddenly challenged and a couple of rifles brought to bear upon them. "Who are you?" — "Friends." — "Don't believe it: dismount!" The Colonel remonstrated. "I am Chief of Artillery of the corps, on a reconnoissance." — "Can't help it. You look like Yanks; down with you, quick!" And the party dismounted in high dudgeon. The officer of the guard coming up, all hands were marched off to Gen. Drayton. Explanations followed, and the party sought our bivouac, thankful for getting off without perforation by even a friendly bullet.

At daylight on the 23d the guns detailed for duty were put in position from left to right as follows: at Beverly ford, one gun of Capt. Anderson's battery, two guns of Capt. Rogers's battery, and the Third company Washington Artillery, Capt. Miller, four guns. At the "*tête de pont*" and the railroad bridge, the First company Washington Artillery, Capt. Squires, four guns; two guns of the Dixie artillery, under Lieut. Chapman; Capt. Stribling's battery of four guns ; and two guns of the Donaldsonville Artillery, under Lieut. Landry, — nineteen guns in all.

The fog was lying heavily over the river when the guns took position, but at sunrise, it having lifted, Capt. Miller was ordered to open fire upon one of the enemy's batteries opposite. This was the signal for all the guns to open along the line, and the guns to the right of Capt. Miller, that had been placed under the command of Major Garnett, immediately opened upon the "*tête de pont*" and the batteries on the opposite shore. The enemy's guns were not long in replying, and their fire was rapid and accurate. The battery opposite Miller's position engaged him hotly and well, but its fire had almost been silenced when the guns of Rogers and Anderson, on his left, that should have engaged the battery in their front, were withdrawn from the field without orders. The enemy's battery, thus disengaged, turned its guns against the Third company Washington Artillery, whose front was changed to meet this new antagonist. The battery opposite, which had been supposed silenced, reopened, and under this cross-fire our battery suffered considerably in men and horses, and was withdrawn by half battery from the field. At the railroad bridge Squires, Stribling, Chapman, and Landry were hotly engaged, and in about two hours, the enemy was driven across the river, abandoning his "*tête de pont*."

The brigades of Gens. Evans and D. R. Jones, the latter under Col. G. T. Anderson, moved forward to occupy this position. It was found untenable, however, being exposed to a cross-fire of artillery from the other bank. The troops were therefore partially withdrawn,

The Artillery Duel.

and Col. S. D. Lee was ordered to select positions for his batteries, and joined in the combat. The enemy's position was soon rendered too warm for him, and, after setting fire to the railroad bridge and the private dwellings in the vicinity, he retreated in haste.

This was an artillery battle only, as our infantry was not engaged, and the losses in the two batteries of the reserve, the First and Third companies Washington Artillery, were, in proportion to the number of cannoneers at the guns, very heavy.

The withdrawal of Rogers's and Anderson's guns, for the reason of "having one of the guns of the former choked by a ball," led to the heavy loss in the Third company, under Capt. Miller.

As Miller's guns were being brought off, the enemy shelled him vigorously, and, one shell bursting directly over the heads of Col. Walton and myself, wounded my horse, killed that of the bugler, and a fragment ripped open the shoulder of Sergt. Collins's jacket.

A wounded horse dashed by us with an officer's sabre strapped to the saddle. I recognized it at once as that of Lieut. Brewer, who was brought off the field in a dying condition.[1]

---

[1] REPORT OF COL. WALTON.

HEAD-QUARTERS ARTILLERY CORPS, RIGHT WING,
DEPT. NORTHERN VIRGINIA,
August 25, 1862.

I have the honor to report that, in obedience to an order received from Major-Gen. Longstreet, on the evening of the 22d instant, accompanied by Major J. J. Garnett, Chief of Artillery, on the staff of Brig.-Gen. D. R. Jones, and Capt. C. W. Squires, commanding the First company Washington Artillery, I made a reconnoissance of the position of the enemy in the vicinity of Beverly's Ford and

At night a burial detail performed the last sad rites to our dead comrades by the flickering light of a blazing fire of logs and rails, having made rude coffins of the pews of " St. James's church," which, meaning no sacrilege, were appropriated for that purpose.

Rappahannock station, on the Rappahannock river, with the view, as instructed, to place the long-range guns under my command in position to open upon the enemy's batteries early on the following morning. Having, during the night, made all necessary preparation, at daybreak, on the morning of the 23d, I placed in position on the left, at Beverly's Ford, Capt. Miller's battery Washington Artillery, four light 12-pounder Napoleon guns, a section of two 10-pounder Parrott guns, under Capt. Rogers, and one 10-pounder Parrott gun, under Capt. Anderson; and on the right, Capt. Squires's battery Washington Artillery, four three-inch rifles; Capt. Stribling's battery, one three-inch rifle and three light 12-pounder Napoleon guns; a section of Capt. Chapman's battery, one three-inch rifle and one light 12-pounder Napoleon gun, under Lieut. Chapman, and two Blakely guns of Capt. Maurin's battery, under Lieut. Landry.

The heavy fog prevailing obscured the opposite bank of the river and the enemy's positions entirely from view until about 6 o'clock A.M., at which hour, the sun having partially dispelled the fog, I opened fire from Capt. Miller's battery upon a battery of long-range guns of the enemy, directly in front, at a range of about one thousand yards. By previous arrangement the batteries on the right and left of Capt. Miller's position immediately opened, and the fire became general along the line. We had not long to wait for the response of the enemy, he immediately opening upon all our positions a rapid and vigorous fire from all his batteries, some in positions until then undiscovered by us. The battery of the enemy engaged by Capt. Miller was silenced in about forty minutes. Notwithstanding the long-range guns under Capts. Rogers and Anderson, on the left, had, shortly after the commencement of the engagement, been withdrawn from action and placed under shelter of the hill on which they had been posted, thus leaving the battery of the enemy, which it was intended these guns should engage, free to direct against Miller, and the batteries on the hill on the right, a most destructive fire. At this time Capt. Miller changed position and directed his fire against the opposing battery, when one on the right of that which had been silenced opened upon him, subjecting him to a cross-fire, and causing him to lose heavily in men and horses. The fire was continued by Miller's battery alone on the left until 7 o'clock, when, after consultation with Gen. Jones, and the fire of the enemy having greatly slackened, I ordered him to retire by half battery, which was handsomely done, in good order.

At this time Lieut. Brewer fell, mortally wounded. The combat on the right was gallantly fought by the batteries there placed in position.

Capt. Squires assumed command of that part of the field, and won for himself renewed honors by the handsome manner in which he handled his batteries, and for the good judgment and coolness he displayed under the heavy fire of the enemy, to which he was subjected during four hours without intermission.

It was far into the night when the following order was received : —

HEAD–QUARTERS LONGSTREET'S CORPS, August 23, 1862.

COLONEL, — Our brigades are ordered to move at 4 o'clock in the morning. If you are ready by daylight it will do.

As heretofore, follow in rear of the column.

Very resp'y,   G. M. SORREL,

A.A. Gen'l.

COL. WALTON, *Chief of Artillery.*

The object sought to be obtained by this engagement, I am happy to say, was fully accomplished by driving the enemy from all his positions before nightfall, and causing him to withdraw from our front entirely during the night.

I have to lament the loss, in this engagement, of a zealous, brave, and most efficient officer, in Lieut. Brewer, Third company Washington Artillery, who fell at the head of his section at the moment it was being withdrawn from the field, and of many non-commissioned officers and privates. The officers and men in all the batteries engaged are deserving the highest praise for their gallantry upon the field. The attention of the general commanding is respectfully directed to those named particularly in the reports of Capts. Miller and Squires. Too much praise cannot be awarded to Capt. Miller and his brave company for the stubborn and unflinching manner in which they fought the enemy's battery in such superior force and position on the left, and to Capts. Squires and Stribling, and Lieuts. Landry and Chapman on the right. I am indebted to Capt. Middleton, of Brig.-Gen. Drayton's staff, to Lieut. Williams, of Gen. D. R. Jones's staff, and to Lieut. William M. Owen, adjutant, Washington Artillery, all of whom were constantly with me under fire during the engagement, for their valuable assistance and zealous conduct on the field. There are none more brave or more deserving consideration than these gentlemen. I annex a list of casualties, and have the honor to be,

J. B. WALTON,

Col. and Chief of Art., Right Wing.

REPORT OF CAPT. MILLER.

I proceeded with my battery of four smooth-bore 12-pounder Napoleons to Beverly's ford, on the Rappahannock, one thousand yards from the river. My position, on a hill sloping towards the river, was not such a one as I would have desired, though doubtless the best the locality afforded. At sunrise I discovered a battery of the enemy in position immediately in front of us, on a hill on the north side of the river, and I opened on it with spherical ease. The enemy replied briskly, and for half an hour the firing was very spirited. During this time I was considerably annoyed by an enfilading fire of a long-ranged battery, posted to our right, and entirely beyond our range. After nearly an hour's engage-

At 11 o'clock in the morning of the 24th we marched as ordered, in the rear of the brigades, crossed Hazel river and camped.   On the 25th the swollen condition of the Rappahannock was such as to prevent the army from

---

ment, I was gratified to notice that the fire in our front had perceptibly slackened, indeed had almost entirely ceased. Up to this time but one of my men had been wounded, and two horses killed. The batteries supporting me at this time retired from the field, subjecting me to a galling cross-fire from the enemy's rifle battery in their front. I immediately changed front on the left and replied. The enemy, having our exact range, replied with terrible precision and effect. For some time we maintained this unequal conflict, when, having nearly exhausted my ammunition, and agreeably to your orders, I retired by half battery from the field.

My casualties were: Killed—First Lieut. Brewer, privates Thompson, McDonald, Joubert (mortally wounded), and Dolan.

Wounded—Corporal P. W. Pettiss ; privates James Tully, Levy, Fourshee, Maxwell, Crilly, Kerwin, Lynch, — eight.

Twenty-one horses killed ; 356 rounds of ammunition expended.

I would be pleased to pay a tribute to the coolness and intrepidity of my command, but, where all acted so well, it would be invidious to particularize. I should be wanting in my duty, however, where I not to mention Lieuts. Hero and McElroy, and my non-commissioned officers, Sergts. McNeil, Handy, Collins, Ellis, and Stocker, and Corporals Coyle, Kremmelburg, Pettiss, and DeBlanc, who, by their coolness and close attention to duty, contributed not a little to the efficiency of my battery.

Respectfully,

M. B. MILLER,
Capt. Commanding 3d Co. B. W. A.

REPORT OF CAPT. SQUIRES.

Early on the morning of the 23d of August, the artillery, composed of the First company Washington Artillery (four three-inch rifles), and Captain Stribling's battery (three Napoleon guns and one three-inch rifle), marched in the direction of the hill opposite to Rappahannock station. . . . The batteries were formed in line from right to left in the following order: First company Washington Artillery, four three-inch rifle guns ; Dixie artillery, one Napoleon gun and one three-inch rifle ; Stribling's battery, three Napoleon guns and one three-inch rifle. This had scarcely been accomplished when the signal was given from your position to "commence firing," which was quickly responded to by the enemy. The combat was briskly carried on by the artillery directly in our front for half an hour, when the enemy placed a battery on the extreme left, and had partly succeeded in enfilading our batteries when I withdrew the section of Lieut. Galbraith and directed him to engage the enemy on

crossing at any of the fords, so it moved to the left, up stream. Pope was on the opposite bank moving parallel with us. We camped at sundown near Jeffersonton. During the evening the enemy treated us to a little artillery

---

the left. Lieut. Galbraith accomplished this under a heavy fire, and was partly forced from his first position when Lieut. Landry, with a section of Capt. Maurin's battery, reported, and was sent to assist Lieut. Galbraith, the four guns being placed under Lieut. Galbraith, who managed to keep a heavy enfilading fire from the main batteries, by the coolness and bravery with which he manœuvred this battery. The fire on both sides now became general and rapid. The enemy placed more artillery in position, and for some time I thought I should have to retire; but the enemy soon after slackened his fire, and it was evident he was worsted by the projectiles with which our artillerists assailed him. An officer now came from the right, and informed me that the infantry were preparing to charge, and to cease firing as soon as they appeared. I kept up the fire, returning shot for shot with the enemy, who appeared willing to give up the combat.

Seeing this, and being informed that Gen. Evans (commanding the infantry) was advancing to attack the enemy, I ordered the four (reserve) guns of Lieut. Galbraith in position to engage the enemy's artillery and draw his attention while our troops were advancing. The enemy finally gave up his position, retired across the Rappahannock, and only replied occasionally to our fire, and in an hour after ceased firing altogether.

It is with pleasure I am enabled to speak of the gallantry with which Capt. Stribling, officers and men, behaved on this occasion. Lieut. Chapman, with his section of Dixie artillery, behaved with great coolness, and handled his guns with effect. To Lieut. E. Owen, J. M. Galbraith, and those under their command, I would especially call your attention. Both officers commanded full batteries, and handled them with coolness, bravery, and good judgment, which have so often on previous occasions won the confidence of their men. Sergts. T. Y. Aby, C. L. C. Dupuy, and L. M. Montgomery rendered me efficient service; the latter, on previous occasions, has placed me under many obligations for his voluntary services.

First company battery Washington Artillery, killed: privates W. Chambers, R. T. Marshall, J. Reddington, and H. Koss. Wounded, Corporal W. H. West, privates, John R. Fell, T. S. Turner, M. Mount, and W. R. Falconer.

Dixie artillery, wounded: privates, John Eddins, Westley Pence, John Knight, and Daniel Martin.

Stribling's battery, wounded: Lieut. Archer and one private.

First company battery Washington Artillery, horses killed, 1; wounded, 1.

Stribling's battery, horses killed, 4; wounded, 0.

Dixie battery, horses killed, 1; wounded, 0. Total, 6 killed, 1 wounded.

One three-inch rifle gun exploded during action. The batteries were engaged from about 7 o'clock A.M., to 11 o'clock A.M., and expended the following ammunition: —

practice, which did no damage except frightening the colored cooks and some of our teamsters almost out of their senses.

On the morning of the 26th the enemy had disappeared. We were careful in marching to keep out of view of the enemy's signal stations, so we kept under the shelter of woods, and moving through Amissville crossed the Rappahannock at Hinson's Mill and camped at Orlean. Lee was making every effort to circumvent Pope. It was reported that old "Stonewall" was very near Manassas. We must have it out with the general having his "headquarters in the saddle" in a very few days.

At 9 A.M. on the 27th, the army moved, passing through Salem, and camped at White Plains, placing guns in position to guard against surprise. On the march to-day the column halted on the outskirts of Salem, and many men and officers, Gen. Lee among them, went into the village to get some refreshment. While thus engaged a cry was raised, "The Yankee Cavalry! Yankee Cavalry are upon us!" And then there was "hurrying to and fro"

First company Washington Artillery, 400 ; section of Dixie artillery, 209 ; section of Maurin's artillery, 119; Stribling's artillery, 354; Leake's artillery, one gun. Total, 1,182.

Capt. Leake reported after the enemy had retired with one rifle and three smooth-bore guns. He sustained no loss. About 2 o'clock P.M., Major Garnett rode up and requested me to send four rifle guns to Col. S. D. Lee, who was on the right, near Central Railroad. For this purpose I detached Lieut. Owen with one section of the Washington Artillery, and one section of Maurin's battery. In obedience to your orders, at 5.30 P.M., I ordered all the guns back to their respective commands.

Very respectfully, Colonel, your obedient servant,

C. W. SQUIRES,
Capt. Commanding First Co. Bat. W.A.

To COL. WALTON, *Commanding.*

at a great rate as a squadron of horse dashed down the
main street of the town.   Some of our people — about fifty
— were taken, and Gen. Lee himself narrowly escaped. Not
knowing but the enemy might be in force, a line of battle
was formed, and two pieces of artillery were placed to
sweep the road; but they came not, so all visions of
captures of horses, pistols, and silver watches had to be
abandoned.   Upon reaching Thoroughfare Gap in the afternoon of the 28th, Col. G. T. Anderson, commanding the
Georgia brigade, was ordered to clear it of the enemy, who
was found there.   Col. Beck, with his regiment (Ninth
Georgia), was ordered to advance, and sent forward two
companies as skirmishers on a reconnoissance.   Proceeding
cautiously he drove a mounted picket before him, killing
three of them, and cleared the pass, moving some quarter
of a mile beyond, and held his position until attacked and
driven back by a whole brigade and a battery.   The whole
of Anderson's brigade was now ordered forward, and,
moving rapidly to the front, met Col. Beck falling back
very slowly before the large force of the enemy, and he
was at once ordered to form his regiment on the right of
the railroad, and the other regiments were formed on the
left as fast as they came up.   The line being formed, and
skirmishers advanced to the front, the brigade moved forward gallantly, the men climbing the rough mountain sides
on their hands and knees to reach the enemy, who were occupying the crest of the hill and delivering a murderous fire in
their faces as they made the perilous ascent.   From the
nature of the ground and the impenetrable thickets of laurel
and brush, but one regiment obtained a favorable position,

that being the First Georgia, which inflicted a severe loss upon the enemy. Capt. Patton brought down five men with his pistol, killing three of them.

After Anderson had entered the Gap, Gen. D. R. Jones ordered in the remainder of his division, placing Drayton's brigade and two regiments of Toombs's brigade. on the right of the gorge, holding the other two regiments of Toombs in reserve. The enemy appeared in force upon the plateau in front of the Gap, and opened an artillery fire upon the troops now emerging from it. The artillery fire was kept up until after nightfall, when the enemy retreated, and Jones's division bivouacked beyond the Gap unmolested by the enemy.[1]

During the afternoon Gen. Hood, with his own and Gen. Whiting's brigade, was ordered by a footpath over the mountain to turn the enemy's right, and Gen. Wilcox, with his own, Featherstone's and Pryor's brigades, was ordered through Hopewell Gap, three miles to our left, to turn the right and attack the enemy in rear. Both commands bivouacked beyond the mountain, but the enemy had already retreated.

---

[1] Early in the morning, cavalry were sent to the Gap to reconnoitre, and, on their report that the enemy were advancing through the Gap, Rickett's division, which was to bring up the rear, and which was to have followed on King's left, and marched to Manassas Junction, was detached and sent to the Gap by way of Haymarket, where it arrived at 3 P.M.

Ricketts was seriously delayed by wagon-trains in marching from his bivoua? of the night before, west of Buckland Mills to the road, where he turned off to the left to go to Haymarket and the Gap.

However, his troops delayed the passage of Longstreet's troops through the Gap during the rest of the day and early part of the evening, and the enemy were obliged to send three brigades through Hopewell Gap to the north of Thoroughfare Gap before our troops retired. After dark, Ricketts fell back to Gainesville. — *Army under Pope.* ROPES.

August 29. — Gen. Longstreet slept in a small cottage last night, on the mountain, near the Gap, and his staff, Col. Walton, and myself on the porch in front of his door. I don't believe the General slept a minute, as he was tramping up and down the floor, it appeared to me, all night.

Just before day, when it was very dark, he opened his door, and, stalking across the gallery, disappeared in the darkness. Presently he called his orderly, Morris, and ordered his bay horse saddled, which being done he rode away alone. Sorrel and Fairfax were sleeping soundly. I gave each a kick with the toe of my boot, and told them "they had better be crawling out, that the General was off and in the Gap by this time." Then came the hurrying and scurrying of busy feet; horses were saddled, blankets rolled, and off we all scampered. It was often noticed that the General would, upon occasions when his mind was much occupied, mount and ride away, not noticing whether his staff was following or not; but when he turned his head to the right or to the left, he expected staff officers to be at hand, and they generally were there.

At daylight no enemy was in sight at or near the Gap. Hood and Wilcox joined the column of march early in the morning, as it moved in the direction of Gainesville. Noticed a few dead Federals in the Gap, one a captain, said to be named Carpenter; he was a fine-looking man, fully six feet in height.

Our two reserve batteries, the First and Third companies Washington Artillery, marched at the head of the column, immediately in rear of Gens. Lee and Longstreet and their escorts.

We are nearing Haymarket and Gainesville, and can hear the roar of cannon and small arms over on our left, towards Bull Run, where Jackson is supposed to be. If Pope has locked horns with him he must be hard pressed; but he has a way of taking care of himself.

The heat and dust are something terrible, and the men suffer much for water, some stooping down and drinking from the pools of dirty water by the road-side and from the cow tracks.

A squadron of cavalry emerges from a piece of woods on our left. Not knowing whether they are friend or foe, the column is halted. But soon the cross of St. Andrew is recognized upon their guidon, and a body of officers approaches rapidly. We soon distinguish the manly form, flowing beard, and plume of Gen. J. E. B. Stuart.

Gen. Lee greets him, and says: " Well, General, what of Jackson?"

"He has fallen back from Manassas, and is holding the enemy at bay at Sudley's ford."

"We must hurry on and help him," said Lee. "Is there no path by which we can move our tired men and get them out of the heat and dust?" Evidently there was none, and the troops were once more put in motion. The roar of the guns and the rattle of the small arms fill every heart with that indescribable emotion a soldier feels when he knows a battle is at hand. It is not fear nor anxiety. What is it? Let others answer. It is a glorious feeling, however, and the men step forward briskly, " eager for the fray."

At 11.30 A.M. the reserve batteries (First and Third companies Washington Artillery) reach Gainesville, where we come into the Warrenton turnpike, and, turning to the left in the direction of Groveton, move along a mile or two, when we are turned off into a piece of woods on the left of the pike and halted.

The infantry then deployed in line of battle : Hood, the first to arrive, with the Texans, on the right and left of the turnpike, at right angles with it, and supported by Gen. Evans's brigade. Then come Kemper's division, with his own brigade under Col. Corse, Pickett's brigade under Col. Hunton, and Jenkins's brigade, who form on the right of Hood ; then D. R. Jones's division of the brigades of G. T. Anderson, Drayton, and Toombs, forming on Kemper's right, with his own right resting on or near the Manassas Gap Railroad.

Wilcox's division arrives last, — having followed the rear of the column, — with his own brigade and those of Featherstone and Pryor. He passes through the woods on the left of the pike, where our reserve batteries have been halted, his men going through our guns, and deploys in a field in front of us, his right on the turnpike near Hood's left. Jackson's right is just in front of Wilcox, his line extending along an unfinished railroad cut, leading off towards Sudley's ford, where he rests his left.

As soon as the head of our advancing column of infantry is seen by the enemy they retire from the high ground in front of us, where they have been attacking Jackson's right, and change front to meet Hood and Evans

At 1 o'clock Gen. Longstreet sends for Col. Walton, and we find the General, with his staff, in the field where Wilcox is forming his lines, dismounted and standing behind their horses, for the sharp-shooters are popping away vigorously. He orders " all the long-range guns that can be gotten up to occupy the hill just abandoned by the enemy, and to open upon the enemy's left."

Capt. Miller's Third company Washington Artillery, with four Napoleon guns, was at once sent forward, passing through Wilcox's unformed line, much to his disgust, and immediately took position and opened fire. Capt. Squires, with the First company Washington Artillery, with three rifle-guns, under Lieut. E. Owen, followed and took position on Miller's left. These were followed by Riley's battery, four guns ; Bachman's battery, four guns ; one rifle-gun of Capt. Anderson ; one Napoleon of Capt. Chapman, and two Blakeley guns of the Donaldsonville Artillery, under command of Lieut. Landry, — nineteen guns in all. These guns filled the space between Jackson's right and Longstreet's left, and opened a terrific fire on the enemy's infantry and some of his artillery at Groveton. Jackson's men hear the welcome sounds and know that Longstreet and his brave men are near. A mighty yell of recognition surges from thousands of throats along the battle line above the sounds of cannon. Lee's grand army of brave Southern hearts is reunited ! Who can stand before his veterans ?

Upon the ground now occupied by the nineteen guns of Longstreet's corps the enemy has left his dead and

SCALE OF Miles
0   1   2

BULL

Cat Harpin Run.

Sudley Rd.

Sudley Sp.

Sudley, Ch.

RUN

Stone Bridge

Page Land Lane

Sudley Road

Line of Cavalry

Jackson

Independence and Groveton Road

Sudley Road

BRANCH

Stone

Gen'l. Pope Hdq.
Stone House

Turnpike

Robinson

Dogan

Warrenton

Henry

W.A.
1st C.
1P.M.

Groveton

Young's Lane No. 2

Chinn

Gainsville

Lewis Lane No. 1

YOUNG'S

Holkum Branch

Sudley Road

Washington Road

Gen'l Lee Hdq

Wid. Lane No. 1

Meadow Lane

W.A.
4th C.

Conrad

Manassas and Alexandria and

Newmarket

Old Warrenton

Longstreet

Mt. Pond

W.A. 2nd C.
Carmack

SECOND BATTLE
OF
MANASSAS
Aug. 29 & 30th 1862

N

S

Lawley's Mills Road

DAWKINS BRANCH

MANASSAS

Manassas and Gainsville

GAP

Manassas Gap Sudley and

RAIL-ROAD

Bethlehem Church Road

Leod

Sudley

╌╌╌ Confederate forces
▬▬ Federal forces

W. J. Hardee, C.E.

wounded; the latter are helped out of the way, but, the grass having caught fire, many are badly burned.

The enemy's artillery fire having slackened greatly, and an attack upon Jackson's left by the enemy's infantry having been broken up, I was sent to report the condition of affairs to Gen. Longstreet, then with Gen. Lee on a hill a little in the rear of our infantry, on the right of the Warrenton turnpike. I found the General, and reported. Old "Stonewall" was with him. Gen. Lee was evidently anxious to attack the enemy at once, and said to Longstreet, "Hadn't we better move our line forward?" But Longstreet replied, "I think not; we had better wait until we hear more from Gen. Stuart about the force he has reported moving against us from Manassas;" and our line was not moved. Gen. Jackson paid a compliment to our artillery, saying, after having observed the practice of the nineteen guns, "Gen. Longstreet, your artillery is superior to mine." Our timely arrival probably caused him to look most favorably upon the batteries engaged, to the detriment even of the fine artillery organization in his own corps.

As Col. Walton, "Bliffkins," and I were sitting on our horses in the road behind the batteries, a shell exploded over our heads, killing a poor fellow who had been enjoying the luxury of see-sawing in a rocking-chair. But a moment before we had observed him, remarking that he was the picture of ease and comfort; the next instant he had joined the great majority.

The nineteen guns were withdrawn from their positions upon the hill at 3.30 P.M., to refill their chests with ammunition from the ordnance wagons, which had just come up. It is always a comfort to know that plenty of ammunition is to be had, and Capt. Fred Colston of the ordnance is always on hand. "Give me plenty of ammunition, and unlimited horses, and I will fight my batteries day in and day out," said Col. Snowden Andrews.

While refilling the chests Gen. Longstreet sent for a battery to go over to his right, and the Third company Washington Artillery caissons were hurriedly filled, and the battery sent over.

Wilcox's three brigades were also marched over to our right, as an attack was apprehended in that quarter from Manassas; but nothing came of it, and Wilcox's men and our battery were returned to the left again.

Hood's two brigades, supported by Evans, and joined by Wilcox, moved forward about 4 o'clock, and made a gallant attack against a force of the enemy advancing to attack Jackson. There was a severe brush: one piece of artillery, several regimental standards, and a number of prisoners were taken, when the enemy retired, and at midnight Hood, Evans, and Wilcox resumed their former places in line. The army bivouacked in line of battle; water was scarce, and much suffering was experienced in consequence.[1]

On the morning of the 30th the enemy again advanced,

---

[1] One thing, however, is certain, and that is that the presence of Porter's corps that afternoon not only retained Jones on the railroad, but for a certain space of time brought over Wilcox also from the turnpike.

It is understood that Gen. Lee wanted to attack that day, and that Gen. Longstreet was opposed to it. If he had attacked that day he would have had certain advantages which he did not have the following day.

The divisions of King and Ricketts, as well as those of Porter, were all out of position on Friday. — *Army under Pope.* ROPES.

and began skirmishing along the whole line. Jackson
and Longstreet maintained the same position that they did
yesterday. Gen. R. H. Anderson's division had arrived
at Gainesville, where it was held in reserve.

Stephen D. Lee's battalion of artillery occupied the
same ground our nineteen guns occupied yesterday, and
engaged the enemy until noon, when all firing ceased, and an
ominous silence prevailed. At about 3 o'clock the enemy
advanced against Jackson's left in heavy force, his glittering lines of battle in magnificent array. Jackson's men
keep under cover of the railroad embankment until the
enemy come in close range, when all along their front suddenly comes a crash of musketry. The enemy wavers and falls
back. Our men behind the railroad cut are running short of
cartridges, and many run out and strip the dead and wounded
of their cartridge-boxes. A second and third line of the
enemy, of great strength, move up to support the first, and
come forward with apparently irresistible force. Jackson's
men, having no ammunition to spare, again await them
until at close range, and then pour their volleys into them
with unerring aim; but the enemy fights doggedly and
well. Many Confederates, getting out of ammunition, pick
up great stones, and throw them into the faces of the foe
with deadly effect. The result of the fighting seems to tremble
in the balance, and Jackson sends for reinforcements, when
the enemy fortunately comes in range of the left flank of
Longstreet, who quickly orders four of the batteries of
Col. S. D. Lee's battalion to open upon him. The effect
is instantaneous : the heavy columns, until now holding
their own or gradually pushing the hard-fought and tired

troops of Jackson, break and fall back in great confusion. Their efforts to rally are unavailing, and, thus relieved of the pressure, Jackson's men leap out of the cut, and, pressing forward against the foe with wild shouts and yells, drive him in confusion and dismay. Then Longstreet, riding down his lines, gives the command to charge the enemy's centre and left.

The men, eager and anxious for the fray, like bloodhounds unleashed, leap forward to help " Old Stonewall." [1] Hood, with his Texans, followed by Evans, leads the attack. Anderson gallantly supports Hood, while Wilcox takes care of the left and Kemper the right; D. R. Jones on the extreme right. Forward sweeps the line, steadily, determinedly ; no halting, but " Forward ! " " Forward ! " always " Forward ! " No other order is necessary. The reserve batteries (Washington Artillery) follow, but so rapid is the advance that they cannot get a shot. On the right the Second and Fourth companies Washington Artillery are fully engaged. The Fifth Texas strikes the Fifth New York Zouaves, and short and bloody is the work. Kemper pounces upon a battery of " Napoleons." Richardson's cannoneers of the Second company Washington Artillery run forward and man the pieces, and open them upon their late owners. Eshleman, with the Fourth company Washington Artillery, following Rosser's and Stuart's cavalry, sweeps around the enemy's extreme left, and en-

---

[1] Porter meantime, about 4 o'clock, pushes Morell's division in front. They drive the enemy from the outlying woods back upon the old railroad embankment. Sykes's division of regulars is in reserve. To the right Hatch pushes in King's division. The attack is made with great resolution. Jackson's veterans resist them with their never-failing tenacity and pluck. — *Army under Pope.* ROPES.

gages him, moving from hill to hill. On, on, the fiery line advances ; volleys and yells, shell and canister, — the slaughter is terrible. The enemy breaks from one position after another, and at last retreats to the opposite bank of Bull Run.

But over there, upon the well-known "Henry-house Hill," [1] stands like a wall of glittering steel the division of

---

[1] The slope of the hill behind the village (Groveton) was covered with a mass of men without order. Beyond these were other troops posted at right angles with the first, and among them the Zouaves, who were then half a mile away from where they were posted in the morning. The Confederate line came out on the open ground, moving in fine order, and firing as it advanced. The insignificant force opposing it was swept from the field in a few minutes, leaving the hill-side strewn with dead, a great number of whom were of the Zouave regiment. The fugitives fled towards the turnpike and towards the next ridge, and the Confederate line halted to re-form the ranks, and the batteries advanced to the open ground.

. . . .

The Second brigade moved along with the mass into the road and down to the toll-gate at the foot of the Henry Hill. Near this spot a little brook enters Young's branch from the south.

Beside the turnpike, and on the opposite side of this brook, stood Col. Warren and sixteen Zouaves of the Fifth New York Volunteers, with the regimental colors, — the remnant that came out of the battle intact. Warren sat immovable on his horse, looking back at the battle, and as if paralyzed, and the sixteen men, formed in files of four, blackened with dust and smoke, stood under their colors silent as statues, and gazed vacantly at the tumultuous concourse passing by. —*Recollections of a Campaign.* WM. E. DOUGHERTY, *Capt. U. S. Army.*

We pass now to the struggle for the Henry-house Hill. Here were Sykes's regulars, in first-rate order, and ready to receive the enemy. Buchanan, an old veteran of the war with Mexico, who had with his own hand forced open the door of Molino del Rey, commanded one brigade ; Chapman, his comrade in the same gallant fight, the other. Here, too, were gathered all the troops that could be collected from the front. It was a post of the last importance. We could not afford to lose it. There was no position west of Bull Run which offered such advantages for defence as this. The army was in full retreat, though in orderly retreat ; but that orderly retreat would be changed into a rout if the enemy should drive us from our position on the Henry-house Hill and its neighborhood. There would be nothing between them and the stone bridge across Bull Run. And they did not carry it. Their exertions had been severe before they reached this position. They had marched a considerable distance, and over difficult country. They attacked, however, with their accustomed energy and courage, and, while they suffered much, they inflicted heavy losses upon the regulars of Sykes. But, fortunately for the Federal army, darkness came on, and the exhausted Confederates ceased from farther assaults upon their obstinate antagonists. — *The Army under Pope.* JOHN C. ROPES.

regulars, the rear-guard of the volunteer army of Gen. Pope. Their perfect discipline and steadiness render them no mean adversaries for our exultant troops. That wall of fire stands immovable, while our arms beat against it with gigantic blows. It alone stands between Lee and a rout like unto Bull Run. At last, after long waiting, night spreads its mantle over the scene of blood. Batteries near the Chinn House, and our Fourth company at the Conrad House, with Rosser's cavalry, continue the cannonade, until finally the brave regulars move steadily off the field, and passing over Bull Run at the stone bridge the battle is ended, and Pope has found "*lines of retreat*," and has not seen the "*backs*" of Lee, Longstreet, "Stonewall Jackson," and their men.

Lee has scored another victory. With 49,000 men, of all arms, he has defeated Pope with 75,000, and put him to inglorious retreat on the road to Washington. Seven thousand prisoners have been taken, besides 2,000 wounded left on the field. Thirty pieces of artillery, and upwards of 20,000 small arms, numerous colors, and a large amount of stores, besides those taken by Jackson at Manassas Junction, were captured.

REPORT OF COL. WALTON, OF SECOND BATTLE OF MANASSAS.

HEAD-QUARTERS BATTALION WASHINGTON ARTILLERY,
November 30, 1862.

To MAJOR G. W. SORREL, *Assistant Adjutant General, Right Wing, A. N. V.:* —

I have the honor to transmit the following report of the operations of the Battalion Washington Artillery, of New Orleans, under my command,

on the 29th, 30th, and 31st of August last, at and after the second battle
of Manassas. On the 29th of August, 1862, the four batteries composing
the battalion were assigned and served as follows: The Fourth company, consisting of two 6-pounder bronze guns, and two 12-pounder
howitzers, under Capt. B. F. Eshleman, Lieuts. Norcom, Battles, and
Apps, with Pickett's brigade; the Second company, with two 6-pounder
bronze guns, and two 12-pounder howitzers, under Capt. Richardson,
Lieuts. Hawes, DeRussey, and Britton, with Toombs's brigade; the
First company, with three 3-inch rifle-guns, under Capt. C. W. Squires,
Lieuts. E. Owen, Galbraith, and Brown, and the Third company, with
fonr light 12-pouuder guns (Napoleons), under Capt. M. B. Miller,
Lieuts. McElroy and Hero in reserve.

About noon on the 29th the two batteries in reserve, having halted
near the village of Gainesville on the Warrenton and Centreville turnpike, were ordered forward by Gen. Longstreet, to engage the enemy
then in our front, and near the village of Groveton. Capts. Miller and
Squires at once proceeded to the position indicated by the General, and
opened fire upon the enemy's batteries. Immediately in Capt. Miller's
front he discovered a battery of the enemy, distant about twelve hundred
yards. Beyond this battery, and on a more elevated position, were
posted the enemy's rifle-batteries. He opened upon the battery nearest
him, and, after a spirited engagement of three quarters of an hour, completely silenced it, and compelled it to leave the field. He then turned
his attention to the enemy's rifle-batteries, and engaged them until, having exhausted his ammunition, he retired from the field.

Capt. Squires, on reaching his position on the left of Capt. Miller's
battery, at once opened with his usual accuracy upon the enemy's
batteries. Unfortunately, after the first fire, one of his guns, having
become disabled by the blowing out of the bushing of the vent, was sent
from the field.

Capt. Squires then placed the remaining section of his battery under
command of Lieut. Owen, and rode to the left, to place additional guns
(that had been sent forward to his assistance) in position. At this time
the enemy's infantry were engaged by the forces on the left of the
position occupied by our batteries, and, while the enemy retreated in
confusion before the charge of our veterans, the section under Lieut.
Owen poured a destructive fire into their ranks.

The enemy's artillery, having withdrawn beyond our range, the section was ordered from the field. Both batteries, the First and Third, in this action, fully maintained their well-earned reputation for skilful practice and gallant behavior. With this duel ended the operations on the left of our line for the day.

The next morning, 30th of August, the Second company of Capt. J. B. Richardson was ordered forward, from its position on the Manassas Gap Railroad, to join its brigade (Toombs's), then moving forward towards the enemy. Capt. Richardson pushed forward until, arriving near the Chinn House, he was informed that our infantry had charged and taken a battery near that position; but, owing to heavy reinforcements thrown forward by the enemy, were unable to hold it without the assistance of artillery. He immediately took position on the left of the Chinn House and opened on the enemy, who were advancing rapidly, in large numbers. After firing a short time he moved his battery forward about four hundred yards, and succeeded in holding the captured battery of four Napoleons, forcing the enemy back, and compelling a battery immediately in his front, and which was annoying our infantry greatly, to retire. He then turned the captured guns upon their late owners, and at night brought them from the field with their horses and harness.

Capt. Richardson, in his report, makes special mention for gallantry of privates J. B. Cleveland and W. W. Davis, who were the first to reach the captured battery, and, with the assistance of some infantry, fired nearly twenty-five rounds before being relieved by their comrades. Lieut. Hawes had his horse shot under him during this battle. While Richardson, with the Second, was doing such gallant services near Chinn House, Eshleman, with the Fourth, with his short-range guns, was doing good work in the same neighborhood. Following his brigade (Pickett's), he shelled the woods in their front, while they advanced in line of battle against the enemy, whose skirmishers were seen on the edge of the wood. Finding it would be impracticable to follow the brigade, owing to the broken nature of the ground, he passed rapidly to the right and front, going into battery and firing from every elevated position from which he could enfilade the enemy, until he had passed entirely to the right of Gen. Jones's position (overlooking nearly the whole space in front of Chinn House), from which his shells fell into the ranks of the enemy with great execution. A persistent attack on the front and flank drove the enemy back into the woods, and now the immense clouds of dust rising from Centreville road indicated that he was in full retreat. He was directed by Gen. D. R. Jones to move forward and shell the wood and road, which he continued to do until directed by Gen. J. E. B. Stuart to send a section of his battery to the hills in front of the Conrad House, and to fire into a column of cavalry advancing in his rear. The section under Lieut. Norcom was detached, took position on the left of the Conrad House, and fired into the enemy until directed to cease by Gen. Stuart, his object having been accomplished.

The remaining section of the battery, under Lieut. Battles, was then ordered by Capt. Eshleman across the Sudley road, firing, as it advanced, into the retreating enemy. At this time Capt. Eshleman's only support was one company of sixty men of Gen. Jackson's sharp-shooters, under Capt. Lee.

After a short interval the enemy again appeared in force near the edge of the wood. Capt. Eshleman immediately changed his front to the left, and poured into the enemy's ranks two rounds of canister, with deadly effect. Those not killed or wounded ran in disorder. After throwing a few shells into the woods Capt. Eshleman retired about two hundred yards to the rear, being unwilling to risk his section with such meagre support. In a few minutes an order was brought from Gen. Stuart directing the section to be brought again to the vicinity of the Conrad House.

It was now dark, and Capt. Eshleman kept up from this last position a moderate fire until 9 o'clock, in the direction of the Centreville road, when he was directed to retire, with Lieut. Norcom's section, that had joined him on the field, and rest his men. Capt. Eshleman, in his report, applauds highly the conduct of his officers, non-commissioned officers, and men, to whose coolness and judgment he was indebted for the rapid evolutions of his battery and precision of his fire.

The next day, August 31, 1862, Lieut. Owen, with two guns of the First company, accompanied Gen. Stuart, commanding cavalry, in pursuit of the enemy to and beyond Germantown. They came up with the enemy at several points, driving him ahead of them and capturing five hundred prisoners.

Capt. Squires, on the same day, with one gun, accompanied Col. Rosser to Manassas, going in rear of the enemy, capturing a large amount of stores (quartermaster's and surgical), ambulances, horses, etc.

My casualties in this battle were, one killed, — private H. N. White, — of Second company, and nine wounded.

Thus ended the operations of this battalion in this great second battle of Manasses, fought almost on the same ground and in sight of the field where our guns first pealed forth a little more than a year before.

I have the satisfaction, in conclusion, to say that all the officers and men gave in this important battle renewed evidence of their devotion, judgment, and cool bravery, in most trying positions.   No eulogy of mine can add to the reputation they so worthily enjoy, earned upon bloody battle-fields.

I am under obligations to Lieut. W. M. Owen, my always devoted and brave Adjutant, for distinguished services under fire.

I have the honor to be your obedient servant,

J. B. WALTON,
Colonel Commanding.

Our army bivouacked upon the battle-field, and this morning (August 31) it is raining hard, as it always does after a heavy cannonade, making everybody uncomfortable.

Richardson has appropriated the battery that Kemper captured yesterday, preferring the new guns to his old ones.

Yesterday Gen. Lee sent the following order to Gen. Longstreet, who referred it to Col. Walton : —

The General commanding directs that you economize greatly your ammunition of all kinds, but especially artillery, as it cannot be replaced immediately.

By order of Gen. Lee,

R. H. CHILTON,
A. A. G.

All the battle-field orders that we receive are written on little scraps of paper, torn sometimes from memorandum-books, without envelopes.

We occupy ourselves riding about the field, observing the effects of the battle, which has been fought on the same ground fought over in July last, with the positions of the opponents reversed. The dead are lying thickly around, and where the Fifth Texas encountered the Fifth New York Zouaves, the dead of the latter are distinguished by their gay uniforms. We were told that the body of the adjutant had been identified. Our forges have been kept busy all day repairing damages, and shoeing the horses.

In the afternoon we received the following order : —

HEAD–QUARTERS, Aug. 31, 1862.
COLONEL : — General Longstreet wishes you to move your batteries after the column this evening to Sudley Ford, halting and parking just this side of the ford.   Yours truly,

G. M. SORREL,
A. A. G.

COL. WALTON *comd'g, etc.*

Get a guide and take the shortest route to the ford. All the batteries that are not with the brigades are to be brought on by you.

G. M. SORREL,
A. A. G.

We bivouacked at Sudley Ford.

On September 1st all the army crossed Bull Run at Sudley Ford, moving towards Germantown. Gen. Lee has taken to his ambulance, as his hurt wrist, sprained yesterday, does not permit him to control his horse. Jackson is moving at the head of the columns, and trying to get in on the flank of Pope at Fairfax Court-House. At Chan-

tilly he encountered the enemy, and had a sharp engagement in a driving rain.

Ex-Governor Smith, of Virginia,—"Extra Billy " as he is
called,— was the cause of much merriment to-day. Although
wearing his uniform as a Colonel, he insists on sporting a
high beaver hat of the stove-pipe order, and a blue cotton
umbrella. To-day, while it was raining, he rode about with
his umbrella raised, and on all sides came the cry from the
troops : " Come out of that umbrel ; I see your legs ! Come
out of that hat ; want it to boil the beans in," etc., etc.

Gen. Phil. Kearney was killed to-day, and his body is
in our hands, lying upon the porch of a cabin near the roadside.   He is a very soldierly-looking man, with heavy
mustache and goatee ; one arm is gone, — lost at the
gates of Mexico.   Lee, Longstreet, and many others, knew
him well.   He was killed in the thick woods at dark,
Having evidently mistaken our troops for his own he rode
up to our lines, and asked, " What troops are those ? " The
reply came, " Louisiana Brigade ! "   At that he turned his
horse at full speed to escape, when a shot fired after him
brought him to the ground.

On the morning of the 2d his body was returned to the
enemy, under flag of truce, together with his horse.

The weather is now clear and cool.   I rode forward to
see friends in the Louisiana brigade, and saw Col. Penn,
Tom Morgan, Flower, and others.   My old and intimate
friend, Eugene Janin, was killed on the 30th, while charging with his men.[1]

---

[1] Eugene Janin was the son of the late Louis Janin, Esq., one of the most
distinguished and learned members of the Louisiana and Washington city bar,

Three days' rations ordered to be cooked. On the 3d of September the army marched at daylight, and bivouacked at Dranesville. The two corps of the army are now united, and the enemy is peeping over his forts in front of Washington.

"On to Maryland!" is now the cry, and the heads of columns are directed towards the Potomac, — the First corps bivouacked near Leesburg. On the 5th of September the march was resumed, and the banks of the Potomac reached. On the 6th the army began early in the morning to ford the river into Maryland.

---

a contemporary of Grimes, Roselius, S. S. Prentiss, and Benjamin, a gentleman of the old French school; he bore a national reputation.

The captain of Eugene's company, Company C, Capt. T. N. Powell, having been shot through both thighs on the 29th, Eugene had command of his company on the 30th, and early in the engagement had been wounded slightly in the hand or arm. When the enemy made their last determined assault upon Jackson's front they came close to a common fence which separated the two opposing lines, and over which the engagement raged the fiercest. Soon the enemy began to scatter, and Janin, observing this, climbed the fence, calling upon his company to follow him, and tried to seize the enemy's colors just in front. He had almost accomplished his object when he was struck by a bullet full in the forehead, and was killed instantly. But his death was not unavenged, for the Federal soldier who had shot him was bayoneted by a soldier named Burns, of Company D, Tenth Louisiana regiment, who had followed Janin's lead.

On the 18th of August, in a pleasant letter written from camp on the Rapidan, he said, "The banks of most of the little brooks about here are lined with mint, suggestive of the 'Sazarac' and happier days; but whiskey and sugar are scarce articles, or I would drink copious libations to the health of yourself and other absent friends."

He adds: "I presume the expected battle cannot be far distant. We have about 80,000 men up here of the oldest troops of the Confederacy, led by its most experienced generals. Burnside has joined Pope, and between the two they doubtless can bring 100,000 men in the field; but the difference between the character of the troops will more than compensate for the difference of numbers." Little did he think that in the "expected battle" he would be called upon to offer up his young life upon the altar of country. He died, as he had lived, a brave and noble gentleman. He was buried upon the field where he fell.

CHAPTER VII.

" MARYLAND, MY MARYLAND."

Explosion of Ammunition. — Boonesboro. — Hagerstown. — Dr. Maguire. — Jackson to Harper's Ferry. — D. H. Hill at Boonesboro. —
Sharpsburg. — Lost Order of Gen. Lee. — Washington Artillery again
in Battle. — Longstreet and Staff as Gunners.

AFTER all the batteries were safely across the Potomac
this morning, I immediately straggled, with Kursheedt and " Bliffkins," to get something to eat, as of late
the army has been on short rations, living mostly on
roasting ears of corn, plucked from the fields on the
march.   We call this, even now, the " Green-corn
Campaign."

Every one we meet says he is a " rebel," and we are
most hospitably received wherever we go.   We get plenty
to eat and to drink.   The young ladies are wild to see
Gen. Lee, and we agree to find him for them ; so in the
afternoon a caravan is made up of all the old family carriages in the country, and filled with pretty girls, and we
escort them to where " Uncle Robert " is resting.   He is
immediately surrounded, and kissed, and hugged, until the
old gentleman gets .very red in the face, and cries for
mercy.   We young ones look on, and only wish they
would distribute those favors a little more " permiscus," so
to speak ; but the fair ones, though coy, are very agreeable,
and we each forthwith select one whose colors we shall wear

until we reach the next town. But all pleasures have an end, and the bugle sounds "Forward," and away we march upon the soil of Maryland, wondering if she is now going to "breathe and burn." "Maryland, my Maryland!" On the 7th of September we crossed the Monocacy river, and encamped near Frederick.

Jackson's "foot cavalry" has been here before us, and has gobbled all the plunder; but we found a grocer, a good, sensible fellow, with "rebel sympathies," and we invested a few hundred dollars, "Confederate scrip" in coffee, sugar, whiskey, Scotch ale, champagne, and a few other "necessaries of life," much to the disgust of his partner, who did not take a bit of stock in "Jeff Davis," and who felt remarkably sore when the last of his stock of groceries, was exchanged for Confederate notes. We told him when Maryland began to "burn" they would be good in New York for gold.

Oh, what a time we had in camp that night! Oh, my!! Green-corn dinners, hard marches, thirst and fatigue, — all were forgotten. "Champagne flowed like water" (not too much water, but just enough), the "crystal goblets were filled to the brim," and we "sipped the nectar," and felt mighty good, not to express it in stronger terms.

Final result, by a mental calculation, a headache in the early dawn; but a plunge in the cold waters of the Monocacy brought us about all right again.

We are encamped (the two reserve batteries of the Washington Artillery) in a beautiful grove of oaks. On one side of us the head-quarters of Gen. Longstreet are established, and with him is Gen. Lee. On the other side " Stonewall " has pitched his tents. The latter passes our camp and our tent several times a day. " Old Jack," as the boys call him, is rather an ungainly person on foot. It is only when the roar of battle breaks forth that his eye lights up and he looks the " mighty man of war " he is. He told Gen. Longstreet that " he (L.) was the only commanding officer he ever knew who had a body guard of artillery." He thought it a good joke, — it was for " old Jack." The engineers are destroying the railroad bridges across the river, and Gen. Lee has issued a proclamation to the people of Maryland, asking them to come and " breathe and burn." They haven't burned much so far.[1]

---

[1] HEAD–QUARTERS ARMY NORTHERN VIRGINIA,
NEAR FREDERICK, Sept. 8, 1862.

TO THE PEOPLE OF MARYLAND : —

It is right that you should know the purpose that has brought the army under my command within the limits of your State, so far as that purpose concerns yourselves.

The people of the Confederate States have long watched with the deepest sympathy the wrongs and outrages that have been inflicted upon the citizens of a Commonwealth allied to the States of the South by the strongest social, political, and commercial ties.

They have seen, with profound indignation, their sister State deprived of every right, and reduced to the condition of a conquered province.

Under the pretence of supporting the Constitution, but in violation of its most valuable provisions, your citizens have been arrested and imprisoned upon no charge, and contrary to all forms of law. The faithful and manly protest against this outrage, made by the venerable and illustrious Marylanders, to whom, in better days, no citizen appealed for rights in vain, was treated with scorn and contempt. The government of your chief city has been usurped by armed strangers; your Legislature has been dissolved by the unlawful arrest of its members; freedom of the press and of speech has been suppressed; words have been declared offences by an arbitrary decree of the Federal Executive, and citizens ordered to be tried by a military commission for what they may dare to speak.

Believing that the people of Maryland possessed a spirit too lofty to submit to such a government, the people of the South have long wished to aid you in throwing off this foreign yoke, to enable you again to enjoy the inalienable rights of freedom, and restore independence and sovereignty to your State.

The 10th of September was a bright, beautiful day, and the army of Lee, with bands playing and colors flying, marched through Frederick. The citizens crowded the streets and windows to see the troops pass. Ladies were demonstrative, and waved their handkerchiefs; but the men looked coolly on as though afraid to express their feelings either way. The artillery boys marched in front of their batteries, and sang their choruses, led by Lieut. Frank McElroy.

The army passed through in good order, and all in the merriest and jolliest mood possible, indulging occasionally in good-natured chaff, as was their wont. Any peculiarity of costume or surroundings of any person was sure to bring out some remark that would set whole regiments in a roar. On a small gallery stood a buxom young lady, with laughing black eyes, watching the scene before her; on her breast she had pinned a small flag, the "stars and stripes." This was observed, and some soldier sang out, "Look h'yar, miss, better take that flag down; we're awful fond of charging breast-works!" This was carried down

---

In obedience to this wish our army has come among you, and is prepared to assist you with the power of its arms in regaining the rights of which you have been despoiled.

This, citizens of Maryland, is our mission so far as you are concerned. No constraint upon your free will is intended; no intimidation will be allowed.

Within the limits of this army, at least, Marylanders shall once more enjoy their ancient freedom of thought and speech. We know no enemies among you, and will protect all of every opinion.

It is for you to decide your destiny, freely, and without constraint.

This army will respect your choice, whatever it may be, and while the Southern people will rejoice to welcome you to your natural position among them, they will only welcome you when you come of your own free will.

R. E. LEE,
General Commanding.

the line amid shouts of laughter. The little lady laughed herself, but stood by her colors.[1]

The columns were soon upon the high road towards Boonesboro', and we were all struck with the beautiful scenery of this section of the country. As we climbed the hills long stretches of valley extended as far as the eye could reach in the direction of the Potomac. How still and peaceful it all looked; and yet armies were to tramp over it, and the desolating foot of war was to stamp out, ere long, all its sweet freshness.

As we were marching to-day over the turnpike road the rear chest of a caisson exploded. Although against the orders of his officers, private Alsobrook seated himself for a ride upon the caisson and smoked his pipe. Presently came the explosion, and he was hurled twenty feet into the air, and fell upon the road, entirely denuded of all his clothing, and burned from head to feet. Strange to say he received no serious injuries. He had hardly been removed when the shells in the chest began to explode, and caused a stampede of officers and men. Then Corporals Kursheedt and Ruggles, of the First company, stepped to the front, and, going deliberately up to the smoking-chest, emptied their canteens of water upon the burning cotton used for packing; then taking the shells, some already ignited, threw them into the ditch of water alongside the road, where some exploded, making an awful scatteration of mud and water, but fortunately hurting no one. The

[1] The poet J. G. Whittier has written a poem called " Barbara Frietchie," the scene of his story being laid in Frederick on this day. If the events he relates occurred it is strange we did not know it. "Poets have license, but not always reason."

danger over, the march was resumed. For this gallant act these corporals quite modestly received the warm approbation of their comrades, and no more was thought of it. But the "Victoria" and the "Cross of the Legion of Honor" have been pinned to a soldier's breast for acts of lesser heroism. On the 11th the march was continued towards Boonesboro' and Hagerstown. We find that our welcome along the road is not cordial, and the "general rising" of "down-trodden Maryland" will not be on hand. On the 12th we reached Hagerstown, and find the people here are more demonstrative, and we have much polite attention shown us. Many young girls approached us as we marched through the streets, and presented us with beautiful flowers. We remember gratefully the kind attention of Dr. Maguire and his charming family.

At Boonesboro' the command of Gen. D. H. Hill was left to guard Turner's Gap, and Jackson and A. P. Hill have marched towards Harper's Ferry, to take that place. We did some "shopping" in Hagerstown, devoting ourselves chiefly to the "dry-goods line," and bought water-proof cloth and some dress patterns to present to our lady friends in Richmond, where they were in great need of such things. I should have liked to carry a wagon-load back. One merchant had upon his top shelves, where they had lain for many years, about one hundred old-fashioned, bell-crowned beaver hats, with long nap upon them, just the style our fathers wore, and caricaturists are wont to place upon the head of Brother Jonathan. These were discovered by some funny fellow, who appeared upon the street with one upon his head. The new "mode" took like wildfire, — as new fashions always do, — and the store was soon relieved of the stock of beavers, and the streets were thronged with men with the new "Brother Jonathan" hat. They wore them upon the march, and went into the battle of Antietam with this most peculiar head-gear for warriors.

On the 13th it was reported that a cavalry skirmish had occurred at Frederick, and that McClellan with a large army, was following in our wake. We found excellent lager beer and cigars in Hagerstown, and the "secessionists" entertained us hospitably. On the 14th the enemy, under McClellan, reached Turner's Gap, near Boonesboro', and attacked D. H. Hill's division of 3,000 men. Longstreet's corps marched at daylight from Hagerstown to his relief. McClellan has caught us in a bad fix, for Jackson and A. P. Hill are still away at Harper's Ferry. Our column (Longstreet's) moves as fast as it can, and the firing at Boonesboro' is distinctly heard. As we reached the outskirts of Boonesboro', at 3 o'clock, we met an ambulance, conveying the body of Gen. Garland, who had been killed during the afternoon. Upon reaching the gap, two divisions (D. R. Jones's and Hood's) of Longstreet's corps were sent up the mountain to aid D. H. Hill; but it soon became manifest that our forces were not sufficient to resist McClellan's entire army, and, in view of this, Gen. Lee, at dark, ordered the troops to withdraw. Gen. Fitz Lee, of the cavalry, estimate McClellan's force at 100,000 men.[1]

---

[1] As we have now reached the point at which the nucleus of Lee's army has taken position in front of Sharpsburg, while two divisions of McClellan's army have formed up for the attack, the time seems to have come for some remarks upon the character of the two armies. There is no occasion for saying much about the rank and file of either side, for the soldierly qualities of both are too well known. After eighty years of peace, the surface of which had been

At 11 P.M. Longstreet and D. H. Hill, having been withdrawn, are marched in the direction of the Potomac to Sharpsburg, so that they may connect with Jackson and Hill when they shall come from Harper's Ferry.

The road is blocked with wagons and our movements are necessarily slow. Gen. Lee and staff pass by and urge every one to move along as fast as possible. Reports are received that the enemy's cavalry occupies Sharpsburg.

We reached the vicinity of that town early in the morning of the 15th, crossed the Antietam by a stone bridge, and formed line of battle along the range of hills between the town and the stream, with our backs to the Potomac.[1]

---

scarcely ruffled by the war of 1812 and the Mexican war, the men of the North and of the South had shown that they still possessed the soldierly qualities of the Anglo-Saxon race. For fourteen months they had been opposed to each other, and from the first and second Bull Run, at Williamsburg and Fair Oaks, and Gaines's Mill and Malvern Hill, and in all the campaigning which came between the first clash of arms and the last struggle at South Mountain, they had displayed intelligence, courage, endurance, tenacity, and patriotism. The qualities which enabled the South to win the first Bull Run, and had made Massachusetts men "stand in the evil hour" at Ball's Bluff, had been developed and disciplined by the experience of war, and Lee and McClellan now had each an instrument to work with, which had been not perfected, but much bettered, by the tempering process of the field.

When we pass from the men to the commanders there is more to be said.

[1] Lee had Longstreet, and D. H. Hill, and Hood, and Stuart with him, while Jackson, A. P. Hill, McLaws, Anderson, and Walker, were hastening to join him.

McClellan had, for corps commanders, Hooker and Sumner, and Porter and Franklin, and Burnside and Mansfield, while his division commanders were Cox, Couch, Doubleday, French, Greene, Hatch, Meade, Merrell, Richardson, Ricketts, Rodman, Sedgwick, Slocum, W. F. Smith, Sturgis, Willcox, and Williams.

If a student of military history familiar with the characters who figured in the war of secession, but happening to be ignorant of the story of the battle of the Antietam, should be told that the men we have named held the high commands there, he would say that with anything like an equality of forces the Confederates must have won; for their leaders were men who made great names in the war, while the Federal leaders were, with few exceptions, men who never became conspicuous, or became conspicuous only through failure. Their names are for the most part unknown to the public, and few can say who among them are alive or dead. — *Gen. F. W. Palfrey, p. 52.*

On the opposite shore of the Antietam the banks are quite steep, and afford good position for artillery. Longstreet's corps forms on the right of the main road, and D. H. Hill on the left. All the batteries present are placed in position along the ridge. Longstreet says, "Put them all in, every gun you have, long range and short range."

The guns of the Washington Artillery were posted as follows : on the ridge east of Sharpsburg, and on the right of the turnpike which runs through the town, was the First company, under Capt. Squires, Lieuts. E. Owen, Galbraith, and Brown, with two 3-inch rifles and two 10-pounder Parrotts ; on Squires's right came the Third company, under command of Capt. Miller, Lieuts. A. Hero and McElroy, with four 12-pounder Napoleons ; across a ravine on the right, in an orchard in front of Gen. D. R. Jones's division, was the Second company, under Capt. Richardson, Lieuts. Hawes, Britton, and DeRussey, with two 12-pounder Napoleons and two 12-pounder howitzers ; near Richardson, and still farther to the right, was the Fourth company, under Capt. Eshleman, Lieuts. Norcom, Battles, and Apps, with two 6-pounder bronze guns and two 12-pounder howitzers. On the ridge near the First company were the batteries of Bachman and Riley, and here Gen. Lee established head-quarters.[1]

A courier arrives in hot haste, with news that Jackson

---

[1] The National Cemetery at Sharpsburg is situated upon the crest of a hill to the eastward of the town, and just outside the houses. It fronts upon the main road from the town to Keedysville, and lies on the southerly side of the road. It commands a view of remarkable beauty and extent. Within its enclosure is a small mass of limestone, upon which it is said Lee stood to direct the battle. — *Antietam and Fredericksburg.* PALFREY, *p. 50.*

has captured Harper's Ferry, with its garrison of 12,000 men, 70 pieces of artillery, and 13,000 small arms.

"This is indeed, good news," said Gen. Lee; "let it be announced to the troops;" and staff officers rode at full gallop down the line, and the announcement was answered by great cheering.

Our lines were scarcely formed when the enemy appeared upon the opposite bank of the Antietam, and our artillery opened upon him a few guns, just to let him know that we were going no further, and were at bay.

Couriers were sent to Jackson and Hill to come to us as soon as possible. Our numbers in their absence are fearfully small, hardly 15,000 men, being those of Longstreet, D. H. Hill, and Stuart's cavalry; and McClellan has 100,000; but they must be but hastily raised militia regiments, and don't count for much. Where do all these men come from? Pope had but 50,000 after the battle at Groveton last month.

All this day our thin line faced the whole of McClellan's army, and it closed with a little artillery practice on each side.

The Colonel and I quartered ourselves in a dwelling-house on the edge of the town. Gen. Toombs was under the same roof, and Gens. Lee and Longstreet were in a house on the opposite side of the street.

For some unknown reason Gen. Lee expressed his belief that there would not be much fighting on the morrow. He did not then know, as we learned afterwards, that McClellan held the key to all his movements, by having in possession a most important order, lost by Gen. D. H. Hill at

Frederick, and expected, from the information obtained, to crush Lee's army. McClellan was reported as saying, "If I don't crush Lee now, you may call me whatever you please." [1]

At daylight, on the morning of the 16th, the enemy is

---

[1] Major Marshall, of Gen. Lee's staff, mentioned to me as one of the greatest misfortunes which has happened to them during the war (greater, he thought, than the fall of New Orleans), the accidental loss, through carelessness, by a general of division, of a very important order of Gen. Lee's. McClellan, who had been slowly and carefully feeling his way, totally ignorant of Gen. Lee's plans and the whereabouts of his main force, is said to have exclaimed, on finding this order, "Well, if I don't destroy Lee this time, you may call me what you like;" and he immediately pushed on as fast as he could march, and caught the Confederates before they were ready. The drawn battle of Sharpsburg, or Antietam Creek, followed; and Lee, not destroyed, but thwarted in the main object of his campaign, soon afterwards recrossed the Potomac. In the meantime, however, Jackson had captured Harper's Ferry, with its garrison of 12,000 men and immense stores, so that Lee still reaped some advantage from his ably-conceived plan of campaign. McClellan alludes to this matter, in his evidence before Congress on the conduct of the war, in the following terms : —

"When at Frederick we found the original order issued to Gen. D. H. Hill by direction of Gen. Lee, which gave the orders of march for the whole army, and developed their intentions. The substance of the order was, that Jackson was to move from Frederick by the main Hagerstown road, and, leaving it at some point near Middleburg, to cross the Potomac near Sharpsburg, and endeavor to capture the garrison of Martinsburg, and cut off the retreat of the garrison of Harper's Ferry in that direction. Gen. McLaws was ordered, with his own command and the division of Gen. Anderson, to move out by the same Hagerstown road, and gain possession of the Maryland heights, opposite Harper's Ferry. Gen. Walker, who was then apparently somewhere near the mouth of the Monocacy, was to move through Lovettsville, and gain possession of Loudon's height, thus completing the investment of Harper's Ferry. Gen. Longstreet was ordered to move to Hagerstown with Hill, to serve as a rear-guard. Their reserve trains were ordered to take a position either at Boonesboro' or Hagerstown, I have now forgotten which. It was directed in the same order, that after Jackson, Walker, McLaws, etc., had taken Harper's Ferry, they were to rejoin the main army at Hagerstown or Boonesboro'. That order is important in another sense. It shows very plainly that the object of the enemy was to go to Pennsylvania, or at least to remain in Maryland. Upon learning the contents of this order I at once gave orders for a vigorous pursuit," etc.

Singularly enough, the same general lost an equally important order before the seven days' fighting around Richmond, and it was found on a prisoner who was captured at Gaines's Mill. Unaware, perhaps, of its importance, he had not sent it on to head-quarters, or it would have done incalculable mischief. — *Ross's Camps and Cities of the Confederate States.*

in plain view on the high ground upon the opposite bank of the Antietam. His batteries are in position. They open fire, and become annoying. We reply with Squires's, Bachman's, and Riley's batteries of long-range guns; but the distance is too great to make a duel effective, and the firing is stopped by order of Gen. Lee.

The long-range guns of the enemy, however, make their shot whistle over our heads, and plunge into the town, setting fire to some houses.

Riding through the town, to find Gen. Longstreet, I met Gen. Lee on foot, leading his horse by the bridle. It was during the artillery firing, and the shells of the enemy were falling in close proximity to him, but he seemed perfectly unconscious of danger. He directed us to keep the artillery ammunition for the enemy's infantry only.[1]

During this evening, 16th, Gen. Jackson arrived with Ewell's division (Gen. Lawton commanding), and Jackson's division (Gen. J. R. Jones commanding), and his men were placed on the left of Gen. Hood, who had been sent over to the left from our extreme right, and had formed on the left of D. H. Hill. A battery of the enemy opened fire upon Jackson's division, but it was silenced in a few minutes by a well-directed fire from Poague's battery.

---

[1] Tuesday, the 16th, was a terribly hot day in its early hours, with a burning sun and no breeze; but at about eleven the sun became overcast, and a little air stirred from time to time. It was a day of mere idleness throughout for a large part of the army, and no one but the gunners had anything to do in the forenoon. We lay about on the eastern slope of the ridge which interposed between us and the valley of the Antietam, and occasionally we would go to the crest of the ridge to see what we could see. There was plenty to see, but unfortunately that was not all of it. The Confederate batteries were wide awake, and their *practice was extremely good*, and projectiles flew over the crest so thickly that mere curiosity was not sufficient to keep any one there long." — *Gen. F. W. Palfrey, p. 56.*

Other batteries opened soon after upon our lines, and the firing continued until dark.   About 10 P.M. Lawton's and Trimble's brigades relieved Hood, who had been more or less engaged during the evening.

This afternoon our strength was less than 18,000 men, consisting of the commands of Longstreet, D. H. Hill, the two divisions under Jackson, and two brigades under Walker.

Couriers were sent to hurry up A. P. Hill, Anderson, and McLaws, from Harper's Ferry.

The troops slept that night upon their arms, disturbed only by occasional picket-firing.

The Federal corps of Gen. Hooker had crossed the Antietam in the afternoon, and were bivouacking in front of our lines.

We made our head-quarters in the Dutch Reformed church in the town where our friends, the "surgeons," have also established themselves.   They treated us to a good supper, and we smoked our pipes, and spread our blankets within the chancel and slept soundly.

At daybreak on the 17th skirmishing commenced in front of our left, and the Federal batteries opened a severe and damaging fire.   This was replied to by Poague, Carpenter, Brockenbrough, Raines, Caskie, and Wooding. About sunrise, Hooker's corps, now being reinforced by Mansfield's corps, advanced to the edge of the woods on the eastern side of the Hagerstown turnpike.   Batteries were opened in front, and for an hour a terrific storm of shot, shell, and musketry was poured into our men.   Gen. Jones, commanding Jackson's division, was wounded, and

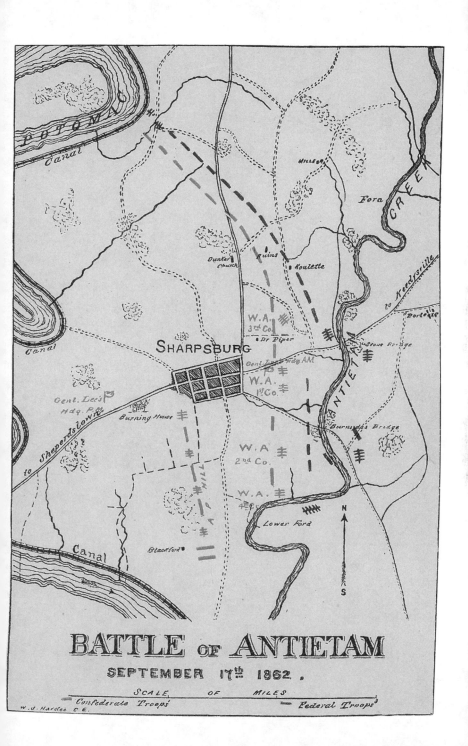

BATTLE OF ANTIETAM

SEPTEMBER 17ᵗʰ 1862.

SCALE   OF   MILES

Confederate Troops   Federal Troops

W.J. Hardee C.E.

compelled to leave the field, and the command devolved upon Gen. Starke.

With heroic spirit our lines advanced, at times driving the enemy, and at times being compelled to fall back before his destructive fire. At this early hour Gen. Starke was killed. More than half the brigades of Lawton and Hays were killed and wounded, and more than a third of Trimble's, and all the regimental commanders in these brigades, except two, were killed or wounded.

Thinned in their ranks and their ammunition exhausted, Jackson's division, and the brigades of Lawton, Hays, and Trimble, retired, and Hood again took the position from which he before had been relieved.

Early now took command of Ewell's division, and determined to hold his ground if reinforcements could be sent to him. A small command under Col. Grigsby kept in check the advance of the enemy on the left flank, while Gen. Early attacked, with great vigor and gallantry, the columns on his right and front. The force in front was giving way under this attack, when another heavy column of Federal troops was seen moving across the plateau on his left flank. It was Sedgwick's division of Sumner's corps, which had crossed the Antietam after Mansfield, and joined in the fight, advancing with spirit near the woods in which was the Dunker church, planting a battery across the turnpike near the edge of the wood.

But now the expected reinforcements come with a rush upon the field, — Semmes's, Kershaw's, Barksdale's, and Cobb's brigades of McLaws's division, — and the whole, including Grigsby's command, now united, charge upon the enemy, checking his advance, and then drive him back with great slaughter at all points, sweeping the woods with perfect ease. The enemy was driven not only through the woods, but over a field in front, over two high fences beyond, and into another body of woods, more than half a mile distant from the ground where the fight began, our forces regaining and occupying their original position.

No other advance, beyond demonstrations, was made by the enemy on the left. This was about 10 o'clock.[1]

Sedgwick's Second division of Sumner's corps, having crossed the Antietam and attacked our left under Jackson, and been beaten back, the First and Third divisions of the same corps, under French and Richardson, followed, and, moving southerly and parallel to the Antietam, encountered three small brigades of D. H. Hill's command, near the Rullet House, and, pushing them back, advanced upon the centre of Lee's line.

The brigades were Colquitt's, Ripley's, and Garland's (under McRea), and they were fighting gallantly when Capt. Thompson's Fifth North Carolina cried out, "They are flanking us!" This cry spread like an electric flash along the ranks, bringing up recollections of the flank fire at South Mountain. In a moment they broke and fell to

---

[1] "Thus," says Gen. Palfrey, " by about 10 o'clock the successes of the morning were lost. Our lines had been withdrawn almost altogether to the east of the turnpike, though we had more or less of a lodgment near the Dunker church, and some of Sedgwick's men were west of the turnpike in the neighborhood of the Miller House, or nearly as far north. Two corps and one division of the Federal army had been so roughly handled that but small account could be made of them in estimating the available force remaining." And it was here some old opponents were met, for Gen. Palfrey adds : " The Fifteenth and the Twentieth Massachusetts had been at Ball's Bluff, but their fate at Antietam was harder yet."

the rear. Thus three of Hill's brigades had been broken, and much demoralized, and all the artillery had been withdrawn from his front.

Gens. Rodes's and G. B. Anderson's brigades still held the line on an old road, and some stragglers had been gathered up and placed upon their left. It was now apparent that the enemy was massing on Hill's front, and that their grand attack would be made upon his position, which was the centre of our line. Reinforcements were sent for, but before any arrived a heavy force, consisting of the divisions of French, Richardson, and Smith's division of Franklin's Sixth corps, advanced "in three parallel lines with all the precision of a parade day." They met with a galling fire, however, recoiled, fell back, and finally lay down behind the crest of a hill and kept up an irregular fire.

By some unfortunate misunderstanding of orders Gen. Rodes's brigade was moved to the rear, and finally retreated in confusion. Gen. D. H. Hill immediately intercepted them and rallied a few men, not more than forty in all, and the remainder of the brigade disappeared from the field. This small number, together with some Mississippians and North Carolinians, about one hundred and fifty in all, were stationed behind a small ridge, leading from the Hagerstown road. Gen. G. B. Anderson still nobly held his ground, but the enemy began to pour through the Gap made by the retreat of Rodes. Anderson himself was mortally wounded, and his brigade was totally routed.

Col. Bennet, of the Fourteenth, and Major Sillers, of the Thirteenth, North Carolina regiments, rallied a portion of their men, and the Third Arkansas and Twenty-seventh

North Carolina, of Walker's division, steadfastly held their ground.

The enemy crossed the old road, which we had occupied in the morning, and took position in a cornfield and orchard in advance of it. They had now got within a few hundred yards of the hill which commanded Sharpsburg and our rear. Affairs looked very critical. Longstreet, who had ridden rapidly to the centre, saw at once the condition of affairs, and sent for a battery. The Third company Washington Artillery, Capt. Miller, was ordered to him. As Miller went into position a well-directed shot of the enemy's battery exploded one of his caissons; he immediately unlimbered and opened upon the enemy, who was advancing in force. This attack was met by the troops of Walker, Miller's battery of the Washington Artillery, and two guns of Boyce's South Carolina battery, and the enemy was driven back in some confusion.

Our weak line, with enthusiasm, made an effort to pursue. Col. Cooke, of the Twenty-seventh North Carolina, very gallantly charged with his own regiment, but his supply of ammunition being exhausted, and he being un-unsupported, returned to his position in line.

Miller suffered considerably under the fire of the Federals, losing two of his gunners, and several cannoneers were wounded. The enemy having fallen back beyond effectivè range our guns ceased firing.

In about twenty minutes the enemy advanced again. Cooke stood with empty guns, and waved his colors to show that his troops were in position. Miller played upon their ranks with cannister. Lieut. Hero was wounded, and Lieut. McElroy having been sent to watch the enemy's movements on the right, Capt. Miller found himself the only officer with his battery. With only men enough left to work a section, he opened upon the enemy with two guns with fine effect, and placed the remaining section under Sergt. Ellis, directing him to take it completely under cover. He then continued the action until his ammunition was nearly exhausted, when Sergt. Ellis brought up the remaining caissons.

The enemy had made two determined attempts to force our line, and had been twice signally repulsed. They were now advancing the third time, a little to the right of the last, when Sergt. Ellis, who had succeeded in rallying some infantry to his assistance, gallantly brought one of the guns of his section into action on Miller's left, and the two batteries played upon the enemy over the heads of R. H. Anderson's men, who had come to their support. The enemy was again signally repulsed, and withdrew.[1] Miller's guns remained in position, supported by the troops of R. H. Anderson, until about 4 o'clock, when he withdrew to refill his chests.

This defence of the centre lasted an hour and a half.

When Miller became short-handed, by reason of his loss of cannoneers, the staff officers of Gen. Longstreet,

---

[1] Musketry fire ceased about 1 o'clock. Richardson, still holding Piper's house, withdrew his line to the crest of a hill, and at about the same time received a mortal wound. Why he withdrew his line, and whether his wound was the cause of the cessation of operations at this part of the ground does not appear. Hancock was placed in command of his division. A sharp artillery contest followed the withdrawal of Richardson's line, in which a section of Robertson's horse battery, of the Second artillery, and Graham's battery, of the First artillery, were engaged on the Federal side." — *Palfrey, p. 101.*

Majors Sorrel, Fairfax, and Thomas Walton, dismounted from their horses and helped work the guns. Sorrel and Walton were wounded, and the horse of Fairfax was killed. Gen. Longstreet directed the fire of the guns in person, and by example animated the soldiers near him.[1]

The corps of Hooker, Mansfield, Sumner, and Smith's division of Franklin's corps (Sixth) had been rendered *hors du combat*, and had no spirit in them.[2]

---

[1] One line of the enemy's infantry came so near us, that we could see their colonel on horseback waving his men on, and then even the stripes on the corporal's arms. How it made our blood dance and nerves quiver as we saw their colors floating steadily forward, and how heroically and madly we toiled at our guns! Our men worked that day desperately, almost despairingly, because it looked for a time as if we could not stop the blue wave from coming forward, although we were tearing it to pieces with canister and shell. Longstreet was on horseback at our side, sitting side-saddle fashion, and occasionally making some practical remark about the situation. He talked earnestly and gesticulated to encourage us, as the men of the detachments began to fall around our guns, and told us he would have given us a lift if he had not that day crippled his hand. But, crippled or not, we noticed that he had strength enough left to carry his flask to his mouth, as probably everybody else did on that terribly hot day, who had any supplies at command to bring to a carry.[1]

Finally the blue line disappeared from our front, and we managed to hobble off with our pieces, though with the loss of a good many men, horses, and some wheels of our gun carriages. — *Bartlett.*

[2] The heavy masses of the enemy again moved forward, being opposed by only four pieces of artillery, supported by a few hundred men belonging to the different brigades, rallied by Gen. D. H. Hill and others, and parts of Walker's and Anderson's commands; Col. Cooke, with the Twenty-seventh North Carolina regiment of Walker's brigade, standing boldly in line without a cartridge. The firm front presented by this small force, and the well-directed fire of the artillery under Capt. Miller, of the Washington Artillery, and Capt.

---

[1] Gen. Longstreet says, in his report, that the enemy on the 17th renewed an attack commenced the night before on Hood's brigade, — a handful compared with those before him. Hood fought desperately until Jackson and Walker came to his relief, the former soon moving off to flank the enemy's right. The enemy "now threw forward his masses against my left; met by Walker, two pieces of Capt. Miller's battery of the Washington Artillery, and two of Boyce's battery. The enemy was driven back in some confusion; an effort was made to pursue, but our line was too weak. From this moment our centre was extremely weak. The enemy's masses again moved forward, and Cook's regiment stood with empty guns, moving his colors to show his regiment was in position. The artillery played upon the enemy with canister. Their lines hesitated and after an hour and a half retired.

"Another attack was quickly made a little to the right of the last. Capt. Miller, turning his pieces upon these lines, and playing upon them with round shot (over the heads of R. H. Anderson's men) checked the advance, and Anderson's division, with the artillery, held the enemy in check until night."

Hooker was wounded and Mansfield killed.

There is little more to be said of the operations of the Federal right. The serious fighting there ended at about 1 o'clock.

In the afternoon, in obedience to instructions from Gen. Lee, Gen. Jackson made a move towards the Potomac with a view of turning the enemy's right, but found his numerous artillery so strongly and judiciously posted as to render it inexpedient to hazard the attempt.

At the close of the day Jackson held the ground he had held in the morning.

Boyce's South Carolina battery, checked the progress of the enemy, and in about an hour and a half he retired.

Another attack was made soon afterwards, but was repulsed by Miller's guns, which continued to hold the ground until the close of the engagement, supported by a part of R. H. Anderson's troops. — *General Lee's report.*

CHAPTER VIII.

ANTIETAM.

Left Attack. — Burnside's Bridge. — A Ride for Gen. Lee. — Attack of
Enemy. — Squires, Richardson, and Eshleman Engaged. — D. R.
Jones's Division Pressed Back. — Arrival of A. P. Hill. — Garden's
and Riley's Batteries Engaged. — Defeat of Enemy. — Meeting of
Generals. — Lee Dubs Longstreet his "Old War Horse." — Quiet
Day after the Battle. — Army Crosses the Potomac. — Enemy Fol-
lows. — Is Beaten Back. — March to Martinsburg. — Forces Engaged.
— Address of Lee to the Army.

WHILE standing with Col. Walton in Squires's
battery, about noon, Gen. Lee walked over to
us. One hand was in a sling, it not having recovered
from the accident at the second Manassas ; the other held
his field-glass. He said, in his quiet way, " Well, Colonel,
what do you make of the enemy : what is he going to
do ? " The Colonel replied, " They seem to be moving a
battery more to our right." At this moment a courier
rode up, holding in his hand a despatch, which he held out
to the General, and, both of his hands being engaged, I took
it from the courier and read it to him. It was as follows :
" The enemy is moving a six-gun battery to our right,
evidently with the intention of covering with it their
crossing." It was signed " Johnson, Engineer Officer."
" Yes," said the General, " I see they are. Colonel, can you
spare this young officer (myself) to ride for me ? None of
my staff are present." Of course the Colonel said " Yes,"

and I modestly awaited my instructions, feeling considerable pride that I was about to do something for Gen. Lee. Turning to me the General said, "Go to Gen. D. R. Jones, and tell him I wish that battery" — indicating with his field-glass the one he meant — "moved farther to the right, to cover the lower ford, where the enemy will soon endeavor to cross. Let it be done at once." Saluting, and springing upon my horse, I plunged down the ravine, and up the other side to the orchard, found Gen. Jones, and delivered the order. "Where is my chief of artillery?" he asked. No one knew. "This is bad; the battery must be changed at once; Lieutenant, won't you do it for me?" Of course I would, and went over the ground like a flash. I passed Richardson (Second company Washington Artillery), then firing at the enemy, who was endeavoring to cross the stone bridge opposite Toombs's brigade, and found that the battery indicated by Gen. Lee was our Fourth company, under Eshleman. Giving him his instructions, and leaving him in the act of receiving the first fire of the six-gun battery, I rode back to where I had left Gen. Lee, and, dismounting, reported "the order had been obeyed." He replied, "I see it has. Thank you, '*Captain.*'" Of course I felt taller in stature for having ridden for "Uncle Robert" on a battle-field, and under a hot artillery fire, too, from the enemy's batteries on the opposite bank of the Antietam.

From an early hour in the morning heavy masses of men had been observed in front of Gen. D. R. Jones's position, who endeavored to cross the Antietam at the lower bridge to attack the right wing of our army. Gen. Jones had stationed at the bridge, to prevent the enemy's crossing, two small regiments, the Second and Twentieth Georgia, numbering only 403 muskets, and Richardson's battery, Second company Washington Artillery. The attempt of the enemy to effect a passage was repulsed again and again, and he manœuvred as if to cross below, at the "lower ford," where Eshleman, with the Fourth company Washington Artillery had been posted by order of Gen. Lee. Jones's force at noon consisted of the two regiments of Toombs (Second and Twentieth Georgia), and the brigades of Kemper, Drayton, and Jenkins, the latter under command of Gen. Joseph Walker. Gen. Jones gave his strength in the early morning, with six brigades, as 2,430 men. At this time two more of Toombs's regiments, the Seventeenth and Fifteenth Georgia, joined him, accompanied by five companies of Anderson's brigade, and were at once placed at Gen. Toombs's disposal to aid in the defence of the bridge. Before, however, they could be made available for that purpose, the gallant Second and Twentieth Georgia, having repulsed five separate assaults, and exhausted their ammunition, fell back, leaving the bridge to the enemy.

The advance troops of Gen. A. P. Hill were now coming on the field, and McIntosh's battery, of Hill's division, was sent forward, and opened fire from the ridge.

The enemy, now swarming over the bridge, received the fire of Squires's guns (First company Washington Artillery) from the hill east of the town, together with that of Garden's and Moody's batteries. Together they poured shell and canister into the heavy columns of the enemy, inflicting serious loss upon them as they deployed in lines of battle for the assault; but, undeterred, except momentarily, by this fire, he advanced in enormous masses to the assault of the heights. Sweeping up the crest they were mowed down by the fire of Richardson's, Brown's, and McIntosh's batteries.

They overcame, however, the tough resistance offered by the feeble forces opposed to them and gained the heights, capturing McIntosh's battery. Kemper and Drayton were driven through the town. The Fifteenth South Carolina, Col. De Saussure, fell back slowly through the town, and in good order, forming the nucleus on which the brigade (Drayton's) rallied.

Jenkins's brigade, under Gen. Walker, held its own, and from its position in the orchard poured a destructive fire on the enemy. Gen. Toombs, with a portion of his brigade, with Richardson's and Garden's batteries, joined Jones's troops, forming on their right.

None too soon did the head of A. P. Hill's column reach the battle-field, at 2.30 P.M., having marched a distance of seventeen miles in seven hours, from Harper's Ferry, coming by the road crossing the Antietam near its junction with the Potomac. Pender, in advance, was joined by Eshleman, with the Fourth company Washington Artillery, near the Blackford House, where he had been engaging the enemy at the "lower ford."

Hill's line was immediately formed, with Pender and Brockenbrough on the extreme right, and Branch, Gregg, and Archer, extending to the left and connecting with Toombs, who had joined hands with D. R. Jones on his left. Gen. Garnett, with Pickett's brigade of only 200 men and a few men he had picked up among many who had lost their commands, came upon the field and joined Gen. Drayton.

Quickly the line was formed to check the advance of the victorious enemy, — the Ninth corps of the Federal army, 14,000 strong, under Gen. Burnside.

Hill's batteries, under Braxton, Pegram, and Crenshaw, were placed in position along the line, and guns from different batteries of the Washington Artillery and others, who had borne the brunt of the fighting all day long, having replenished their ammunition, were put in position to assist the movements of A. P. Hill to check the enemy.

There were the Fourth company Washington Artillery, under Eshleman, four guns; one rifle of the First company, under Lieut. Galbraith; one Napoleon of the Second company under Lieut. Britton; two Napoleons of the Third company, under Lieut. McElroy, and two guns of Riley's battery. These six guns were placed under command of Capt. Miller, of Third company Washington Artillery: two 12-pounder howitzers of the Second company, under Lieuts. Hawes and De Russey, and Capt. Garden's battery of four guns.

The enemy was advancing in three lines of battle and in full tide of success, when, with a yell of defiance, Toombs and Archer charged; all the guns along the line opened a furious fire. McIntosh's battery was retaken, and the enemy was driven pell-mell, while Branch and Gregg, with their sturdy old veterans, held their ground and poured in destructive volleys, till the tide of the enemy surged back, and, breaking in confusion, passed out of sight.

But 2,000 of Hill's "Light division" were engaged in this, the final conflict of our troops with the enemy upon this sanguinary field. At night Lee's army slept upon the ground it had occupied in the morning.[1]

This battle was fought against great odds, and such straggling of our men had not been seen before. The

---

[1] It is now necessary to look to the other end of the Union line, held by the Ninth corps, under Gen. Burnside. This force lay massed behind the heights on the east bank of the Antietam, and opposite the Confederate right, which it was designed he should assail, after forcing the passage of the Antietam by the lower stone bridge. . . . . . .

Gen. McClellan, appreciating the full effect of an attack by his left, directed Burnside early in the morning to hold his troops in readiness to assault the bridge in his front. Then, at 8 o'clock, learning how much opposition had been developed by Hooker, he ordered Burnside to carry the bridge, gain possession of the heights, and advance along their crest upon Sharpsburg as a diversion in favor of the right.

Longstreet, having removed the entire divisions of McLaws and Walker from the Confederate right to the left, left on that entire wing but a single hostile division of 2,500 men, under Gen. D. R. Jones, and the force actually present to dispute the passage of the bridge did not exceed *four hundred*. Nevertheless, it was 1 o'clock before a passage was effected, and this being done, two hours passed before the attack on the crest was made. This was successfully executed at 3 o'clock, the Sharpsburg ridge being taken, and a Confederate battery that had been delivering an annoying fire captured. (McIntosh's battery.)

It was one of the unfortunate results of the long delay in their operations on the left, that, just as this success was gained (taking the ridge and Sharpsburg), the division of A. P. Hill, which Jackson had left behind to receive the surrender of Harper's Ferry, reached the field from that place by way of Shepherdstown, and, uniting his own reinforcement of 2,000 men with the troops of Jones, that had been broken through in the attack, he assumed the offensive, recaptured the battery (McIntosh's), and drove Burnside over all the ground gained, and to the shelter of the bluff bordering the Antietam.

It was found that the losses on the Union side made an aggregate in killed and wounded of 12,500 men, while the Confederate loss proved to have been above 8,000. — *Army of the Potomac, p. 221.* SWINTON.

The enemy fled in confusion towards the river and bridge, making two or three efforts to rally, which were soon defeated by the vigorous charges of our troops, aided by Capt. Richardson's battery (Second company Washington Artillery), which I ordered up immediately upon the recovery of the heights, and which, with its accustomed promptness and courage, was rapidly placed in position and action.

The enemy, to cover his retreating columns, brought over the bridge a battery and placed it in position. I ordered Capt. Richardson's battery to open upon it,

forced marches had used the men up, and hundreds upon hundreds were unable to keep up with their colors.

In endeavoring to turn our left the enemy attacked with three full corps of their army, numbering at least 40,000 men.   To have resisted this mass of men so successfully, with reduced numbers, shows the stuff our soldiers were made of.

Leaving orders with the battery officers to bivouac where they had ended the battle, the Colonel and I rode to find Gen. Lee's head-quarters.

Lieuts. John Britton and Edward Owen were severely wounded this evening, as were privates John Holmes, McCartney, and Michel.

As we were riding through the fields an infantry soldier passed by, having in charge a Federal colonel of infantry, prisoner.   We asked his name and regiment.   He gave it as "Col. Jones, One Hundred and Twentieth Ohio Volunteers, of Columbus, Ohio."   I had known Col. Jones years before as captain of a militia company, styled the "Columbus Fencibles;" so we renewed our acquaintance under these remarkable circumstances.   I relieved the infantryman of his charge and took Col. Jones with us to Gen.

---

and at the same time ordered the Fifteenth and Twentieth Georgia forward, who pursued the enemy so close to his guns as to bring them within range of musketry, which compelled his battery, after a few shots, to join his flying infantry, and retreat across the bridge.   Capt. Richardson and his officers and men, of the Second company of Washington Artillery, attached to my own brigade, were conspicuous throughout the day for courage and good conduct.   Capt. Richardson clung to the infantry amid every danger, and, being nobly seconded on every occasion by his officers and men, largely contributed to every success. During the whole connection of this battery with my command its officers and men have so conducted themselves everywhere — on the march, in the camp, and on the battle-field — as to meet and receive my special approbation. — *Gen. R. Toombs's Official Report.*

Lee, where Col. Chilton endeavored to "pump" him ; but he knew nothing except that he was a "prisoner," and didn't exactly know how it all had happened. His regiment had gone to smash, —he knew that. I consigned him to the care of the provost-marshal, and bade him good-by.

We found head-quarters established in an open field back of the town. A large number of general officers and staff-officers were assembled about Gen. Lee. The occasional crack of a rifle, the groans of wounded men being carried by on stretchers, the crackling of the timbers of a burning house near by, which cast a lurid glare upon the group, made it a scene not soon to be forgotten.

Old "Stonewall" was talking to Gen. Lee when we approached. The two Hills, Hood, Jones, and Early, were there. "But where is Longstreet?" Gen. Lee inquired anxiously. "I saw him at sundown, all right," said Col. Venable. Just then Longstreet rode up, smoking the cigar which he had held all day, unlighted, between his clenched teeth, as was his custom when business "was pressing and urgent." Gen. Lee stepped forward as Longstreet dismounted, and, grasping him by the hand, said, "Ah ! here is Longstreet ; here's my old *war-horse !* Let us hear what he has to say ; " and they conversed in a low tone together.

Everybody was saying what a pity "old Jack" had not been able to get around the flank of the enemy this afternoon ; but it could not be done on account of the superior positions of the Federal artillery, and their line having been extended to the banks of the Potomac.

Had it been accomplished we would have scored a great victory.[1]

We found our friends, " the surgeons," on the edge of the group ; took a " nip," lit our pipes and enjoyed a soothing smoke, then sought our ambulance, after visiting Dr. Drew's field-hospital, ate a little supper, stowed ourselves in our blankets, and slept well.

At daylight on the 18th it was reported that the enemy was preparing for another attack ; but Longstreet said, judging from the position in which they had massed their artillery on the heights across the Antietam, it appeared as though they were fearful *Lee would attack them.* Our guns were returned to their old positions east of the town, from which they had been forced back by Burnside last evening. We saw Gen. Jones at his position at the orchard, and found him exceeding sad, having learned from prisoners that his brother-in-law, Col. Kingsbury, was in the Federal attacking column and had been killed at the bridge. Some ammunition was received for the artillery this morning, but not enough for a long engagement.

---

[1] If Lee had been in McClellan's place on the 17th of September, and had sent Jackson to conduct the right attack, and Longstreet to force the passage of the lower bridge and turn the Confederate right, the Army of Northern Virginia, though commanded by a second Lee, a second Jackson, and a second Longstreet, would have ceased to exist that day. — *Antietam and Fredericksburg. p. 17.* PALFREY.

In painful contrast to the passive attitude of the principal Federal army on the afternoon of the 18th is the undoubted fact, that the indomitable Lee and Jackson, unaffected by the terrible losses which their troops had suffered, actually the one ordered, and the other attempted to execute, that afternoon a turning movement of the Federal right.

.   .   .   .

The Federal artillery was found so judiciously posted in their front and near the Potomac, that it was thought inexpedient to hazard the attempt. — *Gen. Palfrey, p. 123.*

This ammunition supply is a serious one, and we always like to have enough to make things comfortable and pleasant for us and the enemy.

The day passed away with nothing done except a little firing now and then between the skirmishers and sharpshooters. On the top of the highest mountain the enemy had cut down an acre or so of trees, and had established a signal station, so he could see everything that was going on within our lines.

At dark we received the following order from Gen. Longstreet : —

HEAD–QUARTERS, Sept. 18, 1862.

COLONEL : — All ordered to the rear at once. Put your batteries on the road to Shepherdstown ford, except one, to be left in the main street of Sharpsburg for Gen. Stuart's cavalry, marching to the rear. Rifled guns, if possible. Order all cannoneers to walk, and have all your staff occupied getting everything along. No vehicle must double, however, on another.

Please exert yourself and staff to the utmost to prevent delay.

Most respectfully,

J. LONGSTREET,

Major-General.

COL. WALTON, *Chief of Artillery.*

Orders having been issued to the batteries to move out, I was ordered to go and secure one to report to Stuart. The fog was dense, and the camp-fires burning alongside the road were blinding. Proceeding in the direction of Sharpsburg, I met a constant stream of troops marching, and had great difficulty in passing through; and when my horse ran against some infantry man I was saluted by curses loud and strong, and it was suggested that I was a " cavalry man going after buttermilk." At length I pushed my way through, as far as I thought necessary to carry out my orders, and halted. Presently the noise of a battery was heard, and when it approached I hailed it: "Whose battery is that?"—"Capt. Riley's," was the reply. " Ah, Captain!—just looking for you. The chief of artillery directs you to halt here, and report to Gen. Stuart as he comes by with the rear-guard." And I tipped myself a wink. " Devil take it now," said the Captain; " can't somebody else do this? My men are tired out, — let me get beyond the river."—" Couldn't think of it, Captain; this is the post of honor. Report to Stuart. Good-by, and good luck to you!" As I rode away in the fog I could hear the Captain blessing his eyes and d—g all " posts of honor." But I knew the soldierly qualities of the Captain, and that he would never desert a place he was told to hold as long as he had a shot left.

When I at last reached the Potomac the army was crossing the ford at Shepherdstown. Artillery, infantry, ambulances, wagons, all mixed up in what appeared to be inextricable confusion in the water; and the ford, too, was full of large bowlders. Immense fires were blazing on the banks, which had the effect of blinding both men and animals. Staff-officers stood on either bank, shouting to the drivers of vehicles and artillery where they should land. Drivers were whipping their animals, and loudly urging them on. Altogether there was a terrible racket. By dint of patient effort I safely landed on the Virginia shore, and made up my mind to look out for number one. It was impossible to find our head-quarters, so I would do the best possible thing under the circumstances, — I would " straggle."

I turned into a road leading up a hill, and began my journey. A piece of artillery belonging to a battery in front of me had tumbled into the ravine below. After I got away from the fires on the bank of the river the darkness and fog were intense, so I determined to stop at the first wagon-camp I came to. I soon espied the light of a camp-fire, and, riding up to it, to my great delight, I found it was our own quarter-master, Lieut. Gieger. He was as glad to see me as I was to run across him, and I was soon partaking of his good cheer, and my horse was munching his corn, the first he had received that day. He (Gieger) pressed me to enlighten him in reference to the doings of the " boys " in the battle, having heard but little at his camp in the rear ; but I was so tired I begged to be allowed to go to sleep ; so, providing me with an empty wagon, into which he put plenty of hay, I crawled in and had a good night's rest, although the wagon-mules, fastened to it, would stick their big heads inside and eat my bed.

On the 19th the enemy followed us closely,[1] and Gen. A. P. Hill, who commanded the rear-guard, told me he thought at times he would be compelled to turn about

---

[1] On the 19th the Fifth Corps was ordered to support the cavalry. It was found that the Confederates beyond the river had artillery well posted to cover the fords. Porter determined to clear the fords and try to capture some guns. He lined the eastern bank of the Potomac with skirmishers and sharp-shooters, supported them by the divisions of Morell and Sykes, and by guns so posted as to command the opposite bank. Volunteers from the Fourth Michigan, One Hundred and Eighteenth Pennsylvania, and Eighteenth and Twenty-second Massachusetts, crossed the river under charge of Gen. Griffin.

Sykes was ordered to advance a similar party, but by some misunderstanding the orders did not reach him seasonably. The attempt was made at dark, and resulted in the capture of five guns and some of their appurtenances.

Among the guns taken was one of Battery D, of the Fifth Artillery, which had been lost at the first Bull Run." — *Palfrey, p. 128.*

and fight. The General appeared to have the contents of a whole sutler's store in one of his wagons, part of the "loot" of Harper's Ferry. His aide-de-camp, Dick Morgan, furnished me with a goodly supply of stationery, of which I stood in need.

The batteries of Squires and Miller moved from Shepherdstown about noon, and went into bivouac a short distance from the town.

This morning I took the "Second Rhode Island" ambulance into Shepherdstown, and to the mill at the dam where all of our wounded men were, filled it with all that it would carry, and sent them off to Winchester. There were Lieuts. Hero, Britton, Owen; privates Holmes and Muntinger. The enemy began shelling the town as we were moving out. On the road, army-wagons, ambulances, and private conveyances, with citizens and their families, were marching in three columns abreast.

A good deal of confusion existed as to the whereabouts of the different commands. They got somewhat mixed crossing the ford last night. Officers and couriers are riding the country over. Gen. Longstreet and staff will share our bivouac to-night. He was furious this afternoon at the stragglers, and ordered a gun put in position in the road with orders to fire upon them if they didn't go back; he checked the stream effectually. During the night the enemy crossed the river with a brigade of infantry, and captured four of Gen. Pendleton's guns of his reserve artillery. Early this morning (20th)[1] Gen.

---

[1] A reconnoissance in force was sent across the river the following morning (20th) at 7 o'clock under Morell and Sykes. The cavalry ordered to coöperate

A. P. Hill attacked and drove the enemy through Shepherdstown, killing, wounding, and drowning large numbers of them. Such as escaped reached the Maryland shore in a demoralized condition. We marched this evening towards Martinsburg, and encamped two miles from the town, on the Opequan creek.

Here we had a good rest, and enjoyed the charming society of Col. Faulkner's family and others.

REPORT OF COL. WALTON OF THE BATTLE OF SHARPSBURG.

HEAD–QUARTERS BATTALION WASHINGTON ARTILLERY.

MAJOR G. M. SORREL, *A.A.G. Right Wing Army Northern Virginia :* —
[EXTRACT.]

.   .   .   .

On the morning of the 17th of September, our batteries still remaining in the position of the day before, the enemy crossed large bodies of infantry in front of Capt. Squires's position. They also opened their batteries upon him. Paying little attention to the artillery practice of the enemy, he quietly awaited the advance of his infantry, and concentrated his fire upon them, and succeeded in driving them from view. He then withdrew his guns and allowed the batteries of the enemy to expend much ammunition. Shortly afterwards the enemy advanced one regiment of infantry. Capt. Squires then turned all his guns and those of Garden's battery upon him, which drove him back; he rallied a second time, but again he was driven behind his hill. Here he was reinforced, and advanced again. He was again broken, but rallied within four hundred yards of the batteries, from which position he deployed skirmishers, and annoyed our men with the bullets of his sharpshooters. He again sounded the charge and advanced within canister range. We opened a heavy fire upon him. He broke, and our support,

---

failed to do so, and the enterprise was unsuccessful. The troops were attacked sharply, and driven back across the river with considerable loss, — the loss falling principally upon the One Hundred and Eighteenth Pennsylvania. It lost in all 282 out of 800, of whom 64 were killed. It had been in service just three weeks. It was known as the "Corn Exchange Regiment."— *Palfrey, p. 128.*

under Gen. Garnett, charged him.   Being nearly out of ammunition, Capt. Squires withdrew his battery, to refill his chests.

. . . .

During the action Capt. Squires was deprived of the valuable services of Lieut. E. Owen, who was wounded in the thigh by a piece of shell while acting with his usual gallantry at his guns.   .   .   .   .

Sergeant-Major C. L. C. Dupuy went into action with this battery, and did gallant service.

. . . .

Too much praise cannot be bestowed on Capt. Miller, for his stubborn defence of the centre for several hours ; to Lieuts. Hero and McElroy, Sergts. Ellis, Bier (chief artificer), and Dempsey (artificer), for their gallantry.

. . . .

Capt. Richardson, in his report, expresses himself entirely satisfied with the conduct of his officers, non-commissioned officers, and men. They behaved in such a manner as to reflect credit upon the " Second," and the corps of which they are a part.

The " Fourth," under Eshleman, was not idle during this eventful day.   About noon on the 17th he was directed by Gen. Jones, in front of whose position he was placed, to remove his battery to a position to guard the lower ford below the bridge held by Gen. Toombs.   The battery was placed in position between the Blackford House and the ford, and opened fire upon the enemy, who was crossing in force.   A long-range battery of the enemy on the opposite bank of the stream opened upon and enfiladed his guns, and he was compelled to retire, not, however, before he had driven the enemy back from the ford.   He then received orders from Gen. D. R. Jones to hold the enemy in check, if possible, until the arrival of Gen. A. P. Hill, whose division was near at hand.   The enemy soon made another attempt to cross with infantry and cavalry.   Capt. Eshleman took a position near the ford, and, under cover of a hill, which protected him from the enemy's battery, opened fire upon him with shell.   At this juncture Gen. Pender, of Hill's division, came to his support.

. . . .

Always ready, and ever watchful and zealous, Adjutant W. M. Owen has again placed me under obligations for services on the field.   Frequently, in my capacity as chief of artillery, during the two days, had I occasion to send him to distant parts of the field under the heaviest fire. Gallantly and unhesitatingly he executed every order. Color-Sergeant Montgomery, as at the battle of Manassas, served me as an aid, and was under fire during the engagement of the two days. He is a deserving and brave gentleman. Ordnance-Sergeant Brazelman deserves special mention for his assiduity and unflagging devotion in supplying ammunition, and in the performance of all his duties.

I am, Major, very respectfully,

J. B. WALTON,

Colonel Commanding.

Casualties in the Battalion "Washington Artillery" from the 23d of August to the 17th of September, 1862, inclusive[1] : —

1 officer killed.

3 officers wounded.

12 enlisted men killed.

48   "   " wounded.

2   "   " missing.

Total,   66

---

[1] The name of every officer, non-commissioned officer, and private who has shared in the toils and privations of this campaign should be mentioned.

In one month these troops had marched over two hundred miles upon little more than half rations, and fought nine battles and skirmishes, killed, wounded, and captured nearly as many men as we had in our ranks, besides taking arms and other munitions of war in large quantities. I would that I could do justice to all of these gallant officers and men in this report.

At Sharpsburg Capt. Miller, of the Washington Artillery, was particularly distinguished; Col. Walton, of the Washington Artillery, at Rappahannock station, Manassas plains, and Sharpsburg. — *Gen. Longstreet's Official Report.*

HEAD–QUARTERS, ARMY OF NORTHERN VIRGINIA,

October 2, 1862.

GENERAL ORDERS, No. 116 : —

In reviewing the achievements of the army during the present campaign the commanding general cannot withhold the expression of his admiration of the indomitable courage it has displayed in battle, and its cheerful endurance of privation and hardship on the march.

Since your great victories around Richmond you have defeated the enemy at Cedar Mountain, expelled him from the Rappahannock, and, after a conflict of three days, utterly repulsed him on the plains of Manassas, and forced him to take shelter within the fortifications around his capital.

Without halting for repose you crossed the Potomac, stormed the heights of Harper's Ferry, made prisoners of more than 11,000 men, and captured upwards of 70 pieces of artillery, all their small arms, and other munitions of war.

While one corps of the army was thus engaged, the other insured its success by arresting, at Boonesboro', the combined armies of the enemy, advancing under their favorite general to the relief of their beleaguered comrades.

On the field at Sharpsburg, with less than one-third his numbers, you resisted, from daylight until dark, the whole army of the enemy, and repulsed every attack along his entire front of more than four miles in extent.

The whole of the following day you stood prepared to resume the conflict on the same ground, and retired next morning, without molestation, across the Potomac.

Two attempts, subsequently made by the enemy, to follow you across the river, have resulted in his complete discomfiture, and being driven back with loss.

Achievements such as these demanded much valor and patriotism. History reecords few examples of greater fortitude and endurance than this army has exhibited, and I am commissioned by the President to thank you, in the name of the Confederate States, for the undying fame you have won for its arms.

Much as you have done, much more remains to be accomplished.

The enemy again threatens us with invasion, and to your tried valor and patriotism the country looks with confidence for deliverance and safety.

Your past exploits give assurance that this confidence is not misplaced.

R. E. LEE,
General Commanding.

From the official reports of the two armies engaged, we gather the strength of each : —

Longstreet's command was	6,262
Jackson's "	5,000
D. H. Hill's division	3,000
R. H. Anderson's "	3,500
A. P. Hill's "	3,400
McLaws's "	2,893
J. G. Walker's "	3,200
Cavalry and artillery, estimated	8,000
Total	35,255

Gen. McClellan, in his report, says that he had in action 87,164 men, of all arms.

Those 35,000 Confederates were the very flower of the Army of Northern Virginia, who, with indomitable courage and inflexible tenacity, wrestled for the mastery in the ratio of one to three of their adversaries, and with consummate skill were they manœuvred and shifted from point to point as different parts of the line of battle were in turn assailed with greatest impetuosity.

The right was called upon to go to the rescue of the left; the centre reduced to a mere shell in responding to the demands of assistance from the right and left; and A. P. Hill's command, the last to arrive from Harper's Ferry, reached the field just in time to restore the wavering right.

At times it appeared as if disaster were inevitable; but succor never failed, and night found Lee's lines unbroken, and his army still defiant.

The weapon used was admirably tempered; but, much as we may praise the blade, we should not forget the extraordinary skill and vigor with which it was wielded in that memorable engagement by the great Confederate leader. — *Four years with Lee.* TAYLOR.

CHAPTER IX.

FREDERICKSBURG.

Martinsburg. — Culpeper. — March to Fredericksburg.—Alarm Guns.— Boots and Saddles. — City bombarded. — Enemy crosses the Rappahannock. — Attack on Marye's Hill. — Great Battle fought. — Enemy beaten. — He recrosses the River. — Winter Quarters.

AFTER waiting a week at Martinsburg, thinking McClellan might follow the army into Virginia, we moved on to the neighborhood of Winchester, where the Battalion went into camp at Stephenson's spring, the finest and largest we had seen in Virginia.

During the second day at Sharpsburg some of the cannoneers saw a body of mounted officers of the enemy riding about, and from time to time halting and surveying our lines through their glasses. One officer was distinguished from the others on account of his white horse. " Let's give them a shot," said a cannoneer. " No," said the gunner ; " that's the Chief of Artillery ; whenever you see him on his white horse look out for a battery. He's a brave man, and I won't fire at him. Wait until the battery comes, and we'll fire at that." And the boys confidently believed it was Gen. Hunt, Chief of Artillery of the Federal army, whom they saw on the white horse. There was some chivalry in that gunner's composition.

On the 11th of October Col. Walton went to Richmond on leave of absence, and Capt. Eshleman was left in command of the Washington Artillery ; all the four batteries being now in camp together once more, as the campaign was over. Our trip into Maryland didn't cause her to throw herself into the arms of the Confederacy "breathing and burning" one bit. A number of our wounded were in Winchester, at the residence of Mr. Carson. Miss Julia Carson was another "Florence Nightingale," and nursed the boys and dressed their wounds with her own hands, and the boys in turn idolized her. Owen, Hero, Britton, Holmes, Muntinger, were all there. They came through on the "Second Rhode Island."

On the 13th of October Wilcox's division and the Washington Artillery were reviewed by Gen. Longstreet, out of compliment to Col. Wolseley[1] of the British army and two or three members of the English Parliament, who were visiting the army. Notwithstanding the war-worn appearance of the troops the review went off creditably. Of course the Washington Artillery did its level best. We were hard-looking cases though, as compared with the finely equipped British troops Col. Wolseley serves with.

---

[1] SIR GARNET WOLSELEY. DESCRIPTION OF HIS MEETING WITH LEE AND JACKSON, AND HIS OPINION OF THE SOUTHERN CHIEFS. — In September, 1862, having some leisure from his duties in Canada, Col. Wolseley took a notion to visit the Confederacy, and note the progress of the war from that side, and make the acquaintance of the southern generals of note. He had only six weeks' time, however, but made the most of it. He ran the blockade into Virginia. He was received with open arms by the Southern ladies, and the various officials and generals of the Confederate army whom he met. He visited Gen. Lee's head-quarters, then near Winchester. Of the great Southern captain Gen. Wolseley says: "He is a strongly built man, about 5 feet 11 in height, and apparently not more than 50 years of age. His hair and beard are nearly white; but his dark-brown eyes still shine with all the brightness of youth, and beam with a most pleasing expression. Indeed, his whole face is kindly and benevolent in a high degree. . . . We sat with him for a long time in his tent, conversing upon a variety of topics, the state of public affairs being, of course, the leading one. You have only to be in his society for a very brief period to be convinced that whatever he says may be implicitly relied upon, and that he is

On the 17th of October the enemy came out of Harper's Ferry in force, and we were under arms all day. Our outposts were driven in at Charlestown.

On the 18th all was quiet again. It is reported that Bragg has gained a victory over Buell, in Kentucky, for which there is great rejoicing. We are having a splendid rest, but the weather is getting to be very cold and frosty and the wind very piercing. There is but one tent in the command, and that is at head-quarters. No tents were allowed the army during the last campaign, except for head-quarters and adjutant-general's work. The boys are in the woods, and large fires are constantly burning.

Miss Belle Boyd was in camp to-day.

At last McClellan has begun a forward movement, and has transferred his army to the south bank of the Potomac, on the east of the Blue Ridge mountains.

Upon learning of this, Longstreet's corps was ordered to Culpeper Court-house, and the Washington Artillery encamped near that town. Here we were furnished with a few tents.

On November 4 McClellan occupied Ashby's Gap, and concentrated his whole army near Warrenton.

---

quite incapable of departing from the truth under any circumstances." He was especially struck with the absence of "the pomp and circumstance of war" at Gen. Lee's head-quarters, which consisted of a fence corner tent, with no sentries on guard, and no aids loitering about. On leaving Gen. Lee the Colonel paid a visit to Stonewall Jackson, who was at Bunker's Hill, six miles nearer Martinsburg. Of him Wolseley says: "Dressed in his gray uniform he looks the hero that he is; and his thin, compressed lips and calm glance, which meets yours unflinchingly, gave evidence of that firmness and decision of character for which he is so famous. . . . Altogether, as one of his soldiers said to me, when speaking of him, 'he is a glorious fellow,' and after I left him I felt that I had at last solved a mystery, and discovered why it was that he had accomplished such almost miraculous feats. With such a leader men would go anywhere, and face any amount of difficulties."

Our newly organized "Literary and Dramatic Association" gave their first entertainment in this camp. An immense fire was built, around which logs were placed, in horseshoe form, for the audience. Upon a platform, seated in an arm-chair improvised from a flour-barrel, sat the President, Corp. R. McK. Spearing.

The President opened the meeting by stating the objects of the society, which were, by the contribution of whatever varied talent the boys possessed, to assist, upon stated occasions (when we were at leisure), in the amusement and instruction of the command. A certain number were booked for the opening night, and in all sincerity it can be recorded, the entertainment was highly creditable. George Meek was especially praised for his recital of Poe's " Raven."

The society afforded a fine opportunity for our young lawyers and students to display themselves.

The President announced the fact that a dramatic company was in course of organization, and would be heard from at some future day. As cold weather comes on apace we will have different amusements to help pass the idle hours of a winter camp.

Owing to the absence of " Chief Editor " St. Paul, the " Waltonville War-cry " cannot be resurrected.

On November 7th we experienced the first snow of the season.[1]

---

[1] HEAD–QUARTERS RIGHT WING A. N. VA.,
November 7, 1862.

GENERAL ORDERS, No. 47 : —

The inclement season having set in commanders will take every method of

On November 10 we heard heavy firing in front, and were under arms all day.

I visited Mr. Ned Gaines, who has a large farm near this place, and enjoyed a good dinner. Gaines had a tilt with Gen. Pope last summer, at the time of the Cedar Run fight. Pope cursed him, and Gaines told him if he would kindly take his uniform off and come outside of his tent he would give him a thrashing he would long remember.

Pope declined the invitation, and called Gaines a " d—d rebel scoundrel" and threatened to hang him.

McClellan has been relieved, and Burnside appointed to the command of the Federal army.

Lee, seemingly by intuition, has discovered that Burnside proposes marching to Fredericksburg, and has, there-

---

protecting and guarding their men from the weather in their present exposed situation.

To this end company and regimental commanders will take care that fires are kept burning during the entire day, and will at night see that they are moved to a short distance, so that the men can make their bivouacs on the earth thus warmed during the day.

The bivouacs made in this manner are warmer and dryer than any that can at present be devised.

The attention, forethought, and ingenuity of commanders can at all times be exercised to advantage in anticipating the wants and preparing for the hardships and necessities to which their men are unavoidably exposed.

It having been found impracticable, at the present juncture, to fully supply this army corps with shoes, the attention of commanders is directed to the advantageous employment of the raw hides of slaughtered cattle in the manufacture of a strong and warm covering for the feet.

Experience has shown that an excellent substitute for the shoe can be made out of this material. Hides are hereby authorized to be used for this object, and the energy, and practical judgment, and the experience of the commander will always be shown in making the most of small resources for the comfort and protection of his men.

By command of Lieut.-Gen. Longstreet,

G. M. SORREL, *A. A. Genl.*

fore, ordered Longstreet's corps to that point. We shall soon have lively work again on our hands.[1]

The Battalion was ordered to march at 4 P.M., November 19; night rainy and "dark as Erebus," roads deep with mud. Boys keep up their spirits by singing firemen's songs and choruses, led by private Mount. It was too dark to travel, and we turned into a field and barn-yard, and bivouacked. Head-quarters appropriated a deserted chicken-house, the boys the barn and hay-lofts. Raining in torrents.

We hear that Jackson, who is still in the valley, is ordered to move rapidly to Orange House.

On November 20 we marched, at 7 A.M., in a cold rain, forded the Rapidan at Raccoon Ford, at 10 A.M., and camped on Mine Run, at Bartley's Mill.

In crossing the ford much difficulty was experienced in getting the pieces and caissons through the mud-holes, and W. A. Randolph, up to his waist in water, was particularly zealous in his efforts to help. When the Battalion came into camp, to his infinite disgust, he found that his blanket-

---

[1] HEAD-QUARTERS FIRST ARMY CORPS, A. N. VA.,
November 16, 1862.

GENERAL ORDERS, No. 49 :—

The troops of this command will be held in readiness for battle upon a moment's notice. Commanders will see that provisions, ammunition, and transportation are at hand, and in such quantities as may be wanted to meet their necessities.

The Commanding General relies upon the valor and patriotism of these well-tried troops to sustain them in the struggles that they may again be called upon to encounter.

Officers! be cool and take care of your men. Soldiers! remain steady in your ranks, take good aim, and obey the orders of your officers!

Observe these simple injunctions, and your Generals will be responsible for the issue.

By command of Lieut.-Gen. Longstreet,

G. M. SORREL, *A. A. Genl.*

roll was missing from the caisson to which he had fastened it before going into the water. It, no doubt, was now floating down the Rapidan.

A contribution from the already small stock of comfortable clothing in camp was collected for the unfortunate one.

We pitched the head-quarters' tent, but it was a very small addition to our comfort; a more drenched and disgusted set was never seen. We knew full well that "Drugs" had a stone jug of *spiritus frumenti* in the ambulance, and we begged and entreated him for a dose as we could conscientiously have been placed upon the "sick list;" but he was obdurate and wouldn't give us a drop. Never mind, "Dr. Drugs," we will not forgive you for your stony (jug) heartedness.

The van of Burnside's army reached Fredericksburg on the 17th, in the afternoon, but has not crossed the river yet.

November 21. It rained without cessation all night, and we had to lighten our wagon this morning, throwing out all superfluous articles. Bivouacked at Chancellorsville.

On the 22d we reached the hills back of Fredericksburg at 1 P.M. A grand exodus is going on; all day long we met people, old and young, leaving the city, carrying their household gods with them. Carts and wagons containing their bedding, etc., going to the rear. Children and women all in the procession.

Lee's army now confronts the Federal Commander, who can see the bristling bayonets of the Army of Northern Virginia, 78,000 strong, surmounting the range of hills that overlook the plain and city of Fredericksburg.

The enemy shows a large force on Stafford Heights, across the Rappahannock; but Lee, Longstreet, and Jackson, and their men, stand before them and again bar their way to Richmond.

The line of heights on our side is being strengthened with earth-works, rifle-pits, and redoubts for artillery.

The Washington Artillery has been assigned to Marye's Hill, which juts out towards the town, forming a sort of salient, and nearer to it than any of the other fortifications. Behind it rises Guest's Hill, and on the right, looking towards the town, is Lee's Hill. The plank road passes over the former, and the telegraph road to Richmond over the latter.

At the foot of Marye's Hill the telegraph road runs, and then turns abruptly at right angles and branches off into the town. In front of Marye's Hill it is a sunken road, and on the side towards the town is a stone wall about breast high. The field beyond is flush with the top of the wall.

Before Marye's Hill is an open plain, with a few cottages and market-gardens, and divided up into lots by board fences until the outskirts are reached.

In front of the town flows the Rappahannock, and opposite are the Stafford Heights, upon which the enemy has posted more than a hundred pieces of artillery, commanding the town. Thus, between our position on Marye's Hill and the enemy on Stafford lies the old-fashioned revolutionary town of Fredericksburg.

For the first time our army will fight behind dirt.

On " Marye's " the engineers have laid out works for

three of our batteries, *en barbette*, — that is, with the work only as high as a man's breast, or as the muzzle of a cannon, — but we improve upon their work by raising the earth higher, and arranging embrasures to fire through. The engineers say we spoil their work, but as we, not they, have to stand here in case Burnside comes across, they will remain as we have altered them. Longstreet says, "If we only save the finger of a man, that's good enough."

As the position is enfiladed by the enemy's batteries at Falmouth, strong traverses are built to protect us from a flank fire.

Officers of other batteries have already dubbed our position a "slaughter-pen." It may turn out so; but the old "war-horse" (Longstreet) says he hardly thinks Burnside will cross here and make a direct attack, but go around our left flank.

We ride into Fredericksburg almost daily, and visit a few of the citizens who are still at home, among the rest Temple Doswell and T. S. Barton, a venerable citizen, who says he will stay in his old house, and die there if need be. He keeps open house for all who choose to call, and his dining-table is always set with cold saddles of mutton, bread and butter, flanked by bottles of old wines from his ancient stock in the garret. He says he would rather we would consume every bottle of it than let the Yankees get it. We will try and carry out the patriotic idea.

Barksdale's Mississippi brigade is in the town on picket, and the enemy's pickets across the river only a biscuit's toss. There is no firing, so they "chaff" each other fearfully.

Our camp is about a mile back from the line.

The redoubts are all ready on " Marye's " for our occupation, and we are to go into position at once should the enemy attempt to cross the river. Each officer knows the position to be occupied by his guns. The signal is to be two guns fired in quick succession, and the army will go into the works without further orders.

On the 9th of December Col. Walton returns from Richmond and assumes command of the Battalion. Accompanying him are Cols. George Deas, P. T. Moore, and Messrs. Adam Giffin and Henry Florence. The two latter have sons in the command.

Our "Literary and Dramatic Association" has erected a stage and side-scenes for a theatrical performance in the open air. The side-scenes are blankets, and the drop-curtain an old tent-fly, with crossed cannons and " W. A." in charcoal letters. The circular enclosure is protected from the cold winds by pine brush; the seats are of logs, and huge fires light the house and warm it at the same time. The play is the "Lady of Lyons," with Lieut. Stocker as *Claude Melnotte* in braided artillery jacket and red kepi, and Sergt. John Wood as *Pauline*.

The play went off admirably well, both parts being well performed; but where the sergeant got his petticoats from he won't tell !

The after-piece was a "roaring farce." Our guests were much pleased; and the boys say they are well organized now, and will soon give a series of entertainments.

We have at last persuaded old Mr. Barton to pack up what he can and retreat to Richmond.

Lieut. Norcom, Capt. Barton, and myself devoted a day and night to packing up his library, some of his old wines, and clothing, etc., and saw him aboard the cars and out of harm's way. The citizens are still leaving the town, to avoid the coming clash of arms, and very rightly, too.[1]

December 11. It was a late hour last night when our guests retired, as a game of " euchre " was in progress and a bowl or two of hot punch was brewed.

Before daybreak the boom of a heavy gun was heard. Old Mr. Florence, hearing it, rose bolt upright, as though he had a pocket catapult under him. I watched him from my blankets, for I didn't feel a bit like taking an early start. There was a short interval, when " boom " went the second gun, the signal that the enemy had begun his preparations to cross the river. The bugles immediately sounded the "*Reveille*" and " Boots and Saddles," and the camp was immediately astir, horses harnessed, haversacks packed ; the men fall in at their post, and the Battalion was on the road to Marye's hill. The roads were frozen and slippery, and the weather intensely cold.

The First company, under Capt. Squires, the Third under Capt. Miller, and the Fourth under Capt. Eshleman,

---

[1] HEAD–QUARTERS FIRST ARMY CORPS,
December 10, 1862.

COLONEL : — The Lieut.-General commanding directs that you have your battery hitched up at daylight to-morrow morning.

I am, Colonel, very respectfully,

G. M. SORREL, *A.A.G.*

COL. J. B. WALTON,
Commanding Washington Artillery.

took their allotted positions in the redoubt on Marye's; while the Second, under Richardson, marched off to report to Gen. Pickett, near Lee's Hill.[1]

In the sunken road at the foot of Marye's Hill was posted the brigade of Gen. T. R. R. Cobb, of McLaws's division, and the Twenty-fourth North Carolina regiment, of Ransom's brigade; and supporting the position was Ransom's division of North Carolina troops, held out of sight in our rear.

At a little before day the enemy began launching his boats and laying his pontoon bridges, but was thrice driven from them by the accurate fire of Barksdale's Mississippi riflemen, stationed in the houses lining the edge of the river in Fredericksburg.[2] At 7 o'clock the enemy opened a furious fire from his batteries posted on Stafford Heights, endeavoring to drive Barksdale's men away; but the guns could not be sufficiently depressed to damage the houses in

---

[1] HEAD–QUARTERS FIRST ARMY CORPS,
December 11, 1862, 6 A.M.

COLONEL : — If you have not already done so, Gen. Longstreet wishes you to have your batteries placed in position at once.

Very respectfully,

G. M. SORREL, *A.A.G.*

COL. WALTON, *Commanding Washington Artillery.*

[2] HEAD–QUARTERS FIRST ARMY CORPS,
December 11, 1862, 7.15 A.M.

COLONEL : — The enemy are building a pontoon bridge about one-half mile below the creek, which empties into the river about one-half mile below the town.

At the lower end of Water street, the lower end of town, and at the street above the town-bridge, which is at the foot of Commerce street. This latter is a double bridge.

Gen. Longstreet does not wish you to enter into an artillery duel. Fire deliberately and with effect at the infantry and pontoons.

Very respectfully,

G. M. SORREL, *A.A.G.*

which the sharp-shooters were concealed, and the effect of the bombardment was only the destruction of a few houses, which were set on fire. Gen. Barksdale sends word back to Gen. Lee, that "if he wants a bridge of dead Yankees he can furnish him with one."

In the afternoon, after a severe shelling from one hundred and fifty pieces of artillery, which set fire to a number of houses, the enemy sent across a force of infantry in boats (not being able to complete their bridges, owing to the sharp-shooters), who having effected a landing under the shelter of the banks of the river, Barksdale's men withdrew. The bridges are now completed, without further molestations, and at nightfall the enemy has occupied the town.[1] We can hear the bands playing and the men cheering in the streets, and request to be allowed to open our guns and shell them; but Gen. Lee forbids it, as he is under the impression that there are many men and women still in their houses. We think, after the bombardment of to-day, there must be but few remaining that could be injured by our guns.

We established "head-quarters" in a room in Marye's

---

[1] (Received 7.10 P.M.)

HEAD-QUARTERS FIRST ARMY CORPS,
December 11, 1862.

COLONEL:— The enemy has now possession of the town, and may be expected to make an advance at any hour of the night.

Gen. Longstreet wishes you to be in readiness with your batteries to open on them, and thoroughly rake the streets of the town.

Gen. R. H. Anderson is on the left, with pickets on the canal, and Ransom on his right, supporting the batteries near the telegraph road.

Very respectfully,

G. M. SORREL, *A.A.G.*

COL. WALTON, *Commanding Artillery.*

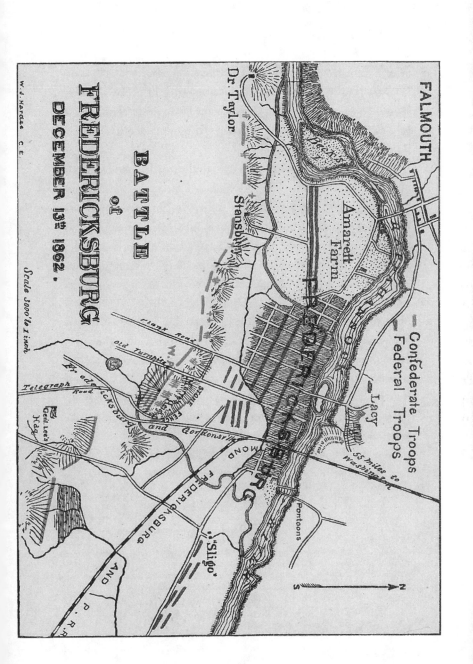

BATTLE of FREDERICKSBURG

DECEMBER 13ᵗʰ 1862.

W.J. Hardee C.E.

Scale 3000'to 1 inch

FALMOUTH

Confederate Troops
Federal Troops

Dr. Taylor

Stansbury

Beck's

Amarett Farm

Lacy

55 miles to Washington

Pontoons

Plank Road

old Turnpike

Telegraph Road

Fredericksburg and Gordonsville

Fredericksburg and Gordonsville

Genl Lee's Head'q's

AND P. R. R.

FREDERICKSBURG

RICHMOND

"Sligo"

N

S

house, and Mr. Giffin comes to us with the "Second Rhode Island," and the "Major Domo" with our suppers.

This afternoon Mr. Mitchell, who has been left by Mr. Barton in charge of his property, was with us on the hill. During a lull in the firing he concluded to ride into town and see if any damage had been inflicted upon Mr. Barton's house.

When the enemy's guns again opened we saw him coming down the telegraph road, whip and spur. Two white bags hung across his saddle, and they flapped up and down at a great rate. On he came, the shells of the enemy seeming to follow him as the fairies did "Tam O'Shanter." Bets were freely taken that he wouldn't make the trip. The whole command was watching him with intense interest. By dint of great exertion he reached the sunken road, and finally reached us safely on the hill. Here he made his report that a cannon-ball had passed through Mr. Barton's sideboard and knocked the dining-room to "demnition smash." He found the old colored cook in the cellar; but she had provided him with two pillow-slips full of biscuit, and had also put in them two bottles of Barton's Old Madeira. We enjoyed the lunch, and drank Mr. Barton's health "standing."

It was now quite evident that Burnside intended to come straight at the heights back of the town, just where Lee wanted him. We are confident of holding our position, although it may be the "slaughter-pen" the other battery officers have termed it. Our boys are content to try it.

Our guns are all in position; our embrasures and traverses are as complete as we can make them, in the absence of necessary tools, fascines, etc. The ammunition chests have been taken off the limbers and placed behind the traverses, so as to be convenient, and our horses and carriages have been sent to a ravine in the rear, where they will be secure from the enemy's fire.

To-day the enemy sent up a large balloon, secured by stout ropes, to make an observation of our position. The balloon ascended from the Stafford Heights.

When day dawned on the 12th the whole valley between us and the town was covered with a dense fog, which shut everything from our view. At 2 P.M. it finally cleared away, and we could see the Stafford Heights densely crowded with troops. At 3 P.M. a column was observed marching down to cross one of the pontoon bridges; but a few well-directed shots from our guns checked it, and caused it to halt and then retire.[1]

At 4 P.M. a large force of the enemy appearing near the gas-works, our guns opened, and, being fired with an accurate aim, soon scattered it. Our position on the hill afforded fine opportunities for the gunners to show their marksmanship, and all were trying to do their best, for,

---

[1] (Recd. 6.20 A.M., Dec. 12, 1862.)

HEAD–QUARTERS FIRST ARMY CORPS,
December 11, 1862.

COLONEL : — As soon as the enemy's infantry comes in range of your long-range guns Gen. Longstreet wishes you to open upon them with effect.

Be particular in acquiring the bearing and range of the streets of the town.

The enemy passing through them will give you an opportunity to rake him, which you will, of course, take.

Very respectfully,
G. M. SORREL, *A.A.G.*

COL. J. B. WALTON,
Commanding Battalion Artillery.

when a good shot was made, the boys applauded. Gunners John Payne and Parsons made the best shots to-day.

In return for our firing upon the troops at the gasworks the enemy opened his guns upon us, and, after firing some fifteen minutes, ceased, as much as to say " *There now!* "

A fragment of shell struck Sergt. John Wood, our *Pauline* of yesterday, and so severely wounded him that he never returned to duty in the army.

Gen. George Deas and Frank Vizetely, the war correspondent and artist for the "Illustrated London News," were with us to-day upon the hill, and Vizetely sketched the town and bombardment from the Fourth company's position. They arrived during the firing, and their presence was made known to us by a loud Indian war-whoop, "Hi-yah!" from Deas as a shell went over their heads.

Vizetely was a rollicking fellow, full of fun, and said he enjoyed this " sort of thing, don't you know?" immensely.[1]

The morning of the 13th December broke with the same dense fog covering our whole front, so that the movements of the enemy were not visible to Lee's army. The Colonel and I rode to the extreme right of the lines, at Hamilton's crossing, to see what was going on, and saw

---

[1] After visiting the different armies of the Confederacy Vizetely left for Nassau, and thence went to Europe. He afterwards sketched for his paper during the Franco-Prussian war, and was at the bombardment of Alexandria and the battle of "Tel-el-Kebir," in Egypt, with Sir Garnet Wolseley. He was with Hicks Pasha when his command was defeated at El Mejid by the False Prophet, El Mahdi, and at last accounts was one of the few survivors of that ill-fated army, and a prisoner in the hands of the enemy.

many old friends. When near Jackson's line we heard the movements of the enemy, marching through the fog. The jingling and rattling of accoutrements and the commands of the officers, " Forward ! Forward, men ! Guide centre ! " were quite distinct.

The cannoneers of Walker's battalion were at their post by their cannon, and the infantry were trying to peer through the fog, and were grasping their rifles tightly.

The clash was close at hand, and we hastily returned to our places on Marye's Hill to await it.

Almost immediately the battle opened in front of Jackson and A. P. Hill on our right, near Hamilton's crossing, and the roar was incessant, but our view was obstructed by the intervening fog.

At noon, while sitting in Marye's garden, overlooking Fredericksburg, the fog had lifted, and we were in momentary anticipation of an attack upon our position, as the enemy could now be seen in immense force in the town. A note came from Gen. Longstreet for Gen. Cobb, but for our perusal. It read as follows : —

" If Anderson, on your left, is badly pressed, he will fall back to the second line of heights. Conform to his movements."

The contents of the note looked ominous.

I went down the terraced hill and into the road, and found Gen. Cobb near a small house on the edge of the road and fields, and delivered the order. He read it carefully, and then said : —

" If they wait for me to fall back they will wait a long time."

Just at this moment (12.30) the firing of the sharp-shooters became brisk, and looking over the stone wall, in the direction of the town, we saw our skirmishers falling back and the enemy's skirmishers advancing. Presently, with loud cries of " Hi! Hi ! " columns of the enemy came charging through the streets of the town, with their muskets at a " right shoulder " and their colors aslant the shoulders of the color-bearers. They began rapidly to deploy behind a ridge that partially hid them from our view. Now our time had come.

I left Gen. Cobb, climbed the hill and rejoined Col. Walton, where I had left him, in Marye's yard. Then mounting our horses, and directing Lieut. Galbraith, who with one 3-inch rifle-gun of the First company was close to the plank road, to open fire as soon as the enemy came within good range, we rode to the centre of the batteries and joined Capt. Squires in his redoubt. Our horses were left with the bugler, behind the brick wall of Marye's graveyard, upon the hill, just behind our position.

The artillery in position upon the hill was as follows : — On the right, the Fourth company, under command of Capt. Eshleman, Lieuts. Norcom, Battles, and Apps, with two 12-pounder howitzers and two 12-pounder Napoleons. On the left of the Fourth company came the Third company, under Capt. Miller, Lieut. McElroy, with two 12-pounder Napoleons. On the left of the third Capt. Squires was posted, with one 3-inch rifle, and one 10-pounder Parrott gun (Richmond make), of the First company, assisted by Lieut. C. H. C. Brown ; and on the plank road Lieut. Galbraith was posted, with one 3-inch rifle of the First company, — nine guns in all of the Washington Artillery.   Beyond the plank road Capt. Maurin's battery, the Donaldsonville cannoneers, with four guns, were in position to aid in repelling the attack of the enemy. On the extreme left was Col. Alexander's artillery battalion, and the heavy guns of the general reserve.

At last the Federal line is formed, and appears above the ridge and advances.   What a magnificent sight it is ! We have never witnessed such a battle-array before ; long lines following one another, of brigade front.   It seemed like some huge blue serpent about to encompass and crush us in its folds, their musket-barrels gleaming brightly in the sunlight, their gay colors fluttering in the breeze.   The lines advance at the double quick, and the alignments are beautifully kept.   The board fences enclosing the gardens fall like walls of mere paper.   Then the loud, full voice of Col. Walton rings out, " 'tention ! Commence fir-i-ng ! ! " and instantly the edge of Marye's Hill is fringed with flame. The dreadful work of the Washington Artillery has begun. The boys soon warm up to their work and aim and fire coolly and deliberately.   Nearer and nearer the enemy's line advances, and now they are within range of canister and we give it to them.   Now they are near enough to the infantry in the sunken road, the Georgians and the North Carolinians ; and they are unseen by the enemy, for the smoke is beginning to cover the field.   All at once the gray line below us rises ; one moment to glance along the trusty rifle-barrels, and volley after volley is poured into the enemy's ranks.   Great gaps appear ; we give them canister again and again ; a few leave the ranks — more follow ;

the lines halt for an instant, and, turning, are seen running in great disorder towards the town. The first assault has been met and repulsed. The field before us is dotted with patches of blue; they are the dead and wounded of the Federal infantry.

It was the division of French that had charged the hill, and was shattered, with the loss of half their numbers.

Hancock's division now advances in splendid style, and being joined by remnants of French's command, pushes on valiantly to and beyond the point French had reached, and then, in little more than fifteen minutes, like our first assailants, are forced back. Of the 5,000 men Hancock led into action 2,000 fell in the charge. With Hancock came the Zouaves and the Irish brigade of Meagher, bearing aloft the green flag with the golden harp of Ireland. The brave fellows came within five-and-twenty paces of the stone-wall and encountered such a fire of shot, shell, canister, and musketry as no command was ever known to live through. The result was that two-thirds of this splendid and gallant brigade was left upon the field killed and wounded.

To relieve Hancock's and French's hard-pressed battalions Howard's division now came up, with the division of Sturgis and the brigade of Carroll, and again assailed the hill. Observing this movement Gen. Ransom brought up the three reserve regiments of his brigade to within a hundred yards of the crest of the hill, and pushed forward the Twenty-fifth North Carolina volunteers to the crest. The enemy, almost massed, moved to the charge heroically, and met the withering fire of the Washington Artillery and small arms with great steadiness.

On they came to within less than one hundred and fifty paces of our line ; but nothing could live before the storm of lead that was hurled at them from this distance. They wavered, broke, and rushed headlong from the field. A few, however, more resolute than the rest, lingered under cover of some houses and fences, and annoyed us with a scattering but well-directed fire. The Twenty-fifth North Carolina volunteers reached the crest of the hill, where Miller's guns were posted, halted, dressed their lines, and poured a few volleys into the enemy at a most deadly range, and then dashed down the hill and took position, shoulder to shoulder, with Cobb's and Cooke's men in the road. Men of the Twenty-fifth North Carolina had fallen upon Miller's redoubt, and he had to drag their bodies away from the muzzles of his guns.

During this attack the gallant Gen. Cobb was mortally wounded, and almost at the same instant Gen. Cooke was wounded and taken from the field.

In passing through our guns some North Carolinian has dropped a fine blanket, and Corporal Ruggles runs out and secures it, saying, " It will be a good thing to have this to-night."

Gen. Kershaw, at the head of one of his regiments, now dashes up to the new road leading from the telegraph road, near the mill, and leads it into the fight at Marye's house, where he assumed command of the troops in the road. A second regiment of his brigade followed. Gen. Ransom then advanced his regiments to the rear of Marye's house.

The enemy, now reinforced by the divisions of Getty and Griffin, who have come to the support of Sturgis, again moved forward. Our infantry held their fire until it would be fatally effective. Meanwhile our artillery was again spreading havoc among the enemy's ranks. Still he advanced under the destructive fire of our line, and, even more resolute than before, madly pressed on. At length, broken and dismayed, he retreated to the town.

We received the following note during the attack just repulsed : —

HEAD–QUARTERS FIRST ARMY CORPS.

COLONEL : — Don't be uneasy about your position. Gen. Anderson has been ordered to hold the heights on the left, with his whole force if necessary.

Very respectfully,

G. M. SORREL,

COLONEL WALTON, *Chief of Artillery.* *A.A. General.*

Have all necessary arrangements made to replenish your ammunition-chests at once. Do not get out of ammunition.

(PRIVATE.) — We have been looking at your practice ; it is very pretty, and I congratulate you on it.

We are fighting under the very eyes of Lee and Long-street. "Now, boys, do your level best !" A solid rifle cannon-ball tears its way through the redoubt, scattering dirt and dust in our faces. Kursheedt picks it up, and says, laughingly, "Boys, let's send this back to them again.'' An instant later it is in the gun, and despatched on its mission back to the enemy.

Corporal Ruggles, who, with sleeves rolled up, has been ramming his gun, suddenly throws up his hands and falls backwards with a ball in his spine.   Perry seizes the sponge-staff as it falls from Ruggles's hands, and takes his place.   The sharp ring of a bullet, striking the face of the piece, is heard, and Perry's arm, having been shot through, drops helpless at his side ; he has been severely wounded. Rodd is holding vent; his elbow-joint is shot away. Everett steps into his place ; a bullet strikes him and he falls.   As he is laid in a corner of the work with Ruggles, he said, "Let me do something, boys ; let me cut fuses."

Falconer passes in rear of the guns, and is struck by a bullet behind the ear, and falls a corpse.   These casualties occurred in rapid succession from the accurate fire of the enemy's sharp-shooters.

We are now so short of men necessary to work Squires's guns that infantry soldiers are called in to help.   The ground, which had been frozen hard, is now converted into mud and slush, and all hands, officers and men, have to put their shoulders to the wheels to run the guns up to the embrasures.   There is a little brick house alongside of Squires's guns, and in it our wounded have taken shelter.   A cannon-shot comes crashing through the work, and, striking the edge of the 'wall, knocks brick and mortar right and left.   Old Mr. Florence had been looking around the corner where the shot struck only a moment before, to see how his son was getting on at the gun.   We think the old gentleman has gotten his quietus, but out comes his gray head again, as lively as ever.

Major Latrobe rides up to us, sent by Longstreet, to see how we are doing.   We tell him, "All right, except we

are running short of ammunition," and that we have not
been able yet to get any sent to us, and asked to be supplied; but how can it be done under such a fire and the
ammunition-train so far away? He promises to see about
it, and, as our place is "too hot for him," he gallops away,
only to get into a hotter one; for he rode over to Maurin's
battery, and had one gun brought outside the work (where
it could not bear upon the enemy attacking Marye's), and
opened fire. In a minute every man was killed or
wounded at the gun, and with difficulty it was withdrawn.[1]
At this time Capt. Squires is struck full in the chest
by a spent ball, and reels and falls into my arms. Thinking he is dreadfully hurt, he says, "Send for Galbraith to
take command, I'm wounded;" but he is soon reassured,
and gazes complacently at the leaden-bullet mark upon his
gray overcoat. Kursheedt and Rossiter are at this moment
badly wounded.

Eshleman now comes over from the right, and reports
his battery almost out of ammunition, only a few solid shot
left. The other batteries are in the same condition.
Nothing to do but send to Col. Alexander for his limbers containing the ammunition we need to be sent to us.
I scribbled a note to him, and Frank, the bugler, is despatched with it. The enemy keeps up a brisk fire from
his advanced lines behind the ridge, aiming at our embra-

---

[1] Lieutenant Landry, of Captain Maurin's battery, I believe called the "Donaldsonville artillery," by direction of Captain Latrobe, took his piece from
behind the epaulement, in order to dislodge a body of the enemy upon whom
the battery could not play. Most effectually he performed this service, but, in
doing so, lost several of his men, and had his piece disabled. His conduct was
admirable, for during the time he was exposed to a direct fire of six and an
enfilade fire of four guns. — *Official Report of General R. Ransom, Jr.*

sures.   Gunner Payne dislodged some sharp-shooters from a frame house, with solid shot.

The enemy's batteries have been firing at us from positions they have taken upon the plain ; but we pay no attention to them, as they do us no harm, reserving our fire always for the masses of infantry.

A flask of spirits in my saddle-pocket, behind the grave-yard wall, was considered the correct thing to have just now, and I made a run for it, got back safely, and passed it around.   It seemed to do a power of good to all hands, both the wounded and the sound.

An officer came from Col. Alexander to say, in answer to my note asking for ammunition, that "he thought it better to send some of his guns to relieve ours, as the limbers might mistake the guns they were intended to supply."

At 5 P.M. we drew out our nine guns, which were immediately replaced by Alexander's, from the batteries of Woolfolk, Moody, and Jordan, with fresh men and plenty of ammunition.   Our batteries were retired out of range, and finally returned to our old camp.   We had been under an uninterrupted and hot fire for nearly five hours, and our ammunition-chests were empty.

The last charge against Marye's Hill was made at dusk by Gen. Humphreys's two brigades, supported by Sykes's division of regulars of the Fifth corps.   These troops, out of sheer desperation, charged with the bayonet, but the deadly fire of the artillery and musketry broke it after an advance of fifty yards, and the united efforts of Gen. Humphreys and Gen. Tyler, their staffs, and other officers, could not arrest the retiring mass.[1] Save an occasional cannon-shot, or the crack of a sharp-shooter's rifle, the battle in front of Marye's Hill was over. The only troops of Longstreet's command engaged in the defence of Marye's Hill and the "sunken road" were the nine guns of the Washington Artillery, which were relieved at 5 P.M. by the same number of Alexander's battalion; the battery of four guns of the Donaldsonville artillery, to the left of the plank-road, where they were, for the most part, unable to reach the enemy with their fire; the brigade of Gen. Cobb; the division of Ransom; and the two regiments of Kershaw's brigade of McLaws's division, amounting to between 2,000 and 3,000 men.

The loss in the Washington Artillery engaged was three killed and twenty-four wounded (27). The position was a hot one, and very like a "slaughter-pen," as it had been called. The little brick house alongside of Squires's guns, which was white at the beginning of the

---

[1] The Fifth corps, under command of Gen. Hooker, consisted of the following: First division, Gen. Griffin; Second division, Gen. Sykes; Third division, Gen. Humphreys. All three divisions were engaged, and lost 2,500 men.

Gen. Hooker thus states the result of the attack: "Finding," says he, "that I had lost as many men as my orders required me to lose, I suspended the attack."

In reference to his opinion of our army he reported as follows:—

"Our artillery had always been superior to that of the Confederates, as was also our infantry, except in discipline, and that, for reasons not necessary to mention, never did equal Lee's army. With a rank and file inferior to our own, intellectually and physically, it has, by discipline alone, acquired a character for steadiness and efficiency unsurpassed, in my judgment, in ancient or modern times."

"We have not been able to rival it, nor has there been any near approximation to it in the other Confederate armies." — *General Hooker's testimony before the Committee on the Conduct of the War.*

battle, was perfectly red with bullet-marks at its close, its paint being scaled off. There was an old cooking-stove in front of the house, exposed, as was the house, to the fire of the enemy. The balls striking it kept up a perpetual "bing, bing," equalling the varied notes of a hand-organ.

Poor Ruggles used his blanket that night, but it was his winding-sheet. He had been cautioned about exposing himself so much while ramming his gun. He laughed and said, "Oh! they can't hurt me. I've been here before." The words were hardly spoken when he fell.

The president of our lately formed literary society, Corp. R. McK. Spearing, was also killed at his gun. He was a noble gentleman.

He ranked high as a splendid gunner, and was serving his piece when struck by a bullet. His comrades advised him to go at once to the surgeon, but he insisted upon having another shot. He had sighted his piece, when, in the act of raising himself to an upright position, he was struck in the breast by a solid cannon-ball, and was instantly killed.

After the command was placed in camp the colonel and I rode over to Lee's Hill, where we saw Gens. Lee and Longstreet and their staffs, who praised the conduct of the battalion upon Marye's Hill to-day.

We met here Captains Phillips and Woodruff of the "Coldstream Guards," English army. All unite in saying it was the grandest panorama of a battle-field ever seen. The impression was that Burnside had fully 100,000 men in line to-day. Less than 20,000 of Lee's army were engaged upon the whole line from Taylor's Hill to Hamilton's Crossing.

We also met Doctors Cullen and Barksdale; and, being tired out, accepted their kind invitation to pass the night with them, and accompanied them to their tents, where we had a good supper, smoked our pipes, took a "night-cap," and slept soundly under our blankets.

On the 14th December our batteries were held in reserve. The second company was not engaged yesterday, being in position on Gen. Pickett's lines. Prisoners have been taken from six divisions which attacked Marye's Hill yesterday. They numbered probably 40,000 men. Our force was certainly not over 3,000 men defending the hill.

On the 15th all remained quiet. The enemy don't seem likely to attack again, although Gen. Lee thinks that their repulse was so easy they might try it again; but, to the amazement of the whole army, when day broke on the 16th, the whole of Burnside's army had crossed the bridges and were once more safe on Stafford Heights. The town of Fredericksburg had been sacked, and the streets filled with broken furniture. Of all the battles this was the most easily won. In front of Marye's Hill, upon the plain over which the Federal columns advanced, we counted 1,498 dead bodies. The artillery and infantry fire was certainly very destructive.

To-day Cols. Sorrel and Fairfax crossed the river to request Gen. Burnside to send over and bury his dead. This he agreed to do; and on the 17th a regiment was sent over for that purpose. A soldier of Meagher's Irish brigade [1] was the nearest body to the stone-wall, and by actual measurement it lay twenty-five paces only from the wall.   The brigade was led, as we were informed, by Col. Robert Nugent, in the absence of Gen. Meagher, who was prevented by sickness from commanding it in person.   The men wore green sprigs in their caps.

The entire fifteen hundred dead bodies, without marks or recognition, were buried in long trenches, until they became full, with a slight covering of earth.   One ice-house on the edge of the town was found filled with bodies, and temporary works were constructed by laying the dead in rows and covering them with earth, behind which men lay down and fired.

The burying party continued their work on the 18th. Capt. Cutts, of Burnside's staff, and other officers who availed themselves of the flag of truce while their dead were being buried, said they attacked Marye's Hill with 60,000 men, and that their loss all along the line, from the beginning to the ending of the battle, was estimated at 20,000 men. [2]

---

[1] "Meagher's Irish brigade attacked Marye's Hill with a gallantry which was the admiration of all who beheld it, but they were literally annihilated by the Washington Artillery and the Confederates lining the sunken road, who themselves suffered hardly any loss.   Fourteen hundred and sixty Irish were buried, who in this attack had fallen on a piece of ground about forty yards deep and three hundred broad." — *Ross's " Camps and Cities of the Confederate States."*

[2] Here we met Gen. Ransom, who had commanded one of the brigades on Marye's Heights which had sustained the principal shock of the assault; and the general's polite offer to show us the battle-field, and give us a description of the fight, was gratefully accepted.

The sight was, indeed, a fearful one, and the dead bodies lay thicker than I had ever seen before on any field of battle.   This was chiefly the case in front of the stone-wall which skirts the sunken road at the foot of Marye's Heights. The dead were here piled up in heaps six or eight deep.   Gen. Ransom told us

On the 19th Cullen gave a grand dinner-party, and amongst the guests were Generals Longstreet, Pickett, and Deas. Big time! Plenty of captured sherry and champagne, and Deas led off in the war-dance.

On the 27th of December the Washington Artillery was marched to the rear, and went into winter-quarters twenty-five miles from Fredericksburg.

We have had a lively time of it since leaving Waltonville.[1]

---

that our men were ordered not to commence firing until the enemy had approached within a distance of eighty yards; but that, from the moment they advanced within this, the hostile ranks had been completely mowed down by our volleys. The nature of the ground towards the town is open and flat, broken only by some plank fences, and dotted with a few wooden houses scattered here and there. All these objects, and even the very ground, were so thickly riddled with bullets that scarcely a square inch was without its dint; and it became incomprehensible to me how even that small few of the most dashing assailants, who had run up within fifteen paces of our lines, could have survived this terrific fire long enough to do so. Many of the Federal soldiers had found death seeking shelter in the small court-yards of the houses behind the wooden plank fences surrounding them, but which, of course, offered not the slightest protection; and heaps of the corpses of these poor fellows filled the narrow enclosures. On a space of ground not over two acres we counted 680 dead bodies; and more than 1,200 altogether were found on the small plain between the heights and Fredericksburg, those nearest the town having mostly been killed by our artillery, which had played with dreadful effect upon the enemy's dense columns. More than one-half of these dead had belonged to Meagher's brave Irish brigade, which was nearly annihilated during the several attacks.— "*Memoirs of the Confederate War for Independence,*" *by Heros Von Borcke, Chief of Staff to General J. E. B. Stuart.*

[1] The following address to the First corps has been issued:—

HEAD–QUARTERS FIRST ARMY CORPS,
NEAR FREDERICKSBURG, Dec. 18, 1862.

GENERAL ORDER, No. 53. — The General commanding the First corps desires to express his gratitude for the good conduct of his troops in the late encounter with the enemy. They had so often attested their valor upon the battle-fields of Virginia and Maryland that he looked for nothing less than steadiness in them when the shock of battle should come; yet, notwithstanding he knew them to be steadfast veterans, they still kindle in him a new admiration by the remarkable firmness with which they defended Marye's Hill.

A more frightful attack of the enemy has not been seen during the war.

They approached within thirty paces of your lines, again and again, returning with fresh men to the assault. But you did not yield a step; you stood by your post, and filled the field before you with slain.

The General commanding congratulates the troops upon the humiliating retreat to which the invader has been forced. Every such disaster to his arms brings us nearer to the happy and peaceful enjoyment of our homes and our families. At the same time he hopes to interest officers and men of this command in the afflictions which have come upon the people of Fredericksburg. Their conduct from the time the two armies appeared before the town has been marked with the most self-sacrificing devotion to their country; and now that their homes have been sacked by the foe, let not not their patience and cheerfulness under these calamities remove from our minds the remembrance of their losses and their wants.

The General, therefore, directs that the commanding officers of this corps will open subscription-lists for the relief of the sufferers of Fredericksburg.

By command of Lieut.-General LONGSTREET.

G. M. SORREL, *A.A.G.*

COL. J. B. WALTON, *Commanding Battalion Washington Artillery.*

Brig.-Gen. R. Ransom, Jr., commanding division, says in his official report : — "Though no part of my command, I will not pass over the already famous Washington Artillery. Its gallantry and efficiency are above all praise."

In Col. Walton's official report, he says : —

"It is my duty, as well as my pleasure, to say, in behalf of my officers, cannoneers, and drivers, that upon no field during this war have men behaved more gallantly.

"To Capts. Eshleman, Miller, and Squires, and the brave officers and men under them, is the service indebted for the gallant defence of Marye's Hill against the stubborn and overwhelming assault of an army of over fifty thousand men.

"To Lieut. W. M. Owen, my Adjutant and only aid, I am, as usual, indebted for zealous and fearless conduct on the field in the performance of all his duties. Before closing this report I may be permitted, without being invidious, to direct the attention of the General commanding, to the gallant conduct of Capt. Eshleman in directing, and Lieut. Norcom, Fourth company, in executing the order, in taking one of the Napoleons from the work, where it was out of range, and placing it between two of the redoubts, on the open field, there continuing it in action, entirely exposed to the enemy's infantry and sharp-shooters, during the greater part of the engagement."

It was at this gun that Lieut. H. A. Battles was severely wounded in the arm.

"As the fog lifted on the 13th of December, the Confederates beheld the Army of the Potomac drawn up in most imposing array, fully 100,000 strong, stretching from above Fredericksburg to Deep Run.

" It was a grand and beautiful sight; rarely is one more glorious vouchsafed to mortal eye.

" And now, as the command is given to the Federal troops to advance, a new interest, a spirit of intense excitement, is added to the scene; and, as the whole line of blue, solid and regular, bristling with glittering bayonets, moves steadily forward, accompanied by the deafening roar of artillery, the eye takes in the whole panorama at a glance; men hold their breath, and realize that war is indeed as glorious as it is terrible.

" The Federal soldiers advanced right gallantly to the desperate work assigned to them; time and again was the assault renewed on the right and on the left of the Confederate line, but all in vain.

" The cool, steady veterans of Lee, under the protection of their hastily-constructed or extemporized works, made terrible havoc in the ranks of the assailing columns; and division after division recoiled under the terrible shock, shattered, discomfited, and demoralized. Their allotted task exceeded human endeavor, and no shame to them that, after such courageous and brilliant conduct, their efforts lacked success. Less than 20,000 Confederate troops (about one fourth of the army under Lee) were engaged.

" It was certainly the most easily won of all the great battles of the war, and it was indeed the most exhilarating and inspiring to look upon, as beheld from the summit of one of the hills occupied by our troops, where army head-quarters were temporarily established." — " *Four Years with Lee.*" — Taylor.

" The attack on the 13th had been so easily repulsed, and by so small a part of our army, that it was not supposed the enemy would limit his efforts to one attempt, which, in view of the magnitude of his preparations and the extent of his force, seemed to be comparatively insignificant.

" Believing, therefore, that he would attack us, it was not deemed expedient to lose the advantages of our position, and expose the troops to the fire of his inaccessible batteries beyond the river, by advancing against him." — *Gen. Lee's report.*

Gen. Lee, in his report to the Secretary of War, Dec. 14, 1862, says : —

" Soon after his repulse on our right, he commenced a series of attacks on our left, with a view of obtaining possession of the heights immediately overlooking the town. These repeated attacks were repulsed in gallant style by the ' Washington Artillery,' under Col. Walton, and a portion of McLaw's division."

Swinton, in his " Army of the Potomac," says of the battle of Fredericksburg, December 13, 1862, as follows : —

" There is little need of comment on this battle, or for other reflection than must spontaneously arise from the simple recital of its incidents.

" Such slaughters stand condemned in the common voice of mankind, which justly holds a commander accountable for the useless sacrifice of human life."

CHAPTER X.

CHANCELLORSVILLE.

Contribution to Fredericksburg. — On Recruiting Service. — "Battle House," Mobile. — Manassas Club. — Admiral Buchanan's Ball. — Confederate Guards. — New Orleans Refugees. — Lieutenant E. Owen. — Montgomery. — News from Camp. — Theatricals. — Back to Old Virginia. — Enemy Moving. — Chancellorsville. — General Jo. Hooker. — Sedgwick at Fredericksburg. — Barksdale's Brigade. — Early's Division. — Hays's Brigade. — Washington Artillery on Marye's Hill. — Flag of Truce. — Enemy Attack. — Guns Lost. — Hooker Defeated. — Diary of a Captured Officer.

THE battalion having been called upon to subscribe money for the poor and homeless of Fredericksburg, contributed a goodly sum, as the following letter from head-quarters will show : —

HEAD-QUARTERS, 1ST ARMY CORPS,
NEAR FREDERICKSBURG, Dec. 28, 1862.

COLONEL : —By direction of the Lieutenant-General commanding I have the honor to acknowledge the receipt of your check for thirteen hundred and ninety-one dollars ($1,391), the contribution of your command to the fund for the relief of the Fredericksburg sufferers.

In making this acknowledgment, I am directed to express his admiration for the generous and feeling manner in which your battalion has responded to the call for relief. The members of the " Washington Artillery " show that they have hearts to feel as well as hands to fight. I have the honor to be, Colonel,

Very respectfully,
Your obedient servant,
G. M. SORREL, *A.A.G.*

COL. J. B. WALTON,
  Commanding Battalion Washington Artillery.

This is the second time the Washington Artillery in Virginia has been called upon to subscribe their meagre pay as soldiers for the relief of our distressed countrymen; and right cheerfully and heartily do they respond to all calls of this nature.

We are now in winter-quarters, but not in huts, as we were at Waltonville, in 1861. Here each mess is thrown upon its own resources and ingenuity to make themselves as comfortable as they can. Some dig a deep square hole or cellar, with a fireplace and chimney at one end. Over the hole is stretched a tent " fly," and then, by covering the floor with clean straw, a comfortable dwelling-place is made. Others are in Sibley tents, with large mud fire-places and chimneys; and, as wood is plenty, all hands are enjoying a much-needed rest. Head-quarters are in tents, and the whole camp is in a large pine woods.

Our losses in battle have been heavy during the year just passed.

From August 23 to 30, inclusive, they were: —

    1 officer killed (Lieutenant Brewer).

    4 non-commissioned officers and privates killed.

  23   "   "   " wounded.

From September 14 to 17: —

    3 officers wounded.

    4 non-commissioned officers and privates killed.

  25   "   "   " wounded.

   2   "   "   " missing.

From December 11 to 13: —

    1 officer wounded.

24 non-commissioned officers and privates wounded.

3   "   "   " killed.

Making a total of 94.

As our number for duty never exceeds 300 men, and often a less number than that, these casualties show a loss of thirty per cent. of the entire command in one year. The two or three hours' artillery-fighting at Rappahannock Station by the 1st and 3d companies on the 23d August, was especially severe, exceeding that of the great battle of Fredericksburg, December 13.

The batteries of Capts. Miller and Squires are reduced to a section each (two guns), the latter having two 3-inch rifles, and the former two 12-pounder Napoleons. Capts. Eshleman and Richardson have each batteries of two 12-pounder Napoleons and two 12-pounder howitzers. Total guns in the battalion, 12.

To recruit the command from the young men of New Orleans Col. Walton applied for leave of absence for a recruiting detail, and upon his application the commanding general of the corps placed the following indorsement : —

HEAD–QUARTERS 1ST ARMY CORPS,
December 26, 1862.

There is no finer command than the Washington Artillery, and I think that every effort should be made to recruit its ranks.

I approve the suggestion of Col. Walton, and recommend the detail as soon as possible.

J. LONGSTREET,
Lieut.-Gen., Commanding.

Without any unnecessary delay a recruiting detail, consisting of Col. Walton, the Adjutant, a commissioned and non-commissioned officer from each battery, was ordered South for recruits, and on the 7th of January, 1863, we bade good-by to army life, and left camp in high spirits.

After a rough journey by rail we arrived at Mobile, and officers were sent to their recruiting-stations adjacent to the city of New Orleans, now in possession of the enemy, under Gen. Butler.

The Colonel and I made the Battle House our head-quarters, and found the change from Marye's Hill to our present abiding-place decidedly pleasant. We once more enjoy comfortable rooms and beds, bells, servants, and all the conveniences of civilized life, to which we have been strangers for several months while in Virginia.

Word has been sent through the lines into New Orleans that we need more young men of spirit, and they are coming out daily to enroll themselves.

We are enjoying Mobile society hugely. Immediately upon our arrival we were visited by the Hon. John Forsyth, Dr. Ketchum, and others, and were introduced to the Manassas Club, where we were quite lionized and *fêted*. A night or two after our arrival Admiral Buchanan, of the Confederate navy, gave a grand ball, to which we were invited, and where we met most charming and beautiful women. But for the uniforms of the officers present one could scarcely realize that these were war times. Gen. S. B. Buckner is in command of the city, and his staff are having a gay time. At the Battle House we found quite a little colony of New Orleans gentlemen refugee-ing. Nearly all of them had been members of the Confederate Guards in the city, — a command composed of cotton factors and members of the Boston Club, all of mature years. It is said when they went into camp near the city it was better than a play to see them go through the details of soldier-life. They lived luxuriously, — tents floored, cots, sideboards, etc., plenty of servants, but had, at times, great privations, for Joe Lovell told me that "once it rained very hard, and there wasn't an umbrella in the whole regiment." When the city fell, Butler gave the members of the regiment permission to leave the city if they desired to go, and so they are having a good time of it at the Battle House and Manassas Club.

My brother, Lieut. E. Owen, who is on sick leave, on account of wounds received at Sharpsburg, is sojourning at Montgomery, and came down to see me, and I have promised to return with him. He offers special inducements, promising to introduce me to some lovely girls.

In due time I was presented ; and, although I went to Montgomery "heart whole and fancy free," my "wings were scorched," and I surrendered. The sojourn at Montgomery was most delightful ; we had no end of creature comforts at the beautiful country home of some friends of my brother's. Here I was first introduced to the luxury of peanut coffee, and found it excellent ; sometimes it was called cocoa, but it answered for both. A beverage made of sweet potatoes was considered very fine. While at Montgomery I had the honor of being presented to Mrs. Jefferson Davis, and became much attached to her and her immediate family.

But our leave of absence came to an end, and, having forwarded our recruits, — and a goodly number of them, too, — we, with great reluctance, left hospitable Mobile for Richmond, Virginia.

That the boys we left behind in camp were enjoying themselves in our absence a letter received from one of them will show : —

CAMP WASHINGTON ARTILLERY,
NEAR FREDERICKSBURG, Feb. 22, 1863.

We are still in camp where you left us in January. I am writing in my tent almost suffocated by the smoke, that will insist on coming out of the wrong end of the stove.

Old Solomon was right when he said, "a smoky chimney and a scolding wife were evils." I know all about the first, but nothing of the latter, and don't want to.

We are having a regular Arctic snow-storm. Old mother Earth is already covered to the depth of many inches, and still no indications of a clear-up. The men are all comfortably fixed for this cold snap, many of them having built log-huts, with fireplaces and chimneys, and, wood being plentiful, they are as snug as can be.

Our horses are protected by shelters of pine branches.

You have heard, I presume, of the second performance of the "Washington Artillery Varieties" company. It was a complete success; even better than the one we had just prior to the battle of Fredericksburg. In fact, the army has declared the "Varieties" an institution. It was attended by a score of ladies from the surrounding country, a special railroad train having been run for their accommodation. Gen. Longstreet and staff were present. Gen. Lee was prevented by business from being present, but sent his regrets in an autograph note, thanking the managers for their kind invitation, and wishing them success in their efforts to introduce these entertainments into the army.

Representatives from all the divisions of the army were present, some of Jackson's men walking twenty miles, so great was their desire to see the show.

Our theatre being out of doors, we could, of course, accommodate the largest kind of audiences. There was no danger of crowding the house and announcing to the public that "standing-room only" could be furnished at the box-office.

The stage was tastefully decorated with the Battalion colors and the guidons of the four batteries. The battle-flag presented to us by Gen. Beauregard was conspicuously displayed. The side-scenes were blankets, and a tent served as a drop-curtain, on which was handsomely sketched the badge of the Battalion, the cross cannon and motto, " Try us."

The whole scene was illuminated, not by the " soft light of alabaster lamps," but by tallow-dips hung in Chinese lanterns, that some thoughtful fellow managed to bring from Maryland last summer.

The united bands of the Twelfth and Sixteenth Mississippi regiments, under the leadership of Professor Hartwell, furnished delightful music.

The programmes were handsomely printed in Richmond, and distributed throughout the army. The programme opened with "Pocahontas, or Ye gentle savage," — a demi-savage, semi-civilized extravaganza, with music dislocated and reset through the instrumentality of Seignor Knighti.

Private W. P. N——, of Third company, sustained the part of " Powhatan, first king of the Tuscaroras," and " one of the original F.F.V.'s."

Private Bob Many, of Third company, was capital as " Pocahontas," and Corp. W——, of First company, as " Capt. John Smith," was excellent.

" Toodles " was the after-piece, — Corp. H——, of Second company, as Toodles, and Sergt. B——, of Second company, as Mrs. Toodles.

Of course, throughout the play, the house came down any number of times, and the audience appeared delighted.

The band played the " Bonnie Blue Flag," and the audience scattered to their camps.

The bills announce that the " Lady of Lyons " is to be performed again; but, as " Pauline " was wounded at the battle of Fredericksburg, and is now confined in the hospital, it is puzzling the managers who to cast for the part. The choice will fall upon Bob Many, we suppose. Recruits are arriving, and are fine fellows, and will become good Washington Artillerymen.

Come to us soon.

Yours fraternally,

BOLIVAR WARD.

During the month of February the light batteries of artillery of the army were organized into battalions, each commanded by field-officers, and reporting direct to the chiefs of artillery of the army corps.

The assignment of single batteries to brigades, as was the case during the summer campaign, is done away with; for it is considered that a brigadier-general has about all he can attend to in fighting his infantry.

The following general order has been issued by Gen. Lee : —

HEAD-QUARTERS ARMY NORTHERN VIRGINIA,
February 15, 1863.

GENERAL ORDER NO. 20 : —

I. The following organization of the Artillery of this army is made in accordance with requirements of Par. II., General Order, No. 7 (current series), from A. & I.G.O.

The batteries forming the battalions of each corps, with the officers assigned to their command, are designated in the following table. *All the battalions of each corps will be under the command of, and will report to, the chief of artillery for the corps.* The whole in both corps will be *superintended by*, and report to, the general chief of artillery.

II. A medical and ordnance officer and an assistant quartermaster, the latter to perform also the duties of commissary, will be assigned as soon as practicable to each battalion.

By order of Gen. LEE.

R. H. CHILTON,
A.A. & I.G.

BATTERIES OF ARTILLERY IN THE ARMY OF NORTHERN VIRGINIA.

FIRST CORPS.

Lewis's Battery,
Grandy's   "   Major J. J. Garnett,
Maurin's   "   Major Richardson.
Huger's   "

Manly's Battery,
McCarthy's "
Coalter's "
Reid's " } Col. H. C. Cabell,
Major S. P. Hamilton.

Blount's "
Macon's "
  (Richmond Fayette Artillery),
Bradford's Battery,
Stribling's "
Caskie's " } Major James Dearing.

Bachman's "
Garden's "
Reilly's "
Latham's " } Major Kemper.

SECOND CORPS.

Carter's Battery,
Bondurant's "
Page's "
Fry's " } Lieut.-Col. T. H. Carter.

Braxton's "
McIntosh's "
Davidson's "
Crenshaw's "
Pegram's " } Col. R. L. Walker.

Carpenter's "
Brown's "
Raine's "
Dement's " } Lieut.-Col. Snowden Andrews.

Thompson's "
  (Louisiana Guard),
Garber's Battery,
  (Staunton Artillery),
Carrington's Battery,
Latimer's " } Lieut.-Col. H. P. Jones.

RESERVE FIRST CORPS.

Squire's Battery,
Miller's   "
Eshleman's Battery,   } Col. J. B. Walton.
Richardson's   "
  (Washington Artillery),

Jordan's   Battery,
Rhett's   "
Moody's   "   Lieut.-Col. E. P. Alexander.
Parker's   "   Major J. R. C. Lewis.
Wolfolk's   "
Eubank's   "

RESERVE SECOND CORPS.

Hardaway's Battery,
Johnson's   "   } Major D. G. McIntosh.
Wooding's   "
Lusk's   "

Poague's   "
Smith's   "
Dance's   "
Watson's   "   } Col. J. Thompson Brown.
Hupp's   "
Brooks's   "

GENERAL RESERVE.

Lane's Battery,   } Lieut.-Col. A. S. Cutts,
Ross's   "   } Major T. Jefferson Page.
Patterson's "

Massie's   "
Kirkpatrick's Battery,   } Major Nelson.
Milledge's   "

NOTE. — 14 battalions; 60 batteries; 240 guns. First corps, 17 batteries; Second corps, 17 batteries; Reserve, 20 batteries; General reserve, 6 batteries.

Hardly had the month of April relieved the tedium of winter-quarters when, by direction of Gen. Lee, orders were issued for the artillery to get rid of all *impedimenta*, and again "strip for the fight;" and we do not doubt but we shall have our hands full again as soon as the warm April sun shall have dried the roads so the armies can move.

The following is the order, as issued by Gen. Pendleton, Chief of Artillery of the Army of Northern Virginia : —

HEAD—QUARTERS ARTILLERY CORPS,

April 15, 1863.

ORDER NO. —

In obedience to the direction of the Commanding General, transportation and baggage of the artillery will be immediately reduced to the lowest amount consistent with necessary supplies. So important is it to remove every horse that can be spared, and every wagon not essential to the support of the army and its necessary horses, that even general officers are called upon to take only such baggage as may be borne on their horses.

General Jackson takes no trunk himself, and allows none in his corps.

The clerks in Gen. Lee's office are not mounted, and for all his voluminous papers, and all the accommodation of his staff, only three or four wagons are employed.

Examples so significant may well be followed throughout the army.

. . . . .

W. N. PENDLETON,
Brig.-Gen'l and Chief Arty., A.N. Va.

On the 30th of April, all the recruiting detail having returned to duty again, the battalion is ordered by Gen. Lee from winter-quarters to Fredericksburg, it being reported that the enemy is moving again. On the morning of the 1st of May we learn that the enemy has crossed the

Rappahannock on our left flank, at Chancellorsville, and Gen. Lee has gone there with the bulk of the army, leaving Early's division and Barksdale's brigade at Fredericksburg, about nine thousand men.

Longstreet's corps is absent, so we are that much weaker. Heavy firing heard to-day in the direction of Chancellorsville.

Capt. Richardson, with three guns of the Second company Washington Artillery, and one gun of the Fourth company Washington Artillery, under command of Lieut. Battles, is ordered to report to Gen. Early at Hamilton's Crossing.

On the 2d of May orders were received from Gen. Pendleton, Chief of Artillery, to move the First, Third, and Fourth companies, Washington Artillery, to the front, and their guns are placed in position in earthworks opposite Falmouth. Large bodies of Federal troops can be seen on the right, — some on the south (our) side of the Rappahannock. About noon a *corps d'armée* of Federals moved through Falmouth, in front of our guns, going apparently to reinforce Hooker at Chancellorsville, leaving a corps on our right. All very quiet in front of Fredericksburg, but heavy firing heard towards Chancellorsville.

In the evening the enemy on the right began pushing in our skirmishers and advancing on the hills towards Hamilton's Crossing, where Early's division is posted. We were ordered by Gen. Pendleton to leave our positions and take the three batteries to the telegraph road. He then ordered Col. Walton to fall back to some safe place. We marched about a mile, when we met Gen. Barksdale's brigade moving in the direction of Fredericksburg. It was now dusk. Gen. Barksdale called out : "What artillery is that ?" Col. Walton told him. He then said : "Col. Walton, you are not going to desert me, are you ?" The Colonel replied : " General, I am the last man in the world to desert you or anybody else. I am acting under orders." — " Then will you obey an order from me ?" — " Yes," was the reply. " Then reverse your column and come back with me to Fredericksburg. We must hold this point to the last." We immediately countermarched and retraced our steps. It was now quite dark, and, to deceive the enemy, innumerable camp-fires were lighted all along Lee's Hill, to make it appear that there was a heavy force bivouacking there, — that we had been heavily reinforced. There can't be less than 20,000 men in front of us, perhaps more. A deserter came in and told us it was the *corps d'armée* of Sedgwick. We are evidently playing a big game of bluff to keep these 20,000 men off of Lee at Chancellorsville.

About 2 o'clock in the morning of May 3d Capt. Miller, with the two guns of the Third company, Washington Artillery, was ordered to take position on Marye's Hill, on the plank-road. Col. Walton protested against this order, and told Gen. Barksdale it was not right to send the guns to this exposed position when the supports were so meagre, — that on December 13 we were supported on Marye's Hill by the whole corps of Longstreet. The general insisted, and the guns were sent.[1]

---

[1] About midnight I went to Gen. Barksdale's bivouac on Lee's Hill to learn the result of the consultation with Gen. Early. I found him wrapped in his war

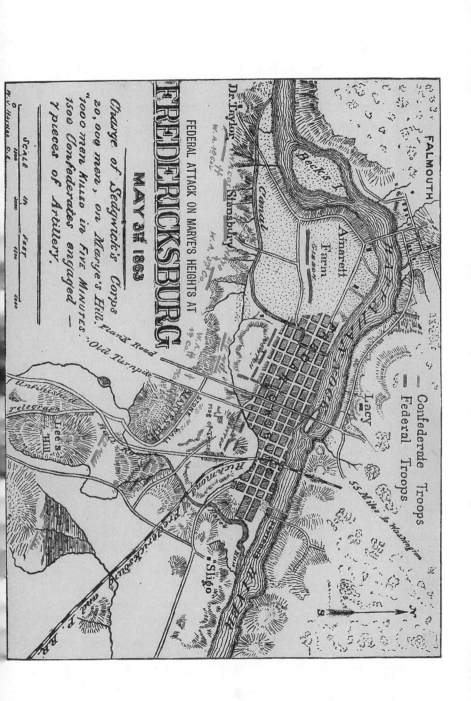

FEDERAL ATTACK ON MARYE'S HEIGHTS AT

FREDERICKSBURG

MAY 3RD 1863

Charge of Sedgwick's Corps
20,000 men, on Marye's Hill.
"1000 men killed in Five Minutes."
1500 Confederates engaged —
7 pieces of Artillery.

SCALE   IN   FEET

H. J. Hardie. C.E.

— Confederate Troops
▪▪▪ Federal Troops

FALMOUTH

55 Miles to Washington

On the morning of the 3d of May the troops defending Marye's Hill and the line of heights back of the town of Fredericksburg were as follows : —

To the left of the plank-road the Twenty-first Mississippi regiment, 330 muskets, under command of Col. B. G. Humphreys. Behind the stone-wall at the foot of Marye's Hill, the Eighteenth Mississippi regiment, Col. Griffin, 318 muskets. At the foot of Lee's Hill, the Seventeenth Mississippi regiment, Col. Holden, 330 muskets, and the Thirteenth Mississippi regiment, Major Bradley; two 12-pounder Napoleons, of the Third company Washington Artillery, and two guns of Parker's battery, under Lieut. Brown, on Marye's Hill. Gen. Early, with his division, was at Hamilton's Crossing, where it was thought the enemy would attack, and Gen. Wilcox's brigade was at Banks's Ford, a few miles above the town.

Early in the morning the enemy made an advance in very strong force against the hills, and were gallantly repulsed by the Mississippians and Miller's and Brown's guns on Marye's Hill.

Of this advance Gen. Doubleday, of the Federal army, says : " At dawn Newton deployed Wheaton's brigade and made a demonstration to develop the enemy's line. As the fortified heights commanded the plank-road by which Sedgwick was to advance, it became necessary to attack

---

blanket, lying at the root of a tree. "Are you asleep, general ?" — "No, sir. Who could sleep with a million of armed Yankees all around him ?" he answered, gruffly. He then informed me that it was determined by Gen. Early to hold Marye's Hill at all hazards; but that his brigade and a portion of the Washington Artillery had to do it. — *Gen. B. G. Humphreys, ex-Governor of Mississippi and Colonel Twenty-first Regiment.*

immediately.   The plan of assault, which had been devised by Newton and approved by Sedgwick, was to attenuate the rebel force by attacking it on a wide front, so that it could not be strong anywhere, and to use the bayonet alone.   Accordingly Gibbon was directed to advance on the right, to turn their flank there if possible, while Newton was to demonstrate against the centre, and Howe to act against the left.

" Newton deployed Wheaton's brigade, opened fire along his front, and kept the enemy employed there.   But Gibbon was unable to advance on the right because a canal and a railroad lay between him and the rebels, and they had taken up the flooring of the bridges over the latter.

" Howe did not succeed any better on the left, as, in attempting to turn the first he encountered the fire of the second line (Seventeenth Mississippi) in rear and in *echelon* to the first, which took him directly in flank, so that the combined *attack was a failure.*"

And this attacking column of three divisions, numbering nearly 20,000 men (for it was the beginning of a new campaign, and the ranks were undoubtedly full), met and was repulsed by Wilcox's brigade, which had come down from Banks's Ford, in front of Gibbon, the Twenty-first and Eighteenth Mississippi regiments of Barksdale's brigade, about 650 men, in front of Newton, and the Thirteenth and Seventeenth Mississippi, also of Barksdale's brigade, in front of Howe, and a few pieces of artillery along the heights.

About 8 A.M. the First company Washington Artillery, Capt. Squires, with two 3-inch rifles, was ordered to

Marye's Hill, on the right of the dwelling. When the second gun came into position the enemy opened fire from a battery. The first shell killed Sergt. West, passing entirely through his arm and body.

At 9.30 A.M. a flag of truce came out of the town, and was met about one hundred yards in front of the stone wall by Capt. Robert Brown, of the Brown rifles, and Sergeant-Major William Blake, of Company K, Eighteenth Mississippi regiment. The enemy requested permission to take off their killed and wounded, but Col. Griffin very properly refused their untimely request; but it was noticed by Blake that the bearers of the flag peered intently at the foot of the hill where our infantry were, and our men would lift their heads above the stone wall, showing plainly how small their numbers were. This was just what the enemy wanted to discover, and, being satisfied, retired to their own lines.

Gens. Pendleton, Barksdale, and Col. Walton were at this time on Lee's Hill, overlooking the plain below.

Gen. Harry Hays, with three regiments of the Louisiana brigade passed by, going from Hamilton's Crossing, on the railroad, towards our left, in the direction of Falmouth, where Wilcox was, and where the enemy was demonstrating.[1]

By order of Gen. Pendleton, one of Miller's guns

---

[1] Gen. Barksdale applied to Gen. Pendleton, who had control of a large train of artillery on the telegraph road on Lee's Hill, not a mile off, and not in position, to send a battery to Taylor's Hill to command the two bridges that spanned the canal. Instead of sending a battery from his train that lay idle during the whole engagement, he ordered a section of the Washington Artillery from the redoubt on the plank-road, where it was needed. (Miller's gun sent under command of Lieut. Hero.) — *Gen. B. G. Humphreys.*

(Third company, Washington Artillery) was removed from the plank-road near Marye's House, and sent with Gen. Hays, under command of Lieut. Hero.

Lieuts. Apps and De Russy, with two howitzers, occupied a small earthwork beyond the plank-road, and Capt. Norcom, Fourth company, with two guns, was still farther to the left.

Hays halted his brigade for a short rest in a ravine behind the crest of Lee's Hill, and we had the pleasure of meeting some old friends. Among them was the Adjutant-general, Major Seymour. The Major rode up to the work where we were standing, and took an observation of the enemy's position. Not to be considered deficient in hospitality, I proposed that we should take a few drops for "auld lang syne," to which proposition he acquiesced. I went to my saddle-bag, produced the leather-covered bottle, and, unscrewing the top, was extending it to him, when Col. Walton cried out, "Take that blessed horse away from here; you will draw the enemy's fire!" Just then "boom!" went a gun, and a solid shot struck the ground disagreeably close, scattering dirt all over us.

The Major's horse took fright, and dashed off towards and into the ravine. "Hollo!" I cried; "take that drink before you go. What's the matter with you?" As he disappeared from view, his reply was wafted back through the sulphurous air, "See you later!"

At about 10 o'clock, emboldened by the discovery of our weakness, made under flag of truce, the enemy suddenly appeared to spring out of the ground, in line of battle, from behind the ridge near the town. At the same time thirty or forty guns opened upon our positions from the Stafford Heights. It was a beautiful sight, but a terrible one for us. On the columns charged, with a rush, with loud shouts and yells. The Eighteenth Mississippi behind the stone-wall, and the guns of Miller and Squires on the hill, the Twenty-first Mississippi, with the howitzers of Apps and De Russy on the left of the plank-road, banged away as fast as they could be served, checking the assaulting columns; but their efforts to stay the tide were unavailing against such great odds. As the enemy advanced, Gen. Barksdale sent me to the foot of Lee's Hill to order Lieut.-Col. Fizer to go at once to the assistance of Col. Griffin, with the Seventeenth regiment; but just as I reached him, and delivered the order, Gen. Barksdale cried out, "Too late; fall back here." I climbed back on the hill as fast as I could, and found it deserted; all had left it except a battery, and that was being withdrawn, and on its limber was the body of its Lieutenant (Habersham), with his head shot off by a cannon-ball. We had been talking together but a few moments before the attack commenced. My horse was in the ravine where I had left him with the Orderly, who could not tell me which way the Colonel had ridden. Looking towards Marye's Hill, I saw it was crowded with the enemy; they had evidently overrun our small force. And our guns and the boys of the Washington Artillery, what of them? The uncertainty as to their fate was dreadful. To my right the Thirteenth and Seventeenth Mississippi regiments were marching off to the rear in good order; on the left Gen. Barksdale was rallying the remnants of the

Eighteenth and Twenty-first Mississippi regiments. I turned my horse's head towards Marye's Hill, and started to ride in that direction. I had an idea the Colonel might have gone that way. I was in a very belligerent state of mind, and much excited; for the first time we had lost guns in action. I was recalled to my senses by the orderly, who was following me, calling out: "No use going any farther, Adjutant, the Colonel hasn't gone this way." We had approached the enemy too closely, and the minies were flying about our ears; evidently the sharpshooters were taking notice of us. We turned and rode back up the Telegraph Hill, and just as we reached the crest what a glorious sight greeted us! — the Second company, Washington Artillery, coming down the road at a gallop, cannoneers mounted, Walton on his black stallion, and Richardson at the head. "Hurrah!" I yelled and shouted; here was somebody left who would fight. They had heard of the danger the boys on Marye's Hill were in, and had come gallantly to help them if they could. As they dashed up in splendid style, the Colonel cried out: "Adjutant! you know the ground; put Richardson in!" — "All right! come along, old fellow, glad to see you; come on! Go in here." — "Where shall I fire?" said John. — "Yonder! Marye's Hill; full of them; give it to 'em good!" and the guns opened upon the dense mass of the enemy, the cannoneers working with a will.

By direction of the Colonel, I rode over to where Gen. Barksdale was rallying the infantry, and asked him "if he considered it safe to keep the battery where it then was?" He replied, "Our centre has been pierced, that's all; we will be all right in a little while." I rode back to the road, and there, to my amazement, the Second company was going to the rear as fast as they could travel. A line of the enemy had climbed the hill right under the muzzles of their guns, and appeared suddenly before their very faces. A volley at close range wounded some men and horses, and Lieutenant Battles had to leave behind his gun, two of his horses having been shot, and it was no time to " swap horses."

After the first surprise, everything was rallied into shape again, and we fell back in good order, and retired, firing, to the line of the mine road, from Hamilton's Crossing, where were concentrated Early's division, including Hays's brigade and the remnants of Barksdale's brigade. Wilcox had fallen back to Gest's Hill. To our great astonishment we saw there all of Gen. Pendleton's reserve artillery, about twenty guns, that hadn't fired a shot during the whole engagement.[1]

---

[1] Gen. Barksdale, as soon as he saw Marye's Hill was lost, the Eighteenth regiment shattered, the Washington Artillery captured, and the Twenty-first regiment cut off, ordered the Thirteenth and Seventeenth regiments to fall back to Lee's Hill. Adjutant Owen, of the Washington Artillery, rallied the Second company, under Capt. Richardson, to the telegraph road on Lee's Hill, and opened upon the blue mass on Marye's Hill. Barksdale rallied the remnant of the Eighteenth regiment, and three companies of the Twenty-first regiment, and posted the Thirteenth regiment on the right of the telegraph road; the left wing, under Major Bradley, resting its left company immediately on the road. Col. Holder posted the Seventeenth regiment on the left of the telegraph road, the right wing under Lieut.-Col. Fizer, and immediately engaged the advancing enemy. This timely and judicious disposition of our troops, and their stubborn daring, checked the enemy and enabled me to reach the telegraph road with the Twenty-first regiment. The enemy, however, pushed forward his troops under cover of the brow of the hill, and, concealed by the smoke of the artillery, almost to the muzzles of the guns of the Second company of the Washington Artillery, shot down some of the horses, wounded several of the men, and forced them to limber to the rear, leaving one gun. The ranks were rapidly wasting away under the deadly fire. Gen. Sedgwick was pushing his blue lines over

In reference to this day's work Gen. Doubleday says : —

It was now 10 A.M., and there was no time to be lost; and Gen. Warren, who represented Hooker, urged an immediate assault, and Newton formed three columns of assault in the centre, and Howe three on the left. To Col. Johns, of the Seventh Massachusetts, who was a graduate of West Point, was assigned the direct attack on Marye's Hill, with two regiments of Eustis's brigade, another column consisting of Shaler's brigade, and four regiments under Col. Spear of the Sixty-sixth Pennsylvania, was directed to act farther to the right, and the right division, under Col. Burnham of the Fifth Massachusetts, attached to Newton's command, was ordered to deploy on the left against the base of the hill. Spear's column was enfiladed and *broken by the artillery,* — indeed, almost literally *swept away,* — and Spear himself was killed.

Johns had the most difficult task, for he was compelled to advance up a broken, stony gulch swept by *two rebel howitzers* above. The head of his column encountered a terrific fire, and was *twice broken,* but he rallied it each time. Then he was badly wounded, and there was a brief pause; but Col. Walsh, of the Thirty-sixth New York, rallied the men again, and they kept straight on over the works.

Burnham, with his light brigade of four regiments, captured the entrenchments below, which had been so fatal to our troops in the previous battle of Fredericksburg, and went into the works along with the others.

General Shaler's reserve regiments entered on the right at a less exposed point, where, however, the cross-fire was very severe.

Sedgwick, Newton, and Shaler rode into the works almost simultaneously with the men.

The fortified heights on the right of Hazel Run, held by Barks-

---

Marye's Hill and up the plank-road. His serried lines were fast encompassing Lee's Hill, and it was apparent that the Thirteenth and Seventeenth regiments would soon be enveloped and crushed.

Barksdale yielded before the impending shock, and ordered a retreat. We fell back along the telegraph road about two miles to the mine road. It was now about the middle of the afternoon, and Barksdale's brigade of 1,500 Mississippians, and seven guns of the Washington Artillery, with less than 200 Louisianians, and one (two ?) gun of " Parker's battery," with about twenty Virginians had been struggling and holding back from Lee's flank and rear Sedgwick's army, variously estimated from 18,000 to 30,000. — GEN. B. G. HUMPHREYS, *Colonel of Twenty-first Regiment.*

dale's brigade, being now occupied by our men, those to the left were necessarily taken in reverse, and therefore Sedgwick thought it useless to attack them in front. Nevertheless, Howe carried them gallantly (with his division of two brigades), but with considerable loss of life (he was opposed by the Thirteenth and Seventeenth Mississippi regiments).

The coveted heights, which Burnside had been unable to take with his whole army, were in our posssession, together with about one thousand prisoners; but the loss in the Sixth corps was severe, for nearly *one thousand men were killed, wounded, and missing in less than five minutes.*

The attack was over so soon that Early did not get back Hays's brigade, which had been detached to oppose Gibbon in time to assist in the defence. Newton says, "*If there had been one hundred more men on Marye's Hill, we could not have taken it.*" One of our boys, who had stood by his gun until all hope was gone, was passing through Gen. Pendleton's reserve artillery; he was as mad as he could be, and his hands and face covered with burnt powder. One of the reserves called out, "Hello, Washington Artillery! where are your guns?" He replied sharply, "Guns be damned! I reckon now the people of the Southern Confederacy are satisfied that Barksdale's brigade and the Washington Artillery can't whip the whole damned Yankee army." They left him alone. He had about told the story of the fight. Early had under his command about nine thousand men, but less than two thousand were engaged with Sedgwick's corps. When the remnant of the troops that had been engaged fell back, Early formed line of battle on the mine road at right angles with the telegraph road, and prepared for the enemy's coming. Just at dusk we saw coming towards us what appeared to be a battery of artillery.   Gen. Early inquired of Gen. Pendleton if all of our batteries had been brought in.   Pendleton replied that they had. Just at this moment the supposed battery made a sudden countermarch, and Early cried out, "It is the enemy! open the artillery upon him!" and in an instant twenty guns were sending shells after the retreating enemy, Sergt. Brinsmaid of Second company, Washington Artillery, firing the first.   In the morning we gathered in the fragments of four battery wagons and forges, and the headquarter wagons of Gen. Sedgwick, that had been knocked to pieces by the shells.   The drivers had taken the wrong road, and run right into us.   This little incident afforded some amusement after the depressing events of the day.

After driving our troops from Marye's Hill Sedgwick took up his line of march along the plank-road towards Chancellorsville, to aid Gen. Hooker, whose army Gen. Lee was furiously attacking, and successfully.

The loss in the Washington Artillery, as near as can be ascertained this evening, is fifty cannoneers, officers, and drivers.   The guns on Marye's Hill are certainly captured, with their officers and men.   Some of the Eighteenth Mississippi, who escaped, reported that the boys, when last seen by them, were fighting heroically at their guns, apparently with no idea of deserting their posts. The charge of the enemy was so sudden that but few succeeded in getting away from the stone-wall at the foot of Marye's Hill.   Sergt.-Major William Blake and Lieut.-Col. Campbell, of the Eighteenth Mississippi, took advantage of the confusion to escape when the Federals leaped into the road, and, finding two horses tied behind Marye's house, — supposed to be those of Capt. Squires and Lieut. Owen, — mounted them and rode off. They passed the enemy, now re-forming his line, and thought themselves almost safe when they were fired upon, and Col. Campbell was shot through the body, but kept his seat upon the horse until Blake got him safely away and into an ambulance.

Lieut. Apps reports that when the enemy charged up the plank-road, from which Miller's gun had unfortunately been removed, he suddenly saw a Federal flag upon a work between his guns and the road. A deep ravine was in his rear. The enemy's skirmishers were fast closing in upon him when he gave orders to abandon the two howitzers, and for the men to save themselves and the battery-horses if possible. A gallant driver, named Keegan, rode his team off down the line of Federal skirmishers, they firing at him all the while, and he waving his cap and whipping up his horses, meanwhile delivering a volley of oaths at the enemy, and taunting them to "Shoot me if you can, you bloody blue divils!" He saved his team. Lieut. Apps reports Corp. Lewis and Bob Many wounded and left on the field.

At sunrise on the 4th of May, in obedience to the orders of Gen. Lee, Early moved forward, and again reoccupied Marye's Hill, where a few of our boys were found, some dead, some wounded. Leaving Barksdale behind the stone-wall to look out for any of the enemy who might still be in Fredericksburg, he thence followed Sedgwick with his division. Yesterday, at Salem Church, Sedgwick was met by Gen. McLaws, with five brigades detached by Gen. Lee for this purpose, including Wilcox's. To-day Gen. Anderson was sent to re-enforce McLaws with three additional brigades.

Meanwhile Gen. Early had connected with these troops, and in the afternoon Sedgwick was assailed, Early attacking the left, making the main assault.

At dusk the Federal General crossed to the north side of the river, and he never got to Hooker at all, and left Lee to finish off the finest army on the planet without interruption.[1] But in this battle we have lost Gen. Jackson, — "Old Stonewall," — and it has filled all hearts with great sorrow; his place can never be filled. His very name was the synonym of victory.

This has been Lee's greatest battle. With 57,000 men, including the troops under Early, at Fredericksburg, — 9,000, — he has beaten 132,000[2] of the enemy under "fighting Joe Hooker," on ground chosen by Hooker himself, and partially fortified, and compelled him to leave the field and recross the Rappahannock with great loss. Nothing but a heavy rain-storm coming up prevented Gen. Lee from crushing him completely.

---

[1] Owing to the sudden rise in the river, the bridges became too short, and there was some doubt as to the practicability of passing over them, but by taking down one and piecing the others with it the difficulty was overcome, and the army retired, without being followed up, under cover of thirty-two guns posted on the heights on the opposite bank. Meade's corps acted as rear guard.

Hooker left his killed and wounded behind, and had lost fourteen guns and 20,000 small arms. — *Chancellorsville, by Gen. Doubleday.*

[2] Swinton, p. 269.

On the 9th of May, all being again quiet along the Rappahannock, the Battalion Washington Artillery is ordered to Stannard's Farm, to pitch our tents on the river "Po," to rest the men and graze the horses. We are completely tired out, and the splendid bathing in the cool, pure waters of the little river is very welcome. Our horses revel in the fresh fields of clover, and my faithful steed, "Sam," is buck-leaping all over the pasture. I hope, in this exhibition of his exuberant spirits, he won't break his back.

Our losses on May 3d were as follows : —

3 Non-commissioned officers, killed ;
3 Non-commissioned officers, wounded ;
7 Privates, killed and wounded ;
3 Commissioned officers, captured ;
2 Non-commissioned officers, captured :
21 Privates, captured ;
6 Drivers, captured.
___

Total, 45.

Guns captured by enemy from Washington Artillery : —

First Company, 2 3-inch Rifles ;
Second   "   1 12-pounder Howitzer ;
Third   "   1 12-pounder Napoleon ;
Fourth   "   1 12-pounder Howitzer ;
  "   "   1 12-pounder Napoleon.
          ___

Total,   6

These officers and men were killed, wounded, and captured while bravely fighting their guns, and from no lack of courage and devotion on their part ; but, owing to the exigencies of the case, they were put in exposed positions, with meagre infantry support, and were run over by mere weight of numbers, after repulsing again and again the enemy's attacks.

The one gun of the Third company on the plank-road, with the Twenty-first Mississippi regiment, twice broke the two regiments of Col. Johns, who also received the fire of the two howitzers of the Second and Fourth companies.

The First company, with two rifle guns, held its post on Marye's Hill, supported by the Eighteenth Mississippi (who were in the road behind the stone-wall), firing at the enemy until he came to the very muzzles of its guns, almost literally sweeping away the column of four regiments under Col. Spear, who was killed, and with no faltering, no thought of falling back, surrendered only when completely surrounded, front and rear, by the Sixth Maine regiment of Burnham's Light Division (which had overcome the Eighteenth regiment, killing and capturing half of them), — not one man leaving his post to seek safety, thus preserving the honor and distinction of the Washington Artillery, gained on many battle-fields.

The sacrifice was worthy of the object attained, delaying, as it did, twenty thousand men from reaching Gen. Lee's flank at Chancellorsville, until too late to succor his adversary.[1]

---

[1] List of killed, wounded, and missing in the Battalion Washington Artillery, May 3, 1863 : —

FIRST COMPANY.

Killed. — Sergeant W. H. West, Corporal T. J. Lutman, Private J. E. Florence.

As a solace for our woes, caused by the loss our six guns on Marye's Hill, we have received the following letter from the Chief Ordnance Officer of the Army of Northern Virginia, which we appreciate : —

ORDNANCE OFFICE, A.N. VA., May 7, 1863.

COL. J. B. WALTON, *Chief of Artillery, First Army Corps :* —

SIR, — I have the honor to acknowledge the receipt of your letter of May 5. I have as yet received no official report of the number of guns captured in the recent engagement. I have only heard of eleven pieces. I regret that I can-

---

Wounded. — Corporal C. A. Everett, — taken prisoner.

Captured. — Captain C. W. Squires; Lieutenants Edward Owen, J. M. Galbraith; Sergeant W. T. Hardie; Privates R. Alsobrook, H. B. Berthelot, Jno. Bozant, Wm. Fellowes, Jr., J. R. Harby, M. E. Harris, Jas. McCormack, A. Micou, J. Myers, N. B. Phelps, E. Peychaud, C. Peychaud, P. Siebrecht, T. S. Turner, Sumpter Turner, Van Vinson, John Eshman, John Hoch, James Kennedy, P. Rierson, E. W. Smith.

SECOND COMPANY.

Wounded. — Lieutenant George B. De Russy. Privates Barton Kirk, Phil Von Coln.

Captured. — Privates H. D. Summers, Wm. Giffin, H. D. Coleman.

THIRD COMPANY.

Wounded. — Corporal R. P. Many, and prisoner; Privates, L. Adam, Otto Frank.

Captured. — Sergeant Jno. T. Handy; Privates, W. P. Noble, Benjamin Dick.

FOURTH COMPANY.

Killed. — Corporal L. L. Lewis.

Wounded. — Corporal J. Valentine, Artificer J. Callahan, Driver J. Anderson.

Of all the battles fought by the Army of Northern Virginia, that of Chancellorsville stands first as illustrating the consummate audacity and military skill of the commander, and the valor and determination of the men.

General Lee, with 57,000 troops of all arms, intrenched along the line of hills south of the Rappahannock, near Fredericksburg, was confronted by General Hooker, with the Army of the Potomac, 132,000 strong, occupying the bluffs on the other side of the river.

. . . .

General Hooker, with the bulk of his army, crossed at the upper fords, and in an able manner and wonderfully short time had concentrated four of his seven corps, numbering 56,000 men, at Chancellorsville.

. . . .

not give you much encouragement as to the prospect of your Battalion getting a portion of them, as those batteries of the Second Corps that were engaged at Chancellorsville have already laid claim to all of them. I will, however, lay your communication before the General commanding for his decision. While there is universal regret expressed at the misfortune which your fine Battalion has met, I have not heard an insinuation of blame to be attached to the officers or men of your command. Common-sense and justice would be shocked at such an idea.

Very respectfully,

BRISCOE G. BALDWIN,
Lieutena -Colonel and Chief of Ordnance, A.N. Va.

Lee at once determined on the movement, the least expected by his opponent. The advance of the enemy was attacked with vigor and soon put on the defensive.

. . . .

On the 5th, Hooker sought safety beyond the Rappahannock."— *Taylor's four years with Lee, page 85.*

Extract from the Diary of Lieutenant Edward Owen, First Company, Washington Artillery, captured at Marye's Hill, Fredericksburg, May 3, 1863: —

May 3. About 10 o'clock the enemy (Sedgwick's corps) suddenly charged our position on Marye's Hill. We had two guns of First company, two guns of Third company, and two guns of Parker's Battery, under Lieutenant Brown, and the Eighteenth Mississippi regiment, three hundred and eighteen muskets strong. At the same time a very heavy body charged opposite Falmouth.

We poured canister into them from our works, and drove them back in great confusion, when, much to our astonishment, we were fired upon from the rear by the Sixth Maine, which had run over our infantry on our left, in front of Marye's House, and came in our rear while we were busy with those in our front, and took us in at our posts. Our last gun was fired by Sergeant W. T. Hardie and Sumpter Turner, when six or eight Federals were trying to get into the embrasure. It blew them to atoms. They also captured Lieutenant Brown with the two guns of Parker's Battery, and one gun of the Third Company, Washington Artillery.

The enemy were very much frightened and excited when on Marye's Hill. They fired on us after we had surrendered, killing Corporal Lutman and wounding J. C. Florence severely in the hip; they fired off their guns in the air, etc. Wanted to turn our guns on Lieutenant Brown. Some one told them they were spiked, and they left them alone. They were not spiked, however.

We had thirty men captured, and Captain Squires, Lieutenant Galbraith and myself. Corporal Everett wounded in the arm. Adjutant Oscar Stuart, of the Eighteenth Mississippi, was killed after he had surrendered with a white flag, his brains deliberately blown out by a drunken soldier. One soldier of the Eighteenth Mississippi (Blake White, Company D), lying on the ground wounded in the leg, had his skull mashed by a Federal soldier with the butt of his musket. The enemy had evidently been filled up with whisky. The Eighteenth Mississippi was posted four paces apart along the stone-wall. On the left the Fourth company lost two guns and the Second company one, on the telegraph road. Our caissons got off safely.

We were taken to General Patrick's (Provost-marshal) head-quarters, near Falmouth, and paroled, although we were still under guard. Were treated very well and hospitably by Capts. Kimball and Cox, of General Patrick's staff.

May 4. Reached Washington, and were marched through the streets to the police-station.

. . . .

In the evening the officers were taken to the old Capitol prison, and very well fixed, six of us in a room, with beds. Three hundred and twenty-nine in our crowd.

May 6. The Washington Artillery boys have been sent to Fort Delaware.

May 9. Papers are full of Hooker's strategic move, some denouncing him, and others trying to shield him. Our rations are coffee and salt meat for breakfast. Bread and meat at dinner.

May 12. The "Richmond Examiner," of the 7th, says: "The Washington Artillery lost their guns on Marye's Hill by the pusillanimity of some infantry regiments." Such is by no means the case. The Eighteenth Mississippi, Col. Griffin, our supports, fought like tigers. Some fought with stones after the enemy reached the stone-wall. They had a hand-to-hand fight, clubbing their guns; many were bayonetted after the enemy got over the stone-wall. They did all that men could do, but were overpowered by the heavy columns of the enemy. Many were killed after they had surrendered, so infuriated were the Yanks at the stubborn resistance they had met.

May 14. It is very amusing to read the Northern reports of the capture of Marye's Hill. They admit their assaulting column was three thousand strong. Our force was less than four hundred (Eighteenth Mississippi). They speak of "Lieutenant-Colonels riding up on black horses, and, waving swords over us, ordered us to surrender, and that we were cowed at the determined bravery of their men." I never saw such a frightened and excited mob as they were.

From their accounts I almost doubt of my being taken on Marye's Hill, they are so different from what I witnessed.

May 20. Have been exchanged, and leave Washington for "Dixie land," — about three hundred of us, — and a happy set we were.

May 23. Reached Richmond.

May 27. Call on Miss S——, Mrs. Davis, and was introduced to the President. Miss H—— will be here to-morrow, so will wait and see her.

May 29. Return to duty in the field, and was settled before night same as before trip to Washington. The balance of our men captured at Marye's are beginning to arrive in camp.

Extract from a letter of Gen. Fitz Lee, dated Richmond, June 1, 1883.

. . . .

In my address on Chancellorsville I dealt particularly with Jackson's flank march and attack on the enemy. The guns of the Washington Artillery did not participate in that movement, but were left behind with Early at Fredericksburg, and fought with their accustomed dash and courage against Sedgwick.

. . . .

Indeed, I can truthfully say that no soldiers of the Army of Northern Virginia incurred greater hardships with more cheerfulness, or stood steadier when the lightning scorched the very ground under their feet than the justly celebrated Washington Artillery. It was their Miller Owen, I believe, who spoke humorously of the late war " as a little difficulty between the Washington Artillery and the United States." Suppose it was, the Artillery, at any rate, has no reason to be ashamed of the record. Oh no! the Battalion has no better friend than yours respectfully and truly. — FITZ LEE.

CHAPTER XI.

GETTYSBURG.

Army in Motion. — Culpeper. — Stuart's Cavalry Review. — Death of Pelham. — Chester Gap. — Ewell in Winchester. — Defeat of Milroy. — Fording the Potomac. — Lee's Orders. — Chambersburg. — Gettysburg. — Gen. Reynolds Killed. — Lee on Seminary Hill. — Col. Freemantle. — Capt. Ross. — Gen. Barksdale Killed. — Hood Wounded. — Grand Cannonade. — Pickett's Charge. — Retreat. — Williamsport. — Pettigrew Killed. — Crossing the Potomac.

THE use of a flag of truce by the enemy on the 3d of May, in front of the Eighteenth Mississippi Regiment, has caused much just indignation at head-quarters. It was unfair and unusual, and brought forth the following order : —

HEAD-QUARTERS FIRST ARMY CORPS,
NEAR FREDERICKSBURG, May 23, 1863.
GENERAL ORDERS NO. 13 : —

. . . .

II. Flags of truce will not be received unless they are sent by the Commanding General of the enemy's army. Parties sending flags of truce to make arrangements for surrender will be allowed five minutes to stack arms and surrender as prisoners of war. Bearers of *other* flags *will be arrested and held as prisoners of war, or as spies*, as the circumstances may warrant.

By command of Lieut.-General Longstreet,

G. M. SORREL,
A.A.G.

To COL. J. B. WALTON, *Chief of Artillery, First Army Corps.*

On the 4th day of June, 1863, the Battalion Washington Artillery, after having had a long rest at Stannard's Farm, resumed active operations, with ten guns, under command of Major Eshleman. Col. Alexander, with his battalion of artillery, twenty-five guns, joined the column of march, moving towards Spottsylvania Court-House. These two battalions, thirty-five guns, form the reserve artillery of Longstreet's *corps d'armée*, and are under the immediate command of Col. J. B. Walton, Chief of Artillery.[1]   On the 5th of June the march carried

---

[1] HEAD–QUARTERS FIRST ARMY CORPS, June 2, 1863.

COLONEL: — The Lieut.-General commanding desires you to move for Culpeper Court-House, *via* Raccoon Ford, with Alexander's and Eshleman's Washington Artillery Battalions, at daylight, on the morning of the 4th instant.

Cabell's battalion will move with McLaws's division, and you will please direct the commanding officer to report to-morrow to Gen. McLaws to receive instructions for his movement.

The battalions of Dearing and Henry will be left with the divisions with which they are at present serving, and will receive orders from Maj.-Gens. Pickett and Hood.

It will be important for you to move promptly with the two battalions above directed, so as to be out of the way of the troops that will probably move on the same day.

I am, Colonel, very respectfully,
G. M. SORREL,
A.A. Gen'l.

To COL. WALTON, *Chief of Artillery.*

The following orders were issued: —

HEAD–QUARTERS ARTILLERY CORPS, June 2, 1863.

GENERAL ORDERS No. —

I. Under the recent organization of the Army of Northern Virginia into three corps a corresponding adjustment of the artillery battalions becomes necessary. And under special directions from the Commanding General the following arrangement is ordered: —

First Corps. — Lieut.-General Longstreet: Cabell's battalion, Dearing's battalion, Henry's battalion, Alexander's battalion (reserve), Eshleman's battalion (reserve).

Second Corps. — Lieut.-General Ewell: Carter's battalion, Jones's battalion, Andrew's battalion, Brown's battalion (reserve), Nelson's battalion (reserve).

Third Corps. — Lieut.-General A. P. Hill: McIntosh's battalion, Garnett's battalion, Walker's battalion (reserve), Cutt's battalion (reserve).

us by the old Wilderness Tavern, where we learned that Gen. Longstreet slept last night. Fording the Rappahannock at Raccoon Ford, our march on the 6th brought the battalions to Culpeper Court-House, where they went into camp. Our whole force is being transferred to this place, leaving Gen. Hooker behind us at Stafford Heights, opposite Fredericksburg. Yesterday Gen. Jeb Stewart had a grand review of his cavalry corps; 10,000 sabres in line, — so said.

Took occasion to ride to our friend Mr. Ned Gaines, and dined with his charming family. Miss Nettie is as lovely as ever.

The Chiefs of Artillery of the First and Second Corps remain as heretofore, and the battalions designated in these corps will report through their chiefs. The battalions designated in the Third Corps will report through the Chief of Artillery who may be nominated by the corps commander and approved by the Commanding General.

II. Towards forming the new battalion required for the Third Corps, Cols. Brown and Alexander will each report one of their batteries to be detached, and these two batteries will be by them directed to report to the Chief of Artillery for the Third Corps, that they may, with Wyatt's battery, now with Gen. Pettigrew's brigade, be formed into a battalion. Field officers will soon be assigned.

W. N. PENDLETON,
Brig. Gen'l, Chief of Artillery.

HEAD-QUARTERS ARTILLERY CORPS, June 4, 1863.
ORDER NO. : —

In accordance with General Orders No. 43, June 13, 1862, A. & I. G. O., First Lieut. Joseph Norcom, Fourth company Washington Artillery, being strongly recommended as fully competent for the position, is hereby announced as Captain of said company, vice Capt. B. F. Eshleman, promoted, to date from March 26, 1863, the date of Major Eshleman's promotion.

Second Lieut. George E. Apps to be a First Lieutenant from same date, in said company, being also strongly recommended for promotion.

Second Lieut. Andrew Hero, Third company Washington Artillery, is hereby announced as First Lieutenant, vice First Lieut. Isaac W. Brewer, killed in action 23d August, 1862. His promotion to date from that period.

By command of Brig.-Gen. Pendleton.

D. D. PENDLETON,
A.A. Gen'l.

On the 8th A. P. Hill's corps arrived from Fredericksburg. Hooker must feel lonesome without neighbors. He is left alone in his glory.

The first sound that saluted my ears upon awakening this A.M. (9th) was the reports of artillery in the distance. It appears that the Federal cavalry crossed the Rappahannock at Beverly Ford, and at daylight attacked Stuart. Our people were surprised, and a good many were captured, but rallied and drove back the enemy.

The Second South Carolina and the Fourth Virginia Cavalry were engaged. General Butler, of South Carolina, lost a leg. The engagement lasted all day, fighting from

---

HEAD–QUARTERS ARMY NORTHERN VIRGINIA, June 4, 1863.
GENERAL ORDERS NO. 69 : —

.   .   .   .

IV. For harmony of movement on the march and in action on the battle-field, the artillery of each corps will be under the orders of the corps command-ers. The same rule will apply to cavalry when attached to any corps for duty.

The general Chief of Artillery, acting under the immediate orders of the commanding general, *may*, in battle, command the artillery on any part of the ine, and use it at such points as may be needed.

By command of Gen. Lee,
R. H. CHILTON,
A.A. Gen'l.

HEAD–QUARTERS DEP'T NORTHERN VIRGINIA, June 4, 1863.
SPECIAL ORDERS NO. 151 : —

.   .   .   .

X. In accordance with the recommendation of the Chief of Artillery, made under Par. II., General Orders No. 69, current series, from these head-quarters, the following-named officers are assigned to the command of the artillery under the recent organization : —

Col. J. B. Walton, of the First Corps.

Col. V. Crutchfield, of the Second Corps, his place to be filled, while disabled by his wound, by Col. J. T. Brown.

Col. R. L. Walker, of the Third Corps.

By command of Gen. Lee,
W. H. TAYLOR,
A.A.G.

Brandy Station to Beverly Ford. The gallant Colonel John Pelham, of the artillery, was killed to-day. His death is greatly deplored.[1]

During the engagement all of our infantry and some artillery were moved out from their quarters to be on hand if needed. At dark all was quiet, and the troops returned to camp. Some of the old officers say this was a very creditable cavalry fight.

Dined again to-day with Miss Nettie, and had ice-cream.

On the 10th, rode over the battle-field of yesterday with General Stuart; saw about fifty of the enemy's dead. Stuart was looking for the body of Colonel Percy Wyndham, who is reported to have fallen. Went down to Beverly Ford, and gathered strawberries in view of the

---

[1] Next morning, about an hour before daylight, I was aroused from my slumbers by hearing some one riding up to my tent, and startled out of bed by the voice of one of the couriers Stuart had taken with him, who, with much agitation of manner, reported that the General had been engaged with Fitz Lee's brigade in a sanguinary battle against far superior numbers of the enemy, and had beaten them, but at the cost of many lives, and among them that of Pelham, the gallant chief of our horse artillery. Poor Pelham! He had but just received his promotion to the rank of Lieutenant-Colonel, and now met his death in a comparatively small engagement, after passing safely through so many great battles. Being on a visit of pleasure, he had been taken unprepared, and, at the first sound of the cannon, hastened, unarmed, on a horse borrowed from Sweeney, to the field of action. His batteries had not come up to answer the enemy's cannon, but his ardor would not allow him to wait for their arrival, and he rushed forward into the thickest of the fight, cheering on our men and animating them by his example. When one of our regiments, advancing to charge, was received with such a terrible fire by the enemy as to cause it to waver, Pelham galloped up to them, shouting, " Forward, boys! forward to victory and glory! " and at the same moment a fragment of a shell, which exploded close over his head, penetrated the back part of the skull, and stretched the young hero insensible on the ground. He was carried at once to Culpeper, where the young ladies of Mr. S.'s family tended him with sisterly care; but he never again recovered his senses, and the same evening his noble spirit departed. — *Van Boercke's Memoirs.*

enemy's pickets.   Saw our battle-field of last year, and the graves of our comrades in St. James's church-yard.

Requiescat in pace.
" They have fought their last battle."

On the 4th, Ewell's corps left Culpeper, and no one appears to know where he will " figger now."   We are all in the dark as to what our summer campaign is to be.   The enemy don't seem to be badly disposed.   Some talk of going into Maryland again ; but I don't think the move a popular one.

On the 15th our marching order came,[1] and we hitched up and took the road towards the valley, and camped near Woodville.   On the 16th passed through Sperryville and Little Washington.   Dined with our old friend Mr. Lane, at his beautiful house, " Rose Hill."   While at dinner a small but inquisitive child broke my field-glasses into remarkably small bits.

On the 17th we crossed the Blue Ridge Mountains at Chester Gap, and enjoyed a magnificent view from the

---

[1] HEAD-QUARTERS FIRST ARMY CORPS,
CULPEPER COURT-HOUSE, June 14, 1863.
Midnight.

COLONEL : — The Lieutenant-General commanding, directs that you move your command to-morrow afternoon for Winchester, taking the turnpike from here as your route.   Have all your needful preparations made to-morrow morning, and advise me early of the hour at which you will probably move.
I am, Colonel, very respectfully,
Your obedient servant,
G. M. SORREL,
A.A. Gen'l.

By your command is meant, for the present, the battalions of Alexander and Eshleman.   The others will move with the divisions to which they are temporarily assigned.

crest. We could see for miles on either hand. We marched through Front Royal and encamped on the banks of the beautiful Shenandoah. Here we enjoyed a pleasant swim in its waters, and refreshed ourselves to our hearts' content. News from Ewell came to-day. He has captured Winchester with 4,700 prisoners, 30 cannon, and a large amount of quartermaster's stores. Hays's Louisiana brigade led the charge upon the principal fort with their usual vim and gallantry.[1] Just our luck to be behind when

---

[1] Our line having meanwhile lengthened until it reached from Fredericksburg to the valley, Ewell suddenly pounced down on Winchester, and stormed its heights, taking 4,000 prisoners and a large amount of war material.

The way in which this was accomplished, according to Gen. Early's report, was by an assault made on a hill to the north-west of the enemy's works. A position having been selected, — that is, the side from which the attack should be made, — Early led his guns and infantry by obscure paths to within a short distance of the hill to be stormed. His movements thus far had been concealed by the woods, and he had been fortunate enough to miss meeting any of the enemy's scouts. Meanwhile Gordon had been making an advance from the opposite side of the town.

Jones's Artillery (twenty guns) were now put in readiness to support the charge on the storming side, and Hays's Louisiana brigade, which had many times before enjoyed the honor of being selected for similar work, was put under cover, and allowed to gaze at the hill in front, covered with recently felled timber, at the bastion works with which the fort was crowned, and at the two lines of breastwork with which the fort was crowned, and at the two lines of breastwork further beyond.

It was now an hour by sun, and the men were burning with impatience. Twice Gen. Hays made ready to move, and was detained by Early's orders; a third time the detaining order was sent to him by Early, who could not believe but what the enemy were keeping a better look-out than they did. But finally the twenty guns opened simultaneously, which was the *laisser faire* for action, and the next moment, before the enemy had recovered from his astonishment at seeing troops in this direction, and, in spite of orders, Hays and his men were crawling through the brushwood, and up the steep slope. "He drove," says Gen. Early, "the enemy from his fortifications in fine style," and with some of his infantry, who had been, purposely for such occasions, trained as cannoneers, he opened with the enemy's own rifled pieces, thus preventing all efforts at recapture. The enemy abandoned the whole town the next morning. Milroy fled towards the Potomac, but too late to save his infantry, who now found themselves intercepted by Johnson's division. Twenty-five guns were captured, and only a few horsemen, who were with Milroy, succeeded in reaching the Potomac. — *Bartlett's Story.*

there's any plunder to be gathered. We can imagine Ewell's men regaling themselves on champagne and peaches and cream.

On the 18th we forded the Shenandoah at Morgan's Ford and camped at Randolph's Grove, at Millwood, — one of the loveliest spots we ever saw, plenty of large trees, green grass, and a mountain stream of cool water running in front of our tents. We enjoyed bathing in a natural stone bath-tub, where the water rushed in at one end with a fall of several feet, affording us a fine shower. We have been marching to-day through Clark county, the most beautiful part of Virginia. The fine residences and plantations give evidence of wealth and comfort. Gen. Longstreet and the surgeons have pitched their head-quarters near us. We learn that the enemy are following along after us and watching our movements with their cavalry, on the other side of the Blue Ridge, and our cavalry and theirs indulge in skirmishing at long-taw daily.

The following order was received to-day : —

Ashby's Gap, Encamped at Millwood,
Head–quarters, Paris, June 18, 1863.

Colonel : — Please send Col. Alexander to me early in the morning, — say daylight, — to aid me in selecting line of battle in this (Ashby's) Gap. Have your horses ready during the early part of the day to move at a moment's notice. If not called before three o'clock turn out the horses to grass. Let the horses have grass as much as possible at night. Your battalion (Washington Artillery) will probably be required to-morrow at Snicker's Gap, and Alexander's here.

Most respectfully,
J. LONGSTREET,
Lieut.-Gen., Commanding.

To Col. J. B. Walton, Chief Artillery.

On the 19th we remained in camp all day, with horses harnessed and ready to move out at a moment's notice. Three hundred and fifty prisoners passed by under guard. One of them was aid to Gen. Hooker, — a Major Stewart. On the 21st I managed to get permission to ride into Winchester. The plunder was all gone, of course, but a soft-hearted quartermaster presented me with a pair of blue cavalry pantaloons, and my wardrobe needed that addition exactly. "Thanks much, Ewell's men ! — we 'owe you *one* '*!* " On the 22d the enemy moved away from the other side of the mountain, and our cavalry has gone in pursuit.[1] On the 24th we were again on the road, and, passing through Winchester, encamped at Bunker Hill, after a march of twenty-two miles. While passing through Winchester I called to see Miss Josie Carson and Miss Hattie H., and breakfasted with the latter. On the 25th we passed through Martinsburg on the march, where we saw Miss Belle Boyd. As usual she wanted buttons, but we "cut and ran." She apparently has "no soul above buttons." In the afternoon we crossed the Potomac at

---

[1] HEAD-QUARTERS, FIRST ARMY CORPS,
MILLWOOD, VA., June 23, 1863.

The division and reserve artillery of this corps will move to-morrow morning, at three o'clock for Hagerstown, Maryland, via Berryville, Smithfield, and Williamsport, in the following order of march : —

    1st. Pickett's division.
    2d. Walton's reserve artillery.
    3d. Hood's division.
    4th. McLaws's division.

The movement of each command will begin punctually at the hour named. The daily march will be about fifteen miles.

. . . .

By command of Lieut.-Gen. Longstreet.
G. M. SORREL,
A.A. Gen'l.

Williamsport, Maryland, and encamped one mile outside of the town in a very heavy and driving rain. When the army started to ford the river the brigades filed off to the right and left, and the men denuded themselves of their nether garments and shoes, making a bundle of them, and carrying them and their cartridge-boxes upon their shoulders. A number of carriages containing ladies, mostly young and guileless, crossed the ford, coming from Maryland, as our men were crossing to the other side. The sight of thousands of " Confeds " in the water and in the fields, "*sans culotte*," must have been astounding and novel in the extreme, and something the young ladies would not soon forget. Fifty thousand men without their trousers on can't be passed in review every day of the week.

As we marched through Martinsburg McElroy led the chorus, and the boys sang " Upi dee ! " and some reference was made to hanging the President of the United States " on a sour-apple tree ; " but of course they didn't mean it.

On the 26th we marched, in a drizzling rain, to Hagerstown, and on to Greencastle, Pennsylvania. The farmers apparently did not know a war was going on. Gen. Lee's orders are positive against any appropriation of private property ;[1] even chickens, milk, and butter were sacred.

---

[1] HEAD–QUARTERS ARMY NORTHERN VIRGINIA,
CHAMBERSBURG, PA., 27th June, 1863.

GENERAL ORDERS No. 73 : —

The Commanding General has observed with marked satisfaction the conduct of the troops on the march, and confidently anticipates results commensurate with the high spirit they have manifested.

No troops could have displayed, or better performed, the arduous marches of the past ten days.

Sergeant Ellis was detected by the officer of the day with a pair of fat geese; but he convinced the Lieutenant that it was "all on the square," and that he had paid for them; we believe the officer dined with him that day. We established head-quarters for the night at a very fine large farm-house, and were well entertained by the hospitable occupants, man and wife. The couple were German, and were employed at one hundred dollars a year to attend to the farm in the absence of the owners. Upon taking leave of our hosts in the morning we handed them two silver half-dollar pieces, which they received with expressions of surprise and delight. Hans said, "Johanna, put dis silber mit der du-bit piece dot you got last Christmas. Py jimminy, dis war is big luck for some peebles!"

Their conduct in other respects has, with few exceptions, been in keeping with their character as soldiers, and entitles them to approbation and praise.

There have, however, been instances of forgetfulness on the part of some that they have in keeping the yet unsullied reputation of this army, and that the duties exacted of us by civilization and Christianity are not less obligatory in the country of the enemy than in our own.

The Commanding General considers that no greater disgrace could befall the army, and through it our whole people, than the perpetration of the barbarous outrages upon the unarmed and defenceless, and the wanton destruction of private property that has marked the course of the enemy in our own country.

Such proceedings not only degrade the perpetrators and all connected with them, but are subversive of the discipline and efficiency of the army, and destructive of the ends of our present movement.

It must be remembered that we make war only upon armed men, and that we cannot take vengeance for the wrongs our people have suffered without lowering ourselves in the eyes of all whose abhorrence has been excited by the atrocities of our enemies, and offending against Him to whom vengeance belongeth, without whose favor and support our efforts must all prove in vain.

The Commanding General, therefore, earnestly exhorts the troops to abstain with most scrupulous care from unnecessary and wanton injury to private property, and he enjoins all officers to arrest and bring to summary punishment all who shall, in any way, offend against the orders on this subject.

(Signed)   R. E. LEE,
                            General.

We moved on to Chambersburg, passing many fine houses, and large barns full of grain and forage; but "Massa Robert" won't permit any confiscations, and not a fence-rail is disturbed, much to the disgust of the negro cooks, who cannot understand why the army should act so differently from the Federal armies in Virginia. As we entered Chambersburg we met many scowling faces of men who, we thought, were in good enough condition to be in the Federal army, and be carrying a musket.

On the 28th we lay in camp all day; in the evening rode over to Gen. Lee's head-quarters on the Gettysburg road.

The General has little of the pomp and circumstance of war about his person. A Confederate flag marks the whereabouts of his head-quarters, which are here in a little enclosure of some couple of acres of timber. There are about half-a-dozen tents and as many baggage-wagons and ambulances. The horses and mules for these, besides those of a small — very small — escort, are tied up to trees or grazing about the place. The General has a private carriage, or ambulance as it is called, of his own; but he never uses it. It formerly belonged to the Federal Gen. Pope.

He was evidently annoyed at the absence of Stuart and the cavalry, and asked several officers, myself among the number, if we knew anything of the whereabouts of Stuart?

The eyes and ears of the army are evidently missing and are greatly needed by the commander.

On the 30th of June the two battalions of reserve artillery marched from Chambersburg towards Gettysburg and camped at Greenwood; raining all day and sloppy.

On the 1st of July the following note was received : —

HEAD–QUARTERS FIRST CORPS, July 1, 1863, 10 A.M.

COLONEL : — The Commanding General desires you to move your command out this morning, following Gen. Hood, and camping near him on the other side of the mountain.

Gen. McLaws will move first, when Johnson's division, now passing, shall be out of his way, and Gen. Hood will follow Gen. McLaws.

It will accordingly be some hours before you will have to move out.

I am, Colonel, very respectfully, your obedient servant,

G. M. SORREL,

To COL. J. B. WALTON, *Chief of Artillery.*   *A. A. G.*

The two battalions (Washington Artillery and Col. Alexander's) remained in camp all day, and at midnight the following note was received by courier : —

HEAD–QUARTERS, NEAR GETTYSBURG, July 1st, 5.30 P.M.

COLONEL : — The General Commanding desires you to come on to-night as far as you can without distressing your men and animals.

Ewell and Hill have sharply engaged the enemy to-day, and you will be wanted for to-morrow's battle.

Let us know where you stop to-night. The action to-day has been vigorous and successful.

The enemy was driven two or three miles and out of Gettysburg without hesitation.

Gen. Rodes now occupies the town.

The enemy's loss in prisoners and casualties considerable; ours light.

Maj.-Gen. Heth wounded, not dangerously.

I am, very respectfully,

G. M. SORREL,

COL. J. B. WALTON, *Chief of Artillery.*   *A. A. G.*

Immediately upon receiving this order the batteries were hitched up, and, after waiting until 2.30 A.M. for a clear road, began our march, and at 8 A.M. reported, ready for action, to Gen. Longstreet on the field. The battalions were ordered to halt in an open field close by, and await orders.

It is said the enemy is on Cemetery Hill, and that Ewell could have taken it last evening. Now we will have a tussle for it.

Gen. Lee and his staff are on Seminary Hill, near the town of Gettysburg, and with him are Generals Longstreet, A. P. Hill, and Heth. The last was wounded yesterday in the head, and has it bandaged up this morning.

Here we also met the Hon. Francis Lawley, of the English Parliament, and correspondent of the "London Times," Capt. Ross, of the Austrian Huzzars, and Col. Freemantle, of the Coldstream Guards, British army. They are all equipped with field-glasses and *pocket-pistols.*

At about 4 P.M. rode to the right of our line, where Gen. Longstreet was forming, in a small wood, his corps for attack. Alexander's, Cabell's, and Henry's battalions of artillery accompanied the corps, Col. Alexander commanding. The Washington Artillery will be held in reserve on "Seminary Hill," near Gen. Lee's head-quarters.

Gen. Longstreet rode up and down the line, occasionally dismounting and going forward to get a better view of the enemy.

The ground before us was plain and open, but beyond were hills covered with rifle-pits, and bristling with cannon. The Federals also had possession of the open ground below in front of their works, and their foremost guns were about a quarter of a mile from the wood we were in. A battery in a peach-orchard was firing at one of ours not far off.

As we passed Barksdale's Mississippi brigade the General came up and said to Longstreet, " I wish you would let me go in, General ; I would take that battery in five minutes."—" Wait a little," said Longstreet ; " we are all going in presently." Gen. Barksdale said to me, skaking me by the hand, "I hope we will have better luck this time with your guns than we had on Marye's Hill." He referred to the 3d of May.

The men were as eager as their leader, and those in the front line began to pull down the fence behind which they were lying. "Don't do that, or you will draw the enemy's fire," said Longstreet. Soon afterwards the General called for his horse, mounted, dashed to the front, gave the word, and, waving his hat, led the line forward himself. We all followed him.

It was a glorious sight ; the men who had been lying down sprang to their feet and went in with a will ; not one fell out of line unless he was really hurt. On swept the line, breaking out with a yell when they came face to face with the foe, but, on the whole silently. The guns in the peach-orchard were pounced upon, and half of them taken in a trice ; the rest limbered up and made off in a hurry.

Hundreds of prisoners were taken, and everything was going on so satisfactorily that, for a time, it was thought that we would drive the enemy to and beyond the heights.

But, at a critical moment, Gen. Hood was severely wounded, and Gen. Barksdale killed, and their men, at the very moment of apparent victory, hesitated, halted, and at length fell back, losing thereby more men than they would have done had they continued the advance. But still we gained decided advantages, taking many prisoners and four guns, and getting possession of the ground up to the foot of the hill, and the Emmittsburg turnpike.

I rode back to where the Washington Artillery was halted, near Gen. Lee's head-quarters. Col. Freemantle and Gen. A. P. Hill had climbed high trees, and were trying to see the operations on the right through their field-glasses.

At 7.30 P.M. Longstreet sent for the Washington Artillery, and we went at a quick pace over a bad road along the borders of Willoughby Run, over stumps and logs. It was quite dark when we reached Longstreet's neighborhood, and, by his orders, the command was placed in bivouac for the night. The firing had ceased, and all operations were over for the day.

I rode back towards Seminary Hill, to find, if possible, the field where our wagons and the Second Rhode Island ambulance had been parked, to get my blanket. On my way, I overtook Major Fairfax, of Gen. Longstreet's staff, conducting, under guard, nearly a thousand prisoners. Fairfax is a little puzzled about his locality, and asked me to stay with him; so I remained, and between us we got the prisoners and guard safely to Seminary Hill. Among the prisoners was Brig.-Gen. Graham, who asked us the name of the general officer who led the charge to-day. We told him it was Longstreet. He said, " Our generals don't do that sort of thing." He seemed very civil, and Fairfax dismounted a courier and gave the horse to Gen. Graham to ride.

It was one o'clock when I found our head-quarters

and Colonel Walton. I fed my horse, ate a little supper, and crawled under my blanket. I had been in the saddle twenty-three hours, and was very tired, and slept without rocking.

At daylight on July 3d we were awakened by the roar of artillery on the right of our lines. So, after swallowing hastily a cup of black coffee, and cramming a few biscuits into our haversacks, away we galloped to the front. Arriving at the field where we had left the battalion last evening, we found it had been removed by Col. Alexander, and, upon looking farther, found it in position on the Emmittsburg turnpike, on the left of the peach-orchard, on the ground gained yesterday, and on a line with the other batteries of the First Corps, that had already been placed in position along the Emmittsburg turnpike. The guns we had heard were ours (Washington Artillery). They had engaged in an artillery duel with a battery of the enemy. Capt. Norcom had been knocked down and slightly wounded. Two of Capt. Miller's best horses and their driver, Smith, had been killed. The enemy fired a few shots at us. A solid 12-pound ball ricochetted just over our heads.

The enemy occupied this part of the field yesterday when Longstreet charged, and their dead were still lying around. A barn close by was full of wounded. Later it was burned by shells from the enemy's guns.

Gen. Longstreet sent for Col. Walton, and we rode to where the general officers were assembled, and there learned the plans of attack about to be made upon the enemy's position. At a given signal, to be arranged by

Col. Walton, Chief of Artillery, all the guns on the line of the First and the Third Corps — one hundred and thirty-seven — were to open simultaneously upon the batteries of the enemy opposite. After they should be silenced, Pickett's divison (just arrived from Chambersburg), supported by Heth and Wilcox, was to advance and endeavor to pierce the enemy's line, who, we hoped, would be demoralized by our fire.

The signal agreed upon was two guns fired in quick succession by the Washington Artillery, at the peach-orchard. The commanders of all the batteries and battalions of artillery in position were notified, and information of the fact communicated by me to Gen. Longstreet, who was standing with Gen. Pickett in front of the latter's division, which was lying down concealed by the woods from the enemy's view. Gen. Longstreet said, "All right; tell Col. Walton I will send him word when to begin."

At 1.30 P.M. this note was brought by a courier to Col. Walton, as we were sitting on our horses in a grove of oaks on the Emmettsburg pike, opposite the peach-orchard : —

HEAD-QUARTERS, July 3, 1863.

COLONEL : — Let the batteries open; order great care and precision in firing. If the batteries at the peach-orchard cannot be used against the point we intend attacking, let them open on the rocky hill.

Most respectfully,

J. LONGSTREET,
Lieut.-Gen. Commanding.

To COL. WALTON, *Chief of Artillery.*

Instantly orders were given to Major Eshleman to fire

the signal guns, which was done ; and then began the most
furious cannonade the world ever saw. The one hundred
and thirty-seven Confederate guns were belching fire upon
the enemy's lines,[1] who replied with eighty guns more.
Our batteries fired nearly two hours, when the enemy's
guns suddenly slackened their fire, until they hardly returned shot for shot.[2]

---

[1] The guns of the First Corps, engaged in the bombardment at Gettysburg,
July 3, 1863, were as follows : —

Alexander's battalion	25 guns.
Washington Artillery	10 "
Cabell's battalion	15 "
Dearing's "	18 "
Henry's " one battery engaged (full armament, 18 guns)	6 "
	74 "

Report of Col. J. B. Walton, Chief of Artillery, First Corps,
July, 1863 : —

Armament of Third Corps engaged, as reported by Col. R. L. Walker, Chief of Artillery	63 "
Total engaged in artillery duel	137 "

Number and calibre of the guns in First Corps at this date : —

15	3-inch rifles.		
13	10-pounder Parrotts.		
39	12	"	Napoleons.
10	12	"	howitzers.
4	20	"	Parrotts.
5	24	"	howitzers.

Total, 86 guns.

[2] In reference to the cannonade, John Esten Cooke says : "For nearly two
hours this frightful hurly-burly continued, the harsh roar reverberating omi-
nously in the gorges of the hills, and thrown back in crash after crash from
the rocky slopes of the two ridges."

Gen. Hancock says : "Their artillery fire was the most terrific cannonade I
ever witnessed, and the most prolonged. . . . It was a most terrific and
appalling cannonade, — one, possibly, hardly ever paralleled."

Doubleday says : "Battery C., 4th U.S., Lieut. E. Thomas, was in the line
of the Second Corps on July 3. Some of the batteries were so nearly demol-
ished that there was no officer to assume command at the close of the battle."

Soon all was still as death itself. It was but the calm before the storm. Pickett's division, heroes of many battles, had been lying down during the cannonade. They now arose and dressed their lines, the men fully comprehending the serious work before them. Many were heard bidding good-by to comrades a few files from them.

Upon a signal from Col. Alexander, who had been observing the effect of the artillery fire upon the enemy, under the direction of Gen. Longstreet, the whole line moved forward out of the woods in common time. They had nearly a mile of open plain to cross in full sight of the enemy, and in range of his artillery, which had opened again, and to ascend the Cemetery Hill and attack the works thereon.

Steadily they moved forward. McDonald's charge at Wagram was eclipsed. The enemy rose in their works, and from behind stone fences, and poured a storm of lead into them. Men fell by scores, still on they pressed without faltering. Heth's division, commanded by Gen. Pettigrew, now emerged from the woods in *echelon* going to Pickett's support. They went in steadily at first for that purpose, but soon were shaken by the storm of shot and shell that met them. Presently a small column of the enemy emerged from a wood and began to form on their flank. The men saw it, wavered, stopped, and then fell back in a panic, getting terribly punished as they did so. In vain were all efforts to stop them.

Longstreet, who had seen the threatening move, sent Latrobe to warn Gen. Pettigrew, but the rout had commenced before he could meet him. His horse was shot

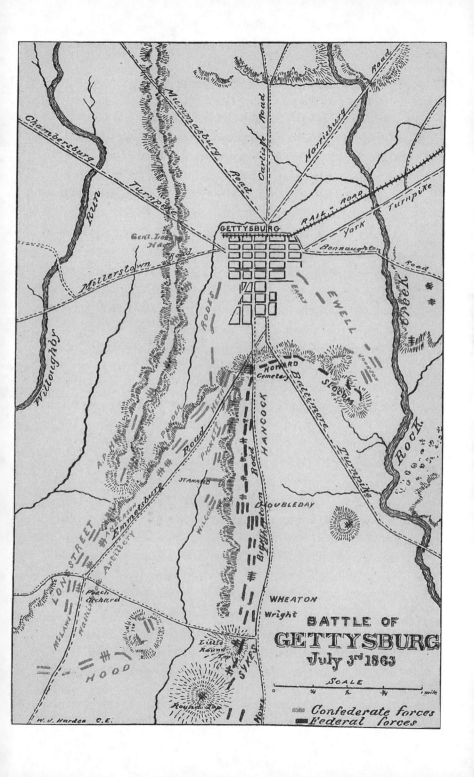

BATTLE OF
GETTYSBURG
July 3rd 1863

SCALE

Confederate forces
Federal forces

under him as he rode across the plain. Pickett, whose men were now well in, and in the flush of victory they deserved, galloped down and implored the men to rally. Many other officers did the same; but it was all in vain. It was a panic such as will, at times, strike the best and bravest troops, and no efforts could induce them to form anew while under that terrific storm of fire. The division lost frightfully, but the worst effect was that Pickett's men, who had behaved so gloriously, were now left to fight alone against overwhelming odds.

Encouraged by their success, the enemy, freshly reinforced, now turned upon them with redoubled energy and courage. Pickett's men continued the charge without supports, and in sight of the enemy, and, moving steadily forward, leaped the breastworks, and, driving back the foe, planted their battle-flags upon eleven captured cannon, amid shouts of victory, — dearly won and short-lived victory.

Then Pickett, who had so proudly said to Longstreet: "I shall lead my division forward, sir!" when he reached the ridge his men had so gallantly charged, had but to look around him to see that the ground could not be held. His supports all gone, his men falling around him, his trusted Generals, Garnett, Armistead, and Kemper, and all the field-officers dead, or wounded unto death, his men fighting over the guns with clubbed muskets and banner-staves, the enemy in front and on each flank, and crowding upon them in overwhelming numbers, he threw away his empty pistol, and, with his great soldier heart almost bursting, gave the order for his remaining braves to fall back.

But they had won undying fame by their glorious on-slaught; and as long as this war is remembered so long will the charge of Pickett and his brave Virginians be spoken of with the same proud satisfaction with which Englishmen tell of the charge of the six hundred at Bala-klava.

Wilcox's division, that had been engaged the previous day, was to have supported Pickett's right, and moved splendidly forward; but, not observing an oblique move-ment of Pickett's that carried him to the left, Wilcox charged on, only to find himself confronting a very superior force of the enemy, and was compelled to fall back with heavy loss.

The remnants of the attacking division who reached our lines in safety, resumed their old places in line of battle, and were ready to give the enemy a warm reception had he advanced from his works; but he seemed satisfied with hav-ing baffled us, and, with an occasional shot from our artillery, the battle on our right is over.[1]   Our boys worked their

---

[1] When Pickett's division was repulsed, and the whole plain covered with fugi-tives, we all expected that Wellington's command at Waterloo, of " Up, guards, and at them!" would be repeated, and that a grand countercharge would be made. But General Meade had made no arrangements to give a return thrust.

.   .   .   .

Meade rode leisurely over to the Fifth Corps, on the left, and told Sykes to send out and see if the enemy in his front was firm and holding on to their posi-tion. A brigade, preceded by skirmishers, was accordingly sent forward, but as Longstreet's troops were well fortified, they resisted the advance, and Meade — finding some hours had elapsed, and that Lee had closed up his lines, and was fortifying against him — gave up all idea of a counter-attack.

.   .   .   .

He (General Lee) did not for a moment imagine that Meade would fail to take advantage of this golden opportunity to crush the army of Northern Virginia, and end the war.

.   .   .   .

The fact is, Meade had no idea of leaving the ridge. I conversed the next

guns splendidly to-day, and my leather bottles were passed around and received with pleasure. Our loss in the Washington Artillery, in killed and wounded, has been heavy : 3 privates killed ; 3 officers and 20 privates wounded ; 39 horses killed. Our ammunition is well-nigh exhausted, and we have not enough in the caissons to fight two hours more.

Lieut. C. H. C. Brown, who commanded the section of the First Company, Washington Artillery, which fired the signal-guns to-day, made the following report : —

"When the Battalion Washington Artillery was assigned its position on the 3d of July, commanding Cemetery Heights, my section was placed upon the right of all the artillery on the line.

"It was assigned to me to fire the two signal-guns for the artillery duel. My right gun, under W. T. Hardie, was directed by him on a battery directly opposite our position, and, at a distance of from eight hundred to a thousand yards, exploded a caisson.

"The second gun, under Sergt. P. O. Fazende, fired at the same battery and exploded another. The gunners had not compared distance, range, or elevation. Of course the battery gave no further trouble in the action that followed.

"When Pickett's division advanced, our firing ceased. Seeing I could be of no use in the position I was in, I advanced my guns to the open field in front of the right flank of Pickett's division to within three hundred yards of the enemy's lines, being enabled from my position to enfilade their entire line where I knew my guns did most excellent service. I was joined here by a gun of some North Carolina battery, name unknown, which, however did not stay long, as the enemy concentrated a heavy fire upon us.

---

morning with a corps commander who had just left him. He said, " *Meade says he thinks he can hold out for part of another day here if they attack him.*"

. . . .

At 6.30 P.M. the firing ceased on the part of the enemy, and, although they retained their position, the next day the battle of Gettysburg was virtually at an end. — *Chancellorsville and Gettysburg.* DOUBLEDAY.

"When Pickett fell back, having exhausted all my canister, my guns were withdrawn.

"While in this advanced position I was severely wounded, and left in the hands of the enemy when the army fell back. I think our guns were the furthest advanced of any on the field."

This afternoon (3d July) the enemy made a desperate attack, with a force of cavalry, on the Emmittsburg road, against our right flank, where the brigades of Robinson, Anderson, and Benning, of Hood's division, were posted.

They charged through some fields on the left of the road, and were decimated by our fire, which encircled them. Stone fences or walls met them in almost every direction when they turned to retreat, and again and again they rode around in their vain endeavors to escape. To add to the slaughter, Maj. Henry's battalion of artillery, of eighteen guns, opened upon them from behind a stone-wall on the road.

Gen. Farnsworth, one of the Federal commanders in the charge, was left upon the field, desperately wounded.

It was related that when he was approached by some of our men, and was asked if he surrendered, he said, with a defiant air, "He would be d—d if he would," and, before he could be prevented, blew his own brains out with his revolver.

It was a gallant charge of the cavalry, but foolhardy and disastrous.

On the 4th of July, 1863, the rising sun shone on the thousands of dead and wounded men lying between the lines of the two contending armies. The Confederates stand firmly upon the ground held yesterday at the close of the battle.

Batteries are in position, but with only a scanty supply of ammunition, but the enemy apparently evinces no curiosity as to our condition. At about noon I rode over to a hill where Longstreet has taken up his position to overlook the whole field. He is looking well, and seems evidently determined to put on the best face possible. " What o'clock is it?" he asks. — "Eleven fifty-five " is my answer. " General," I added, "this is the 'glorious fourth,' we should have a salute from the other side at noon."

Twelve o'clock came, but no salute. " Their artillery was too much crippled yesterday to think of salutes," said the General. " Meade is not in good spirits this morning."

The General then went on to say that last evening, a little after dark, he rode along our skirmish line near the peach-orchard, where he came across a battery of artillery. He was surprised to find it so far in advance of our line of infantry, and inquired whose it was.

A tall officer, quietly smoking a pipe, approached, and said, " I am the captain." It was "Buck" Miller, of the Third Company of Washington Artillery. When he recognized the General he informed him he "was out there to have a little skirmishing on his own account, if the 'Yanks' came out of their holes." The General laughed at the captain's idea of "skirmishing" with 12-pounder Napoleons. Ever since the battle of Sharpsburg (Antietam), when the Third Company held the centre of our line, and Longstreet and staff worked with the guns, Miller has been a great favorite at head-quarters.[1]

---

[1] At 6 P.M. we heard a long and continuous Yankee cheer, which we at first imagined was an indication of an advance; but it turned out to be their recep-

Wagons and ambulances are passing to the rear towards the Potomac. We cannot remain without ammunition, and must retire. We are in momentary expectation that the enemy will advance and interfere with our quiet and orderly arrangements for moving off. Gen. Longstreet desires the smallest battalion of artillery to accompany General Imboden with the trains to Williamsport, and the Washington Artillery, ten guns, under Major Eshleman, is detached for that service.

At 9 P.M. orders were issued to withdraw all the batteries from the lines, and put them on the road to Williamsport. It was dark and raining, and, being Adjutant of the artillery corps, it was my duty to carry out the order. At midnight the withdrawal was completed, and I sought Col. Walton at Gen. Longstreet's camp-fire on the roadside. There were Gen. Lee and staff, Freemantle, Lawley, Ross, and Phillips, and the surgeons. I made my report that the batteries were all off; and tried to take a nap, coiled up on the roots of a tree, — a decided failure. I then sought Cullen's ambulance, and he kindly filled my canteen. I heard Gen. Lee say to Gen. Longstreet (or

tion of a general officer, whom we saw riding down the line, followed by about thirty horsemen. Soon afterwards I rode to the extreme front, where there were four pieces of cannon, almost without any infantry support. To the non-withdrawal of these guns is to be attributed the otherwise surprising inactivity of the enemy. I was immediately surrounded by a sergeant and about half-a-dozen gunners, who seemed in excellent spirits, and full of confidence, in spite of their exposed situation. The sergeant (Coyle) expressed his ardent hope that the Yankees might have spirit enough to advance and receive the dose he had in readiness for them.

Whilst we were talking, the enemy's skirmishers began to advance slowly, and several ominous sounds in quick succession told us that we were attracting their attention, and that it was necessary to break up the conclave. I therefore turned round and took leave of these cheery and plucky gunners. — *Freemantle.*

perhaps he was speaking to himself), "It's all my fault; I thought my men were invincible!"

Capt. Johnston, of the engineers, rode up. From what I could gather he had been looking for favorable grounds in our rear to lay out a line of battle. Reports were coming in from scouts that the enemy was falling back, and there was nothing in front of us except cavalry, and that the rumbling of guns had been heard that evening. Had Meade had enough of us? We thought then that if Lee had not already withdrawn the troops from our lines an effort might have been made to ascertain correctly what the enemy was about. But it was now too late. The army was on the march, and it was dark, and raining heavily. We all clustered around the fire, and piled on the rails, but it was a miserable, wretched night, and, in spite of India-rubber cloths, we were wet to the skin. I offered my canteen and a tin cup to Gen. Lee, saying, "he must be cold, and a little of its contents would do him good." I never saw him do it before; but, for "his health's sake," he took a few drops. I had intended to keep that cup as a *souvenir*, but lost it on the march.

At daylight on the 5th we took the road, following the troops. The battery-horses are slowly dragging the heavy guns through the roads, axle deep. The infantry are picking their way through the fields.

On the 6th we reached Hagerstown. As we approached the town the enemy's cavalry attacked ours in front, and were driven off towards Williamsport, where all the army-wagons and ambulances are under charge of Imboden's cavalry and the Washington Artillery. The enemy attacked them and were driven off by the artillery, cavalry, teamsters, and quartermasters, together with some wounded men, who were armed with muskets found in the wagons. They made a very gallant fight of it and saved the trains. The artillery had seventeen men wounded and ten horses killed.

On the 7th it was reported that more ammunition had arrived, and communication reëstablished with Richmond. We have gone into camp one mile from Williamsport. The Potomac is too high for the army to cross. Meade has followed us cautiously, but does not seem disposed to trouble us.[1]

Our engineers are having a pontoon bridge built, and to do so are ransacking all the barns for tar, oakum, and tools. On the 8th the river is still booming, and we are in rather a delicate position. Meade on one side, and a big river on the other. Frankly speaking, we are in a decidedly "tight box." We trust to "Uncle Robert" to get us out of it.

On the 10th our batteries are supplied with ammunition, for which we are thankful.[2]

---

[1] Scarcely had we arrived at Williamsport before we were attacked by Kilpatrick, with a body of Federal cavalry, who had already harassed us at Hagerstown, on our retreat, and captured some of our wagons. At Williamsport, the morning after our arrival, there was a sudden dash and hotly contested fight. These assailants were, however, ultimately driven off, with the assistance of the wagoners, who now shouldered the muskets they had been hauling, and fought like Trojans. In this teamsters' fight, the enemy were driven away without doing any serious damage. — *Bartlett's story.*

[2] HEAD–QUARTERS ARTILLERY CORPS, July 10, 1863.

COLONEL : — More artillery ammunition has arrived opposite Williamsport. Have battalion commanders directed to send, immediately, caissons to report at Col. Baldwin's park, and, as he may direct, get the ammunition as soon as it is brought across (the Potomac). It is hoped there is a good supply of rifle ammunition.

On the 11th our army began intrenching their position. Meade is doing the same on his lines in front of us.

On the night of the 13th the pontoon bridge was completed, — an engineering triumph over difficulties, — and the army crossed to the Virginia shore, leaving only two of Major Garnett's guns, and a couple of broken-down wagons, stuck in the mud, — a clean retreat. But we have had the misfortune to lose a gallant officer, Gen. Pettigrew. It had been reported to him that a small body of cavalry, about sixty in number, were riding towards his lines and works. At first they were supposed to be our own men. They displayed a Federal guidon, but our men thought they might have captured it. As they approached our lines they put their horses to the gallop, and began yelling and discharging their pistols. It was then discovered that they were Federals, and, as they charged over our works in their headlong course, Pettigrew's men seized their muskets, and not one of the cavalry escaped, all were shot or bayonetted ; but a pistol-shot had laid low the gallant and chivalrous Pettigrew.

It was presumed they thought our lines were abandoned, and came to see, but they ran into a brigade of infantry, and, while sacrificing their own lives, deprived us of a valuable officer.

On the 16th we encamped at Bunker Hill, and, on the 20th, we once more pitched our tents in our grove at Mill-

. . . .

Act in these matters, if you please, very promptly.

Respectfully, your obedient servant,

W. N. PENDLETON,

Brig.-Gen'l and Chief of Artillery.

COL. WALTON, *Chief Artillery, First Corps.*

wood. We have "seen sights" since we left this delightful spot a few weeks ago. I am better off by two pairs of
pants, and a new pair of riding-boots, which a $5 gold-
piece procured, after many denials, on the part of a store-
keeper of the Israelitish persuasion, in Williamsport, that
such things were to be had in the whole State of Maryland. Oh, the power of gold!

On the 5th of August we encamped at Orange Court-
House, and the campaign is over. General Longstreet,
his staff, and our friends "the Surgeons" are encamped close
by us, and we have a sociable time of it. We contemplate
renewing our dancing-club at the Court-House, *pour
passer le temps.*

Our army at Gettysburg, in Pennsylvania, numbered
62,000 of all arms, — 50,000 infantry, 8,000 cavalry, and
4,000 artillery.[1] The Federal army numbered 105,000.[2]

[1] Colonel Taylor, "Four years with General Lee," p. 113.
[2] General Meade's report.

NOTE.

ARMAMENT OF FIRST CORPS ARTILLERY, A. N. VA., JULY 19, 1863.

BATTERIES.	3-in. Rifles.	10 pounder Parrotts.	12-pounder Napoleons.	12-pounder Howitzers.	20-pounder Parrotts.	24-pounder Howitzers.	Total.
Colonel Alexander's Battalion.							
Captain Jordan	4	. .	. .	. .	. .	. .	4
" Woolfolk	. .	. .	. .	. .	2	. .	2
" Moody	. .	. .	2	. .	. .	4	6
" Parker	3	1	. .	. .	. .	. .	4
" Ficklin (Rhett) . . .	. .	. .	. .	2	. .	. .	2
" Taylor (Eubank) . .	. .	. .	4	. .	. .	. .	4
	7	1	6	2	2	4	22

BATTERIES.	3-in. Rifles.	10-pounder Parrotts.	12-pounder Napoleons.	12-pounder Howitzers.	20-pounder Parrotts.	24-pounder Howitzers.	Total.
Washington Artillery, Colonel J. B. Walton.							
Captain Squires	. .	. .	1	. .	. .	. .	1
" Richardson	1	. .	2	1	. .	.	4
" Miller	. .	. .	3	. .	. .	. .	3
" Norcom	. .	. .	2	. .	. .	. .	2
	1	. .	8	1	. .	. .	10
Major Henry's Battalion.							
Captain Bachmin	. .	. .	4	. .	. .	. .	4
" Garden	. .	1	3	. .	. .	. .	4
" Reilly	1	3	2	. .	. .	. .	6
" Latham	. .	2	2	. .	. .	. .	4
	1	6	11	. .	. .	. .	18
Major Dearing's Battalion.							
Captain Blount	1	1	. .	. .	2	. .	4
" Macon	. .	2	2	. .	. .	. .	4
" Stribling	. .	. .	6	. .	. .	. .	6
" Caskie	. .	. .	4	. .	. .	. .	4
	1	3	12	. .	2	. .	18
Colonel Cabell's Battalion.							
Captain Manly	1	. .	. .	2	. .	1	4
" McCarthy	2	. .	2	. .	. .	. .	4
" Carlton	. .	2	. .	1	. .	. .	3
" Frazer	1	2	. .	1	. .	. .	4
	4	4	2	4	. .	1	15
Total guns	14	14	39	7	4	5	83

WM. MILLER, OWEN,
Adjutant First Corps Artillery.

Camp at Bunker Hill, Va., July 19, 1863.

Report of Inspection made of the Artillery of the First (Longstreet's) Army Corps, Army Northern Virginia, July 25, 1863, at Culpeper Court-House.

COL. CABELL'S BATTALION.

General condition, good. No horses wanted. Ammunition required. Can move at any time. Five new wheels needed.

MAJOR DEARING'S BATTALION.

Thirty-two horses lost at Gettysburg; 36 horses required to fill up. Horses in weak condition, needing a few days' rest. Cannot march under four days unless provided with horse-shoes and corn.

BATTALION WASHINGTON ARTILLERY.

Day after to-morrow horses will all be shod, and will then be able to march; 12 horses required to fill up.

Men badly off for shoes and under-clothing. General condition very good.

MAJOR HENRY'S BATTALION.

All batteries in good order except one; that requires rest; 40 horses needed to fill up. Men all well shod. Ammunition required. Two chests full of ammunition abandoned on the march.

COLONEL ALEXANDER'S BATTALION.

Eighty horses needed to fill. Tolerably well shod up; 170 pairs of shoes needed for men.

N B. Shoes for the men greatly needed. Horse-shoes and nails are needed by the whole Artillery Corps.

J. B. WALTON,
Colonel and Chief of Artillery, First Corps A.N.Va.

W. M. OWEN, *Adjutant Artillery, First Corps.*

HEAD–QUARTERS ARTILLERY CORPS, July 30, 1863.

ORDER NO : —

In accordance with General Orders No. 43, June 13, 1862, A. and I. G. O., the following promotions are announced.

Sergt. William J. Behan, of Capt. Norcom's Company of "Washington Artillery," to be a second lieutenant, vice George E. Apps, promoted March 26, 1862.

By command of Brig.-General W. N. Pendleton.

D. D. PENDLETON,
Captain and A.A.G.

Official : J. B. WALTON, *Colonel and Chief Artillery.*

CHAPTER XII.

CHICKAMAUGA — INDIAN, A "STREAM OF DEATH."

Wm. Preston Johnston. — General Longstreet. — Richmond. — Promotion. — S. W. Virginia. — Abingdon. — Gen. William Preston. — Knoxville. — March through Georgia. — McLemore's Cove. — Dug Gap. — Gen. Bragg. — Gen. Breckenridge. — Fifth Company, Washington Artillery. — Gen. Gracie. — Gen. Polk. — Battle of Chickamauga. — Gen. Wm. H. Lytle killed. — Preston's charge up Missionary Ridge. — Rosecrans in Chattanooga. — President Davis.

AUGUST 10, 1863. — While sitting in front of our tents last evening, chatting, our courier brought me the following letter : —

RICHMOND, Aug. 7, 1863.

LIEUTENANT W. M. OWEN : —

MY DEAR SIR, — I received from my uncle, Gen. William Preston, commanding a district in South-western Virginia, a letter to you, enclosed to me, offering you the place of "Chief of Artillery" with him. He has ten guns, two howitzers, and Saltville is to be fortified with ten guns more, — twenty-two guns.

You would have the rank of Major. You would find the service in some respects rough; but the association with Gen. Preston himself would be agreeable.

On consultation with your friends here we were unwilling to trust to the uncertainty of the mails, especially as Gen. Preston wished immediate action.

It has, therefore, been submitted to the War Department, and I do not doubt that you will receive the appointment.

I write you to learn if it will be agreeable to you.

Very truly yours,

WM. PRESTON JOHNSTON.

Had a shell exploded at my feet I could not have been

more surprised than I was at my sudden promotion. It was totally unsought; but I could not bear the thought of leaving old friends and comrades in the " Army of Northern Virginia," and then —" South-western Virginia ! " a part of the country that seemed out of the world, where I would be buried in obscurity, — would be lost — never heard of again. I half decided I would reject the appointment. However, we took a toddy to " Saltville and Gen. Preston," and turned in to sleep on it.

At an early hour this morning I went to head-quarters to show Colonel Johnson's letter to General Longstreet, and ask his advice.

He told me to accept at once ; that he thought young men should always take promotion when offered. I told him I regretted leaving the old corps, etc. He said, " Oh ! don't be afraid ; we will meet again." I then applied for leave of absence to go to Richmond ; got it, and started immediately by rail.

In the evening, I called upon the president, and was greeted by him as " Major O." The commission was fixed, that was evident. Received the congratulations of the ladies of his family, and passed with them a pleasant evening.

General Preston wants me to report to him as soon as possible ; so I am off to-morrow to camp, for my traps, and then " Ho ! for South-western Virginia," — a " Life Insurance Department."

.   .   .   .

On the night of the 19th of August I found myself at Abingdon, S.W. Va. I was asleep when the train pulled

up at the station, and, although I had requested the conduc-
tor to see that I was notified, he failed to do it, and I was
carried to the next station, seven miles, where I got out,
and marched back the whole distance, over the cross-ties,
to Abingdon. It was ten o'clock when I reached the village. All the officers at head-quarters were asleep, except
a select party, who were in a closed room, from which the
sound of the rattling of ivory checks left a suspicion upon
my mind that something of the nature of "poker" might
be going on; so I went to the village tavern, and was provided with an indifferent bed.

Bright and early, on the 20th of August, I walked into
General Preston's office, and reported for duty, and was
announced in Orders, as "Chief of Artillery of the Department of South-western Virginia" to be "obeyed and respected accordingly." In six weeks I had changed my
locality from the bloody heights of Gettysburg to the
forest-covered mountains of South-western Virginia.

The General is a most agreeable gentleman, and has an
excellent cook, and capital mess.

His staff is composed of young Kentuckians. I think
we will all pull together admirably. Will at once make a
general inspection of the department.

Aug. 23d. — Rumors have been rife for several days that
Burnside is moving this way from Kentucky, and the Gen-
eral and staff, are ordered to Knoxville, to report to Gen.
Buckner.

At Knoxville many wild rumors of the movements of the
enemy are in circulation. This city and our department
are to be evacuated. General Buckner is in command.

While at dinner to day General Preston informed me that General Buckner had offered him the command of a division of infantry, and that he had accepted. He then propounded the question : " Will you go with me as Chief of Staff and Assistant Adjutant-General, on an active campaign, or would you prefer going back to our department, and report to General Sam Jones, at Dublin ? " What an unlooked for opportunity ! Without a moment's delay I decided upon the active campaign. So, farewell to old Virginia ! General Bragg is at Chattanooga, and we will withdraw in that direction. The. quartermaster's stores are being removed from the city as speedily as possible.

On the 24th of August we were busy getting ready to march. The weather was oppressively hot. I am in a bad fix. My "kit" is at Abingdon, and I have with me only one blanket and my cape, and one change of underclothing. My horses are on the journey somewhere between Orange Court-House and Abingdon ; so I am badly prepared for a campaign of, — no one knows how long. I obtained, however, from the quartermaster's department, a little, round-bellied gray horse, and one of the worst Confederate saddles I ever saw. The first chance I get at the enemy it will be " A horse ! a horse ! My kingdom for a horse !" But, like Mark Tapley, I shall "endeavor to be jolly under adverse circumstances."

On the 25th of August we left Knoxville for Loudon, on the Tennessee river, which place is being fortified. Here there is a long bridge, which can be destroyed, should the movements of the enemy render it necessary. Knoxville was given up to-day, and Gen. Buckner and staff

have arrived here. It is a pity to give up this beautiful
country, with its ripening crops, to the enemy. To-day
Gen. Preston took command of his division, in Buckner's
corps, consisting of the brigades of Gen. Gracie, Col.
Trigg, and Col. Kelly, and the Fifth regiment of Kentucky
volunteers, under Col. Hawkins. The division staff is
announced as follows : —

Major W. M. OWEN, A.A.G. and Chief of Staff.

Major EDWARD CRUTCHFIELD, Chief Quartermaster.

Major BRADFORD, Chief Commissary.

Capt. JOHN SANFORD, A.A. General.

Capt. ED. PRESTON, A. Inspector General.

Lieut. S. F. ADAMS, A.A.A. General.

H. RUTHERFORD, Chief Surgeon.

Lieut. H. H. JOHNSTON, A.D.C.

Lieut. ED. WHITFIELD, Ordnance Officer.

Capt. J. C. S. Blackburn, Vol. A.D.C.

The following tabular statement shows the composition
and strength of the division : —

DIVISION OF GEN. WM. PRESTON, AUG. 26, 1863.

	STRENGTH.		
	Regiments.	Brigades.	Present for duty.
First Brigade. Brig.-Gen. Archibald Gracie, Jr.			
63d regiment Tenn. Vols., Col. J. A. Fulkerson.			
43d regiment Ala. Vols., Col. I. M. Moody		3,597	2,206
41st regiment Ala. Vols., Col. M. L. Stansel....			
Hilliard's Alabama Legion, 1st, 2d, and 3d battalions. Lieut.-Col. J. H. Holt. Lieut.-Col. B. Hall, Jr., Major J. A. Sanford...............			
Second Brigade. Col. R. C. Trigg commanding.			
6th regiment Fla. Vols., Col. J. J. Findlay			
7th regiment Fla. Vols., Col. R. Bullock		2,772	1,940
1st regiment Fla. cavalry (dismounted), Col. G. T. Maxwell................................			
54th Va. Vols., Col. Jno. J. Wade.............			
Third Brigade. Col. J. H. Kelly commanding.			
58th regiment N. C. Vols., Col. J. B. Palmer ...	827		
65th regiment Ga. Vols., Col. Moore...........	633	2,327	1,509
63d regiment Va. Vols., Col. J. J. McMahon...	867		
Attached. Col. H. Hawkins.			
5th regiment Ky. Vols.	422	422	296
Morgan's dismounted cavalry, Lieut.-Col. Bowles.			
Totals.................................		9,118	5,951

Artillery.

Leyden's battery.   People's battery.
Williams's battery.   Wollihan's battery.
Eldridge's battery.   Jeffries' battery, with Gracie.

On the 31st of August the division took the field, and the march was begun towards Chattanooga. We encamped on the banks of the Sweetwater, seventeen miles from Loudon.

On the 1st of September the division marched to Riceville, seven miles from Charleston; on the 2d to Carmichael's Ford, on Candy creek; and on the 3d to Georgetown. To-day (the 4th) I rode with Generals Preston and Pegram, to Blythe's Ferry, on the Tennessee river, and observed the enemy's pickets on the opposite bank.

On the 5th the march continued to Harrison, on the beautiful creek called by the Indian name "Ooltowha," where we had a splendid bath, and enjoyed ourselves in the water to our hearts' content. On the 6th and 7th we continued our march; on the latter date some unknown exigencies caused us to march all night, much to the disgust of every one. Gen. Bragg is evacuating Chattanooga, and we can hear the distant cannonading.

On September 8th marched to Ringgold and camped, and on the 9th marched to Pea-vine church.

We — the staff — have now been marching and camping together for the past ten days, long enough to become well acquainted with each other; and, in all my experience in the army, I have never met with a better set of gentlemen than we have assembled here at head-quarters. Gen. Preston himself is a most interesting travelling companion as well as polished gentleman; a handsome, large-framed man, somewhat resembling Col. Walton, my old chief, and has the appearance of what we can imagine a French marshal should have been in the wars of the first Napoleon.

He is chock-full of anecdote, and many an hour have I listened to his experiences and travels of long ago, — before either of us believed we should ever be marching over the dusty roads of Tennessee and Georgia at the head of a column of nearly six thousand stalwart soldiers clad in gray. The General is a Kentuckian, — from that State which has produced so many great orators and statesmen, and has served his commonwealth in the halls of Congress; but what interests me most is the story of his life at the Spanish court, when he occupied the high position of minister plenipotentiary from the United States, and spent each year, in keeping up a grand establishment, fifty thousand dollars over and above the government salary. How he astonished the Dons! And had they inquired of him what that salary was, he could have replied, as Col. John B. Magruder once did to the English officers, whom he was entertaining in princely style at Fort Niagara, on the lakes, when asked what was the pay of a colonel in the United States army, that enabled him to do such magnificent things? "Why, really, now, I don't know; I always hand it over to the servants."

As we jog along, he on his Kentucky thorough-bred, and I, on my round-bellied, quartermaster, nondescript "Rosinante," he tells me of his French cook and the *attachés* of his palace; how the former was brought from Paris regardless of expense, and what dinners he served for state occasions; and when we halted in some patch of woods to bivouac in the open air, and partake of our slice of bacon and dip our crackers in the grease, he would give a sigh of satisfaction, and say, "Ah! Owen, this is just as good.

Now we are *greased* for another day." And so the time passed pleasantly enough as we campaigned together in Georgia. Then, there was Ned Preston, a gallant, handsome young fellow, and Harris Johnston, Ed. Whitfield, Sanford, and Joe Blackburn, — impetuous, gallant Joe, full of snap and vim, and as brave as a lion. They and all the balance of the staff were made of the right stuff.

September 10. — It having been reported at head-quarters that a corps of the enemy (Negley's) has passed through Cooper's Gap, in Lookout Mountain, and entered McLemore's Cove, between it and Pigeon Mountain, Gen. Hindman, with his own and Stewart's and Preston's divisions, with the light batteries of Leyden, Williams, and Eldridge, under my command, are sent to capture or destroy it.

The divisions marched from Pea-Vine church and moved to Morgan's Ford, over the Chickamauga Creek, which runs through the cove and empties into the Tennessee river near Chattanooga.

Here the command bivouacked, and a council of officers was held. Gen. Preston attended, and we of the staff kicked our heels outside of the house where they met until midnight.

While riding to our bivouac the General told me that we were to move at daylight, and attack the enemy as soon as we should find him. We slept upon our saddle-blankets, on the ground in the open field.

On September 11 we were up and stirring at daylight, and the division ready to move. Our cook has not yet overtaken us with the provisions, so we content ourselves

with roasting-ears of corn and water. It is seven o'clock
before the march begins, and then we moved slowly, halting often, and at 11.30 halted to rest. This don't look
like marching to "attack the enemy when we shall find
him," but rather as though we were afraid he would find us.
At 12.15 a single gun is heard in the distance. At 12.45
the column is moved forward, and a line of battle formed,
and there is some skirmishing in front. At 4.35 our line
advances, and the enemy retires rapidly before us, our men
moving at a double quick, and by dusk he is in full retreat
to the gap through which he entered the cove. Our batteries were not used.

Our movements have been so much upon the snail order
that the enemy has been enabled to slip away from our
front, when we should have captured or destroyed him. As
the result of the little skirmishing with his rear-guard, we
found, in a cornfield, one poor little Yank, who had died
that day for his country.

Our expedition having come to naught, we push on
to Dug Gap, over Pigeon Mountain, *en route* for La
Fayette, where Bragg is concentrating and preparing for
battle.

On the 12th we arrived at La Fayette, about 3 P.M.,
having had a hard time getting our troops and wagons over
the mountain. The different corps are concentrating here.
Met Gen. Polk to-day ; the change in his appearance from
a clean-shaved, white-robed bishop to a soldier " bearded
like the pard," and wearing a black slouch hat and a faded
gray uniform, is very striking. His corps is to move to-
morrow in the direction of Pea-Vine church, to attack

Crittenden's corps, said to be moving after us in that direction.

It appears that the Federal army is moving its different corps independently of each other, and Bragg is trying to catch them in detail whenever he can. Hope Polk will be more successful this time than Hindman was on the 10th.

At daylight on the 13th Preston's division was ordered out to support Polk's movements, and marched on the road five miles from La Fayette. At 12.25 some firing is heard in the direction of Rock Spring. At 1 P.M. we are ordered back to La Fayette, to support D. H. Hill, who is skirmishing below the town on the Summerville road. Weather excessively hot, and roads dusty, and our men suffer much for water. At 5 P.M. we were ordered into camp. Another failure. Crittenden has slipped away from Polk, as Negley did from Hindman. Our movements are wretchedly slow. We are not in luck " bagging " corps. I called, with Gen. Preston, to pay our respects to Gens. Bragg, Dan Adams, and Breckenridge.

At 4.15 A.M., September 14, Trigg's brigade and People's battery were ordered to support Helm, on the Summerville road; at 7.30 A.M. they were ordered to rest for the day. We left Abingdon on the 22d of August, and since that date we have marched three hundred and four miles, averaging fourteen miles a day, passing over bad roads and through a mountainous country.

The Fifth company Washington Artillery passed our bivouac, and I was delighted to meet my old friend and comrade, Capt. Slocomb, not having seen him since he left us at Centreville, Virginia, in 1861. He left us then to return to New Orleans on business of the greatest importance, and when the Fifth company was organized, joined it as a private, was elected a lieutenant, and, after the battle of Shiloh, where he was desperately wounded, was promoted to the captaincy, when Capt. Hodgson resigned on account of failing health. I also had the pleasure of meeting Lieuts. Leverich, Chalaron, and Vaught.

The Fifth company has made a brilliant record in this army, as its brothers of the four companies in Virginia have done.

On the 15th we had Gens. Breckenridge and Gracie to dine with us; not much dinner, and no champagne. However, the *piece de resistance* of bacon was passable, and the apple-brandy toddy was good.

Breckenridge is regarded as a fine soldier, whilom an orator, and Vice-President of the United States. Gracie is a rising young General, devoted to his profession, a graduate of West Point. He is justly proud of his brigade of young soldiers, most of whom have never yet been under fire. They will do good work. Passed the evening at the camp of the Fifth company. They are all eager to know what the four companies in Virginia are about.

Becoming tired of the position of Adjutant-General and being awakened at all hours of the night to light stumps of candles and try and decipher incomprehensible despatches, all crumpled from the courier's pocket, where, in all probability, he has stored his pipe and tobacco and his parched corn, I have persuaded the General to announce me as Chief of Artillery of the division, and to let some one else, holding a commission in the Adjutant-General's department, do the candle and courier business.

A battle order from Gen. Bragg has been received, in which he announces his intention to march and find the enemy, and attack immediately.

The army is in fine spirits and full of fight, and it is to be hoped we will find the enemy this time.

On the 17th we marched from La Fayette at 10 A.M., and reached Rock Spring at 3 P.M. Gen. Frank Armstrong reports the enemy˜ at Worthing's Gap, six miles from Rock-spring church.

Encamped to-night on Pea-Vine Creek.

September 18. — Marched at 8.30 A.M. to and beyond Pea-Vine church, and crossed the ridge at Napier's Gap. We are now in the cove ; enemy just in front, across the Chickamauga Creek. Move on to Dalton's Ford, over the creek. Enemy now in full view ; brisk skirmishing. Placed Wollihan's and People's batteries in position to cover our crossing.

At dusk a staff-officer of Col. Kelly's rode up to report a camp of the enemy in full view, and in artillery range, across the creek on our left. At the request of Gen. Preston, I accompanied the officer to the spot, where we could overlook the camp, and, dismounting and throwing the bridle of my horse over my arm, began to use my glasses. Within a thousand yards was a large encampment, with fires burning, and the men evidently preparing supper. I was turning over in my mind how we could stir them up with a battery, when, right at my very feet, there was a flash of a rifle, and a bullet whistled by my ear.   That miserable, round-bellied quadruped had, by his light-grayish color, betrayed my presence to one of the enemy's pickets on the banks of the creek.   I put up my glasses and turned to mount.   The gray pulled back, the picket fired again, and again missed.   The aid-de-camp put off through the woods, and left me and the gray to our fate ; but, by perseverance and cussing, I got alongside, mounted, and was off before my very attentive friend could reload and fire again.   Reported to the General that, if he would lend me Kelly's brigade awhile, I could make that place secure for a battery of artillery.   He *regretted* he could not comply with my request at the moment.

At midnight Gracie's brigade and Jeffrey's battery were put across the creek.

The Chickamauga is crossed by two bridges and three fords.   The plan of attack is about as follows : Gen. Bushrod Johnson's division is to cross at the lower bridge (Breed's), push on up stream, on the opposite side. When opposite the second bridge (Alexander's), Walker's division is to cross and support Johnson's movement. Buckner is to cross at Tedford's Ford.   Polk's corps is at Lee and Gordon's Mill, and D. H. Hill's corps, the extreme left, at Crawfish-spring Ford.

They will conform to the movements of Johnson, Walker, and Buckner.

At daybreak on the morning of the 19th, Kelly's and Trigg's brigades, with Wollihan's and People's batteries, crossed at Tedford's Ford.

At 8.30 A.M., Johnson is already engaged on the right. The firing is heavy.

Forming Line of Battle. Artillery and Skirmishers Engaged.

After crossing the Chickamauga the division is formed in column of brigades at right-angles with the stream. The enemy is in plain view at Lee and Gordon's Mill.

Johnson is forcing the enemy back towards the Chattanooga road. We opened fire upon the enemy at Lee and Gordon's Mill with a rifle-gun. At 10.40 he replied with long-range Parrott guns, causing us to cease firing, and killing a lieutenant and two men in Trigg's brigade, and demoralizing somewhat our men, as it always does troops when lying down under artillery fire awaiting orders.

12 M. Firing very heavy on the right; Johnson and Walker hard at it. At 4 P.M. our division advances. Trigg moved to the right, and the line of battle made to connect. Our forces are swinging around towards the Chattanooga road, and pivoting on Preston's division, the left of the line. Trigg's skirmishers become engaged, and then his brigade, and he loses nearly two hundred men.

7 P.M. Very heavy skirmishing in front of us, and heavy firing on the right. Just as Gen. Preston and staff were taking a rest behind our line, the bullets of the skirmishers came thickly, but flew high, for which much thanks.

With the exception of Trigg's brigade, our troops have been idle. We can hear but little reliable news from the right. We can only judge of the state of affairs by the sound of artillery and musketry. We have all sorts of reports; one is that Hood's division is here, just from Richmond, and has been in to-day. Hurrah for the old army of Northern Virginia!

Longstreet is expected with more troops. The General's

boy (Sam) brought us a canteen of coffee, so called, of which we partook, and, after feeding our horses on corn shucks from a neighboring field, we wrapped ourselves in our blankets, and, with our saddles for pillows, slept soundly behind our line of battle.

September 20th. Polk's and D. H. Hill's corps, finding it impossible to cross the Chickamauga at Lee and Gordon's and Crawfish-spring Fords, moved down during the night and crossed at Tedford's Ford. Moving then, in our rear, to the extreme right of the line, they have taken the places of Johnson's and Walker's tired troops, and Polk has orders to attack the enemy at daylight; but we have not yet heard his guns.

The old "war-horse" Longstreet is here at last, with Hood's and Kershaw's divisions, about 7,000 men. I had the pleasure of shaking hands with him as he was riding along the line this morning. He said, "I told you we would meet again."

His presence is an omen of victory. Latrobe, Sorrel, Goree, and Manning are with him. It is glorious to have these fellows out here. It recalls our old fights. I feel certain we will have a victory to-day.

10.45. Heavy firing on the right. Polk has at last gone in. Should have attacked at daylight,[1] but waited

---

[1] A heavy fog hung over the battle-field during the early morning. Bragg, before daylight, with his staff, took position immediately in rear of the centre of his line, and waited for Polk to begin the attack, waiting until after sunrise with increasing anxiety and disappointment. Bragg then sent a staff-officer to Polk to ascertain and report as to the cause of the delay, with orders urging him to a prompt and speedy attack. Polk was not found with his troops, and the staff-officer, learning that he had spent the night on the east side of Chickamauga Creek, rode over there and delivered his message. Bragg,

for his men to get breakfast. He commands the right wing of the army; Longstreet, the left. Now we will catch it. Trigg's brigade detached to support Hindman. Line parallel to him and in rear.

11 A.M. Buckner's order to remove the enemy's wounded from our front suspended on account of our surgeons and litter-bearers being fired into.

11.30. Our time comes at last. Latrobe gallops up and says, " Gen. Longstreet orders your division to move forward, keeping closed to the right." Trigg, Kelly, and Gracie advance, leaving our batteries to watch the enemy on the banks of the Chickamauga. We are swinging around on Polk's corps, which is now the pivot.

Our division, in advancing, passes the spot where Gen. Bragg is seated upon his horse on the Chattanooga road. He looks pale and careworn, his features rendered more haggard by a white Havelock he wears over his cap and neck.

The enemy seems to be fighting in detached bodies.[1]

---

impatient at the delay, proceeded in person to his right wing, and there found the troops wholly unprepared for the movement. Messengers were sent for Polk in hot haste, and, on his reporting, he was urged to a prompt execution of his orders, and to make a vigorous attack at once.— *The Army of the Cumberland.* H. M. CIST.

[1] Just at this time the order of battle on the enemy's line had reached Longstreet's command, who, seeing this gap, ordered his troops, formed in heavy columns, to advance.

Into this gap they poured, Stewart's, Hood's, Kershaw's, Johnson's, and Hindman's divisions dashing impetuously forward, with Preston's large division as supports.

Our right, disabled as it was, was speedily turned, the line of battle on the enemy's front, extending nearly from Brannan's centre to a point far to the right of the Widow Glenn's house, and from the front of that portion of the line Sheridan's brigades had just been taken.

Longstreet discovers, with his soldier's eye, a gap in their already confused lines, and, forming a solid column of attack, composed of Stewart's, Hood's, Kershaw's, Johnson's, and Hindman's divisions, with Preston's as supports, breaks through and strikes the enemy, and short and bloody is the work. We move steadily forward, no halting. The men rush over the hastily-constructed breastworks of logs and rails of the foe, with the old time familiar rebel yell, and, wheeling then to the right, the column sweeps the enemy before it, and pushes along the Chattanooga road towards Missionary Ridge in pursuit. It is glorious!

We hear that Kershaw's and Hood's men are fighting, as they always do, splendidly. Several thousand prisoners and fifty pieces of artillery reported captured, General Lytle killed. At 2.45 P.M. our exultant troops are halted to rest; our division has followed on, supporting those in front who have so far done the fighting. There is no enemy left except a small force on Horseshoe Ridge, which is a very strong position; those troops of the enemy who were on Longstreet's left, when he broke through the

---

McCook, to resist this fierce assault, had only Carlin's and Hey's brigades, of Davis's division, aud Laibold's brigade, of Sheridan's division.

On finding the rebel troops passing through the space vacated by Wood, McCook ordered Lytle and Walworth to change front and return to assist in repelling the enemy. Wilder and Harrison closed in on Sheridan with their commands as speedily as possible, and aided in resisting the enemy's attack. Davis, being overpowered by the immense number of the rebels, was compelled to retire to save his command. Laibold was in turn driven back in confusion, and the tide of battle then struck Lytle and Walworth, who contended nobly against the overpowering columns, and for a time checked the advance of the enemy on their immediate front. The rebel troops, swarming in, turned the left of these brigades, and they were compelled to withdraw to escape being surrounded. At this point the gallant Lytle was killed. Here our army lost several thousand prisoners, forty guns, and a large number of wagon-trains.— *Army of the Cumberland.* H. M. CIST.

lines, are falling back to positions of greater safety, and are flying to Chattanooga. Longstreet says " They have fought their last man and *he* is running."

3 P.M. While our division was resting at a halt, under an occasional fire of a battery posted on Horseshoe Ridge, I rode to the right and rear of our line, and there saw Gens. Longstreet and Buckner, seated on a log, eating their lunch, which their boy had brought to them. General Longstreet hailed me, and asked for a pipeful of tobacco. I produced my little bag, and he filled his meerschaum pipe. I then asked him what he thought of the battle ; was the enemy beaten or not? " Yes," he said, " all along his line ; a few are holding out upon the ridge up yonder, not many though. If we had had our Virginia army here, we could have whipped them in half the time. By the by," he added, " don't you want some guns for your command? I think my men must have captured fifty to-day." I told him I did, and would like to make a change for better ones, those we have being very indifferent. " Well," he said, " you can have as many as you want." — " General, hadn't you better put that in writing?" He laughed, and instructed Latrobe to write an order for the guns, which read as follows : —

The officer in charge of the guns captured by Lieutenant-General Longstreet's command, and sent to the rear, will deliver them to Major Owen, of Preston's division, upon his receipt.

By order of Lieut.-Gen. Longstreet.

OSMAN LATROBE,

A.A. Gen'l.

BATTLEFIELD, September 20, 1863.

The General then said, " I think there must be some horses, I certainly saw some go by with the guns."—" Oh ! " I said, " include the horses by all means," and the horses were added to the order.

Before leaving the group, Latrobe called me aside, and, with a wink, said, " Owen, old fellow, my horse is lame, not much account any way ; won't you bring me a good one and you shall have my blessing?"—" All right ! " I told him, " you shall have choice No. 2, for No. 1 will replace my old 'Rosinante' ; that is an assured fact, if I live to get to Alexander's Bridge."

It was now 4 o'clock, and the remnant of the Federal army still stubbornly held the Horseshoe Ridge, although during the day they had been assaulted by Breckenridge, Bushrod Johnson, Patton, Anderson, Hindman, and lastly by Kershaw, and all had lost heavily.

Longstreet determined to take the ridge, and sends to Bragg for some of the troops of the right wing, but Bragg says, " they have been fought out and can do him no good."

The position held by the enemy is a very Gibraltar, its sides precipitous, and difficult to climb, but the day is wearing away, and no time should be lost. Longstreet determines to put in his Tenth legion, Preston's 5,000, and sends for the General, and orders an immediate advance. "It shall be done," replies Preston, and the command Attention ! is given down the lines of the three brigades. The young troops spring to their arms ; it is their first baptism of fire, and if they are whipped they won't know it.

The lines are dressed, and at the commands, Forward! forward! the 5,000 move on in beautiful order. The enemy opens a terrific fire; but up the hill our men advance; now the enemy's bullets begin to tell upon the lines, and men fall to the right and left, dead and wounded; but the rest move on undismayed, firing rapidly as they advance; but the artillery and infantry fire is too hot for them, although they have fought most gallantly, and, halting under the crest where some protection is had, the lines are dressed, and General Preston, reassuring them by his presence, rides down the lines and coolly examines each man's cartridge-box, and says, "Men, we must use the bayonet, — the bayonet, — we will give them the bayonet!" The men, one and all cry out, "Go ahead, General! we are not whipped yet!" Confidence restored by the General's cool demeanor, and with the enthusiasm of the troops raised to the highest pitch, Preston rides to the front and centre of his line, and leads the way with splendid dash and bravery, waving his cap above his head, his gray hair floating in the breeze.

With fierce yells and shouts the troops advance,— Gracie on the right, Kelly the centre, and Trigg the left. It is a brave sight. Gracie and Kelly meet a determined resistance; but Trigg, who had been pushed to the enemy's right in the hope of overlapping and flanking him, sweeps down on his flank and rear, capturing 500 prisoners, the colors of the Twenty-first Ohio, the Twenty-second Michigan, and two of regiments unknown, together with Colonels Lefebvre and Carlton, and Lieut.-Col. Glenn. The enemy, assailed on front and flank, falls back, and the battle-flags of Preston's division are planted upon the summit of Horseshoe Ridge, and the battle is won.[1]

It was now growing quite dark, and the last divisions of Rosecrans's army were soon in full retreat on the road to Chattanooga. The troops we had fought upon the ridge were under General Thomas;—the commands of Brannan, Wood, and Granger, men of Ohio, Kentucky, and Michigan.

Our tired men slept upon the field among the enemy's dead and wounded.

September 21. Presenting Longstreet's order for the captured artillery to the officer in charge at Alexander's Bridge, I equipped our batteries with the pick of the new guns, rifles and Napoleons, and divided *pro rata* twenty-six horses, after selecting a mount for Latrobe, my courier, and myself. I have secured a fine animal of power and action, new saddle and bridle, red blankets, curry-comb, etc., etc., etc., as the auctioneer says, too numerous to mention. My old Rosinante has gone back to the quartermaster's department.

Gen. Gracie very proudly showed me this morning the battle-flag of the Second Alabama Volunteers, carried by Sergt. Hiatt yesterday, that was pierced eighty-three times

---

[1] After Hindman was driven back, Longstreet, about four o'clock, determined to retake the ridge. Asking Bragg for reinforcements from the right, he was informed by him " that they had been beaten back so badly that they could be of no service to me."

Longstreet then ordered up his reserve division of fresh troops under Preston, four (?) brigades strong, supported by Stewart's corps, and directed him to attack the troops on the ridge.

Advancing with wild yells, confident of success, Preston dashed boldly up the hill, supported by Kershaw's troops, with Johnson's, part of Hindman's, and, later on, by those of Stewart's. — *The Army of the Cumberland.*   H. M. Cist.

during the contest on the ridge. The Sergeant was not touched.

This battle has been fought upon the highest ridge that divides the Atlantic and the Mississippi river, on the banks of the Chickamauga, an Indian name, meaning the "stream of death." Thomas's, Granger's, McCook's, and Crittenden's corps were all engaged. More than fifty pieces of artillery have been taken, and many thousands of small arms, prisoners, and many stands of colors fall into our hands.

Gen. Bragg's head-quarters are established on the Chattanooga road, at the foot of Horseshoe Ridge, and here he is receiving the captured colors, which are being brought in by the men who have been so fortunate and gallant as to have taken them from their late owners. These men will be mentioned in the General Orders of the Army, and be selected for promotion.

Our division is still bivouacked on the ridge where the battle ended. Burying-parties are ordered out, and small arms are being collected by the ordnance-officers.

Upon the loftiest point of the ridge, where the colors of the enemy's battery had floated, we found the body of the man who had fallen in advance of all his comrades, and buried him there, where he gave up his young life. A board from an ammunition-box was procured and placed at the head of his grave, upon which I inscribed as follows : —

GEORGE W. NORRIS,

Co. E, 2d Alabama Volunteers,

Killed at the head of the command, Gracie's Brigade,

September 20, 1863.

To be buried on the spot where he fell, and where the flag of the Federal battery was planted.

WM. PRESTON, *Brigadier-General.*

There let the young hero sleep until the resurrection morn.

" When the long years have rolled slowly away,
  Even to the dawn of earth's funeral day ;
  When, at the Archangel's trumpet and tread,
  Rise up the faces and forms of the dead ;
  When the great world its last judgment awaits,
  And when the blue sky shall swing open its gates,
  And one long column march silently through,
  Past the great Captain for final review ;
  Then for the blood that's been shed for the right,
  Crowns shall spring up untarnished and bright,
  Then the glad ear of this war-martyr's son
  Proudly shall hear the glad tidings, ' Well done ! ' "

While riding through the woods yesterday I came upon the dead body of Gen. Lytle, of Cincinnati, Ohio. I recognized him at once. We had been friends in the old days, as our fathers were before us. A Confederate soldier was standing guard over the body. From what I learned from the guard it appeared that a brigade of Alabama troops, under command of Gen. Zach. Deas, while advancing in the charge Longstreet made, had struck Lytle's brigade. The latter was behind rude entrenchments of logs and rails. These had been swept by Deas's men, driving Lytle's back. About this time Lytle was struck, and his men, retreating, left his body where he fell. He was recognized by his uniform as a general officer, and Capt. West, of Gen. Deas's staff, took charge of his watch and papers, and placed the sentinel on guard over the body. Dismounting, I asked the man his instructions, and he replied, "I am here to take care of this body, and to allow no one to touch it."

"All right," I said. "I hope you will do it." I then looked to see where Lytle had been struck, and found that one ball had entered his right instep, and another his mouth, knocking out some teeth, and making its exit in the back of the neck. When he was killed he was smoking a cigar. He was dressed in fatigue uniform. His shoulder-straps — one star — indicated the rank of brigadier-general. He wore high riding-boots, a regulation overcoat, dark kid gloves. While standing beside the body, Gen. Preston rode up, and asked, "Who have you there?" I replied, "Gen. Lytle, of Cincinnati."—"Ah!" said Gen. Preston, "Gen. Lytle, the son of my old friend, Bob Lytle! I am very sorry indeed it is so;" and he dismounted and was much affected. After asking the sentinel his instructions, and receiving the same answer I had obtained, he said to him, "See that you do it, my man." We then mounted and rejoined the division, which had halted on the road.

Lytle's body was returned in an ambulance to his friends, under flag of truce, and, as he was known to the gentlemen of the Southern army to be a gallant and chivalrous soldier, as well as the author of the beautiful poem entitled, "Anthony and Cleopatra," all were sincerely grieved at his taking off. As the ambulance containing the remains passed on its way to the enemy's lines the road was lined with officers and men, who testified their respect for the dead General by removing their hats and looking on silently.

During the heat of this battle Gen. Benning, of Georgia, one of the bravest men that ever lived, came charging up to Gen. Longstreet in great agitation. He was riding an artillery horse, and was using a rope trace for a whip. His hat was gone, and he was much disordered. " General," he said, "my brigade is utterly destroyed and scattered." Gen. Longstreet approached him, and said quietly, "Don't you think you could find *one* man, General?"—" One man?" he said, with astonishment. "I suppose I could. What do you want with him?"—" Go and get him," Longstreet said very quietly, laying his hand upon his arm, " and bring him here; then you and I and he will charge together. This is the sacred soil of Georgia, General, and we may as well die here as anywhere." He looked at Gen. Longstreet curiously a moment, then laughed, and, with an oath, lashed his horse with his rope trace, and was off like a flash.

In a few moments he swept by at the head of a command that he had gathered together somehow or other, and he was in the fight again.

Gen. Longstreet does not think it necessary to swear at the men, to whoop 'em up as it were; he always adopts the demeanor of quiet assurance and confidence, which is always better than strong oaths.

On the 22d of September we are once more on the march, moving towards Tyner's Station. At 3 P.M., bivouacked at Red House Ford, over Chickamauga Creek. It is believed we are going into Tennessee.

On the 23d, to our amazement, we are ordered to march to Chattanooga. We thought we were to leave Rosecrans behind, and move on Knoxville, drive Burnside out, and go into Kentucky. But the programme is evidently changed, for reasons unknown to us.

On the 24th we bivouacked at the foot of Missionary Ridge, in full view of Chattanooga, where Rosecrans is fortifying. We should have followed him closely into the town with cavalry and artillery. As it is, our army is encamped around the place, and we have established our head-quarters half way up the mountain.

Capt. Robert Ford, of Kentucky, joins the staff as volunteer aid. He is fresh in the field, and has fine horses, fine saddles, negro boys, and an equipment that makes us ragged fellows quite envious. He is a capital fellow, and an agreeable addition to the mess.

October 10. Since we have been here in front of Chattanooga we seem to have accomplished nothing, save throwing up a few weak works that are already falling down from being washed by the rains.

Enemy still fortifying, and evidently has great difficulty in getting provisions over the mountain roads. We suppose Bragg is trying to starve him out.

We pass our time riding about visiting friends. The Englishmen, Lawley, Ross, and Vizetely, are here, the guests of Gen. Longstreet. They call often, and we like them greatly.

Our guide (the term out here for couriers), Dyer, is a good forager, and the staff made up a purse for him one day to invest in sheep, which he has done successfully.

We have a flock close by, and feast our friends on fine mutton. One day Gen. Longstreet and Latrobe dined with us. We killed the fatted mutton, and had a royal feast, ending up with a liberal supply of hot peach-brandy toddy in the General's own particular pewter quart mug. When the time came for honest folks to part, Latrobe was to be the guide, and he and Gen. Longstreet rode down the mountain side. The General must have been lost in revery, thinking of the last battle probably, or something, when he was aroused by a quick challenge, — "Halt! who comes there?"

Somehow they had reached the pickets of the enemy, and they immediately put spurs to their horses, and got Lookout Mountain over the *right* shoulder quickly. A great wonder the General wasn't captured; that would have been a big thing for our friends in blue.[1]

Have received a letter from Abingdon. My trunk, which I left behind, has been expressed to Richmond to the Spottswood Hotel. My horses are at Abingdon. I am somewhat scattered about the Confederacy, but not demoralized, but would like to gather myself together again some time.

Rode with Gen. Gracie to call on Gen. Kershaw. Called at Gen. Bragg's head-quarters, and at Capt. Slocomb's Fifth Company Washington Artillery camp. The six guns of the battery are in position at the foot of

---

[1] Capt. Ross, of the Austrian Hussars, in his " Cities and Camps of the Confederate States," says : " If any one can boast of a leg of mutton he considers it quite a company dish, to which friends must be invited. One of the most successful caterers is Gen. Preston, and another is his Chief of Artillery, Maj. Owen, an old friend, who, in Virginia, was aid to Col. Walton, Chief of Artillery of Longstreet's corps. Owen is believed to have a flock of sheep hidden away somewhere in the mountain. The General gave us a splendid supper one evening, with a profusion of delicate viands, and more than one bowl of hot punch, made of some capital peach brandy."

Missionary Ridge. They were severely engaged in the last battle, and lost heavily.

President Davis arrived from Richmond, and Gen. Preston and staff rode with him along the lines. Col. Wm. Preston Johnston stayed with us to-night. Gen. Breckenridge dined with us to-day.

October 11. Dined with Cullen, who kindly gave me a tent, which I carried to camp in front of me upon my horse. Have it pitched, and Harris Johnston and I make ourselves quite comfortable. Gen. Preston said he believed if I was shipwrecked upon a barren island I would find all things needful for comfort.

To-day, at the request of Gen. Preston, I took Hiatt, the color-sergeant of the Second Alabama Volunteers, Gracie's brigade, to Gen. Bragg's head-quarters to present to the President, on behalf of that command, the flag that had been so riddled going up Horseshoe Ridge. The President received us graciously, and complimented Hiatt upon his gallantry, saying, "he had never seen a flag so tattered in such a short time." He said, he would take it to Richmond with him, and placed it in the custody of Col. Chestnut. The President instructed Gen. Bragg to have the sergeant announced in orders first lieutenant in his company. The President then turned to me and said, with affected severity, "Major Owen, I thought you were sent to South-western Virginia to take charge of the artillery in that department: how is it I find you here?" I stammered out, "So I was, Mr. President; but Gen. Preston gave me my choice either to stay in Virginia, or go with him on the campaign, and I chose the latter, and here I am." — "Well," said Mr. Davis, "it can't be helped now; but if you had lost your life at Chickamauga, I should have said you were out of your place."

After a little more chat I marched off with Lieut. Hiatt. Gen. Preston laughed when I told him how the President had pitched into me. Hiatt told me that this was his first battle, and I questioned him as to how he felt when he was climbing the ridge with the colors; if he wasn't afraid? He replied modestly, "No; I didn't think of it. The boys kept on crying out ' Go ahead! go ahead! ' and I went ahead." Then, after a moment's reflection, added, "It's mighty queer I wasn't killed, isn't it?" I told him he was a lucky fellow to be so distinguished by his General and the President. To present a good appearance as a staff-officer when I took Hiatt to headquarters I borrowed our surgeon's new kepi, all covered with gold braid, and Ned Preston's new coat. My horse and equipment were *en règle*. On my return it began to rain, and I was dreadfully afraid my borrowed feathers would be spoiled.

On September 17th I rode over the battle-field of Chickamauga, which is seven or eight miles from our camp. The Federal dead are still unburied, which is a shame. Perhaps Gen. Thomas thinks it beneath his dignity to ask permission to bury them; or perhaps he thinks Gen. Bragg will do it for him. This, however, he has no right to expect, as he is little more than a mile farther from the field than Bragg, who, if he sent large details of men eight miles to the rear whilst active operations are going on, would just as much have to demand a truce for the purpose as Gen. Thomas, whose business it is.

On September 18th the welcome order was issued by Gen. Buckner relieving Gen. Preston and staff from duty, on account of the reorganization of the corps, and I immediately took the cars for Charleston, S.C., *en route* for Richmond, glad to leave behind me the mud and rain of Missionary Ridge.

CHAPTER XIII.

EAST TENNESSEE AND DREWRY'S BLUFF.

Charleston. — Wilmington. — Richmond. — *En Route* to East Tennessee. — Lynchburg. — Longstreet at Knoxville. — Dublin. — Gen. Sam Jones. — My Birthday duly Celebrated. — Richmond. — Dinner at the Oriental. — East Tennessee again. — Report to Gen. Longstreet. — Assigned to Command a Battalion of Artillery. — Winter Campaign. — Return to Virginia. — Assigned to Duty with Washington Artillery at Petersburg. — Battle of Drewry's Bluff. — Butler Bottled. — President Davis on the Field. — Gen. Beauregard in Command. — Gen. Heckman Captured. — Belger's Battery Captured. — Flag of Truce. — Col. Otis, Tenth Connecticut. — Petersburg.

ON the 22d of October I reached Charleston, S.C., and called upon Gen. Beauregard, who was in command of the city. He seemed pleased to hear news from Chattanooga. A large portion of the city has been destroyed by the enemy's shells. I dined with two of the General's staff-officers, Capts. Chisholm and Deslonde, but we had to change our restaurant twice to get out of reach of the enemy's fire. After dinner we went to the battery and there witnessed some firing between Fort Sumpter and Morris Island. On the battery were the two 700-pounder guns lately received from England. One had been injured by injudicious loading, and could not be used. In the evening I continued my journey towards Richmond.

Upon arriving at Wilmington I met at the railroad station my old comrade, Surgeon T. Y. Aby, of the Washington Artillery. The Doctor had remained behind with our wounded at Gettysburg, and had been sent to Fort

Delaware, from which prison he escaped, and left the country. He took passage on a blockade-runner which had been chased by a blockader and had been beached. Aby escaped, and came to Wilmington, minus all baggage. He accompanied me to Richmond to rejoin the Artillery wherever it might be.

On the 24th I arrived at Richmond at 7 A.M., after a hard campaign of sixty days, was warmly greeted by Col. Walton and my brother (Lieut. E. Owen), whom I find luxuriating at the Spottswood. Excavate my trunk from the baggage room and once more don the habiliments of a gentleman of elegant leisure. Here I shall await the orders of Gen. Preston and enjoy the society of the capital.

On November 19th I received a letter from Gen. Preston from Abingdon telling me he does not expect to be assigned to duty soon, and advises me to look around for some other sphere. It is likely he will be sent to Mexico, with Capt. Walker Fearn, to interview Maximilian.

I am enjoying Richmond society very much, riding and dancing with the pretty girls, and having a good time generally. I don't believe there ever were so many pretty girls to the square inch as there are now in Richmond; it is remarkable. There is the fascinating Miss H——, at the White House; the petite and charming Miss Lizzie G——, the grand daughter of one of Virginia's ancient governors; the beautiful trio, the Misses Hettie, Constance, and Jennie Carey, from Baltimore and Alexandria; the irresistible Miss Mattie P——, who counts her admirers by the score; the adorable Miss Champ C——, whose brilliant eyes create more palpitation of hearts than does an advance of the foe;

the lovely and sprightly sisters, the Misses Truxie and Fannie J——; the queenly Miss Sallie E——, who entertains with such rare and royal grace in her delightful home; those most perfect of rosebuds in this garden of girls, Miss Norvall C—— and Miss McF——, and a host of others, whose pleasant memories, even after a lapse of years, brighten our retrospection of those dark and gloomy days of war.

We had delightful starvation parties, the men furnishing the music and the hostess the bread and butter. The girls are always prettily dressed, and they don't care if you know what a hard time they have to do it. They say they twist and turn all their old things because they can't get new ones. Fashion-plates are scarce. I had a photograph of a sister sent me through the lines. The costume was peculiar, — some new kind of an overcoat, I think, which attracted the girls' attention, and I was beset by a number to let them use it as a pattern. Such is the tyrant, fashion. If any one receives a box through the lines with gloves, stockings, etc., they have many friends. When I went on recruiting service to Mobile I carried orders for stockings and corsets, and have the sizes still.

While I was in Mobile a joke was perpetrated on a brother officer, who, upon leaving Richmond, had inquired of his belle if there was anything he could bring her on his return from his leave of absence.

The next day a dainty little perfumed note reached his hands as he was leaving on the train, bidding him to think of her, and as a reminder that he had done so he could bring her "Cosette." He read it "Corset," and was

considerably puzzled over what he thought a strange request, and went through a variety of mental gymnastics
about sizes, proportions, etc., and finally took a friend into
his confidence, and between them they managed to select
what they conceived to be the article of proper dimensions.
This treacherous friend, more familiar with the current
literature of the day, knew that the young lady had in view
" Cosette," the last production of Victor Hugo, but, instead of enlightening him, could not resist the temptation
of a joke, and gravely assisted him in the purchase of a
pair of corsets, and sent him on his way rejoicing at getting
through with his difficulty.

Quite elated, thinking he had managed to get the right
thing, on arriving at Richmond he hastened to present his
purchase. One can imagine the blushes and embarrass-
ment of the fair recipient, who, being a young and timid
girl, lacked the *savoir faire* with which a more experienced society girl would have concealed the fact that it
was a mistake. In turn our friend was overwhelmed with
confusion, and from the heights of self-satisfaction and com-
placency he was at once reduced to the deepest pit of mor-
tification. However, the corsets were kept, his visits and
attentions redoubled, and we were apprehending serious
consequences in his defection from bachelor ranks, when he
was ordered to the front and the consummation of his hopes
delayed until the following spring, when our gay but
ragged uniforms contributed their share toward making
his wedding a brilliant one. The joke, however, was too
good to keep, though it became dangerous to mention
Victor Hugo at the mess table. To return to my story.

Everything is growing dearer and dearer in Richmond.

Some of my lady friends, married ones, told me that Confederate money was so depressed that they carried it to market in the market-basket and took home their purchases in their pocket-books. I have not yet felt the want of money, having been so long in the field, and living on Government rations of bacon and crackers. The quartermaster owed me a ton of money when I came from Chickamauga, but it is now going fast. Have just paid the French boot-maker (Francis Thomas) $125 for a pair of top boots, and $18 for a patch on an old pair. Hotel bill $25 a day. I have sold a citizen's overcoat, once very swell, to the colored porter at the Spottswood for $450. And now Bob Ford, of our staff, has arrived here with a trunk full of silver spoons, and whenever we need money we take a spoon down to the Three Balls and our uncle buys it; and mighty glad he is to get it for his scrip. We call this our *Spoon* Campaign, and, being that way inclined, I acknowledge the soft impeachment in more ways than one.

Ford says I shall not go back to the army as long as he has a spoon in the locker.

Just at this time private theatricals were the rage in Richmond, and a performance took place at the residence of Mrs. Ives. The play was " The Rivals." Mrs. Clement C. Clay, of Alabama, represented Mrs. Malaprop; Miss Constance Carey, Lydia Languish; and Capt. Frank Ward, of Maryland, Bob Acres. It was all admirably done.

These performances were followed by fancy dress and dancing parties, the young ladies appearing in the old, resurrected costumes of the Revolutionary period of ancient Virginia belles and grandmothers, and right glad to get them of that or any other period. On one occasion, at a party given at Gen. Cooper's by his daughter, Miss Jennie, I was dancing with a pretty girl, and had been admiring her dress, — lace over blue silk I took it to be, but she told me it was mosquito bar over blue muslin. After a short waltz she suddenly gave a little scream, as girls do when a mouse runs across the floor, and placed her back against the wall. " Quick ! quick ! " she cried, in agonized tones. " My cloak ! Take me home : . my spencer has bursted open in the back." The dress was pretty, but frail. Another young lady at this same ball had made use of a whole piece of mosquito-netting, and with a long train and lots of ruchings and puffings, with concomitants of Turkey red run through the puffs and a single bow of red ribbon to match, really presented a most elegant ball costume, and one which any man could not have told from a Worth or Parisian importation. Confidentially she told me that her skirts were so arranged as not to cut into it too much, as her mother had only loaned it, and designed making use of it for household purposes.

Some demure, long-faced people said it was a shame to be dancing while our soldiers were suffering in the field ; but we danced and had a good time when we could, for who could tell how soon any of us might fill a ditch, yclept a soldier's grave? And we didn't take the trouble to think of it. Besides, Gen. Lee said, " Let the young fellows enjoy themselves : they'll fight all the better for it."

But after all I became tired of inaction, and Ford said it must be that my *affaires du cœur* were going wrong, but says if it is *spoons* that's the matter he has some left. But no; I want to get away from Richmond. The fact is, my girl is looking favorably upon a Brigadier-General, who sports more gold lace than I, as a Major, can afford, and I am miserable. So I apply to my friend, Col. Johnston, to have me ordered off. Where to? Well, no matter; away from Richmond, to South-western Virginia, where I can be good and miserable as possible. So it is all arranged, and I am delighted to get back to the field again, and am told to write my own order, which I proceed to do, and here it is : —

ADJUTANT AND INSPECTOR-GENERAL'S OFFICE,
RICHMOND, December 16, 1863.

EXTRACT SPECIAL ORDERS, No. 298 : —

. . . .

VIII. Major W. M. Owen, Artillery, P.A.C.S., will proceed to Abingdon, S.-W. Virginia, and resume command of the artillery of the district lately commanded by Brig.-Gen. Wm. Preston.

He will report to the senior officer commanding in the district upon his arrival, who will see to the execution of this order.

Should the original batteries have been removed from the district, the commanding officer will, if practicable, place the requisite number of guns under the command of Major Owen.

By command of the Secretary of War,

JOHN WITHERS,

Assistant Adjutant-General.

I immediately prepared for roughing it again, and started upon my journey. After many delays, caused by the destruction of the railroads by the Federal General Averill, I reached Abingdon on Christmas eve, and the members of Gen. Preston's staff, who came here after Chickamauga, and were like so many Micawbers, waiting for something to turn up, greeted me enthusiastically. The General was absent, so I took possession of his comfortable quarters at Mrs. Triggs's, and from thence wrote to Gen. Longstreet, enclosing my orders. He is in East Tennessee, somewhere beyond Bristol. He had been sent by Gen. Bragg to capture Knoxville, but his well-laid plans came to naught by the carelessness or indifference to orders of one of his Generals, who, having been instructed to have his men make and carry *fascines* when they charged the enemy's works, failed to do so.

This officer maintained that his men would go over the works without such nonsense; and when it came to the charge they advanced without them, and approaching the fort ran against lines of telegraph-wire stretched about it, tripping them and causing confusion. Those who did get over and into the ditch found it too deep to get out of again, and the enemy, who had abandoned the front line when the charge was begun, now returned to the parapet, and threw lighted shells and grenades amongst the assailants in the ditch. Col. Fizer, of the Seventeenth Mississippi regiment, always brave, sprang upon the parapet and lost an arm. Capt. Winthrop, an English officer[1] who was with the Washington Artillery at Gettysburg, also distinguished himself. He was shot through the shoulder, and the blade of his sabre was snapped in two by a bullet while he was encouraging, by example, the men to advance.

---

[1] Twenty-second British Infantry.

Gen. Burnside having been reinforced from Chattanooga after Bragg's defeat on Missionary Ridge, Longstreet retired in the direction of Bristol. All this I hear from the staff as the news from the front.

On Christmas-day we were all at a loss what to do for the accustomed eggnog and trimmings, when, at the suggestion of some great genius, we determined to call upon one of the belles of the town, the youngest member of the staff, and the ladies' man, promising to introduce us all. We went, and the young lady was quite charming. We had all the eggnog and plum-cake we desired, and had a pleasant time of it.

On the 27th Capt. Sanford and I rented half of a small cottage and fixed ourselves up in soldier fashion and settled down to await orders. We passed the time reading Pickwick and Shakespeare, — the extent of our library, — and mending old clothes, in which accomplishment I had become quite proficient, having been provided with a collection of needles, thread, buttons, and the like, done up in a little leather case, the gift of a lady in New Orleans.

On the 31st received a letter from Col. Sorrel, Longstreet's Adjutant-General, saying that he has no objection to the immediate return to my command of Jeffries's battery, but that Davidson's battery, now with the battalion of Lieut.-Col. King, cannot be spared. Leyden's battalion, to which Jeffries's battery is attached, is at Bristol, and, being within the department of Gen. Sam Jones, this battery may be ordered to me by him on my application.

On the 7th of January, 1864, I left Abingdon for Dublin, to report to Gen. Jones, and upon my arrival found him absent on a scout, but at head-quarters were Capts. Willie Myers and Jim Fraser, two devil-may-care fellows, who insisted upon celebrating my birthday on the 10th. From a beef-contractor we procured a barrel of milk, and drew upon the commissary for *spiritus frumenti*, and the result was plenty of milk-punch with the invariable next-morning headaches.

On the 15th Gen. Jones returned from the scout, and having no duty to assign me to at present, I applied for leave for a short trip to Richmond. I am restless, and feel that I must go and see the dearest girl in the world, for I hear that there's a General and a Colonel now besieging her. I went, I saw, and I returned with a flea of mastodon proportions in my ear. The Colonel was ahead by several lengths. I was miserable now, thoroughly, and determined to throw my life away in battle with the Yank. I was crushed completely. However, notwithstanding the broken heart, in Richmond I dined at the Oriental restaurant with our English friends, Ross, Lawley, Vizetely, of "Illustrated London News," Capts. Woodruff, of the Coldstream Guards, and Hewitt, of the Royal Navy; and if it hadn't been for this relaxation the most desperate consequences might have resulted.

The bill of fare I preserved as a souvenir. It represents Confederate prices in Confederate scrip. In English gold it was not as much as in peace times, and the bill was settled in English sovereigns. I held one in my hand to see how it felt after the long deprivation of such coin. This is the bill of fare : —

Soup, per plate	$1 50		

Wines.

Soup, per plate $1 50
Turkey, " 3 50
Chicken, " 3 50
Rockfish, " 5 00
Roast beef " 3 00
Roast pork " 3 00
Beefsteaks, per dish . . 3 50
Ham and eggs, " . . 3 50
Boiled eggs 2 00
Fried oysters 5 00
Raw " 3 00
Cabbage 1 00
Potatoes 1 00
Pure coffee, per cup . . . 3 00
Pure tea, " . . . 2 00
Fresh milk 2 00
Bread and butter 1 50
Hot rolls 1 50

Wines.

Champagne, per bottle . . $50 00
Madeira, " . . 50 00
Port, " . . 25 00
Claret, " . . 20 00
Sherry, " . . 35 00

Liquors.

French brandy, per drink . $3 00
Apple " " . 2 00
Rye whiskey, " . 2 00

Malt Liquors.

Porter, per bottle . . . $12 00
Ale, " . . . 12 00
Ale, half bottle . . . 6 00

Cigars.

Fine Havana $1 00

Game of all kinds in season.

Terrapins served up in every style.

PETER K. MORGAN, SR.,

Proprietor.

Nine of us sat down to dinner, and the following is the score : —

ORIENTAL SALOON.

RICHMOND, VA., Jan. 17, 1864.

Soup for nine $13 50
Venison steak 31 50
Fried potatoes 9 00
Seven birds 24 00
Baked potatoes 9 00
Celery 13 50
Bread and butter . . . 14 00
Coffee 18 00
Apples 12 00

Dinner $144 50

5 bottles Madeira . . . $250 00
6 bottles claret 120 00
1 urn cocktail 65 00
Jelly 20 00
Cake 20 00
1 dozen cigars 12 00

Total $631 50

Capt. Hewitt is a Victoria Cross man, having gained it at Inkerman. He had command of the navy battery, and when the Russians charged he stuck to his gun to the last minute, then with a leaden bullet and mallet, spiked it, and got off unharmed. What a pity our boys have no V. C.'s to look forward to! They are doing things every day that deserve decorations.

On the 11th of February orders came for me to join Longstreet in East Tennessee, and by first train I am off, horses and all, to join my old friends at Morristown, where I am met by Latrobe and Surgeon Maury, and my return is duly celebrated. Gen. Longstreet is at New Market, to which place head-quarters are to be moved to-morrow, so I am in the nick of time for the advance.

On the 12th rode with staff to New Market, where I met Gen. Longstreet, who welcomes me back with a cordial grip. He quizzed me considerably, having heard a false rumor that I had become a benedict. I was assigned to the command of the Thirteenth Virginia battalion artillery, 17 guns, 540 men, its commander, Lieut.-Col. King, being absent on sick leave.

The weather is very cold, and the ground covered with snow nearly a foot deep. The enemy is moving near Strawberry Plains, and Col. Alexander's battalion of artillery is ordered to that point. The horses are suffering so much from exposure it is with great difficulty they pull the heavy guns along the road.

Our cavalry has all been sent to Gen. Jos. E. Johnston, and we can do but little without their aid.

While dining to-day at the head-quarters of the surgeons Cullen, Barksdale, and Maury, a young soldier of Kershaw's brigade was brought in with his right hand crushed. He had deliberately placed it upon the railroad track, and allowed a locomotive to pass over it.

The dinner-table was cleared, and the boy placed upon it, and in a little while his hand was flung out of the window. A friend of the boy had wounded himself a short time since, and had been sent home; so this one was trying the same means to accomplish that end. It was the act of a poltroon, and he was made an example of and compelled to remain in the hospital. I had seen a man or two who had shot fingers off in battle to obtain sick leave, but never before one who deliberately allowed a locomotive to run over him.

Received marching orders and reported with the Thirteenth battalion to Gen. Kershaw. After moving a few miles towards Bristol, and countermarching two or three times, reports were received that the enemy was following us, and we finally encamped at Greenville. Here we have terrible weather for men and horses, snowing and sleeting all the time, and the men badly provided with underclothing and shoes. There is much suffering.

The batteries composing the Thirteenth Virginia battalion are the Davidson, Lowry, Ringgold, and the "Otey" battery of Richmond, Va. The latter is a noteworthy organization, composed of the best material of the young men of Richmond and Virginia generally. They are well equipped, well disciplined, and commanded by officers of high standing and ability. The officers are as follows : Capt. D. L. Walker, Lieuts. Bolling, Gunn, Norvell, and Langhorne.

The other batteries are composed of good Virginia boys, who are always willing and trying to do their level best, and not afraid to handle the axe, the pick, or the spade, which all will be called upon to use ere long.

Greenville is the residence of Gov. Andy Johnson, and his tailor-shop was pointed out to us where he worked at his trade. In a house occupied by the surgeons are many hundreds of congressional reports and public documents belonging to the Governor.

We are living in the snow, and have a few old tents. My tent has a large mud chimney, and as the quartermaster has furnished plenty of clean straw we are quite comfortable. Our old friends of Preston's staff paid us a visit as they were *en route* for the Mississippi river.

On the 29th of March we are again on the move towards Bristol. The weather is intensely cold, and some of the drivers are frostbitten. After much hardship, marching over muddy roads, and through snow and sleet, and fording the swollen currents of the Watauga and Holston rivers, with many narrow escapes from drowning of men and horses, we encamp near Bristol and report to Gen. Field.

This campaign, doing nothing but marching and countermarching, has been a hard one, and at a season of the year when other armies are enjoying themselves in comfortable winter-quarters.

President Davis having appointed the 8th of April as a day of fasting and prayer, our cook reports us out of bacon; we breakfast therefore on rice, corn-bread and sorghum, and consequently we are hungry all day.

Am growing very tired of this kind of life : it is too dull. I would rather be in Richmond, fed by Ford's spoons, even if the dearest girl in the world should smile upon the "General" and the "Colonel." On the 12th of April the report reaches us in camp that Longstreet's corps is going back to Lee in Virginia. I immediately apply to go with it, and am referred by Gen. Longstreet to Gen. Alexander, now Chief of Artillery, for assignment. The news of the resignation of Col. Walton has just reached him, and, as there is a vacancy in the field-officers of the Washington Artillery, I am ordered back to my well-loved command. I am delighted, and shall be off like a shot to-morrow by rail, my boy following with my horses. So farewell forever, South-western Virginia !

After travelling night and day I reached Petersburg on the morning of the 15th of April. At the station I found my brother's servant with a horse for me, and I immediately rode to the camp of the Washington Artillery at the Model Farm, where my reception by the boys is quite gratifying, and I am glad once more to get back home.

Officers and men look so jaunty, clean, and neat, and are so well uniformed, that I feel ashamed of the mud of Tennessee upon my boots, and my shabby uniform, all sun-burnt and faded. After presenting my orders to Major Eshleman, the Adjutant (my successor) takes me in charge, and to his quarters, where I enjoy the luxury of a hot bath, and, as my trunk is in Richmond, draw upon my brother, Capt. Owen, for clean clothes, and once again take mine ease.

Model Farm is a collection of houses about two miles

from Petersburg, built before the war for agricultural experimenting. There are a large barn, stables, two rows of cottages, on each side of an open space of about an acre. At the extreme end is the superintendent's house, now used as head-quarters. The company officers occupy the cottages, and the cannoneers the large barn. The guns are parked in the open space in the centre of the group, and as a place for winter-quarters answers admirably.

After my promotion from Adjutant of the Battalion to Major of Artillery, Sergt.-Major E. I. Kursheedt was promoted to the adjutantcy, and Sergt. W. A. Randolph to be Sergeant-Major, — both excellent appointments of well-deserving and brave men.

Col. Walton having resigned the colonelcy of the Artillery, has been appointed Inspector General of Field Artillery of the Confederate States.

Major B. F. Eshleman is in command of the Battalion. The following changes have taken place : —

Capt. C. W. Squires, of the First company, has been promoted to Major of Artillery in the trans-Mississippi Department, and has been succeeded by Lieut. Edward Owen as Captain.

Capt. M. Buck Miller has been promoted to Major, and has been assigned to a Battalion of Virginia Artillery. He is succeeded by Lieut. Andrew Hero as Captain.

Sergt.-Major C. L. C. Dupuy has been appointed to a lieutenancy of Artillery, and has gone to Vicksburg.

First Sergeant Thomas Y. Aby, of First company, has been appointed Assistant Surgeon of the Battalion.

The Major-Domo and wife disappeared when Col. Walton resigned.

On the 16th of April drilling is resumed and preparations pushed forward with a view to putting the command in a condition for service.

Gen. Lee is at Gordonsville, and the Bàttalion is desirous of joining him there; but our wish is not gratified. The command has been at Petersburg since September last, when Longstreet went to Chickamauga. It was to have accompanied him, with the troops of Hood and Kershaw, but got this far and was halted.

Desiring to make a presentable appearance in Petersburg, my good friend Mrs. Dunn has employed a sewing woman to renovate my uniform coat, to turn it inside out, at the cost of $50. This coat was quite stunning when I went to Mobile, — now it is very shabby; but a new one costs $500.

On May 5 we are suddenly aroused to activity. Gen. Pickett, now commanding the Petersburg defences, orders our guns to the City Point road. We are short of serviceable horses, and all the teams in the city are impressed into service. Horses belonging to omnibuses, express-wagons, buggies, — in fact, any animal that can help haul a gun is sent to us and forced to serve.

Thirty transports full of the enemy's troops and five monitors are reported coming up the James river and at Bermuda Hundreds, Gen. B. F. Butler in command. After much trouble with the new horses we get off with the following guns : —

First company, Capt. E. Owen . . . 4 guns.
Second company, Capt. Richardson . . . 3 "
Third company, Capt. Hero . . . . 3 "
Fourth company, Capt. Norcom . . . 3 "

13 in all,

which are placed in works on the City Point road.

May 6. — Enemy reported coming up the City Point road. 5 P.M. — Firing heard across the Appomattox river. Enemy has pushed out a force from Bermuda Hundreds to Walthal Junction, on the Richmond Railroad. Has been attacked and driven back.

The enemy is in large force, and we have but small support, — part of Thirty-first (N.C.) regiment and the city militia. The latter are jolly cases, — have their lunch-baskets with them, and take it all as a big joke. How little they realize the horrors of war, and what may be in store for them at home! Here we met for the first time, in the ranks of the militia, Messrs. Hare, Kevan, Young, Potts, Friend, Duggan, and Cameron, — gentlemen whom we shall probably often meet during our sojourn here.

May 7. — All quiet along the lines this A.M. Lieut.-Col. Eshleman (lately promoted) is ordered at 10.45 across the Appomattox to command the artillery there, taking with him the battery of Capt. Owen, and I am left in charge of the lines of Petersburg.

Guns in position as follows : 9 guns of Washington Artillery, 5 guns of Reid's battalion.

May 9. — At 2 A.M. one section of Capt. Hero's battery is ordered to report to Capt. Sturdevant to attack gun-boats in the Appomattox river. 1 P.M. heavy firing in the direction of Fort Clifton. 11.30 heavy firing across the river in the direction of Swift Creek.

May 10. — A severe engagement is fought again at Walthal Junction, resulting in a repulse of Butler's forces.

May 11. — 7.30 A.M. all the guns of the Washington Artillery ordered across the Appomattox river to positions on the Richmond Turnpike. 9 P.M. all the infantry and artillery march towards Richmond, and bivouac on the roadside near Walthal's. We have been marching in line of battle, skirmishers on our flank towards the enemy at Bermuda Hundreds. The enemy is close at hand, and the strictest silence is enjoined. Drums and bugles not allowed. Gen. Corse is in command, and he bunks with us for the night.

May 12. — March at 3.30 A.M. The *reveille* in the enemy's camp can be heard, less than a mile distant. The utmost silence and caution ordered : we are crossing his entire front. Column halted at the Half-Way House, ten miles from Richmond. 11 A.M. the enemy has discovered our movements, and attacks our rear-guard of South Carolina cavalry. Skirmishing kept up one hour. 12 M. occupy the fortifications around Drewry's Bluff, leaving one section of First company Washington Artillery, under Capt. Owen, at the Half-Way House on picket. The enemy is moving, and has now possession of the road we have passed over, between us and Petersburg. 2.25 P.M. Capt. Owen opens fire upon the enemy's cavalry, and continues firing until dark. One brigade of the enemy is engaged and repulsed by Corse's

brigade and three guns of ours. Enemy's cavalry reported moving around our right towards Chesterfield Court-
House.

May 13. — Heavy skirmishing all along the line. At
4 P.M. Gen. Ransom's position on the right of our outer
line, near the Woolridge House, is flanked by the enemy
under Gen. Gilmore. 6.15 P.M. our guns are withdrawn
to inner line of works.

May 14. — 2 A.M. our whole force of infantry falls
back to the inner line of works immediately around Drewry's
Bluff, leaving our outer line to the enemy, who occupies it
without delay. We now have our backs to the wall, as it
were, and will fight right here. Gen. Beauregard, with
Colquitt's brigade and Macon's battery, arrived from Petersburg *via* Chesterfield Court-House. The entire armament
of the Washington Artillery in the works is as follows : —

On extreme left, two (2) guns of Third company, under
Lieut. Stocker.

In centre, four (4) guns of Second company, under Capt.
Richardson, supported by Hagood's S. C. brigade at Fort
Stevens.

Four (4) guns of Third company, Capt. Hero, supported by Clingman's brigade.

Three (3) guns of Fourth company, Capt. Norcom ; also
four (4) stationary guns, worked by Fourth company, supported by Corse and Ransom.

Four (4) guns of First company, Capt. E. Owen, at
Gregory's Crossing, supported by Colquitt's brigade.

Twenty-one (21) guns in all. Heavy skirmishing all
day along the lines ; the enemy's sharp-shooters sweep

with their rifles the barbette works, causing us a loss of four killed, four wounded, mostly in the Fourth company.

President Davis arrives from Richmond, and visits Gen. Beauregard at Drewry's house. Capt. Owen and I call upon him.

Early this A.M. Col. Eshleman, Adjt. Kursheedt, and I mounted our horses and went out to take a look at the lines. We visited the positions of all our guns, and upon our return, discovering that the sharp-shooters were observing us, we halted behind some log-cabins that had been used as winter-quarters by some troops. To go forward or to retreat was equally hazardous, so we held a council of war, and determined to run the gauntlet across an open field that would take us to the turnpike behind a ridge. We agreed to ride in a bunch, so that we would present but a small mark for the enemy, and, gathering our horses well in hand, gave them the spur and started. Instantly the sharp-shooters began firing, and the bullets flew by us like the buzzing of a swarm of bees. Our good steeds seemed conscious of our peril, and went like the wind. Some close shots were made, but no hits. Finally we heard a " thud " of a bullet, and Eshleman's horse rose up on his hind legs, and Kursheedt and I thought he was a goner, but he came down again, and away we went. We reached the ridge, and were hid from view, right thankful we had run the gauntlet so successfully and with whole skins.

Upon examination we found that the bullet had struck Eshleman's saddle-pocket, leaving a heavy indentation, but had not penetrated. The horse felt it as a sting, and so sprang up and forward.

We rode back to our head-quarters provided with a good appetite for our plain breakfast after our exhilarating exercise.

On Sunday, May 15, sharp-shooting continues all day, and the positions of our guns are hot. This evening the following order for battle was issued : —

HEAD–QUARTERS DEPARTMENT, N. C. AND S. VIRGINIA,

May 15, 1864.

SPECIAL ORDER No. 7 : —

The following temporary organization of divisions for attack is hereby announced : —

Major-General Hoke's Division.— Corse's, Clingman's, Johnson's, and Hagood's brigades.

Major-General Ransom's Division. — Barton's, Gracie's, Kemper's and Hoke's brigades.

Reserve. — Brig.-Gen. Colquitt commanding, Colquitt's and Ransom's brigades.

ARTILLERY. — *Hoke's Division.* — Battalion Washington Artillery, Lieut.-Col. Eshleman.

Ransom's Division. — Lightfoot's battalion, Lieut.-Col. Lightfoot.

Colquitt's Reserve.—Macon's "Richmond Fayette Artillery," Slaten's battery, and the battery under Capt. Martin, all under command of Major W. M. Owen, Washington Artillery.

By command of Gen. Beauregard,

JOHN M. OTEY,

A.A. General.

At 5 A.M., on the morning of the 16th of May, our artillery opens fire all along the line. A heavy fog conceals our movements from the enemy's view. At 5.45 Hoke's division springs over the works and charges the enemy. Ransom, who had advanced upon the river road to strike the enemy's right under Gen. Heckman, did so with spirit, and that Federal General is brought in a prisoner.   The First company (four guns), under Capt. Owen, is ordered to follow Hoke's division down the turnpike, where he engages a heavy battery of the enemy in front and apparently directly on the turnpike.   The guns of the enemy fire high, and ours, having better range, soon pile up his horses and cripple his guns.   Hagood's brigade now goes forward to the charge, and, advancing directly upon the enemy's guns, captures them.   At this moment Capt. Owen and his Lieutenant, Galbraith, **fall wounded, the latter mortally. Slaten's battery of the reserve is now sent to relieve Owen, and its Captain is severely wounded while getting into position.**

Two guns of the Fayette artillery of the reserve, under Lieut. Clopton, are hurried off to the right of our line, where Gen. Corse is severely engaged.

When Hagood secured the enemy's guns, one of them, a 20-pounder Parrott, was most gallantly manned by Col. Eshleman, Adjt. Kursheedt, and Sergt.-Major Randolph of the Washington Artillery, and fired a number of rounds at the enemy.

Gen. Beauregard has established his head-quarters on the turnpike, opposite Fort Stevens, where the Second company Washington Artillery is stationed.   The reserve artillery is in rear of him.   Here reports are received from the field.   Clingman, of Hoke's division, reports the enemy fighting hard, and wants reinforcements.   Johnson and Hagood are driving the enemy, and are fighting splendidly.   " Wait," says Beauregard, "until I get my left (Ransom) well in ! "   Staff-officers are sent out there for news.   Prisoners are passing by in large numbers.   Capt.

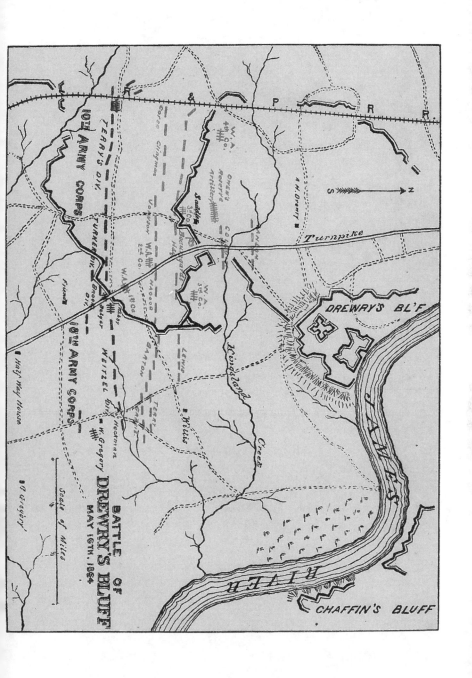

Belger, who commanded the enemy's battery, is a prisoner. The gallant soldier seemed quite dazed at his misfortune, and couldn't comprehend the situation. He asked "What battery was that, that I was fighting?" One of the boys told him, "First company Washington Artillery." The Captain's expression changed, as he replied with emphasis, "D—n that Washington Artillery! I have been looking for it for three years, and have found it at last." Then he moved on to Richmond.

The enemy is giving way, and we listen to the yells and volleys of our troops as they press forward through the timber. Our wounded are being removed to the rear. Capt. Owen passes mounted on his horse, although as bloody as Banquo's ghost from a wound in the head. Dr. Chopin rides forward to examine his hurt, and pronounces it severe but not dangerous. When Owen fell, his brave and brawny Sergeant, Jack McGaughey, carried him upon his back to his horse. Lieut. Galbraith, gallant dashing Johnnie, is mortally wounded. The battery has suffered terribly. Byron Phelps is carried by. He says, in answer to my inquiry after his wounds, "Major, I have six holes through me, and all by one ball;" and so he had, through both his arms and breast.[1] Peychaud is killed, and his brother, running forward to where the body lies beside the road, falls badly wounded. George Chambers, the fourth of the brothers in the Battalion, is mortally hurt. Everett, who is always on the list of wounded, is struck in the foot, and Rossiter is hit again.

---

[1] Phelps's left arm was amputated in New Orleans, in 1885, twenty-one years after the battle, the bone having become diseased.

At 1 P.M. the captured battery was brought in. It consisted of three 20-pounder Parrotts and two 12-pounder Napoleons, and they were presented to the First company upon the field by General Hagood, in recognition of their gallantry in engaging and disabling a heavier battery than their own. Our left has now got well in and the enemy is badly beaten. A small force still holds on at the Half-Way House with two pieces of artillery. Preparations are made to capture them, and two of Capt. Richardson's guns, which have been brought from Fort Stevens, are sent down the road to the skirmish line, and open fire. We soon got a reply, and one of the enemy's solid shot struck at the feet of President Davis and Gen. Beauregard, and they changed their base to the other side of the road, out of range.

The enemy soon limbers up and makes off, and Butler is in full retreat to Bermuda Hundreds.

It was a part of Beauregard's plan, that Gen. Whiting, with a body of troops on the turnpike, near Petersburg, should immediately advance as soon as we had joined battle with Butler, at the first sound of our guns. Marching up the road, he would naturally fall upon Butler's rear. It was now afternoon, and Butler was in full retreat, and we were waiting for Whiting's guns to assure us he was amongst the fugitives.

Gen. Beauregard and President Davis, together with Col. William Preston Johnston, were standing on the works listening intently. Presently a single gun was heard in the distance. "Ah!" said Mr. Davis. "At last!" and a smile came over his face. But that solitary gun was all; no other was heard. Whiting has failed us, and Butler would get back behind his entrenchments at Bermuda Hundreds. At 6 P.M. Johnson's and Clingman's brigades, and the Fayette artillery, and two guns of Martin's battery of the reserve are sent in pursuit. Butler left behind his dead and wounded, his wagons, and thousands of small arms.

Yesterday William Forrest, a driver in Richardson's battery, distinguished himself by replacing the battery guidon on Fort Stevens, where it was shot away twice by the enemy's sharp-shooters. It was an act equal to that of Sergt.' Jasper's in the first Revolution, — though just then times were too stirring with us for it to attract more than passing mention.

Gen. Gracie told me, after the battle, that when his brigade struck Heckman's, on the right of the enemy's line, it broke at once, and as our men pressed forward, firing, a fine-looking man dressed in a blue coat and high black hat of a Federal officer was observed mixed up with our troops, shouting at the top of his voice, " Go in, boys ! Give 'em hell ! " One of Gracie's men stopped, carefully surveyed the stranger, and said, " Look h'yer, Mister, those clothes don't go well with this crowd ! You come along with me. That 'ere hat's a beauty : let's swap." The prisoner was Gen. Heckman. His capture, under the circumstances, caused much merriment at the bivouac that night.

The losses in the Battalion Washington Artillery at Drewry's Bluff were as follows : —

First Company. — Killed : H. Peychaud, George Chambers, T. G. Simmons. Wounded : Capt. E. Owen, Lieut. J. M. Galbraith, Corporal S. Turner, Edward Peychaud, J. J. Norment, C. Rossiter, T. J. Wilson, Joseph Myers, C. A. Everett, Byron Phelps. Captured : P. O. Fazende.

Second Company. — Wounded : M. J. Lapham, George Gessner, I. N. Greenman.

Third Company. — Killed : H. Madden. Wounded : G. Guillotte, A. Guillotte, A. Leefe, James Crilly.

Fourth Company. — Killed : R. G. McDonald, John Faulkes, E. A. Mallard, Edward Condon. Wounded : Sergt. John B. Valentine, J. S. Hood, A. Norcom, William Martin.

Total loss, 30.

On the morning of May 17 we marched towards Petersburg, following the route of the beaten enemy. Counted twenty-five dead horses, and as many dead men, where the captured battery (Belger's) had fought. Bivouacked eight miles from Petersburg. Communication open. Wise's and Martin's brigades join us to-day, under command of D. H. Hill. It is reported we have taken 1,600 prisoners.

In spite of the seriousness of the battle-field some amusing things will occur. Frequently an officer's horse will give him trouble, and raise a laugh at his expense. During the battle of the 16th Col. George Lay, formerly of the old army, and on the staff of Gen. Scott, was serving on the staff of Gen. Beauregard. During the early part of the day the General had dismounted and sat upon the earthwork, giving orders through his staff, and receiving reports from the General commanding the troops engaged on the right, left, and centre. Col. Lay's horse became right restive when the shells would scream past or explode near by, and gave him considerable trouble as he held him by the bridle in the road.

In front of the earthwork was a deep ditch full of water, and the Colonel's horse manœuvred disagreeably close to its edge. Finally a shell burst close by, and the horse backed, and continued backing in spite of his (Lay's) hallooing " Whoa ! Whoa ! " and being dragged at the other end of the bridle. The contest between the two, brain and matter, became so intense that all the staff laughed and watched. The gallant steed was rapidly bringing his rear to bear upon the edge of the ditch, notwithstanding the appeals of the Colonel, when, with one more step too far to the rear, ker-splash ! he went into the muddy ditch, leaving the Colonel upon the bank in a quandary as to what was the next proper move to rescue the brute, — coaxing wouldn't do it, and no other means could be resorted to. And there the Colonel sat on the edge of that ditch during the whole battle watching his horse, who seemed content to be safe from the enemy's fire. When the battle was over a pioneer party dug steps into the ditch and the sensible brute was rescued.

During the battle of the Wilderness Col. Charles Marshall, of Gen. Lee's staff, was riding a parti-colored horse that he had lately purchased in a country town. He happened to be riding through an old field, that had a new growth of scrubby pines and some large stumps in it. When the firing began Marshall found his horse capering about in a queer fashion, and, espying a large stump, he placed thereon his fore feet, and began moving around in a waltzing fashion. The hotter the fire the more he would waltz. The Colonel had no desire to keep the thing up : it was getting monotonous ; but all at once there was a lull in the conflict, and then the well-trained *circus horse* — for such he was — was as easily guided as the Colonel wished ; but he never rode him under fire again.

May 18. — 8.45 A.M. heavy skirmishing in front of Hoke and Hill. One section of Fourth company engaged all day at intervals with skirmishers. In the afternoon a Federal brigade made a forward move, but was driven back.

This P.M. I had concluded to ride into Petersburg to see some lady friends, and had just completed an elaborate toilet, when I received an order to go and construct works for artillery, on Clay's farm, for sixteen guns.

Worked all night with large details with pick and spade, and at 6 A.M. opened fire upon the enemy's lines, firing thirty-three minutes. I don't think we did much damage, save to the wagon-trains and quartermasters in the rear. The front line always "hugs the dirt" during artillery firing, and generally escapes much damage.

May 20, A.M. — Ordered to report to Gen. Bushrod Johnson for duty on his lines in front of the enemy. He places under my command two 30-pounder Parrotts, at the Howlett-House battery, on the James river, and three 20-pounder Parrotts (those captured at Drewry's Bluff) of Owen's battery under Lieut. Brown.

To-day an assault was made upon the enemy's line, which was carried. Gen. Walker is missing. It is supposed he is either killed or a prisoner.

Gen. Johnson's head-quarters are at Mr. Friend's house,

a large dwelling built of brick. He has a pleasant staff, but his mess arrangements are not good; has sharpened sticks for forks, and plates and cups are scarce; but, as I always carry knife, spoon, and fork in my haversack, I am all right. We all sleep in the parlor upon the bare floor. The first night I was with the General, two monitors in the James river opened fire with their 15-inch guns. The shells flew high over our house, went beyond, and exploded. At the first report the General sat bolt upright and said, "Boys! boys! hear that? Those infernal things will hit us sure." We assured him that they did not have our range, and there was no danger; but he said, "But, boys, the blamed thing might wabble!" We had a laugh at the General's expense, who was as brave a man as Julius Cæsar. The idea of a monster gun on a monitor wabbling!

At 2 P.M. on the 21st the monitors opened fire on the Howlett battery. Major W. T. Blakemore, of Gen. Johnson's staff, was struck by a fragment of shell, causing the loss of a foot. His beautiful mare, "Filsey," was killed by the same shell, and they were found lying together on the field. Blakemore was a great favorite with us all, and had served with distinction at Chickamauga and Drewry's Bluff. We were very sorry to lose his companionship and gallant services.

The batteries of Richardson, Hero, and Norcom, of the Washington Artillery, have been ordered to the rear to rest. These batteries were all engaged at Drewry's Bluff, and did most gallant service.

At 10 P.M. the skirmishing upon our front becoming quite heavy Gen. Johnson requested me to ride with him to ascertain the cause. It had ceased when we reached the front, but it is not very pleasant to ride along in the dark expecting every moment the skirmish line to open fire.

At 10.30, May 22, the monitors again throw their immense shells at the Howlett battery. At 5 P.M. there is a flag of truce along our front to bring in the dead lying between the lines, left there after the assault of the 20th. The bodies have become very offensive.

Under the flag of truce I met Col. Otis, of the Tenth Connecticut regiment, and Major Sanford, of the Seventh Connecticut, and from them learned that Capt. Ashby, Third New York Artillery, commanded the three 20-pounder Parrotts, and Capt. Belger the two 12-pounder Napoleon guns taken at Drewry's. Ashby, as was Owen, was wounded in the head.

Gen. Bushrod Johnson is promoted Major-General and put in command of Johnson's, Wise's, Ransom's, and Walker's brigades. For the present I am his Chief of Artillery.

On the 26th of May I apply to be relieved, being completely done up, and am ordered back to the Washington Artillery, at Petersburg.

Then, obtaining leave of absence, go to Richmond to see Capt. Owen and Miss H——. The former is fast recovering from his wound, and is being nursed by our good friends, the Johnstons. I fear the "Colonel," has been in Richmond, as my reception by Miss H—— is decidedly and refreshingly cool, and consequently I am

again in despair, and return to my duties with the Battalion
at Petersburg.[1]

---

[1] Extract from a second letter from a Federal soldier present at the battle of
Drewry's Bluff, dated October 29, 1883 : —

"DEAR OWEN : —

. . . .

" After writing you I succeeded in getting a Government map, made from sur-
veys by the U. S. Engineers in 1867.

" I enlarged the immediate surroundings of Drewry's, of which I send you a
tracing, with such information as I have been able to collect on the subject from
correspondence with the best informed men of all the U. S. regiments east of the
turnpike as well as a personal going over the map with many of them.

" The situation on our side east of the road at the opening of the action is abso-
lutely correct. The position of Gracie's and Terry's and Barton's regiments is
also correct I am satisfied, where the main lines came in contact.

" The pickets of the Ninth New Jersey were in Willis's house and yard when
the skirmish line of the Twenty-third Alabama Battalion routed them out, and
while they engaged the attention of our main line, Col. Stansel, of the Forty-
first Alabama, with his skirmishers, swung around what Gen. Beauregard
calls our 'weak right,' into the road below Mr. Gregory's, when hearing the
heavy firing still in their rear, and realizing the situation, with no unnecessary
delay skipped back by the same route by which they came, into their main line.

" There must have been over an hour's hot work across that little creek before
the Twenty-third Massachusetts at the road, losing their heroic Major Chambers,
went to pieces, under the persistent pressure of Gracie and Kemper, while at the
same time the slackening fire of the Ninth New Jersey, their ammunition being
exhausted, gave fresh hope to Gracie's men, who cried out 'The Yankees have
surrendered!' But Gracie had been too severely handled to overcome even the
feeble opposition, and Terry's men, going over them, opened the gap wider between the Ninth New Jersey and the Twenty-seventh Massachusetts, and went
down the road nearly to Gregory's, then filing westward into the woods, dressed
their line, and advanced upon the rear of the Twenty-seventh Massachusetts,
who, all unconscious of the break in our line, were still holding the Forty-third
Alabama and some of Barton's men at arm's length.

" A few scattering men of the Twenty-third Massachusetts were gathered up in
this grip, but the Virginians saw through the fog a much larger body of men on
their left, from whom, as they faced about, came the hail, 'What regiment is
that?' 'First Virginia!' 'Rebels! Fire!' and eight Virginians, with their
faces almost scorched with the flame of a gallant but unavailing defence, pitch
forward, dead, while their comrades, with the bayonet, rush in upon the astonished Twenty-seventh Massachusetts, and nearly three hundred good and true
men threw up their hands in amazement and despair at this unexpected turn of
affairs.

" The Seventh Virginia, pushing still further westward, first encounters a lone
horseman in blue, who cries out to them, ' Come on, boys, we are beating them
back!' to which a long-haired Sergeant responds, 'Look 'yer, stranger, them

clothes don't go well in this crowd! You come along with me.' Gen. Heck-man, commanding the brigade, refuses to surrender to the Sergeant, who attends him until Col. Floweree comes up, when the General turns over his sword. The Seventh Virginia continues on until well in the rear of the Twenty-fifth Massachusetts, but while attempting a repetition of the success of their com-rades are charged by the Twenty-fifth Massachusetts, whose onset they stop by a well-directed fire, but they cannot overcome it sufficiently to prevent that regiment from slipping through their fingers westward into the thick fog and thicker woods.

"The next regiment, the Ninety-eighth New York, changes front, and, sup-ported by the Eighth Maine and Twenty-first Connecticut, checks the further immediate advance of Ransom's column in this direction. While one of Ran-som's brigades, pushing down the old stage road for the Proctor's Creek Cross-ing, which they were to seize and hold, runs into two detached regiments, the Ninth Maine and One Hundred and Twelfth New York, when the tide is turned, though the eventual abandonment of our line follows later in the morning. Heckman's brigade lost 42 killed, 188 wounded, 458 prisoners."

Of the movements of Belger's battery, the same writer adds : —

"Belger, with his Napoleons, was cavorting about all the P. M. of the 15th in Gregory's orchard and the near woods, but during the night our 'weak right' was still further weakened by his removal to the pike, where he was in-active the most of the morning, until he took the two guns down to '*help out Ashby*,' and *eventually* the Washington Artillery."

CHAPTER XIV.

GRANT IN FRONT OF RICHMOND.

Washington Artillery on the Chickahominy. — Assault at Cold Harbor. — Grant Marches to James River. — Petersburg. — The Siege. — Forts Hell and Damnation. — Shelling the City. — Citizens in Bomb-proofs. — Capt. Dunn. — "*Dum vivimus, vivamus.*" — Gen. Alexander. — Fourth of July. — Col. Walton's Resignation. — Explosion of the Mine. — Negro Troops. — Gibbs's Battalion of Artillery. — Flag of Truce.

ON June 2, 1864, the Battalion was ordered to Richmond by the Secretary of War to report to Gen. Ransom. We marched at 7 P.M. with the Second, Third, and Fourth companies, leaving the First company under Lieut. Brown at the Howlett battery. Bivouacked at Drewry's Bluff.

At 6 A.M. on the 3d we again took the road and at 10 A.M. reported to Gen. Ramson, whose head-quarters were on the Chickahominy, near Richmond, and by his orders went into position at Bottom's Bridge. Grant is confronting Lee at Cold Harbor. We are to protect the lower fords, supported by Fitz Lee's Cavalry. To-day Grant assaulted Lee's lines and was repulsed with very heavy loss. Our loss but slight.

The First company joined us to-day, having being relieved from duty at Howlett's.

June 4. — This is the third anniversary of our arrival in Virginia. "*Tempus fugit,*" sure enough.

June 6. — I rode over to Gen. R. H. Anderson's head-quarters to-day. He commands the corps of Longstreet, who is absent on account of wound received at the Wilderness. Crossed the Chicahominy at McClellan's Bridge, and hunted up Cullen at Dr. Garnett's, dined with him and had a good time.

The loss of the enemy in the last assault said to be 14,000 ; ours, 400.

Dr. Garnett pointed out the ruins of his outhouse and denounced the parties whoever they were who set fire to it and burned it. He was so mad about it I took good care not to tell him my brother did it. The fate of war, Doctor.

The Thirteenth Virginia Battalion of Artillery — the one I was in temporary command of when in East Tennessee with Longstreet — is now in the trenches at Cold Harbor, having come here with Gen. Breckenridge. Lieut.-Col. King is in command.

June 8 to 11. — Gen. Ransom kicks up a great row with Eshleman and d—s the battalion generally because we let our horses loose in a field to graze. He is afflicted with an awfully bad temper.

June 12. — Rode along the lines to-day and visited Col. Walter Taylor at Gen. Lee's head-quarters. Dined with Cullen.

June 13. — Grant is off on another flank movement. This time he has moved towards James river, for he has found the gates of Richmond closed against him on this side. This he might have known before losing so many thousands of his men. He crossed at Long Bridge, forcing Gen. Rooney Lee's Cavalry back to White Oak Swamp, where he holds the bridge. Heth's division confronts him there. Wilcox's and Anderson's divisions move to Riddell's store and toward Malvern Hill. Gen. Custis Lee is placed in command of the "Department of Henrico." Grant is now reported crossing the James river at Harrison's Landing. An attack on Petersburg is apprehended. Heth's division, Ransom's brigade, and Reid's battery ordered to Petersburg. We have applied directly to President Davis to let us go also.

June 16. — Heavy firing is heard this A.M. in the direction of Petersburg. It is reported that the outer works have been taken by the enemy. Longstreet's corps ordered over. Nine Federal prisoners came into camp to-day. They were captured by two Confederates, — all foreigners, — German, French, and Irish. They have had enough fighting, and say they were all drunk when they were "shanghaied," as they term enlisted. We appear to be fighting all the nations of the earth.

June 18. — President Davis has granted our request, and we are ordered over to Petersburg. We marched at once, and upon reaching that city are put in position in the earthworks, and the divisions of Wilcox and Mahone support us.

Here we were destined to remain nearly one year, through the heat and dust of summer, and the mud, snow, and ice of winter, almost daily under fire, losing many of our men. Here Lee's army receives the brunt of Grant's immense forces, and gives up the lines only when our force is so reduced by death, wounds, and sickness that our men stand three yards apart in the trenches extending from Richmond to Hatcher's Run, a distance of thirty miles.

On June 21 three brigades of the enemy march out towards the Weldon Railroad. The cavalry, under our old comrade Dearing, who is now a Brigadier, falls back before them and Wilcox's division, with six guns of Pegram's and six of the Washington Artillery, are sent after them.

The Second company is ordered into a detached work near the Jerusalem Plank Road. This redoubt was afterwards called "Fort Mahone," and by the Federals "Fort Damnation."

The Second company was distinguished in this work for checking the Federals in constructing their works opposite, causing them to draw their lines at a more respectful distance.

They built a heavy work, however, at this point, and called it "Fort Sedgwick," or "Fort Hell;" and "Hell" and "Damnation" were about the hottest places on the lines of Petersburg.

Corporal Myers, of the Second company, was a capital shot, and on one occasion he called attention to the fact that at a certain hour every day a number of officers gathered in "Fort Sedgwick," at a spot where he could see a white tent. He proposed to disturb them, so cutting a shell to burst properly, he carefully sighted his gun, and called all hands to look. The lanyard was pulled, and away went the shell, and so accurate was his aim that the projectile exploded exactly in front of the tent, and it and its occupants gathered no more at that spot. Myers became very annoying to the enemy, and on a bright Sunday

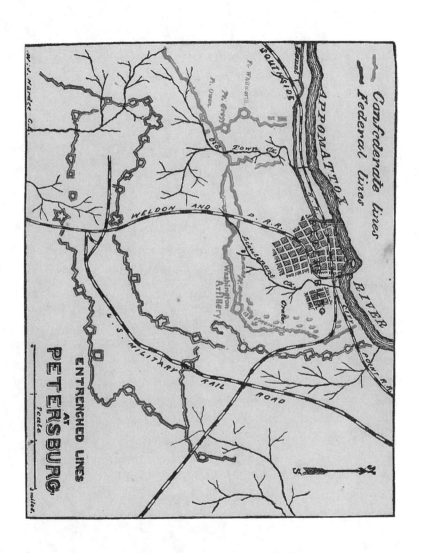

ENTRENCHED LINES
AT
PETERSBURG

morning they had their revenge, as one of their shells exploded near him when sighting his gun, and laid him low.

On June 22d Mahone attacked the Second corps of the enemy on the Jerusalem Plank Road, taking ten stands of colors, four pieces of artillery, and 2,000 prisoners. Our loss was 350.

Urquart, of Second company, was wounded to-day while carrying ammunition.

June 24. — At 7 A.M. some of our guns on the opposite bank of the Appomattox river opened upon the enemy's works.

At 8 A.M. Hagood's brigade and Hoke's division advanced upon the enemy's lines, but, not being supported as they should have been, fall back, after driving the enemy from his rifle-pits. Our loss, 300 to 400.

On June 25 at 2 P.M. the enemy threw a few shells into the city; at 10 P.M. they began shelling again, and continued at intervals all night. Several women are reported killed and a number of buildings struck and more or less damaged.

June 26. — Enemy shelling the city all day. Our headquarters are moved to Banks's house in rear of our guns in the works.

It is sad, but sometimes amusing, — if such things can afford any amusement, — to see the terror evinced by the citizens when a big shell comes hurtling through the air. At the first explosion of a projectile shops are suddenly closed, shutters put up, and the city looks deserted; mounted men gallop through the streets, and footmen seek strong walls or indulge in a walk towards the suburbs for fresh air.

As the siege progressed almost every family had its "bomb-proof" in their gardens, fitted up with bedding, and a fireplace dug out of the clay wall. A "bomb-proof" was a cellar dug about ten feet deep and as many feet square. Over it logs of wood were placed, and on the top of them a lot of earth was thrown; steps were cut on the side away from the direction of the enemy's guns.

Into these holes in the ground the families would retire when the bombardment began, and stay under cover while it continued. The earth roof would keep any shell or fragment from entering.

Some people had bales of cotton piled upon their porches two tiers high. Behind these, families would live in fancied security.

The enemy's fire knocked the gas-works to pieces and set fire to a number of houses; and while the city fire department was endeavoring to extinguish the flames they would be selected as targets by the enemy and fired upon. Nevertheless they worked away courageously, and saved the city on more than one occasion from disastrous conflagration.

Our soldiers were treated with the greatest hospitality by the citizens, and all the "latch-strings hung out." We all remember Capt. Andrew Dunn, Messrs. Hare, Kevan, Cameron, and others with sincere pleasure. Capt. Dunn seemed never to tire having the officers of the army at his residence. He had served upon the staff of Gen. Longstreet, and had been wounded. Now that we were near his home his house was always open, and I fear his good wife was often sorely tried when a number of us were *nolens volens* taken to dinner by the captain. Dunn was one of the few gentlemen who had retained some of his old wines, and it reminded one of the old colonial times to see his venerable father, who always occupied the head of the table, raise his straw-stem glass of Madeira and say, — after the fashion of the " old Virginia gentleman," — "The pleasure of a glass of wine with you!" "Sir, your health," you would reply, and toss off your wine with an air of such innocence that no one would believe that you had ever drunk anything else, — in fact, had never dallied with the beverage called " apple-jack " in all your life.

But now we were coming to a state of siege, and our pleasures were being narrowed down slowly but surely.

We could only say *dum vivimus, vivamus*, and get all the pleasure out of it we could.

Our head-quarters consisted of a large tent, in which Col. Eshleman, Chaplain Hall, and "Frank the bugler" dwelt. The adjutant and I pitched a small shelter tent, about five feet long and three feet high, and under this we crept at night. In front of the large tent waved the beautiful silken colors presented to the Battalion in 1861 by the ladies of New Orleans, when Mr. Benjamin made the presentation speech, and prophesied war, and told every one to go home and prepare for it. How time passes! *Then* it was unfurled in the presence of thousands of fair women ; *now* it floats on the ramparts of a beleaguered city.

Within sight of our quarters are those of A. P. Hill, Wilcox, and Mahone.

During the week ending July 3d some brisk sharp-shooting has been going on, and occasionally the city has been shelled.

Gen. Alexander, the Chief of Artillery of Longstreet's corps, has been wounded, and has gone away on leave of absence. The General was one of the most industrious officers I ever met, and always doing and suggesting something new. At Centreville, in 1861, he established a system of signals between head-quarters and the outposts, using lighted torches at night. After the battle of Manassas, where we found our fuzes far from being satisfactory, he set to work and improved them. He showed us how to use our 12-pounder Howitzers as mortars. He detected and improved upon the enemy's signal code, and often detected their signals.

During the siege of Petersburg he invented all sorts of " contraptions," such as wooden mortars, sharp-shooters' boxes, which were so placed on the works that the men could get an oblique fire and not run the risk of a direct shot from the enemy's quickeyed marksmen. He also furnished the guns in position along the lines with bullet-proof oak shields, which were fastened to the axles at the trunnions, and were as wide as the spread of the wheels. They had a slit cut in them, cross-shaped, through which the gunners could safely aim.

He introduced a system of awards for the men who could collect the largest amount of leaden bullets and fragments of shell fired by the enemy, and would have the men chasing projectiles and fragments even before the former exploded.

It was while collecting bullets himself, going about in

sight of the enemy, with a haversack half filled with lead, that he was dangerously wounded.

For a certain number of pounds of lead turned into the ordnance department the men were either paid in money or received short leaves of absence.

Rumor has it that Wilson's raiders have been routed by Fitz Lee and Hampton. Shelling the city seems to be the chief amusement of the enemy just now. Nearly all of the women and children have gone away from the city.

Gen. Lee evidently expects heavy work to-morrow, the "glorious Fourth of July." We are ready at every point. Gen. Early is said to be marching towards Washington. Visited our pickets to-day within forty yards of the enemy's lines. No firing in our front. Weather hot, and dust intolerable in the trenches. Our horses have had no corn for a week.

Much to our disappointment the enemy does not attack on the Fourth. At daybreak we planted the Battalion colors on "Fort Damnation" as a defiance, and to show that we could also celebrate the day our forefathers made famous, "rebels" though they were.

The enemy was not slow in answering our challenge, and in a few moments every regimental flag opposite us was thrown to the breeze with cheers, which we answered with a vim. A few shots were exchanged but no damage done. Some shells were thrown into the city.

Report says that Mr. Chase, the Federal Secretary of the Treasury, has resigned. Some say this is good for us. How we are beginning to catch at straws!

July 8, 4.30 P.M. — The enemy has remained so quiet

for a few days passed that Gen. Lee ordered the batteries to open to *feel the enemy.* We accordingly *feel* for him, and he announces that he is *felt* by replying vigorously, which burns two houses in the city.

It is reported that fifteen transports loaded with troops have gone down James river, probably to look after Early.

On July 9 Early took possession of Martinsburg, capturing 900 Federals.

We are praying for rain. In the trenches it is terribly hot and dusty. To provide the troops with water, wells have been dug along the lines and good drinking-water obtained. It is raised by supporting long beams on posts so they will swing up and down. To the upper ends are fastened grape-vines or long slender poles; to these are attached buckets or canteens, and pulled down until water is reached. It is a droll sight to watch these long poles bobbing up and down like huge cranes stooping to drink. It is a great blessing to have water so convenient.

At 3.45 P.M. while at head-quarters at dinner a battery of the enemy opened unexpectedly on our front. We were not looking for anything of the kind just there. After firing a few rounds, to which our guns replied, it was withdrawn. Its fire was fatal, however, to one of our best young fellows, as a shell exploding mortally wounded Morgan Harris of First company, my cousin. Word was sent to me, and I immediately went to him in the trenches. He had been struck in the arm and leg by fragments of the shell breaking both. Poor boy! he had crossed the lines from Maryland to join the army. He was an only child, and I tried to dissuade him from joining; but he insisted. Captured on Marye's Hill with his gun detachment, he was afterwards exchanged, and rejoined his battery, and now he had been stricken down by a shot from a battery that had come out to fire at Mahone's head-quarters, from information gained from a deserter. He died bravely, poor fellow, saying, "This is rough on me. If I had been killed in battle I wouldn't have cared, but to be shot in a skirmish it's too bad." Just before he was relieved by death he murmured, "My name is Morgan Harris. If any one wants to find me, go to battery No. 38 on the lines. I am with my gun."

We spread the silken colors over his rude coffin, and buried him in a church-yard in the city, the enemy's shells passing over our heads, making a noisy requiem for the young soldier.

Ah, well! we all may be called upon to take the same long journey; let us do our duty and be prepared, as poor Morgan was, when our time shall come.

July 10. — News of the loss of the steamer "Alabama" was received to-day. It is said Semmes made a good fight, and he and his crew were saved by an English gentleman, who witnessed the engagement from his yacht.

Early's movements are creating quite a stir in the Northern States. President Lincoln has called for more troops.

Mooney, of Fourth company, died yesterday, in the trenches, of a regular case of cholera.

July 15. — Early reported within three miles of Washington. He encountered the Sixth Federal corps at Monocacy Bridge. Great excitement all through the North. Grant again shelling Petersburg.

July 19. — Rain has come at last.   How grateful it is!
It has laid the dust, and the troops welcome it heartily.

Early has retired from Maryland, crossing the Potomac
at Poolesville.   Gen. Joe Johnston has been relieved
from the command of the Army of Tennessee, and Gen.
Hood placed in command.

It is currently reported that Gen. Grant was killed
yesterday by a shell.   Is not this another " straw? "

July 20. — Visited Cullen, Barksdale, and Col. Huger
(acting Chief of Artillery in Alexander's absence), and
dined with Latrobe.   Gen. Longstreet is still absent.
The resignation of our gallant old chief, Col. Walton, has
been accepted.   We shall never cease to regret the circumstances that have induced this action.   All our hearts are so
attached to him that no one, no matter how capable he
may prove himself, can command the Washington Artillery
as he has done, in peace as well as in war.[1]

---

[1] RICHMOND, July 18, 1864.

To the Officers and Members of the Washington Artillery of New Orleans : —

FELLOW-SOLDIERS,— In addressing you a brief statement of the facts connected with my resignation from the army, I trust I shall not incur the imputa-
tion of undue sensitiveness or of unseemly vanity.   I am convinced that the
comrades with whom I came into the field at the beginning of the war, with
whom it has always been my greatest pride to be identified, and to share whose
hardships and perils and glories was my chief ambition, will appreciate my
conduct and sympathize with my motives.

You, my fellow-soldiers, will, I am sure, believe me when I say that only the
sternest and most inexorable necessity could have forced me to sever my
fortunes from yours, and to quit the military service of a country to which I
had dedicated all that the citizen and the patriot can bestow.   I therefore address you, in order that by constituting you the judges of the circumstances, I
may retain your good opinion, and that by briefly recapitulating the events of
my military career, I may vindicate the position I have been forced reluctantly
to assume.

On coming into the field as Major commanding the Battalion Washington
Artillery, I was, I believe, the senior officer of the artillery branch of the ser-

July 22. — During the bombardment this morning a shell struck Captain Dunn's house, in the city, and exploded. The Captain was in his dressing-room, shaving. A fragment entered the room, scattering the plastering about and wounding him. His family, wife and children, were in an adjoining room, and were badly frightened, but not hurt.

They immediately resolved to seek safer quarters, and

---

vice. Certainly my command was larger than any other similar organization in the army.

After the battle of Manassas (1861), in accordance with the application and recommendation of Gen. Beauregard, and under an Act of Congress passed expressly, as was shown by the communication of Mr. Benjamin — then Secretary of War — to Congress, to cover cases similar to mine, and of which mine was selected as the best illustration, I was promoted to the rank of Colonel of Artillery. Immediately thereafter I was assigned to duty as Chief of Artillery of the army of the Potomac remaining however in command of the Washington Artillery. At the same time Colonel Pendleton (made Colonel by *temporary rank* under the law authorizing the President to confer temporary rank upon officers of the regular army), although my junior at the time of entering the service, was promoted to the rank of Brigadier-General of Artillery. Subsequently, on the reorganization of the army, I was announced as Chief of Artillery of the First army corps, commanded by Gen. Longstreet.

In the meantime repeated and pressing applications for my promotion by my commanding Generals — I being, if not the senior Colonel of Artillery in the Confederate army, certainly the senior in the army in which I was serving, — were met with the statement that no more Brigadier-Generals of Artillery were required, and that consequently no more would be appointed. This I learned was the uniform reply to every application in my favor.

Nevertheless, an officer serving upon the staff of Gen. Lee, who, so far as I am informed, had never commanded a gun in action during the war, and who did not belong to the artillery branch of the service at the time, was promoted to be a Brigadier-General in that arm, and was assigned to duty as Chief of Artillery of the Second corps. I submitted to this apparent unjust discrimination in consequence of my desire to remain in the service and my willingness to sacrifice personal advancement to the demands of patriotism. I therefore continued still with the rank of Colonel in the performance of my duties as Chief of Artillery of Longstreet's First corps.

It was then suggested that I could obtain a brigade of infantry, the second Louisiana brigade being indicated; but I was unable to see the reality of a promotion which removed me from the command of more than eighty guns and near 3,000 men, to place me at the head of a brigade numbering about 1,000 men, and which required me to exchange an arm with which I was from ex-

selected the convent at Columbia, S.C., as a place of refuge, where they resided until it was burned by Sherman's
army.

July 30. — At 5 o'clock A.M. was awakened, in our
shelter-tent, by Adjutant Kursheedt shaking me vigorously,
and saying, " Wake up! wake up! Don't you hear the
explosion?" — " Explosion be hanged! What's the matter?" — " Why," he said, " the devil's to pay; the Yanks

---

perience familiar for one with which I had not, for seventeen years, been
connected. To accede to this suggestion would have been equally unjust to
myself, to the service, and to those gallant infantry officers who had so well
earned promotion. I declined the unreal promotion, preferring to remain a
Colonel of Artillery, commanding more than eighty guns and a division of men,
to becoming the Brigadier of less than a regiment. It should be remarked that
I was then, and had been for a long time, performing the duties of Brigadier-
General of Artillery to the satisfaction of the Generals with whom I served.

If competent to discharge those duties with the rank of Colonel, I was competent to discharge them with the increased grade; and if my services warranted
and deserved promotion in a branch with which I was not connected, they certainly warranted and deserved promotion in the branch with which I was identified, and in which I had served from the beginning of the war.

At a later period, in spite of the statement that no more Brigadier-Generals of
Artillery were needed or would be appointed, a distinguished officer, formerly of
the navy was promoted to that grade. Still later, after Gen. Longstreet's corps
had been ordered to reinforce Gen. Bragg in Georgia, an officer, formerly of
the engineers in the old army, then commanding one of my battalions, was also
promoted to be a Brigadier-General of Artillery, and upon being ordered to report to Gen. Longstreet, he was in October last assigned to duty as Chief of
Artillery of my corps. Thus, without the slighest notification to me, I was thrust
from the position I had so long occupied, and it was given to an officer, my
junior in rank, he being taken from my own command. On being informed of
this event I immediately asked to be relieved from duty with the Army of
Northern Virginia. My request was granted, and, at my own suggestion, I was
assigned to duty as Inspector of Field Artillery at large.

Returning from an arduous tour of inspection in the south-west, I learned
that an effort had been made to cause to be declared vacant my position as
Colonel of Artillery. I was informed by Gen. Bragg that in order to guard
against such a conclusion it was necessary to order me again to report to Gen.
Lee for duty in the army of Northern Virginia.

You will not be surprised that I was unwilling to comply with an order in-
volving the very sacrifices from which, for reasons satisfactory to the Adjutant
and Inspector General, I had been relieved. I was content to remain in the service without promotion, and to see my juniors in rank one by one placed above

have exploded a mine down on the left ; " and just then the batteries began to fire. We lost no time in getting to the trenches ; our guns were all ready, but no enemy appeared on our front.

Staff-officers were dashing about, and soon Mahone's men were withdrawn from the trenches near us, and marched off to the left. We could see nothing except a great cloud of smoke, that hung like a pall over the place

---

me. I was willing to do any duty that might be imposed upon me equivalent to the command which for more than two years I had exercised, and I applied for an assignment embracing such duty. But I submit to you, my comrades, that it was too much to ask me to go back to a command identical with that with which I had come into the service, and in an army where I was ranked by and would have to report to officers who had been my juniors and serving under my command. I do not complain of the promotion of those officers; I do not say it was undeserved; on the contrary, I know them to be gallant and meritorious gentlemen; but that they have received promotion while it has been denied to me may be accounted for by a determination, which, I am informed, the President has expressed, to confer the highest grade in the artillery on such officers only who have had the advantages of a scientific military education. I do not possess that advantage. I was not educated at a military institution. But I participated in the Mexican war, and for more than three years have served as an artillery officer, for two years of that time doing the duty and having the command without the rank belonging to the highest grade in that arm.

I may state without vanity, — because you, my comrades, have by your gallantry and conduct illustrated the same fields, — that my experience of war during that time embraces as principal engagements, the battles of Bull Run, Manassas, Rappahannock Station, second Manassas, Sharpsburg, Fredericksburg, second Fredericksburg, or Chancellorsville, Gettysburg, etc., etc. To show that Gen. Beauregard, who will be admitted to be no mean authority, considered me competent to perform the duties of the highest grade in the artillery, I may be excused for quoting his words contained in a communication to me : —

"I regret to hear that you have not been promoted to the rank of Brigadier-General of Artillery, which, in the estimation of your friends, you have won by your efficient services on so many glorious battle-fields, commencing with Bull Run. If my testimony to your efficiency, zeal, and capacity, whilst commanding the Battalion of Washington Artillery in the Army of the Potomac and acting as Chief of Artillery of the First corps of that army, can be of any service to you I willingly give it to you, not as a favor, but as a right to which you are entitled."

And Gen. Longstreet likewise, in a note addressed to me, says : —

"I have on three occasions and several times in conversation expressed my opinion and wishes in favor of having you promoted to the rank of Brigadier.

where the mine had been sprung. We stopped one of the staff-officers riding by, and inquired the particulars. It appears the explosion occurred on General Bushrod Johnson's front, blowing up Pegram's battery of four guns, and the Eighteenth South Carolina regiment. An assaulting column then advanced, with negro troops in front, and occupied our lines; thousands crowded into the crater formed by the explosion, and lost all organization.

I still think your services give you the best claim to the promotion of any officer in the service, and I am quite satisfied you are as well qualified to fill the office. I still hope your promotion may soon come."

It will be thus seen that Gen. Beauregard and Gen. Longstreet, the two Generals with whom I had served, both recommended that promotion which appears to have been studiously and pointedly withheld from me. That by each I was selected to be Chief of Artillery justifies me in assuming that they did not participate in the opinion that only graduates of military institutions are capable of discharging the duties appertaining to the highest grade in the artillery service.

Nor were they able to perceive that the increased grade would diminish the capacity while in no way extending the duties of the officer receiving it. Yet I am forced to the belief that the authorities differ in opinion with these distinguished officers, and concede nothing to the weight of their judgment. If their repeated and pressing applications for my promotion have had no result but in failure — if their unsought testimony to my capacity and efficiency have fallen short of the desired effect, — I am sure that the simple record of my services will ever remain insufficient to procure for me the reward to which it is no less the duty and the right of the patriotic soldier to aspire. I can come to no other conclusion than that the authorities consider me unfit for the position I have so long occupied; and it therefore devolves on me to relieve them from the perpetual annoyance of my seniority, and to guard my own self-respect from the continual assaults with which it is threatened. You, my fellow-soldiers, know full well, that no trifling cause would drive me from the military service of my country; that no ordinary grievance would force me from the side of those with whom I have shared the perils of so many glorious fields. You know that it could have been no motive of mean ambition, no desire for personal advancement, that brought me to the field. At an age of nearly fifty years, and thus, according to ordinary precedent, exempt from military service, I abandoned a lucrative employment and a large income, and left behind me a loved wife and seven children, to answer the first summons of war.

If I had not belonged to the party which desired disunion on its own account I was one of the first to embrace the cause of secession when the election of Lincoln was announced; and the first attack on the authority of the United States in Louisiana, even before the State had seceded, was made by you and other troops composing an expedition under my command.

Col. John Haskell opened upon the mass with his Co-horn mortars, dropping shells right in their midst, doing fearful execution, The Federals could not be induced to advance beyond this point; a few negroes did, however, run across the fields, to our second line of earth-works, where they were taken in and disarmed, as did also some of their white officers. The poor devils were frightened almost to death, and many of them protested that " they

---

I recall these facts in connection with those previously related not to exalt my own services, or to minister to a censurable egotism, but in order that I may vindicate my conduct before those whose opinion I value so highly, and whose esteem I prize beyond anything that wordly ambition can offer. It is with re-luctance I have been forced from the service, with grief that I find myself separated from you, with whom, I had hoped, should Providence permit, to re-turn to the city of our home. Circumstances have denied me this privilege; but harsh as may be their decree, they cannot rob me of the consolatory conviction that while with you I tried to deserve your affection and esteem, nor of the hope that while absent I may retain them.

J. B. WALTON.

HEAD–QUARTERS BATTALION WASHINGTON ARTILLERY,
PETERSBURG DEFENCES, August 29, 1864.

J. B. WALTON, *Late Colonel commanding Battalion Washington Artillery, Chief of Artillery, First Corps Army, Northern Virginia, etc., etc. :* —

DEAR SIR : — Your communication addressed to the officers and members of the Washington Artillery of New Orleans has been received. Dated, as it is, on the third anniversary of the first battle in which we had the merit of participat-ing as soldiers fighting for Southern independence, we are carried back through a long series of events which now form part of the history of our country.

We have a vivid remembrance of those events and of our connection with them during three years as a military organization under your command. The high estimation in which our corps was held at home and what glory we have since attained abroad were due to your personal influences, energy, and organ-izing talent, while the more solid attainments of a soldier — his training and fitness for his post, his previous preparation for the hour of trial — were none the less due to your talents as an officer.

But your communication enlightens us upon matters of which, being more personal in their nature, we were not so fully informed, and in which, as your friends, fellow-soldiers, and citizens, we were deeply interested. While we learn with painful regret of your resignation and retirement from the military

never fired a shot ; " " Look at my cartridge-box, massa, if you don't believe der poor nigger."

The brigades of Mahone and Wright soon cleared the trenches, and reëstablished our lines. As the Federals ran back to their own lines across the intervening space, our guns on the right and left of the crater shot them down by the score. They lost more men in getting back than they did in their advance.

----

service of the Confederacy, our solicitude at the loss of your services as a soldier and as commanding officer, and our sorrow at the severance of the more intimate ties of friendship that existed between us, are in some measure mitigated, by the conviction that your course has been a full vindication of your integrity as a man and your honor as a soldier and a patriot.

The incessant vigilance demanded by our position in the face of a persevering enemy necessitates a painfully brief acknowledgment of your friendship and past services. We all unite in the hope that in some near day of peace we may more fully express to you the sincerity of our sorrow at parting, and the high esteem in which we have long held you.

With a most kindly remembrance of the ties which have been knit so closely by our common danger, and privations in a common cause, and with heartfelt wishes for your future prosperity and success, we subscribe ourselves, with much respect.

Your obedient servants,

> B. F. ESHLEMAN, *Lieutenant-Colonel commanding.*
> W. M. OWEN, *Major.*
> E. I. KURSHEEDT, *Adjutant.*
> E. S. DREW, *Surgeon.*
> THOMAS Y. ABY, *Assistant Surgeon.*
> JOHN WOOD, *Captain and Assistant Quartermaster.*
> B. L. BRAZLEMAN, *Second Lieut. and Ordnance Officer.*
> REV. WILLIAM A. HALL, *Chaplain.*
> WILLIAM A. RANDOLPH, *Sergt.-Major, on behalf of N. C. Staff.*
> C. H. C. BROWN, *Second Lieutenant commanding First company, on behalf of First company.*
> LIEUT. SAM HAWES, *Second company, on behalf of Second company.*
> ANDREW HERO, JR., *Captain of Third company, of behalf of Third company.*
> JOE NORCOM, *Captain of Fourth company.*
> JNO. H. STONE, *on behalf of Fourth company.*

This attack of the enemy was intended as a *coup-de-main*, to have broken our lines, and to have marched straight into the city; but it was an inglorious failure.

We captured eight stands of colors and many prisoners, black and white. This was the first time we had seen black troops; we had fought representatives of every nation on the face of the globe, including Sandwich Islanders and Kannucks, but never negroes. We had some curiosity to see what they looked like, and went over to where they were "corralled." If they ever had any fight in them it was out of them now. They had been told we would hang them if we caught them, and they believed it.

Their white officers had torn their shoulder-straps off, so we should not recognize them as officers; but the fresh marks showed plainly upon their sun-burned jackets, and they could not deceive Major Bob W——, of A. P. Hill's staff, who nearly scared the life out of them by standing them apart from the negroes, and impressing the fact upon them that they were to swing instanter. How they begged! — and, without exception, said "they had been forced in; they could not avoid commanding the blacks," and all that. They were sent to the Libby.

Whitcomb and Mains, of First company, and O. J. Toledano, of Third company, were killed to-day. Kremmelberg, of Third company, was killed on the 23d, while sleeping in his bunk.

Gen. Elliott, of South Carolina, was mortally wounded to-day; and Major Gibbs, also of South Carolina, was wounded while directing the guns of the Thirteenth Virginia battalion artillery, lately commanded by Lieut.-Col. King, whom he succeeded some weeks ago.

July 31. — Am again assigned to command the Thirteenth Virginia battalion; the following order having been received at our head-quarters : —

HEAD–QUARTERS ARTILLERY A. N. VA.,
July 31, 1864.

SPECIAL ORDERS, No. 32 : —

Major W. M. Owen, at present on duty with the Washington Artillery Battalion, is hereby relieved of command with that battalion.

He will report for duty to Lieut.-Col. F. Huger, for assignment to the command of Gibbs's battalion artillery, First Corps Army Northern Virginia.

By command of Gen. Pendleton,
D. D. PENDLETON, *A.A.G.*

Major W. M. OWEN,
(Through Col. R. L. Walker, Chief Third corps artillery).

On August 1st the following was received : —

HEAD–QUARTERS ARTILLERY FIRST CORPS,
August 1, 1864.

SPECIAL ORDERS, No. 24 : —

Major W. M. Owen, having reported to these head-quarters for duty, by orders from Head-quarters Artillery Army Northern Virginia, is hereby assigned to the command of Major Gibbs's battalion artillery.

By command of Lieut.-Col. Frank Huger,
J. C. HASKELL, *A.A.G.*

This morning Gen. Lee allowed Gen. Grant an armistice of three hours, to bury his dead, left in front of our works after the explosion of the mine. A long trench was dug equidistant between our works and the enemy's, and the negro prisoners were made to carry the dead bodies to the trench and throw them in.

I went down to the flag of truce, and there met Gen. Potter, of New York; Col. McElroy, of Ohio; Gen. Ferraro, and Gen. White. These officers were very courteous and chatty, and brought out buckets of lemonade and other refreshments in profusion. They were desirous of getting a glimpse of some of our generals, and had pointed out to them Gen. Bushrod Johnson, clad in a linen duster and a straw hat; and A. P. Hill, in a gray flannel shirt, standing upon the edge of the "Crater." They were anxious to see Gen. Lee, but "Uncle Robert" didn't gratify them.

At the expiration of the three hours a signal-gun was fired, and the armistice ended. We lifted our hats to the Federal officers, bowed, and each retired to their respective lines, ready to renew hostilities.

This afternoon, in conformity to orders, I took formal command of Gibbs's battalion, consisting of three batteries, — Chamberlayne's (late Davidson's), Dickinson's, and Walker's "Otey" battery, 12 guns, 450 men. These are the same batteries placed under my command when in East Tennessee with Longstreet.

The position of these guns is on the Baxter road, immediately to the right of the "Crater." The enemy's lines are scarcely 200 yards off. Heth's division is our support.

August 3. — Went to the lines at 5 A.M. to inspect the position of the guns of the Battalion. Captain Walker pointed out an embrasure that did not permit the guns to bear upon and rake a ravine in front, through which the enemy might approach our works without being discovered.

Mounting the parapet to get a better look, and while standing there, a sharp-shooter of the enemy fired from his rifle-pit twice ; his second shot wounded me in the right cheek. He raised his head to see the effect of his aim, and, being indisposed to gratify him with knowledge of his accuracy, I stood for a moment, and then jumped down into the trench. My wound bled profusely ; but it was a mere flesh wound, and the men running up with canteens of water, I saturated my handkerchief and tied it around my face, and went back to my tent, which was pitched in Mr. Cameron's yard. My servant, "Jacob," was shocked at my "Banquo"-like appearance. He was instructed to mount my horse and ride at once to Col. Eshleman's quarters, and have my flask filled with a "sedative," and notify our surgeon. That worthy soon came, and being put in an ambulance and taken to the house of a friend in the city, Mr. McCullough, I took a delicious warm bath, and was put to bed in a neat, cosey, cool room, and was soon enjoying a refreshing sleep, of which I was so much in need. At 2 P.M. was served with a "Mint Julep" and a broiled chicken. Very nice to be wounded, I find !

Some young girls sent me beautiful flowers and baskets of fruit — God bless 'em ! Think I will remain here until I am all right again. Will retain command of the Battalion, and have the officer of the day report to me daily.

August 4. — Wound not painful, but still in bed at McCullough's. Miss Lizzie G—— sent me fruit and flowers, beautifully arranged in a pretty basket. How charming she is !

Col. Frank Huger and Jo. Haskell, A.A.G., called to see me. They believe the Yanks are mining under my guns. Heavy firing along the lines all night.

August 5. — Gen. Gracie sprung a mine in his front at 6 P.M. My brother, Captain Ned, came over from Richmond to see me; he still suffers from the wound in the head he got at Drewry's Bluff. He had seen a telegram in the newspaper about me, and came prepared to find me much worse off than I am, thank goodness! There was some firing on my batteries to-night, and we had two men killed and one wounded.

August 7. — Though still very weak, took a short walk to-day, and called upon Miss Lizzie to thank her for her kindness in sending me so many nice things. While there my wound broke forth afresh, and she bravely dressed it for me.

August 24. — The past fortnight has been without any event of importance. The enemy still shells the city at intervals. I have reported for duty again in the trenches, and am all right once more. We have established a battery of five Cohorn mortars, and put it under command of Lieut. Langhorne of the "Otey" Battery, — an excellent young officer, — and have laid out and completed a covered way, so we can go into our works with very little risk of being peppered by sharp-shooters.

While at McCullough's convalescing I had a very narrow escape. It was my habit each morning to sit in an easy-chair in the dining-room, and there receive reports and read the news. One bright morning, feeling strong enough, I thought, to visit the lines, I had my horse saddled and rode out to them. While there the enemy threw a few shells into the city; this was an every-day occurrence, and attracted no especial attention. When I returned to the city, and came in sight of my quarters, I was surprised to see "Jacob" shovelling bricks and mortar out of the window of the dining-room, and when I had ridden closer I discovered a hole in the side wall large enough to crawl through.

During the shelling we had witnessed, a shell had struck the house, entered the dining-room, and there exploded. The room was wrecked and the easy-chair shattered. Had I been there in my accustomed place I should have joined the poor fellow we saw enjoying the rocking-chair at "Second Manassas."

It was a beautiful sight at night to watch the shells from the 15-inch mortars, with their lighted fuses, crossing each other in their flight through the air, and I have stood for hours at the window tracing them. One night during the cannonading one battery got the exact range of our street, and made it pretty lively. A church close by was struck, and while standing in our door-way, the negro nurse at my side, a shell burst so close as to blind us, and there was a terrible crash of window-glass.

The nurse turned back-summersaults into the basement kitchen in her retreat. I procured a candle, and went into the parlor to inspect the damage. Half a window-sash was knocked out, and the floor strewn with window-glass. I picked up a large fragment of a shell and placed it on the mantel, as a " curio " for the family when they returned.

General A. P. Hill has attacked the enemy at Reims' Station, and captured 2,500 prisoners and 9 guns from the Second Federal corps. The enemy has seized the Weldon Railroad and hold it. This interferes, very materially, with our procuring food for men and animals from the south.

We are kept busy in the trenches, changing positions of guns, building and repairing bomb-proofs, arranging *abatis*, etc.

September 1. — Obtained leave of absence for a day, and ran over to Richmond and dined with President Davis and family.

On the 12th of October one-half of our artillery-drivers are armed with muskets, and placed on duty in " Battery Gregg," under command of Lieut. McElroy of the Washington Artillery.

All supernumeraries are being armed, and will assist in defending the lines. Every man counts now ; no one can be spared. Our strength is being lessened daily, and there is no material to draw from. We are the " last of the Mohicans," as it were.[1]

---

[1] Organization of the Artillery, Army Northern Virginia, August 31, 1864.

Brigadier-Gen. W. N. PENDLETON, commanding.

First Corps Artillery. — Brigadier-Gen. E. P. Alexander.
Col. H. C. Cabell's Battalion. — Manly's battery, Capt. B. C. Manly; First Company Richmond howitzers, Capt. Anderson; Carlton's battery, Capt. H. H. Carlton; Calloway's battery, First Lieut. M. Callaway.
Major John Haskell's Battalion. — Branch's battery, Capt. H. G. Flanner; Nelson's battery, Lieut. W. B. Stanfield; Garden's battery, Capt. H. R. Garden; Rowan battery, Lieut. E. Myers.

October 27. — Fighting on our right, heavy firing all day. At dark a regiment of Federals entered our lines at the position occupied by the Otey battery, near the "Crater." They were soon driven out. They were supposed to be our relief picket-guards, and came into our lines unmolested. Our lines are now very weak; a force, not a large one either, could break through at almost any time.

We shelled the enemy from our whole front last night with our Cohorn mortars, firing 130 shells.

November 1. — The attack on the 27th instant was evidently intended to gain the Southside Railroad and the Appomattox river.

Northern newspaper correspondents say the troops carried six days' rations and plenty of ammunition.　A. P. Hill

---

Major F. Huger's Battalion. — Smith's battery, Capt. John D. Smith; Moody s battery, Lieut. G. Poindexter; Woolfolk's battery, Lieut. James Woolfolk; Parker's battery, Capt. W. W. Parker; Taylor's battery, Capt. O. B. Taylor; Ficklin's battery, Capt. W. W. Ficklin; Martin's battery, Capt. —— Martin.

Thirteenth Virginia Battalion Artillery. — Major W. M. Owen. Davidson's battery, Lieut. J. H. Chamberlayne; Dickinson's battery, Capt. C. Dickinson; Otey battery, Capt. D. N. Walker.

Battalion Washington Artillery. — Lieut.-Col. B. F. Eshleman. First company, Capt. Edward Owen; Second company, Capt. J. B. Richardson; Third company, Capt. Andrew Hero, Jr.; Fourth company, Capt. Jo. Norcom.

Second Corps Artillery, Brigadier-Gen. A. L. Long.

Major C. M. Braxton's Battalion. — Lee battery, Lieut. W. W. Hardwicke; First Maryland artillery, Capt. W. F. Dement; Stafford artillery, Capt. W. T. Cooper; Alleghany artillery, Capt. J. C. Carpenter.

Lieut.-Col. Thomas H. Carter's Battalion. — Morris artillery, Capt. S. H. Pendleton; Orange artillery, Capt. C. W. Fry; King William artillery, Capt. W. P. Carter; Jeff. Davis artillery, Capt. W. J. Reese.

Major W. E. Cuttshaw's Battalion. — Charlottesville artillery, Capt. J. McD. Carrington; Staunton artillery, Capt. A. W. Garber; Courtney artillery, Capt. W. A. Tanner.

Lieut.-Col. William Nelson's Battalion. — Amherst artillery, Capt. J. T. Kirkpatrick; Milledge artillery, Capt. John Milledge; Fluvanna artillery, Capt. J. L. Massie.

beat them back. So they call it a "reconnoissance." They left behind them their dead and wounded, so must have been in a hurry.

On the 6th of November, after six months' service in the trenches, exposed day and night to the enemy's fire, my battalion was relieved by that of Lieut.-Col. Moseley's.

The enemy, hearing the noise occasioned by getting the guns away from their positions, where they were crowded in by bomb-proofs, traverses, etc., opened a brisk fire ; but, it being quite dark, we had no casualties except one horse killed.

We were ordered to the extreme right flank of the army, and will hereafter act as "flying artillery," attached to A. P. Hill's "Light Bobs." We rejoice in breathing once more the pure air of the woods and fields, and having the

---

Col. J. Thompson Brown's Battalion. — Powhatan artillery, Capt. W. J. Dance ; Second company Richmond Howitzers, Capt. L. F. Jones ; Third company Richmond Howitzers, Capt. B. H. Smith, Jr. ; Rockbridge artillery, Capt. A. Graham ; Salem Flying artillery, Capt. C. B. Griffin.

Third Corps Artillery. —Col. R. L. Walker ; Lieut.-Col. A. S. Cutts's battalion : Ross's battery, Capt. H. W. Ross ; Patterson's battery, Capt. G. M. Patterson ; Irwin artillery, Capt. T. J. Wingfield.

Lieut.-Col. D. G. McIntosh's Battalion. — Johnson's battery, Capt. V. J. Clutter ; Hardaway artillery, Capt. J. F. Hurt ; Danville artillery, Capt. R. S. Rice ; Second Rockbridge artillery, Capt. Donald.

Lieut.-Col. C. Richardson's Battalion. — Lewis artillery, Capt. N. Penick ; Donaldsonville cannoneers, Capt. V. Maurin ; Norfolk light artillery, Capt. C. R. Grandy ; Huger artillery, Capt. J. D. Moore.

Lieut.-Col. W. J. Pegram's Battalion. — Pee Dee artillery, Capt. E. B. Brunson ; Fredericksburg artillery, Capt. E. A. Marye ; Letcher artillery, Capt. T. A. Brander ; Purcell battery, Capt. Geo. M. Cayce ; Crenshaw battery, Capt. T. Ellet.

Lieut.-Col. W. T. Poague's Battalion. — Madison artillery, Capt. T. J. Richards ; Albemarle artillery, Capt. J. W. Wyatt ; Brooke artillery, Capt. W. W. Utterback ; Charlotte artillery, Capt. Williams.

15 Battalions, 61 Batteries. — First corps, 5 battalions, 22 batteries ; Second corps, 5 battalions, 19 batteries ; Third corps, 5 battalions, 20 batteries.

pleasure of stretching our limbs without the risk of receiving a rifleman's bullet.

The young girls of Petersburg are as charming as are those in Richmond. There are not many of them, for the "Feds" have frightened them away. While we were in the trenches, and matters comparatively quiet, we would often slip into town and get the girls together and have a dance. On several occasions, while we were thus enjoying ourselves, a furious firing would break out on the lines, and those officers who belonged to the batteries engaged would have to scamper, but not without securing a partner for a dance after their return. An hour or so would pass, the firing cease, and we would again return to "trip the light fantastic," and say, "You have kept the dance for me, Miss ——? Only a small affair, after all : one man killed, that's all."—"Oh! is that all?" she would reply. "Come, they are forming the set." Riding on horseback was a great sensation for the young girls, and officers' horses were in great demand. On quiet days we would occasionally take them out, so they could see the lines of both armies ; but sometimes the "Feds" would be so ungallant as to fire upon the groups, although their officers must have seen through their glasses that women were there.

We are encamped in a pine thicket, near Ritchie's house, on the Boydton plank road, and are building stables for our horses, and the men are constructing log huts for themselves and making everything as comfortable as possible. We are ordered to turn in to the Ordnance Department two caissons from each battery, for lack of horses. A disease (farcy) has taken hold of our horses, and they die by twos and threes every night. I had my tent pitched, and a big chimney built to it; a wooden door was improvised, and a pane of glass set in it. I could see my whole camp without leaving the tent. I was well off in the way of blankets, but in the mornings would have my mustache covered with ice, as was the case with my water-bucket. I thought it healthier to sleep under canvas than in a stuffy, close hut. My possessions were simple enough : my furniture consisted of a camp-table, a wooden inkstand from Harper's Ferry, one old camp-stool. A small valise contained a change of under-clothing, and a leather haversack, that was always carried on my saddle, held all my toilet apparatus,— looking-glass, comb, brushes, soap, and towel. My blankets were the red artillery blankets of the "Feds," and my large India-rubber cloth, which was rolled about them, when travelling, was a souvenir of "Chickamauga." My pistol and sabre hung on a peg on the rear tent-pole. The sabre was *presented* to me by a Federal officer captured at Drewry's Bluff. In the rear of my habitation was a shelter tent, where "Jacob Faithful" attended to the culinary affairs, when we had anything to eat ; and fhat was becoming a very serious question, which concerned the whole of Lee's army.

Gen. Longstreet has returned and reported for duty, and Capt. Dunn celebrated the event by giving a dinner-party, at which there was a goodly gathering of officers of the First corps. The General still suffers from his wound, his right arm being paralyzed. Among the gayest officers present was the whole-souled, genial Gen. Gracie. It was an event of unspeakable regret when, on the morning of the 2d of December, Gracie was instantly killed upon the lines, by a spherical case shot from the enemy's works. He was one of the best officers I ever saw, and was worshipped by his men. So our numbers are being thinned, slowly but surely. The only question now is, who will see the end?

A few days before Gracie's death Gen. Lee went to the trenches, as was his habit, to inspect them in person. He always went alone. When he came to Gracie's line he stepped upon the "banquette" of the work, and taking out his field-glasses began quietly to examine the position of the enemy. He was in danger, and Gen. Gracie placed himself in front of him and obstructed his view, pretending to be pointing out objects to Gen. Lee. Lee said, "General, you should not expose yourself so much." Gracie replied, "If *I* should not, Gen. Lee, why should you, the Commander-in-chief?" The General smiled, and understood then that Gracie had so placed himself to cover him with his own body in case the enemy had fired. Lee stepped down from the "banquette" and continued his walk down the line.

Col. Walter Taylor, Lee's Adjutant-General, was wont to say, in answering at head-quarters questions as to Gen. Lee's whereabouts, "I can't tell you where the General is; he rode off alone awhile ago. Yesterday he was running the risk of being killed in the trenches; to-day he may be down at Hatcher's Run, running the risk of capture by the Yankee cavalry." There can be no doubt Gen. Lee was very anxious at this time about the state of affairs in the army and at Richmond. We did not think he was in favor of holding on to Richmond for so long a time. Headquarters of the government might as well have been in a baggage-wagon with the army as in Richmond. The holding of that city to the last would be but a matter of sentiment; it held nothing now that could do the army any good.

CHAPTER XV.

IN THE TRENCHES AT PETERSBURG.

Enemy on a Raid. — On the March. — Ice and Snow. — Christmas Dinner. — Virginia Hospitality. — Gen. Pegram Killed. — Gen. J. B. Gordon. — Louisiana Brigade. — Winter-quarters. — Hatcher's Run. — Short Rations. — Fasting and Prayer. — Sherman in Charleston. — Promotion. — Pickett at Five Forks. — Lines Broken. — Defence of Battery Gregg. — Petersburg Evacuated. — Gen. A. P. Hill Killed.

ON the 7th of December, 1864, the enemy started out again on a raid to our right. Our "light battalion" followed, with Gen. A. P. Hill's corps. We marched to Dinwiddie Court-House and towards Stony Creek. Camped at 3 P.M. On the 9th of December we crossed the Nottoway river, and camped seven miles from Bellfield. Enemy reported destroying the Weldon Railroad. We hear some firing, and presume the county reserves have engaged them. Although our march was fatiguing, everything came into camp promptly. During the night it rained, and then froze. The guns, horses, harness, and the men's blankets were covered with ice and frozen hard. We had large fires built to thaw out. Ice formed an inch thick. We slept under our blankets; no tents of any description. This was tolerably severe on men and animals.

On the 10th of December we marched, at 6.30 A.M., towards the Weldon Railroad. Enemy's infantry falling back towards Petersburg. At mid-day we came in sight of a squadron of Federal cavalry and opened a gun on them.

Line of battle formed by our infantry. Gens. Finnegan and Sorrel wounded. Chamberlayne's battery fired sixteen rounds. Enemy retreated rapidly. Troops march in pursuit by the Lebanon road. We are ordered to encamp near the ruins of the Watkins House, destroyed by fire by the Federals to-day. It is distressing to see the ruin and desolation these columns inflict upon inoffensive citizens on their line of march. We cannot believe Americans can do these things, but that it is the work of the refuse of Europe, — the Hessians, that fill the ranks of the enemy. A Federal soldier was taken prisoner this afternoon, and some of our men wanted to throw him into the fire kindled by his own comrades; but better counsels prevailed, and he was marched off to Petersburg.

We cooked our supper in the burning embers of the house, and while smoking our pipes a boy, probably fifteen years of age, came to the fire, and, leaning against a tree, looked around for a few moments, and then burst into tears. We observed him for a little while, then called him up and asked the cause of his apparent grief. He told us, in a quiet, straightforward way, that this house had been his home ever since he was born; he had left here yesterday morning, when he heard the Yankees were coming; he had left behind him grandmother and mother. They had then several head of cattle, a horse, and everything necessary to make a comfortable country home. He had just returned to find everything destroyed, house burned, cattle gone, fences gone, garden and fields beaten down by the tramping of men and the wheels of ordnance wagons. Where his mother was he did not know. He fairly broke down, and sobbed as though his young heart would break, but, soon recovering himself, he clenched his little fist and said, slowly and with emphasis, "If my life is spared I'll get even with these people for inflicting this wrong upon my mother." And, turning to Chamberlayne, he said, "Captain, can't I go with you?" Chamberlayne said, "Yes, come with me. I'll make a cannoneer of you." We shared our supper with the little fellow, and put him in charge of Chamberlayne's sergeant.

December 13. — Gen. A. P. Hill's corps and our Battalion returned to winter-quarters.

1865, January 15. — The last month has passed quietly away, without any event of great importance. The command is comfortably housed, and the blue smoke seen curling from the mud chimneys gives indication of warmth and comfort within the little cabins.

We have had the Christmas dinner the people of Richmond proposed to give to the army. Visions of roast turkey and plum pudding hovered before our eyes. We heard fabulous stories of the thousands of fowls, hams, etc., piled up in tiers in the *commissariat* in Richmond. At last the day came for the distribution, and the men were eagerly awaiting the arrival of the commissary wagons. They came, and our share for 500 men was one loaf of bread to each company. There was a howl of disappointment, and the men said, "The quartermasters and commissaries have eaten all the good things, and we have the crumbs." Members of the Otey battery came to my tent and showed me little slices of bread that were their share, and said they intended to keep them as souvenirs, to show after the war. And it is quite probable these fragments are preserved as reminiscences of soldiering days in many a Virginia home.

Everything being quiet on the lines, and the armies having sought winter-quarters, I took advantage of the situation to obtain a few days' leave of absence, and went to Goochland county to visit Mr. Logan and family. Adjutant Kursheedt and Capt. Owen, of the Washington Artillery, and Capt. Walke, of Col. Walker's staff, accompanied me. What a delicious time we had, and what nice things to eat! Seven different kinds of bread upon the table at once, — "Old Varginny" style, — and the young ladies, Misses Annie and Jennie, were very charming. We were made so welcome that when our leave was up it was hard to tear ourselves away. The enemy has not devastated the James-river country yet, and we hope he never will.

January 29. — On duty in camp again. The men have built a chapel just behind my tent, and have prayer-meetings nightly. The whole army has taken to praying, and if prayers accomplish anything we should whip this fight yet. Peace commissioners started for Washington yesterday. No good is expected from the mission. We will certainly have a campaign in the spring, of some sort or other.

Heard to-day that I had been recommended for promotion to Lieut.-Colonel.

February 5. — Enemy reported moving again towards our right. Battalion ordered to Burgess's Mill. We were put in position by Gen. Gordon, and shelled the woods occupied by the enemy's cavalry, and fired seventy-five rounds; bivouacked near the mill.

February 6. — Marched back to camp. Gen. John Pegram was killed to-day. Only ten days ago he married the beautiful Hettie Carey, and she is now at his camp down by Hatcher's Run.

February 7. — Ordered back to Burgess's Mill. At 2 A.M. reported to Gen. Gordon, who was sleeping in the snow just behind his troops, who were bivouacking in line of battle. The engagement yesterday was a sharp one, our men driving the enemy and holding the ground. Just at daybreak, while marching down the road, we passed a group of ambulances and wagons by the roadside. They were Gen. Pegram's head-quarter wagons, and his wife was with them. She inquired piteously of me if I had heard anything of her husband. Evidently they had not told her the worst. I had not the heart to be the one to break the news to her, and said I had not seen him. She was in the greatest distress.

Gen. Gordon orders our guns to the Brown House, and there we took position so as to enfilade his front in case the enemy should attack him. There is some pretty brisk firing in front of Gen. Sorrel, and he is seriously wounded in the breast. Gen. Gordon said to me, "Major, you are from Louisiana. I will send you the 'Louisiana brigade' to support your guns." Soon after a small body of troops, not over 250, came marching towards me through the ice-covered pines, and I recognized at the head of the column the giant form of Col. Peck. And *this* was all that was left of the "Louisiana brigade," that had numbered over 3,000 muskets before Richmond in the seven days' battles ! Harry Hays's regiment, the Seventh, alone numbered 1,400 men at Manassas. This extraordinary diminution of numbers showed plainly what it had gone through, and the truly gallant, unconquerable Louisiana brigade, now of 250 brave hearts, tempered like fine steel in the fiery blasts of battle, was all that was left for me to depend upon to support my guns.

A few old friends were marching with their men, but, oh, how many familiar faces were gone ! And their bones are buried or bleaching on the fields of Front Royal, Cross Keys, or on the heights of Winchester, Manassas, and Gettysburg !

February 8. — Ordered back to camp, and then to change our winter camp to Hatcher's Run, near Burgess's Mill. Hard at work building cabins and stables, and soon are again settled down. These are the third winter-quarters built by this command this season. Our camp of log huts is well laid out in regular streets, and my little tent, with its glass window and door, is at the end of it all.

I bought in Petersburg to-day a side of French calf-skin for $175, and arranged with a North Carolina soldier, who had been detached as a shoemaker, to make me a pair of riding boots for $75. Total cost, $250. This is considered quite reasonable, as they are selling in Richmond for from $500 to $600 a pair.[1]

---

[1] The following is an abstract from the private expense book of an officer travelling from Richmond to Augusta, Ga., in 1865. Disbursements in Confederate money : —

March 6. 1 curry-comb		$10 00
" 6. Mending pants		20 00

March 10. — We have remained quietly in camp for the
past month.   The enemy does not appear to be in a hurry
to move again.   For some weeks we have been having a
hard time in the eating line, and are now receiving rations
of one-fourth pound of bacon and three-fourths pound of
corn-meal a day ; sometimes coffee and sugar, but not often.

It was at this time that Gen. Jo. Davis, the President's
nephew, and young "Jeff.," the President's son, came to
dine with me.   They were made welcome, but, upon con-
sulting "Jacob" in reference to the contents of the larder,
he informed me that the remains of my day's rations, three-
fourths pound of corn-meal, was all we could boast of.
What under the sun was to be done? What a fix to be in!
The nephew and the son of the President of these Confederate States to dine with me, a Major of Artillery, and
three-fourths pound of meal only in the larder!

However, I was equal to the occasion.   Calling the
Adjutant, I requested him to present my compliments
to Capt. W——, Lieut. L——, and the doctor, and to

March 11.	Meal on road	. . . .	$20 00
"	17.	Cigars and bitters	60 00
"	20.	Hair-cutting and shave	10 00
"	20.	Pair of eye-glasses	135 00
"	20.	Candles	50 00
"	23.	Coat, vest, and pants	2,700 00
"	27.	1 gallon whiskey	400 00
"	30.	1 pair pants	700 00
April 12.	6 yards linen, 2¾ wide	1,200 00
"	14.	1 oz. sulphate quinine	1,700 00
"	14.	2 weeks' board	700 00
"	14.	Bought $60 gold	6,000 00
"	24.	1 doz. Catawba wine	900 00
"	24.	Shad and sundries	75 00
"	24.	Matches	25 00
"	24.	Penknife	125 00
"	24.	1 package brown Windsor soap	50 00

say I would be happy to have the pleasure of their company at dinner at "head-quarters" to meet some distinguished gentlemen; and I added, in a low tone, tell them to bring their own rations with them, their tin cups and plates. And tell the doctor not to forget a modicum of *spiritus.* And giving "Jacob" a few hundred dollars, he was despatched to a Georgia regiment in the outer works for a half bushel of cow-peas for soup.

Meanwhile I entertained my guests by taking them about, and showing them how beautiful my camp was, how *thin* my horses were, and all the objects of interest, keeping an eye all the while upon the kitchen.

At last dinner was served, and, thanks to the officers and the doctor, the *menu* wasn't bad. A large tin bucket held the soup, and we dipped in with our tin cups. We had plenty of bacon and corn-bread, and some excellent coffee made from "Gouber-peas." Our sugar *happened* to be just out; but we explained that to our guests by laying the blame on the "commissary." He also suffered in reputation for not supplying *milk and butter.*

However, we can't have everything at once, and if we can just manage to grease ourselves daily, so that the joints will work, that is all we should expect to do.

We flattered ourselves our guests were pleased, anyhow, and they bade us farewell and said they "would call again," and we said we "hoped they would," and promised them *turkey,* if the commissary would do his duty. We begged to be remembered to the President, and to assure him we were all right and happy. In fact, "although slightly disfigured, we're still in the ring."

This day has been set apart by the President as a day for fasting and prayer. Sheridan has used up Early in the Valley, taken all his artillery, and is now on his way to Lynchburg. Sherman has taken Savannah and Charleston and is moving on Fayetteville. Overrunning is not subjugation. Congress passed a bill yesterday in Richmond to enroll and arm the negroes. Think it a bad move, and too late. Still, if Gen. Lee says it is all right, why, go ahead! Lincoln's inaugural foreshadows nothing but "war to the knife;" no mercy for "rebels." We cannot come back into the Union if we would. Nothing to do but fight it out. Thank God, our desperate state animates the men of the army, but the people at home are getting tired and do not encourage them!

March 12. — Some reports of the enemy making a move. Horses harnessed all day. I sold to-day a diamond ring to a merchant in Petersburg for $1,500 (worth $25 in greenbacks), and contracted for a new uniform coat for $800.

March 22. — Negro troops parade to-day in Richmond for the first time. The darkies are very jubilant, and think it great fun. The music attracts them like flies around a molasses barrel. We are really suffering now for food. Yesterday I had to order some ground corn and shucks to be taken from the horses to be distributed to the men. The distribution of rations is very irregular and unreliable.

While riding down the plank road this A.M. with Col. Lindsey Walker, the Chief of Artillery of Hill's corps, we overtook Gen. Lee, riding with an orderly, going down to see the cavalry below Hatcher's Run. " Good-morning, gentlemen ! " said the General. " I hope you are both well this morning." We returned his kind salutation. We rode in silence for a moment. Col. Walker was expecting daily his commission as Brigadier-General, and he had told me *I* was gazetted for a Lieutenant-Colonel's berth ; but we had not received official notification of our appointments. Presently the General seemed to arouse himself from a revery, and, turning to me, asked, — addressing me as Colonel, — "Colonel, have you seen Rooney Lee lately?" I told him I had not. He then said, "I didn't know but you had, Colonel; he is a gay young fellow like yourself. I thought may be you had seen him last evening at that *ball you attended in the city.*" Then, turning to Walker, he said, " General, have you seen him in your rides?"—"I have not," said Walker.[1] The General soon took a country road leading off to the right, and Walker and I exchanged winks. The General simply desired to inform us that our commissions were all right. Another one of his pleasantries.[2]

---

[1] Gen. Lee frequently thus addressed those around him, not that he attached any importance to, or expected any aid from, what might be said in reply, but in giving expression to that which occupied his own mind, — thinking aloud, so to speak. He at the same time drew from others such information as they might possess, or such views as they might entertain. — *Four Years with Lee.* TAYLOR.

[2] *Promotions in the Artillery Corps Army of Northern Virginia, Gen. R. E. Lee, Petersburg, Va., February, 1865 :* —

To be Brig.-General. — Col. R. L. Walker.

To be Colonels. — Lieut.-Cols. W. Nelson, D. G. McIntosh, Frank Huger, W. J. Pegram.

To be Lieut.-Colonels. — Majors Jno. C. Haskell, W. M. Owen, Jno. Lane, R. V. Chew, W. E. Cuttshaw, M. Johnson, R. M. Stribling.

To be Majors. — Capts. H. W. Ross, T. J. Kirkpatrick, W. J. Dance, B. C. Manly, T. O. Brander, S. T. Wright, N. U. Sturdevant, J. F. Hurt, P. P. Johnson, J. A. Thompson, —— McGregor.

March 25. — By order of Gen. Lee the guns of the Otey and Dickinson's batteries are turned over to the Ordnance Department, and the officers and men are ordered to Richmond to serve stationary guns under command of Lieut.-Col. King, and, having received my commission as Lieutenant-Colonel, am ordered to report to Col. McIntosh as second field officer with his battalion, and to take with me the battery of Chamberlayne.

I consequently removed my head-quarters to the Gregg House, and began the construction of a redoubt for four guns between battery Gregg and the broken dam.

March 28. — We are hard at work, with large details of infantry troops, building the new redoubt. The dam, which had been built with great expenditure of time and labor, has been washed away. It had been constructed with a view of flooding this portion of the line. This new work is the substitute for it.

Lieut. Battles, with two guns of the First company Washington Artillery, will occupy the work when completed.

Lieut. McElroy, Third company Washington Artillery, occupies battery Gregg, with sixty-four artillery drivers armed with muskets.

The enemy is again moving to envelop our right, and Gen. Pickett and his troops are sent off to resist them.

On March 29 Battles occupied the new redoubt, which the men have named " Fort Owen."

10 P.M. — The firing in front of Petersburg is very heavy, the enemy evidently making a desperate attempt to force through our lines and prevent any more troops being

sent to Pickett. Our lines are very weak; the men in the trenches stand two yards apart. Pickett took with him 8,000 men. Rumor says Grant has 200,000 men. Lee has 35,000 only. The odds are certainly fearful.

April 1. — Bad news from Pickett. He has been overwhelmed at Five Forks by the Fifth corps of the Federal army and Gen. Sheridan's cavalry. We are in a tight box now, and only wondering where and when our lines will be broken.[1]

April 2. — There was very heavy firing directly in front of Petersburg all last night; the sky was all aglow with the discharge of cannon and the bursting of mortar shells. Several infantry assaults have been repulsed. We have been told that the Second, Third, and Fourth companies Washington Artillery, under Lieut.-Col. Eshleman, are fighting hard in their redoubts. Capt. Hero reported wounded. At the earliest dawn Lieut. Battles and I repaired to his guns. We heard heavy skirmishing about half a mile to the right. Presently a cannon was fired, and a solid shot struck near us and showered dirt upon us.

Infantry soldiers began to quit the works, where they have been posted three yards apart, and run across the fields. Our boys said that "they were chasing rabbits." A second cannon-shot comes crashing along; a few musket-shots; more men running, and we now realize that it has come at last. Our lines are broken, and the army cut in twain.

At daybreak we can see the heavy columns of the enemy (Sixth corps) marching across the fields towards the

[1] See page 370.

¹ Report showing Losses in Battalion Washington Artillery since its Organization, May 26, 1861, and Present Strength.

COMMAND.	Resigned. Officers.	Promoted out of Battalion. Officers.	Transferred. Men.	Discharged. Men.	Killed or died of wounds received in action and by disease. Officers.	by disease. Men.	Dropped and absent without leave. Men.	Present for duty. Officers.	Present for duty. Men.	Present for duty. Aggregate.	Absent. Officers.	Absent. Men.	Absent. Aggregate.	Aggregate present and absent.	Guns. 12-pounder Napoleons.	Guns. 3-inch Rifles.	Guns. Total.
Field and Staff	2	2	1	2	.	.	.	6	4	10	1	.	1	11	.	.	.
First Company	1	1	4	23	1	26	19	2	67	69	2	32	34	103	.	4	4
Second Company	3	1	2	30	.	14	17	4	69	73	.	25	25	98	4	.	4
Third Company	2	2	4	24	1	27	15	4	75	79	.	38	38	117	4	.	4
Fourth Company	.	.	3	19	.	13	16	4	45	49	.	42	42	91	3	1	4
	8	6	14	98	2	80	67	20	260	280	3	137	140	420	11	5	16

I hereby certify that the foregoing is correct.

(Signed)   B. F. ESHLEMAN,

Lieut.-Col. Commanding Battalion Washington Artillery.

Station: On the lines of Petersburg, Va.

Date: April 1, 1865.

Appomattox river. Battles is ordered to withdraw his guns to Battery Gregg but before his horses can be brought up the enemy charge across the works and captures him and all his men. Lieut. McElroy, in battery Gregg, with his infantry artillerists, opens upon the enemy with musketry, and the force is withdrawn; then leading a charge, McElroy recaptures Battles's guns, and the teams having been brought up, they are moved down the Boydton plank road, and opened fire upon the enemy from a position in rear of the Mississippi brigade of Gen. Nat. Harris, numbering about 500 muskets, that have been posted there by Gen. Wilcox to delay the Federal advance. McElroy, finding his fire is having little or no effect, withdraws with deliberation to battery Gregg, and goes into position in that work. At the same time some guns are put in battery Whitworth, a detached work, like Gregg, to its right and rear.

Harris's brigade is now in danger of being outflanked by the enemy, and is withdrawn from its advanced position. Detachments of the Twelfth and Sixteenth regiments, under Col. James H. Duncan, are ordered into Gregg, as are the fragments of Thomas's and Lane's North Carolina brigades, numbering in all about 200 men. The Nineteenth and Forty-eighth Mississippi regiments are placed in battery Whitworth, and Gen. Harris commands that work.

Preparations were now made to receive the assault, and Lieut. McElroy was instructed to pile up his ammunition upon the platforms, so as to easily handle it, as the caissons had been left outside of the work, and the enemy, having planted a battery in a field seven or eight hundred yards beyond Old Town Creek, had an enfilading fire which covered both Gregg and Whitworth. Their shot that would miss Gregg would strike the other, and prevented all approach to the caissons.

The enemy — a full corps — now advanced in three lines of battle to the charge, and the little garrison repulsed them. The four guns in Whitworth were withdrawn, which the enemy observing, again assaulted both works. The assault was in column of brigades, completely enveloping Gregg and approaching Whitworth only in front.

Gregg repulsed assault after assault; — the two regiments of Mississippians and the North Carolinians, who had won honor on so many fields, fighting this, their last battle, with most terrible enthusiasm, as if feeling this to be the last act in the drama for them.

McElroy, and his men of the Washington Artillery — fighting their guns to the last — preserved untarnished the brilliancy of reputation acquired by that corps.

Gregg raged like the crater of a volcano emitting its flashes of deadly fires, enveloped in flame and cloud, wreathing our flag as well in honor as in the smoke of death. It was a glorious struggle. Louisiana, represented by these noble artillerists, and Mississippi and North Carolina by their shattered bands, stood there side by side together, holding the last regular fortified lines around Petersburg.

The capture of the works was but a question of time. The blue-coats finally jumped into the ditch surrounding

Gregg, and after a delay of half an hour climbed over each other's backs to gain the summit of the parapet. There was a weak point on the side of Gregg, where the ditch was incomplete, and where it had been planned to connect it with Whitworth by rifle-pits; and over this the enemy rushed. Presently six regimental standards were seen waving on the parapet.

While Gregg and Whitworth were holding out, Longstreet was hastening with Field's division from the north side of the James to form an inner line for the purpose of covering Gen. Lee's withdrawal that night. As soon as Harris heard of the formation of that line he withdrew with his little band from Whitworth, cutting his way through.

It was Gibbon's corps of 5,000 men that captured Gregg, and 68 of its brave defenders out of 200 were killed, McElroy losing 6 of his gunners killed and 2 wounded, and the rest taken prisoners. The enemy lost 800 men in the assaults on Gregg and Whitworth.[1]

At 12 o'clock that night the last man and the last gun of the brave army that had defended the lines of Petersburg for a year, passed over the pontoon bridges, and the march began that ended at Appomattox Court-House.

This morning as Gen. A. P. Hill, accompanied by a single courier, was endeavoring to ride to our extreme right, at Five Forks, he ran upon two Federal soldiers of Gibbon's corps, and by them was shot and killed. He, like the French Marshal Ney, was indeed the "bravest of the brave."

---

[1] Gibbon stated this to Gen. Wilcox at the surrender.

CHAPTER XVI.

SURRENDER OF THE ARMY OF NORTHERN VIRGINIA.

On the Last Retreat. — Amelia Court-House. — Forty Hours without
Food. — Pursued by Cavalry. — Wagons Burned. — Army Demoral-
ized. — Fighting, Marching, Starving. — Organization giving Way. —
Marching without Orders. — Appomattox. — Gordon Fighting. —
Artillery Captured. — Custer, Sheridan, and Longstreet. — A Game
of "Brag."

APRIL 3. — Experience a feeling of relief at getting
out of the trenches and on the road once more.
It is reported that Richmond was evacuated last night, and
President Davis and cabinet are on their way to North
Carolina. Our magazines have been blown up and the
bridges burned behind us. Gen. Lee declares that now he
has his little army foot loose, and out of entrenchments, he
will yet evade Grant and eventually hold him at bay in the
mountains.

Our extra caissons, ammunition, and fodder said to be
awaiting us at Amelia Court-House.

April 4. — The Third corps artillery reached Amelia
Court-House this P.M., having marched with scarcely a
halt for forty-four hours. Have not eaten a regular meal
since last Sunday, — three days.

While waiting this A.M. at the pontoon bridge over
the Appomattox, near Amelia, one of the men gave me a
piece of raw bacon and a handful of parched corn, which

he had received from home a few days since. I thought it was an excellent breakfast, and tasted as nice as a tenderloin steak garnished with mushrooms in " Victor's " best style.

Sheridan's cavalry are after us sharply, and have destroyed some wagons.

It is believed that it was the intention to remain here and offer Grant battle ; but it has been discovered that the provisions we expected to have found here have, by some error, been sent on to Richmond, the train being required to bring away the archives. Who cares for archives now? It is food we need. The result of this mismanagement is that the army is without subsistence for men or beast. The men are rapidly becoming demoralized, and are straggling off to find, if possible, something to appease the pangs of hunger.

This A.M. I saw Gens. Lee and Longstreet. As usual they both looked confident.

April 5. — Gen. Lee has decided to push on and try to reach Danville and form a junction with Gen. Johnston. Our extra caissons, full of ammunition, were fired and blown up last night.

The column moved this A.M. Our great wagon-train (much too great) was sent by different roads, and was attacked by the enemy's cavalry and many ordnance wagons burned.

Marched all day and nearly all night. When the batteries halt to rest, the men throw themselves upon the ground and immediately go to sleep. When the order is given to move forward, the horses often move on without their drivers, so hard is it to arouse the men.

Tired and hungry we push on. It is now a race for life or death. We seldom receive orders now. The enemy has the shortest line to Danville and Burkesville, and is heading us off.

April 6. — Marched all day. Enemy close behind. This afternoon our rear-guard was attacked, and Gen. Lee commanded in person. Gen. Custis Lee was taken prisoner, and many men.

The enemy's cavalry appeared in our front at Riceville. We formed a line and fired a few rounds from our artillery, which had the effect of keeping them at a respectful distance.

Gen. Rosser, of our cavalry, captured 800 of the enemy, who had been sent by Grant to destroy the "High bridge" in our front, over the Appomattox river at Farmville.

I was sitting on my horse, watching the men build a rude breast-work of rails and earth, when I heard a familiar voice behind me, inquiring the whereabouts of Gen. Longstreet. I turned to look, and there was Rosser, mounted upon a superb black horse. I had not seen him for months; we shook hands, and I inquired the news. He said, "Oh! we have captured those people who were going to destroy the bridge, took them all in; but Jim Dearing is mortally wounded. He had a hand-to-hand encounter with the commanding officer of the Federals, Gen. Read, and cut him down from his horse, killing him; but Read's orderly shot Dearing through the body, and then he, too, was shot. It was a gallant fight. *This* is

Read's horse and *this* his sabre. Both beauties, aren't they? But I must see Longstreet." Then for the first time I noticed that Rosser was wounded in the arm; but he always made light of such "scratches." We hunted up Longstreet, and then, after Rosser had made his report, I accompanied him to where his cavalry had halted, thence to our bivouac, where I learned that we were to push on again as soon as it was dark.

It was 10 P.M. when we took the road again. It was axle-deep in mud. It was a fearfully trying night.

April 7. — Early this morning we reached Farmville and went into park to rest. Provisions are distributed for the first time, casks of bacon being knocked open on the road-side, the tired and hungry troops helping themselves as they passed by. My orderly, whom I had left behind, to follow the command with my horse "Sam," informed me that some one had stolen him while he was sleeping, but still holding the bridle. I rated him soundly, for "Old Sam" had been a faithful friend. While resting I heard my brother's familiar whistle, coming from a mass of men in the road, and answered him, and immediately we were shaking hands. He had been in Richmond when it was evacuated, and had made his way to Mr. Logan's, in Goochland, where he obtained fresh horses, and then started off to rejoin the army, accompanied by young Logan. I was glad to see him and to get the good mount he had brought me.

We had rested but a little while when orders came to be off again, and then the quartermasters, headed by Col. Corley, chief quartermaster, began to burn the army wagons.

The enemy was following closely over the railroad bridge that our cavalry had, in their hurry, failed to burn. A line of battle was formed and an attack of the enemy repulsed. Matters were looking blue, and some artillery was abandoned.

In the afternoon, while our column was moving through an old field parallel to the wagon road, bullets began to whistle around our ears, and presently a brigade (Laurel) of our cavalry appeared on our flank, crying, " They are coming ! they are coming ! " I was marching at my post in rear of the column of guns, and feeling assured that the enemy was upon us gave the order at the top of my voice, " 'Tention ! Fire to the left, in battery ! " With great promptitude the guns were wheeled into position ready for action just as the Federal cavalry came charging to the crest of the high ground. With shell cut for close range, and canister, our twelve guns were let loose, and such a scattering I never saw before. A brigade of our infantry, about *two hundred men*, came marching from the road to our assistance, and McIntosh and I, now all excitement, drew our sabres and placed ourselves in front to lead them to the charge, when Gen. Walker, whose troops they were, and whom I had not observed, cried, " Gentlemen ! I'll lead my men myself ! " — and we subsided. Chamberlayne, with one gun, then accompanied the charge, and when our troops rejoined the column of march, they had with them, as a prisoner of war, Gen. Gregg, U.S. cavalry. The General was quite chagrined, and said " he had thought he would have had an easy time of it destroying our moving trains, and had not expected to run into the jaws of a whole park of artillery." It was fortunate that we were there just in the nick of time, for had Gregg obtained possession of the road, he stood a good chance of cutting off Gen. Lee and staff and capturing them.

I didn't know that Cullen and Barksdale had been spectators, until we had limbered up and moved on, then they rode up and congratulated us warmly, and inviting me into the bushes, produced a canteen of "medical supplies," from which I took a hearty pull.

We were compelled this afternoon to leave behind, stuck in the mud, the rear chest of a caisson.

We halted awhile to rest and eat something (if we had it), and the surgeons offered to share their coffee and sugar if we would share our meat, which was done; and we all supped together. The march was then resumed, and continued without orders all night, the men falling asleep at every halt.

.   .   .   .

And so the retreat rolls on. We are passing abandoned cannon, and wrecked and overturned wagons, and their now useless contents belonging to the quartermasters. Horses and mules dead or dying in the mud. At night our march is lighted by the fires of burning wagons, and the hoarse roar of cannon and the rattle of small arms before, behind, and on our flanks, are ever in our ears. The constant marching and fighting without sleep or food are rapidly thinning the ranks of this grand old army. Men who have stood by their flags since the beginning of the war now fall out of the ranks and are captured, simply because it is beyond their power of physical endurance to go any farther.

April 8. — We halted just before day near New Store, Buckingham county. Here the Colonel's cook reported us out of provender; so we resumed our march without any breakfast, halting about 9 A.M. on the road to Lynchburg. Riding to the front I was not a little surprised to see the Colonel and his Adjutant eating breakfast in a fence corner. Their cook had discovered provisions in a remarkable manner.

However, I was fortunate enough to meet Col. Edmund Pendleton, Fifteenth Louisiana, who was travelling with the trains, and he shared his breakfast with me, and gave me besides, three large slabs of dessicated vegetables for making soup.

We went into bivouac on Rocky Run, one mile from Appomattox Court-House. Surgeons Cullen and Barksdale joined me at my camp-fire, and we had a bucket of soup for supper.

At Amelia Court-House all of the artillery battalions of the army, except ours and that of Lieut. Col. John C. Haskell, were sent off ahead of the army to try and reach some point in North Carolina to recruit, and obtain fresh horses if possible. These battalions were under the command of Gen. R. Lindsey Walker. After we went into bivouac this evening, the artillery firing, we had heard in front late in the afternoon, seemed to be approaching nearer. It was not a great while before long trains of wagons came tearing down the road from the front, the drivers whipping up their mules and shouting lustily. I mounted my horse and rode forward to see what was the matter. I had not gone far before I came up to a force of infantry that were being aligned across the road and preparing for defence. Here I met some officers and men of the Washington Artillery, from whom I learned that Gen. Walker's column of artillery (about sixty pieces) had been marching in front of the army all day, and at about 4 P.M. halted in a grove just before reaching Appomattox Station, on the Lynchburg railroad. Everything had been so quiet that they concluded to have a good rest, the officers and men taking advantage of the time to wash up and refresh themselves. It was not thought necessary to put out pickets, as the enemy was supposed to be pushing only our rear. While enjoying this supposed security, all of a sudden, a bugle-call rang out upon the air, and a squadron of Federal cavalry was seen preparing to charge. Men rushed to their guns in a hurry, horses were hitched up, and as the enemy advanced they were met by a raking fire of canister, which repulsed them. But again and again the enemy, reinforced, charged. They were Sheridan's cavalry. The artillery that could be gotten off, fired retiring, and fell back to Appomattox Court-House, where in the streets of the town, they met infantry coming to their support, who in turn drove the cavalry back with loss. But the Washington Artillery, fighting to the last, and evading capture with difficulty, destroyed the gun-carriages, buried their guns in the woods, and nearly all the officers and men went to the mountains. They fired their last shot to-day, after three years and nine months' service in the field since Bull Run, July, 1861.

The officers and men who joined me at my camp-fire were Capt. Jo. Norcom and Lieut. George Apps, of

Fourth company, and Sergt. William Fellowes, of First company, Washington Artillery.

April 9. — At 9 o'clock this morning the battalion was moved out into the road to resume the march. Just as we emerged, Gen. Lee was riding by, going towards the rear, accompanied by Cols. Marshall and Taylor of his staff. As I saluted him he reined up his horse and said, " Good-morning, Colonel! How are your horses this morning? Do you think you can keep up with the infantry to-day?" I replied, "I thought I could; that they had had a pretty good feed of shucks, and appeared to be in tolerable condition. But, General," I added, "I have no orders." He replied, "You will find Gen. Longstreet on the hill yonder; he will give you orders." And, touching his hat in acknowledgment of my salute, he continued his ride. I noted particularly his dress. He was in full uniform, with a handsome embroidered belt and dress sword, tall hat, and buff gauntlets. His horse, "Old Traveller," was finely groomed, and his equipment, bridle, bit, etc., were polished until they shone like silver. All this seemed peculiar. I had never seen him before in full rig, and began to think something strange was to happen. He always wore during the campaigns a gray sack coat with side pockets, quite like the costume of a business man in cities; and after the second Manassas I had never seen him carry a sword. Not seeing Col. McIntosh I moved the Battalion forward towards the hill, where I was to find Gen. Longstreet.

From the sound of firing in front it was evident that Gordon and Fitz Lee were attacking Sheridan's cavalry, who outnumbered them four to one, and had also the comforting assurance that the Army of the James was not far off, to support them if needed.

When my march brought me to the hill I espied Generals Longstreet and Alexander, chief of artillery, sitting on a log. Alexander got up and came towards me. I said to him, "Gen. Lee instructed me to stop here for orders. What do you want me to do?" He replied, "Turn into that field on the right and park your guns." Then added, in a low tone, "We are going to surrender to-day!" We had been thinking it might come to that, sooner or later; but when the shock came it was terrible. And was this to be the end of all our marching and fighting for the past four years? I could not keep back the tears that came to my eyes. Alexander cautioned me to keep the news quiet, and I moved on to the field designated, with a heavy heart, and parked the batteries. Col. Haskell's battalion was already in park near me in the same field.

The firing continued in front for some time, and Gordon drove the "invincible troopers" more than a mile, and sent back a large number of prisoners and two pieces of artillery which he had captured. The latter were placed in Haskell's park.

Had it been only Sheridan that barred the way the surrender would not have occurred at Appomattox; but Gordon only drove back the cavalry to find himself confronted by the Army of the James, and their bayonets could now be seen advancing through the trees, and the road was blocked with ten times his number.

It was then that the flag of truce was raised, by an agreement with Sheridan and Gordon.

Presently a Federal cavalry officer was observed coming down the road towards our forces; he wore his hair very long, and it was of a light or reddish color. In his hand he carried a white handkerchief, which he constantly waved up and down. He inquired for Gen. Lee, and was directed to Gen. Longstreet upon the hill. Upon approaching the General he dismounted and said, " Gen. Longstreet, in the name of Gen. Sheridan and myself I demand the surrender of this army. I am Gen. Custer." Gen. Longstreet replied, "I am not in command of this army. Gen. Lee is, and he has gone back to meet Gen. Grant in regard to a surrender."

" Well," said Custer, "no matter about Gen. Grant; we demand the surrender be made to us. If you do not do so we will renew hostilities, and any blood shed will be upon your head ! "

" Oh, well ! " said Longstreet, " if you do that I will do my best to meet you ; " then, turning to his staff, he said, " Col. Manning, please order Gen. Johnson to move his division to the front, to the right of Gen. Gordon. Col. Latrobe, please order Gen. Pickett forward, to Gen. Gordon's left. Do it at once ! " Custer listened with surprise depicted upon his countenance; he had not thought so many of our troops were at hand with Longstreet. He, cooling off immediately, said, " General, probably we had better wait until we hear from Grant and Lee. I will speak to Gen. Sheridan about it; don't move your troops yet."

And he mounted and withdrew in a much more quiet style than in his approach.

As he passed out of hearing, Longstreet said quietly, with that peculiar chuckle of his, "Ha! ha! that young man has never learned to play the game of 'Brag.'" The divisions of Johnson and Pickett were only a myth, and had no existence whatever after the fight at "Five Forks."

Shortly after this little event Gen. Lee, with his two staff-officers, rode through our lines towards Appomattox Court-House, and halted, and dismounted not far from where our artillery was parked. In a few minutes a federal staff-officer, bearing a flag of truce, and who was said to represent Gen. Grant, rode up to where Gen. Lee was sitting in a small orchard by the roadside. He brought word that Gen. Grant was ready to see him at the front, and, accompanied by Col. Marshall only, he rode into the village of Appomattox Court-House.

By a singular coincidence the meeting of the Generals took place in the house of Major McLean, the same gentleman who in 1861, at the battle of Bull Run, had tendered his house to Gen. Beauregard for head-quarters. He removed from Manassas after the battle, with the intention of seeking some quiet nook where the alarms of war could never find him; but it was his fortune to be in at the beginning, and in at the death.

We did not immediately learn what happened at the interview, but it came out later that the two Generals sat at a table to confer together, when Gen. Lee opened the conversation by saying, "General, I deem it due to proper candor and frankness, to say at the very beginning of this interview, that I am not willing even to discuss any terms of surrender inconsistent with the honor of my army, which I am determined to maintain to the last."

Gen. Grant replied, " I have no idea of proposing dishonorable terms, General ; but I would be glad if you would state what you consider honorable terms." Gen. Lee then briefly stated the terms upon which he would be willing to surrender.

Grant expressed himself satisfied with them, and Lee requested he would formally reduce the propositions to writing ; which Gen. Grant immediately proceeded to do.

Gen. Lee read the propositions carefully, and copies were made of the paper by Gen. Grant's secretary and Col. Marshall.

While this was being done, Grant and Lee chatted together, and with the other Federal Generals (Ord and Sheridan) who were present, but nothing bearing upon the surrender, except Gen. Lee stated he had two or three thousand prisoners he would like to get rid of, for whom he had no rations.

Gen. Grant having signed his note, Gen. Lee conferred with Col. Marshall, who wrote this brief note of acceptance of the terms of the surrender offered : —

HEAD—QUARTERS, ARMY OF NORTHERN VIRGINIA,
April 9, 1865.

GENERAL : — I have received your letter of this date, containing the terms of surrender of the Army of Northern Virginia as proposed by you.

As they are substantially the same as those expressed in your letter of the 8th instant they are accepted.

I will proceed to designate the proper officers to carry the stipulations into effect.

Very respectfully,

Your obedient servant,

R. E. LEE.

This terminated the interview, and Gen. Lee mounted his horse and rode back to his quarters, which were three-quarters of a mile north-east of the Court-House.

As soon as he was seen riding towards his army, whole lines of men rushed down to the roadside, and crowded around him to shake his hand; all tried to show him the veneration and esteem in which they held him. Filled with emotion he essayed to speak, but could only say, " Men, we have fought through the war together. I have done the best I could for you. My heart is too full to say more."

We all knew the pathos of those simple words, of that slight tremble in his voice, and it was no shame on our manhood " that something upon the soldier's cheek washed off the stains of powder ; " that our tears answered to those in the eyes of our grand old chieftain, and that we could only grasp the hand of " Uncle Robert," and pray " *God help you, General !* "

And as he rode on to his tent, and disappeared from our view, " the Army of Northern Virginia " passed away, leaving upon the page of history a record of valor and devotion never excelled ; " its battle-flags were furled forever, never lowered in defeat, but in accordance with the orders of its beloved commander, who was himself yielding obedience to the dictates of a pure and lofty sense of duty to his men."

CHAPTER XVII.

DISBANDMENT, AND HOME AGAIN.

Less than 8,000 Veterans with Lee. — Terms of Surrender. — Paroles. — Turning in our Batteries. — On to Mexico. — Lee's Farewell Address. — Dispersion of the Confederates. — On to Richmond. — General Halleck. — Sherman's Army. — Fortress Monroe and Baltimore. — " Barnum's Hotel." — " Maryland Club." — " New York Hotel." — Steamship " Monterey." — Bound for Home. — "Pelicans" Returning. — New Orleans. — Home Again.

APRIL 10. — The army slept soundly last night upon the ground, and obtained the much-needed rest they had been strangers to for many a long day. This morning it is raining, and we, at head-quarters, procured an old wagon-cover and constructed a shelter with the aid of some fence-rails. Seven thousand eight hundred and ninety-two (7,892) men only were in line of battle yesterday, with arms in their hands; the remainder of the army have been unable to keep up for want of food and exhaustion, and have probably been taken prisoners.

All honor to the brave men who, more fortunate than their comrades, were able to stand by Lee to the last moment.

In the absence of Col. McIntosh, who had gone to the mountains, I had the Battalion assembled and informed the men of the terms of the surrender, which were as follows: that each officer and man were to go to their homes after receiving a parole. The officers to retain their side-arms and private horses. The rolls were then called and but few men were found to be missing.

I was informed this morning that my baggage-wagon was burned at Appomattox Station, on the night of the 8th, so I had lost my valise containing my swell $800 uniform, books, and letters too.

I received to-day the following note from Captain Haskell, A.A.G., for Gen. Alexander : —

HEAD–QUARTERS ARTILLERY, FIRST CORPS.

COLONEL : — I send up a sufficient number of paroles for your command, including the Thirteenth Virginia Battalion of Artillery, the Washington Artillery, [1] and Donaldsonville Artillery.

---

[1] There was no formal surrender of the Washington Artillery with the Army of Northern Virginia at Appomattox Court-House. Some of the officers and men succeeded in reaching President Davis, and acted as his body-guard. as the following letter will show : —

WASHINGTON, GA., May 3, 1865.

LIEUT. C. H. C. BROWN, *Washington Artillery :* —

MY DEAR SIR, — The President directs me to return to you his heartfelt thanks for the valuable services rendered him by yourself and the gallant men under your command, as part of his escort.

Very truly yours,

WM. PRESTON JOHNSTON,
Col. and A.D.C.

The names of the officers and men referred to are as follows : —

Chas. H. C. Brown, Lieutenant Commanding, Washington Artillery.
W. G. Coyle, Sergeant, 3d Company, Washington Artillery.
J. F. Lilly, Corporal, 4th   "   "   "
T. J. Lazzare, Private 4th   "   "   "
R. Wilkerson,   "   1st   "   "   "
J. B. McMullan,   "   1st   "   "   "
R. McDonald,   "   4th   "   "   "
—— Webster,   "   4th   "   "   "
R. N. Davis,   "   4th   "   "   "
W. A. McRay,   "   1st   "   "   "
L. D. Porter, Louisiana Guard Artillery.
W. R. Payne,   "   "   "
C. A. Longue,   "   "   "
T. J. Domerty,   "   "   "

You must sign for all except your own, which will be signed by Gen. Alexander.

There is a difference in the form, but they are all the same. One is to be given to each man. No duplicates are to be made. Send back any blanks you don't need, as we are very short.

Yours respectfully,

J. C. HASKELL,

A.A. Gen'l.

To Lieut. Col. W. M. Owen, *Commanding Battalion Artillery.*

With the assistance of Col. Edmund Pendleton, Fifteenth Louisiana, Captains Owen and Norcom, and Lieut. George Apps of the Washington Artillery, I proceeded to parole the men of the artillery command, as directed. The paroles were slips of paper about the size of a bank check, and read as follows : —

Appomattox Court-House, April 10, 1865.

The bearer, Private   , of   Battery of Artillery, a paroled prisoner of war of the Army of Northern Virginia, has permission to go to his home and there remain undisturbed until exchanged.

(Signed)   W. M. OWEN,

Lieut. Col. Commanding Battalion of Artillery.

These passes were respected by all pickets and guards as much as they would have been had they been signed by Gen. Grant himself.

The infantry of the army have been marched to a field adjacent to Appomattox Court-House, and have stacked their arms, and having laid down their tattered battle-flags across the stacks, and hung up their cartridge-boxes, have been marched back to their respective bivouacs.

Forty-five (45) officers and men escaped under Major Buck Miller (the horses having been cut from their harness) by way of Lynchburg and the mountains, to General Jo. Johnston's army in North Carolina.

Another night was spent sleeping soundly in the mud and rain, and this A.M. (11th), according to instructions, I had my teams hitched up and moved my three batteries (12 guns) to the main road, where I turned them over to the Federal officer detailed to receive them. Returning to our "shelter" I was visited by Gen. Jno. G. Hazard, Chief of Artillery of the Second Corps, U.S.A., and his Adjutant-General, Capt. T. Fred Brown.

We couldn't extend to the General much polite attention, but we did the best we could under existing circumstances. Officers and men of the Federal army mingled freely with our officers and men around our camp-fires, and not a harsh word was spoken on either side.

In fact the conduct of the victors was beyond all praise. They sent our starving men provisions, and not a shout of exultation nor the music of a band was heard during all the time we were at Appomattox. A feeling of great and deep sadness filled the breasts of our army, and a feeling of delicate sympathy pervaded the other. Brave men who had looked into each other's eyes for four long years along the shining musket-barrel, and across the deadly, blazing trench, understood and respected one another.

Something was said about our joining together under the "old flag" and marching to drive Maximilian out of Mexico, and I believe we would have gladly gone, but nothing came of it.

On the morning of the 10th, Gen. Meade called to pay his respects to Gen. Lee. The latter reported to his staff after the visit, that the conversation had naturally turned upon the recent events, and that Gen. Meade had asked

him how many men he had at Petersburg at the time of
Gen. Grant's last assault.   He told him in reply that, by
the last returns, he had thirty-five thousand muskets (35,-
000).   Gen. Meade then said, "You mean you had 35,000
men on the lines immediately around Petersburg?" to which
Gen. Lee replied, "No, that he had but that number
from his left on the Chickahominy river to his right at
Dinwiddie Court-House."   At this Gen. Meade expressed
great surprise, and stated that he then had with him, in
one wing of the Federal army which he commanded, over
50,000 men.   The number of Confederates paroled was
between 26,000 and 27,000.[1]

On the morning of April 12th, our battalion and the
remnants of other battalions to be paroled were assembled
for the last time in front of our camp-fire, and I read to
them the farewell address of Gen. Lee, as follows : —

HEAD–QUARTERS ARMY OF NORTHERN VIRGINIA,
APPOMATTOX COURT-HOUSE, April 10, 1865.
GENERAL ORDERS No. 9 : —

After four years of arduous service, marked by unsurpassed courage
and fortitude, the Army of Northern Virginia has been compelled to
yield to overwhelming numbers and resources.

I need not tell the brave survivors of so many hard fought battles
who have remained steadfast to the last, that I have consented to this
result from no distrust of them; but feeling that valor and devotion
could accomplish nothing that would compensate for the loss that must
have attended a continuance of the conflict, I determined to avoid useless
sacrifice of those whose past services have endeared them to their
countrymen.   By the terms of the agreement, officers and men can go
to their homes and remain until exchanged.

You will take with you the satisfaction that proceeds from the con-

---

[1] "Four Years with Lee."— TAYLOR.

Tout perdu.

sciousness of duty faithfully performed, and I earnestly pray that a merciful God will extend to you his blessing and protection.

With an unceasing admiration of your constancy and devotion to your country, and a grateful remembrance of your kind and grateful consideration for myself, I bid you an affectionate farewell.

R. E. LEE.

The men listened with marked attention and with moistened eyes as this grand farewell from our old chief was read, and then receiving each his parole they every one shook my hand warmly and bade me good-by; and breaking up into parties of three and four, turned their faces homeward; some to Richmond, some to Lynchburg, and some to far-off ruined Louisiana.

I watched them until the last man disappeared with a wave of his hand around a curve of the road; then mounting our horses and taking a sad farewell of Generals Lee, Longstreet, Gordon, and Latrobe, Taylor, Cullen, and Barksdale, we rode away from Appomattox. And now—

> "Oh, farewell!
> Farewell the neighing steed, and the shrill trump,
> The spirit-stirring drum, the ear-piercing fife,
> The royal banner; and all quality,
> Pride, pomp, and circumstance of glorious war!
> And O, you mortal engines, whose rude throats,
> The immortal Jove's dread clamors counterfeit,
> Farewell!"

We rode forty miles upon our return journey, and bivouacked in a tobacco-barn near Cumberland Court-House, and obtained some corn-bread and milk from a kind-hearted old negro woman. Our party consisted of Capt. E.

Owen, Lieut.-Col. J. Floyd King, Maj. Thomas Brander, and William Fellowes.

Bright and early we resumed our ride until we crossed the James, and halted at the hospitable home of Mr. Logan, in Goochland, where the family gave us a hearty welcome, yet withal, a sad one; they had lost all hope for the future. We rested well — frequently falling asleep while talking with our hosts.

The night before our lines were broken at Petersburg the boys of the section of the First company Washington Artillery under Lieut. Battles, placed in my possession for safe-keeping, their old battle-flag, as it was too much torn and riddled by bullets to be any longer used. I took it and hung it up in my quarters at Gregg House.

Next morning, when the assaults were being made upon the Fort (Gregg), and the bullets were flying thick and fast, I remembered the flag, and, riding up to the window where it hung, broke in the sash with my sabre and secured it. I carried it in my saddle-pocket as far as Amelia Court-House, where I transferred it to John Logan, who was going home, with instructions to give it to his sisters for safe-keeping. The girls concealed it in a sofa cushion, and after Lee's army had retreated, Federal cavalry came to the house, and officers slept upon the sofa, and laid their heads upon this piece of bunting. The cushion now having been produced, a few cuts with a knife revealed the tattered guidon. While it is very wrong to "kiss and tell," it must nevertheless be recorded that Capt. Owen bestowed a hearty kiss all round.

This little relic now occupies an honored place with other

flags in the arsenal of the Washington Artillery, in New Orleans.

We ended our journey, and rode into Richmond on the 18th of April; and as we passed through Main street furtive glances were cast and little white handkerchiefs were waved at us by the ladies at the windows of their houses. Main street (the business part of it) was in ruins.

Officers in blue were lounging about *our* usual haunts. Soldiers in blue had usurped the places of the boys in gray.

At the outpost, when we entered the city, we were kindly received by the officer in charge, and were informed by him that President Lincoln had been assassinated. We told him that we sincerely regretted it was so. He said, " Yes, I am sorry for you all, for it will go hard with you now, and the whole South."

The 22d of April found us still in Richmond. We are not allowed " to go to our homes unmolested," on account of the assassination.

I sold my horse and a mule, and this put us in funds. Fortunately some kind friends had saved my trunk of reserve clothing, but I thought it prudent to purchase a suit of ready-made garments and a round-top hat.

Some rows having occurred at the " Spottswood Hotel," between Confederate and German Federal officers, we were politely requested to leave, so we hired apartments on Franklin street, and from our windows witnessed the army of Gen. Sherman pass through *en route* for Washington. We finally took the amnesty oath at the State-House, and called upon Gen. Halleck at the " White House," to ask permission to leave the city.

When I crossed the threshold of that house how many pleasant memories it brought to mind, what visions and plans of happiness that were never to be realized!

How my heart went out to Mr. Davis and his family, now in so much trouble and distress!

We laid our request before Gen. Halleck, and were refused unceremoniously; but, nevertheless, the next morning we were, *incognito*, on board the steamboat " Georgiana," bound for Fortress Monroe and Baltimore.

We took leave of our friends in Richmond with sincere regret; all had been so kind to us we had begun to consider it our home. While we were detained in Richmond, awaiting permission to depart, a delegation of officers called upon Gen. Lee to find out what he would say in regard to a half-formed resolution we had made to go to Brazil and enter the army.

The General was indisposed, but Gen. Custis Lee told us that it was the expressed wish of his father that everybody should " go home and help build up the country." The Brazilian army obtained no recruits.

On the 16th of May we arrived at Baltimore, and stopped at " Barnum's Hotel," and were entertained at the "Maryland Club."

The 28th of May found us snugly located at the " New York Hotel," in New York city, and, dropping in at Brooks's, we arrayed ourselves in swell garments, and felt and looked like gentlemen of elegant leisure once more.

I dined with Mr. William Travers, and hunted up my old friends, the Gilmans, all of whom I found, to my unspeakable regret, married; they had a hearty welcome for

me and called me their "rebel friend," and insisted upon
my saying, over and over again, "I am so sorry!"

Latrobe joined us here, but stayed but a day. Happening to see an outrageous caricature of Mr. Davis hanging
in front of Barnum's Museum, on Broadway, he, in great
disgust, hurried away to Boston, and took a Cunarder for
England.

On the 3d of June, Capt. Hilary Cenas, C. S. Navy,
and I, took passage on board the steamship "Monterey,"
bound for New Orleans.

On the third day out we learned, through the Purser,
that a number of "Pelicans" were passengers in the steer-
age. So both of us, taking a bottle of champagne under
each arm, climbed down the companion-way into the
dimly lighted 'tween-decks, and introducing ourselves to
our compatriots we were enthusiastically received, and
popped the corks and had a jolly time.[1]

On the 13th of June, 1865, we walked into the "St.
Charles Hotel," in New Orleans, where we found officiating,
as head clerk, Andy Blakely, an ex-member of the Washington Artillery, who took us in and cared for us, and we
slept once more under a Louisiana sky, and were preyed
upon and bled by the long since forgotten Louisiana mosquito.

In the morning, my last piece of "fractional currency"
(25 cents) was invested in a "Picayune" and a mild refreshing beverage, and stepping out upon the broad stone

---

[1] The names of those returning soldiers were as follows: — John A. Lafaye,
Numa Landry, Ernest Landry, Henry Starr, M. O'Neil, Honoré Flotte, Alfred
Lamothe, Leon Lamothe, Octave Legier.

balcony of the hotel, into the warm, delicious June sunshine, I took up again the broken thread of a business life without a dollar in the world, emphatically and completely "busted."

CHAPTER XVIII.

THE FIFTH COMPANY BATTALION WASHINGTON ARTILLERY.

ON the departure for the seat of war in Virginia of the first four companies of the Battalion, on the 27th of April, 1861, the following order was promulgated by the Major Commanding, the last issued by him previous to mustering into the service of the Confederate States : —

HEAD–QUARTERS BATTALION WASHINGTON ARTILLERY,
NEW ORLEANS, April, 1861.

. . . .

VII. — First Lieut. W. I. Hodgson, of the 4th Company, is hereby specially detailed to remain in New Orleans on recruiting service, and will forward, from time to time, to the seat of war, such recruits as may be required, and hold himself subject to any further orders from these head-quarters.

. . . .

By order,   J. B. WALTON,
Wm. M. Owen, *Adjutant.*   *Major Commanding.*

A reserve force of twenty men was left behind, and Lieut. Hodgson, with their assistance, rapidly organized a Fifth company ; and, in one month from the day of the departure of the Battalion, held an election for officers, casting over 150 votes, with the following result : —

Captain. — W. Irving Hodgson.
Senior First Lieutenant. — Theo. A. James.
Junior First Lieutenant. — Rinaldo Banister.

Senior Second Lieutenant. — Jerry G. Pierson.
Junior Second Lieutenant. — E. L. Hews.

When the Battalion left for Virginia they left the arsenal on Girod street in an unfinished condition, the roof not yet put on, the floors torn up, and everything in the way of camp and garrison equipage, artillery and ordnance stores taken with them. Yet, in order to supply their place, the reserves went to work with a will. They sent special committees to Baton Rouge to the Legislature, to the City Council of New Orleans, and the merchants and capitalists of the city and State. Through handsome donations from the former, a generous appropriation from the Council, and the unbounded liberality of the latter (including the present of a piece of artillery and caisson complete from Gov. Thomas Overton Moore, and a similar gift from John I. Adams, a prominent merchant of New Orleans), they were able within ninety days to complete the arsenal, and pay for it.

They besides perfected the organization of six handsome brass field-pieces, with limbers, caissons and harness all complete, with a serviceable and complete stock of camp and garrison equipage for 160 men; all this without owing a dollar.

From time to time, during the first year of the war, they sent to their comrades in Virginia reinforcements of men and drivers, artificers, etc., always forwarding under the command of an officer of the Fifth company, and always sending them off fully clothed and equipped, free of expense to the Battalion.

A semi-weekly mail was regularly sent also to the command in the field, the cases being packed not only with mail matter, but with clothing, edibles, and everything intended for any member of the command, sent him by his family or friends, and with no expense to the soldier of transportation.

Early in the year 1862, the members of the Fifth company exhibited much military ardor, and felt unwilling to remain longer at home, while their comrades, friends and brothers, were sharing the dangers and toils of camp life.

In February of that year Captain Hodgson addressed a communication to Brig.-Gen. E. L. Tracy, commanding the First brigade, First division Louisiana State militia, to which his battery was attached, asking for a new election of officers, intended for active service in field; in conformity to which, Gen. Tracy ordered an election on the 24th day of that month; and under the supervision and direction of Majors Ignatius Caulfield and John B. Prados, of his staff, the election took place as directed. There were 185 votes cast, with the following result: —

Captain. — W. Irving Hodgson.
Senior First Lieutenant. — Cuthbert H. Slocomb.
Junior First Lieutenant. — Wm. C. D. Vaught.
Senior Second Lieutenant. — Edson L. Hews.
Junior Second Lieutenant. — J. A. Chalaron.

On the first day of March, 1862, the following despatch from Gen. G. T. Beauregard, was published in all of the New Orleans daily papers: —

DESPATCH FROM GEN. BEAUREGARD.

JACKSON, TENN., Feb. 28, 1862.

To Gov. THOS. O. MOORE: —

Will accept all good equipped troops, under the act of 21st August, that will offer, and for ninety days.

Let the people understand that here is the proper place to defend Louisiana.

G. T. BEAUREGARD.

Captain Hodgson immediately called a meeting of his command, which was held on the second day of the month, when it was shown that there was but one unanimous voice to at once offer their services for ninety days, or the war.

All necessary arrangements having been made for their immediate departure for the field, the following order was issued and published in the daily papers: —

HEAD-QUARTERS FIFTH CO., BAT. WASHINGTON ARTILLERY,

NEW ORLEANS, March 5, 1862.

[Order No. 44.]

I. — The officers and members of this corps are hereby ordered to appear at the arsenal on Thursday morning, the 6th inst., at 10 o'clock, punctually, fully equipped, with knapsacks packed, for the purpose of being mustered into the Confederate States service.

II. — Every member of the command is expected to be present. Those failing to appear will not be allowed to leave with the command.

By order of

W. IRVING HODGSON, *Captain.*

A. GORDON BAKEWELL, *O.S.*

On Thursday morning, March 6, 1862, at 11 o'clock, the Fifth company were regularly mustered into the service by the enrolling officer of Gen. Mansfield Lovell's staff, in Lafayette square, with 156 men, rank and file; they left New Orleans for the seat of war in Mississippi and Tennessee on Saturday, March 8, 1862, carrying with them their six guns, with everything perfect and complete, including their camp and garrison equipage, and without the cost of one dollar to the State or Confederate government.

The following is the "Roster" of the Fifth company, as mustered, into service : —

Officers. — Capt., W.Irving Hodgson ; Senior 1st Lieut., C. H. Slocomb ; Junior 1st Lieut., W. C. D. Vaught ; Senior 2d Lieut., Edson L. Hews ; Junior 2d Lieut., J. A. Chalaron ; Assistant Surgeon, J. Cecil LeGaré.

Non-Commissioned Staff. — Orderly Sergeant, A. Gordon Bakewell ; Ordnance Sergeant, J. H. H. Hedges ; Quartermaster's Sergeant, J. B. Wolfe ; Commissary Sergeant, W. R. Barstow.

1st Sergeant, J. W. De Merritt ; 2d Sergeant, B. H. Green, Jr. ; 3d Sergeant, A. J. Leverich ; 4th Sergeant, W. B. Giffen ; 5th Sergeant, John Bartley ; 6th Sergeant, Thos. M. Blair.

1st Corporal, John J. Jamison ; 2d Corporal, S. Higgins ; 3d Corporal, W. N. Calmes ; 4th Corporal, R. W. Frazer ; 5th Corporal, Emmet Putnam ; 6th Corporal, N. L. Bruce.

1st Caisson Corporal, D. W. Smith ; 2d Caisson Corporal, E. J. O'Brien ; 3d Caisson Corporal, A. S. Winston ; 4th Caisson Corporal, L. Macready ; 5th Caisson Corporal, Alf. Bellanger ; 6th Caisson Corporal, E. Charles.

Sergeant Drivers, J. H. Smith; Corporal Drivers, F. N. Thayer.

1st Artificer, W. A. Freret; 2d Artificer, J. F. Spearing; 3d Artificer, W. A. Jourdan; 4th Artificer, John Beggs; 5th Artificer, John Davidson; 6th Artificer, Fred. Holmes.

Privates. — Alex. Allain, V. F. Allain, T. C. Allen, C. A. Adams, N. Buckner, Jos. Banfil, Ben Bridge, A. T. Bennett, Jr., B. Boyden, A. J. Blaffer, John Boardman, Marcus J. Beebe, C. B. Broadwell, T. L. Bayne, Jas. Clarke, J. T. Crawford, W. W. Clayton, Joseph Denegre, J. H. Duggan, J. M. Davidson, M. Eastman, A. M. Fahenstock, E. C. Feinour, E. Fehrenbach, John Y. Fraser, Charles W. Fox, Robert Gibson, James F. Giffen, C. J. Hartnett, C. M. Harvey, W. D. Henderson, H. L. Henderson, Curtis Holmes, John B. Humphreys, Charles G. Johnsen, C. B. Jones, Gabriel Kaiser, W. B. Krumbharr, Minor Kenner, Jr., H. H. Lonsdale, H. Leckie, L. L. Levy, Martin Mathis, Lewis Mathis, H. J. Mather, E. Mussina, Eugene May, E. S. McIlhenny, Milton McKnight, H. D. McCown, D. C. Miller, W. R. Murphy, F. Maillieu, G. W. Palfrey, Robert Pugh, Richard L. Pugh, E. F. Reichert, S. F. Russell, E. Ricketts, J. M. Seixas, W. W. Sewell, G. W. Skidmore, L. Seicbrecht, George H. Shotwell, R. P. Salter, W. B. Stuart, Robert Strong, W. Steven, J. H. Scott, J. T. Skillman, John Slaymaker, Warren Stone, Jr., J. H. Simmons, R. W. Simmons, A. Sambola, E. K. Tisdale, Hiram Tomlin, C. Weingart, T. B. Winston, James White, John W. Watson, C. S. Wing, J. A. Walsh, Charles B. Watt, Charles Withan, Willis P. Williams.

Drivers. — Joseph Byrnes, James Bayle, John Clayton, Richard Farrell, William Dooly, Thomas Lynot, Patrick Long, John Leary, Daniel Moore, James Jordan, Sam. J. Davis, Patrick Kelly, Robert Norris, Geo. A. Turner, William White, Thomas Williams, John Young, Michael Farrel, John Abbott, Thomas Lace, Hugh McCormick, W. P. Hanley, M. Campbell, J. Devernay, J. R. Daley, J. O'Donnell, G. Gillan, B. O'Sullivan, John Singin, Dan. Shillin, Jas. Skalaghen, Wm. Tynen, Henry Day, John Haynes.

Bugler. — Carl Valanconi.

Arriving at Grand Junction, Tennessee, on Monday evening, March 10, 1862, the battery immediately went into camp, under the instruction of Gen. John K. Jackson, Commander of the Post. They were here supplied with their battery horses, and began drilling, and otherwise actively preparing for service. On the 27th day of March, the tents were struck, and the command started over land for Corinth, Mississippi, arriving there on the 1st day of April, 1862, and were immediately assigned to the brigade of Brig.-Gen. Patton Anderson, of Ruggles' Division, Bragg's (2d) Army Corps, and went into camp the same day.

On Thursday, the 3d day of April, the battery filed out through the fortifications with its brigade, and the army, destined for the battle-field of Shiloh.

Of the part taken by the battery in the battle of Shiloh, the following is the official report of Captain Hodgson : —

HEAD–QUARTERS FIFTH CO., BAT. WASHINGTON ARTILLERY,
CAMP MOORE, CORINTH, MISS., April 9, 1862.

To BRIG.–GEN. PATTON ANDERSON, *Commanding Second Brigade, Ruggles' Division, Army Miss.* : —

GENERAL : — In accordance with usage, I hereby report to you the " action " of my battery, in the battles of the 6th and 7th instant.

My battery, consisting of two 6-pounder smooth-bore guns, two 6-pounder rifled guns, and two 12-pounder howitzers, — total, 6 pieces, fully equipped with ammunition, horses, and men, entered the field, just in the rear of Twentieth Louisiana regiment (the right regiment of your brigade), on Sunday morning, the 6th inst., on the hill, overlooking from the south-west the encampments of the enemy immediately to the front of it and to the north-east, being the first camp attacked and taken by our army.

At 7 o'clock A.M., we opened fire on their camp, with our full battery of six guns, firing shell and spherical case shot, soon silencing one of their batteries, and filling the enemy with consternation. After firing some forty (40) rounds thus, we were directed by Gen. Ruggles to shell a camp immediately upon the left of the one mentioned, and in which there was a battery, from which the shot and shell were thrown on all sides of us.

With two howitzers and two rifled guns, under Lieuts. Slocomb and Vaught, assisted by two pieces from Capt. Shoup's battery, we soon silenced their guns, and had the gratification on seeing our brave and gallant troops charge through these two camps, running the enemy before them at the point of the bayonet.

At this point I lost your command, and on the order of General Ruggles to " go where I heard most firing," I passed over the first camp captured, through a third, and on to a fourth, in which your troops were doing sad havoc to the enemy.

I formed in battery on your extreme left, in the avenue of the camp, and commenced firing with canister from four (4) guns, into the tents of the enemy, only fifty (50) yards off. It was at this point I suffered most. The skirmishers of the enemy lying in their tents, only a stone's throw from us, cut holes through their tents near the ground, and played a deadly fire in among my cannoneers, killing three men, wounding seven or eight, besides killing some of our horses, mine among the rest. As soon as we were well formed in battery, and got well to work, we saw them creeping from their tents and making for the woods, and immediately afterwards saw your column charge the whole of them in ambush, and put them to flight.

A visit through that portion of their camp, at a subsequent hour, satisfied me, from the number of the dead, and the nature of their wounds, that my battery had done its duty.

Losing you again at this point, on account of the heavy brushwood through which you charged, I was requested, by Gen. Trudeau, to plant two guns farther down the avenue, say two hundred yards off, to shell a fifth camp farther on, which I did, and, after firing a dozen or more shells, had the satisfaction of seeing the cavalry charge the camp, putting the enemy to flight — killing many, and capturing many wounded prisoners.

Being again without a commanding general, and not knowing your exact position, I received and executed orders from Gen. Hardee and his aid, Col. Kearney, also from Col. Chisholm of Gen. Beauregard's staff, and in fact from other aids, whose names I do not know, going to points threatened and exposed, and where firing was continual, rendering cheerfully all the assistance I could with my battery, now reduced in men and horses.

At about 2 o'clock P.M., at the instance of Gen. Hardee, I opened from the fifth camp we had entered, firing upon a sixth camp, due north; silencing the battery and driving the enemy from their tents. Said portion of the army of the enemy were charged and their battery captured — afterwards lost again — by the Guard Orleans and other troops on our left, under Col. Preston Pond, Jr.

This was about the last firing of my battery on the 6th instant. Taking the main road to Pittsburg Landing, we followed on the heels of our men, after a retreating and badly whipped army, until within three-fourths of a mile of the Tennessee river, when the enemy began to shell the woods from their gunboats. Gen. Ruggles ordered us to the enemy's camp, where we bivouacked for the night.

I received orders on the morning of the 7th, at about 5.30 o'clock, to follow your command with my battery, and at 6 o'clock, being ready to move, could not ascertain your position — so took position on the extreme right of our army, supported by the Crescent regiment of

Col. Pond's brigade, in our rear, and an Arkansas regiment on my front, and I think the Twenty-first Tennessee regiment on my left flank; all under Gen. Hardee, for in fact he seemed to be the master-spirit, giving all orders and seeing that they were properly executed.

At about 9 o'clock, Gen. Breckenridge's command, on our extreme front, had pushed the enemy up and on to within several hundred yards of our front, when we opened fire with shell and shot with our full battery; after firing some seventy (70) rounds, we took position farther on, just on the edge of the open space ahead, and with our full battery, assisted by two pieces from McClung's battery, we poured some sixty (60) rounds into the enemy, who continued to advance upon us, when Col. Marshall J. Smith, of the Crescent regiment, gallantly came to our rescue, charging the enemy at the point of the bayonet, putting them to flight, and saving our three extreme right pieces, which would have been captured but for them.

It was at this point I again met with some losses. Lieut. Slocomb, Sergt. Green, several privates, and many horses fell at this point, either killed or badly wounded.

After the enemy had retreated well in the woods, I had my guns limbered and taken from the field. My men broken down, my horses nearly all slain, ammunition out, and sponges all broken and gone, I was in the act of making repairs and preparing for another attack, when I was ordered by Gen. Beauregard to retire in order to Monterey, which I did that evening, and afterwards to this point, arriving last evening with my battery all complete with the exception of three (3) caissons, a battery-wagon, and forge, which I had to abandon on the road for want of fresh horses to draw them in.

At the request of Gen. Beauregard, I detailed from my command twelve men under a non-commissioned officer, to remain and act with Capt. Byrne's (or Burns') battery, on a prominent hill on the Pea Ridge road, overlooking the battle-field, to cover the retirement of our army. They all came in to-day, safe and sound.

We captured two stands of United States colors, which were handed over to Gen. Beauregard; we also captured several United States horses and mules.

I cannot close this report without again calling to your favorable notice the names of my Lieuts. Slocomb, Vaught, and Chalaron, for their coolness and bravery on the field. Their conduct was daring and gallant, and worthy of your consideration.

I have the honor to be,

Yours, very truly,

W. IRVING HODGSON,

Captain.

The following is the supplementary report of Capt. Hodgson : —

HEAD–QUARTERS FIFTH CO., BAT. WASHINGTON ARTILLERY,

CAMP MOORE, CORINTH, MISS., April 11, 1862.

TO CAPT. WM. G. BERTH, *Acting Asst. Adjutant-General :* —

CAPTAIN, — I herewith tender to you a supplemental report, in regard to matters connected with the battles of the 6th and 7th instant.

My battery fired during said actions, from the six guns, seven hundred and twenty-three (723) rounds, mostly from the smooth-bore guns and the howitzers, a large proportion of which was canister. Some of our ammunition-chests, being repacked from a captured caisson, and other canister borrowed from Capt. Robertson's battery, which he kindly loaned.

The badly torn wheels and carriages of my battery from minie balls, will convince any one of the close proximity to the enemy in which we were. I had twenty-eight (28) horses slain in the battery, exclusive of officers' horses.

I cannot refrain from applauding to you, the gallant actions of the rank and file of my command, all of whom behaved so gallantly on these occasions, that it would be invidious to mention names ; suffice it, they all remained at their posts during the action, and behaved most gallantly ; many of them, for the first time under fire, conducted themselves as veterans.

I have the honor to be,

Yours, very truly,

W. IRVING HODGSON,

Captain.

In connection with the battle of Shiloh, the following extracts are taken from the official report of Gen. Daniel Ruggles, Commanding Division, 2d Corps : —

The Washington Artillery, under Capt. Hodgson, was then brought forward, and two howitzers and two rifled guns commanded by Lieut. Slocomb, and two guns under Maj. Hoop were put in position on the crest of a ridge near an almost impenetrable boggy thicket, ranging along our front, and opened a destructive fire in response to the enemy's batteries then sweeping our lines at long range. I also sent orders to Brig.-Gen. Anderson to advance rapidly with his Second brigade, and as soon as he came up, I directed a charge against the enemy, in which some of the Sixth Mississippi and Second Tennessee joined; at the same time I directed other troops to move rapidly by the right to turn the enemy's position beyond the swamp, and that the field artillery follow as soon as masked by the movement of the infantry.

Under these movements, vigorously executed, after a spirited contest, the enemy's whole line gave way, and our advance took possession of the camp and batteries against which the charge was made.

. . . . . .

The enemy's camps on our left being apparently cleared, I endeavored to concentrate forces on his right flank in his new position, and directed Capt. Hodgson's battery into action there; the fire of his battery and a charge from the Second brigade, put the enemy to flight. Even after having been driven back from this position, the enemy rallied and disputed the ground with remarkable tenacity for some two or three hours, against our forces in front and his right flank, where cavalry, infantry, and artillery mingled in the conflict.

. . . . . .

List of killed and wounded at the battles of Shiloh, fought on the 6th and 7th days of April, 1862, in the Fifth Company Washington Artillery.

KILLED. — 1st Sergeant, John W. Demeritt; 2d Sergeant, Benj. H. Green, Jr.; 4th Sergeant, Wm. B. Giffen; wounded in leg, suffered amputation and died; Private, C. J. Hartnett; Drivers, John Leary, Patrick Long, John O'Donnell. Total, 7 killed.

WOUNDED. — 1st Lieutenant C. H. Slocomb, shot in breast; 2nd Corporal, S. Higgins, spent ball in neck; 6th Corporal, W. L. Bruce, spent ball in side; 4th C. Corporal, L. Macready, shot in the leg; 5th C. Corporal, Alfred Bellanger, lost left hand; Privates, Thos. L. Bayne, shot in right arm; J. M. Davidson, shot in thigh; Octave Hopkins, Curtis

Holmes, Milton McKnight, wounded; Robert Strong, William Steven, John W. Watson, John A. Walsh, wounded in leg; Drivers, Jas. Byrnes, Wm. Dooley, Samuel J. Davis, M. Campbell, John Clayton. Total, 20. Killed, 7; wounded, 20. Total casualties, 27.

After the battle of Shiloh the following men were honorably discharged from the service : —

Second Lieutenant, Edson L. Hews, resigned; 6th Corporal, W. L. Bruce, doctor's certificate; 5th C. Corporal, Alfred Bellanger, wounds received; Privates, T. L. Bayne, wounds received; W. W. Clayton, doctor's certificate; J. M. Davidson, wounds received; J. M. Seixas, by order of Gen. Bragg; Robert Strong, wounds received; Middleton Eastman, by order of Gen. Bragg; John A. Walsh, wounds received; C. S. Wing, H. H. Lonsdale, doctor's certificate.

The resignation of Lieut. Ed. L. Hews having been accepted, Gen. Bragg attached to the battery J. M. Seixas, and appointed him Lieutenant in the Fifth company, to fill vacancy.

EVACUATION OF CORINTH, MISS.

On the 30th day of May, 1862, the army of the Mississippi evacuated Corinth, the Fifth company Washington Artillery, with its brigade, covering the retreat of the army.

The retrograde movement began at about 8 o'clock P.M., continuing during that night, and by 3 o'clock A.M., the last of the troops had passed through the town, on their way to Tupelo, Miss., *via* Clear Creek, a point about forty miles south of Corinth, which latter place they reached on the morning of June the 1st, and immediately went into temporary camp.

The enemy did not pursue the retreating Confederate army more than ten or fifteen miles south of Corinth, and, finding the Confederate forces ready to give battle, they returned to Corinth and went into camp.

On the 5th day of June, ascertaining that the Federal army would not pursue or risk a further engagement in this vicinity, the Confederate army, now under the command of Gen. Braxton Bragg, determined to change their base to Chattanooga, Tenn., for a resumption of hostilities, resulting in the Kentucky campaign, — with a view to a long overland march. The army fell back to Tupelo, where there was an abundance of good water and forage, and went into regular camp, preparatory to said movement.

On the eve of the departure from Clear Creek an order was issued from the head-quarters of the army, that all officers and men who were unable to march twenty miles a day would go to Okalona, Miss., on surgeon's certificate, into the general hospital at that point, by a special train at 5 o'clock the following morning.

It was at this point that Capt. Hodgson, who had been sick and confined to his bed for some days, turned over the command to Lieut. Vaught, as Senior Lieutenant, (1st Lieut. Slocomb, being absent on sick leave, from wounds received at the battle of Shiloh), and went to Okalona.

It was while the battery was in camp at Tupelo (June 6, 1862), Capt. Hodgson, then in hospital at Okalona, forwarded his resignation to Gen. Bragg, commanding the army, which was accepted, and Lieut. C. H. Slocomb was appointed captain in his stead.

Any account of the subsequent history of the Fifth company could not be given in better phrase than that of Lieut. Chalaron, who, when speaking to a toast to the "Washington Artillery, Army of Tennessee," at the reunion of the battalion, held May 27, 1882, to celebrate the twenty-first anniversary of the departure of the first four companies to Virginia, said : —

. . . .

Tupelo is reached, and Slocomb now commands. Suffering is forgotten in recuperation and drilling. Bragg himself acknowledges the Fifth unexcelled in drill, even by his famous battery.

With Adams's brigade we march into Kentucky. Munfordsville is captured, and Perryville is fought. The "White Horse Battery" is known to friend and foe thereafter; and clamorous and enthusiastic recognition salutes it, in the streets of Harrodsburg, from the army passing in retreat. Those shouts shall ever ring in the ears of its survivors.

Through Cumberland Gap, half starving and worn, retreating steps now take us to Knoxville's snow-clad fields. We meet the first blasts of a winter campaign. Our tents are finally pitched, in winter-quarters, on Harpeth's frozen banks, where Rosecrans so rudely disturbed us at Christmas eve. Murfreesboro follows, and Vaught commands; and whether supporting Hardee's crushing blow upon the enemy's right, or holding the pivot of the position, or rushing madly in that deadly charge, when Breckenridge, in grand array and stern devotion, dashed for those heights across Stone river, the Washington Artillery won, on that field, the highest praise that soldiers could expect; and Anthony and Reid are left to mark its passage. Vicksburg is sore beset, and Johnston calls, and Breckenridge is going; the Fifth company ask to follow. Mobile, in passing, gives us new recruits, as, rushing through, we hurry on to Jackson. But Vicksburg falls 'ere we can cross the Big Black; and Sherman tries to intercept, but strikes us only in our works at Jackson. Four stands of colors lie amid a thousand killed and wounded before the muzzles of Cobb's and Slocomb's guns.

Bragg calls in turn and Breckenridge is sent. The Fifth is pushed to Rome and Chattanooga. The echoes of the first guns salute them on arrival. We strike at Glass's Mill, and plunging through the Chickamauga, leave on its banks a holocaust of dead. 'Tis Blair meeting a fate he had just predicted, and Morel, and Anderson, and Belsom, and Bailey, and Daigle! We lay them shrouded in their blankets, and move to strike elsewhere. Morning finds us on the right; Breckenridge turns the Federal left; we cut them off from Chattanooga. Astride the road, we save the day till Liddell can be brought up; and Graves has fallen in our midst, and bending over him Breckenridge laments his loss. Around him lie Brocard and Bayle, and Reichert, and Duggan, and Stakeman, and Greenwood, and Woods, with shattered carriages and crushed guns, that show what fire we took unflinchingly, while pouring canister alone upon their charging lines. Breckenridge thanks us on the field. To replace Blair, Johnsen now stands promoted.

And Chickamauga's victory leads us but to Missionary Ridge. Dissensions and rivalries have brought about defeat. The Fifth, unmoved, indignant, and devoted, their battery sacrificed, seize the first guns abandoned in their rear, and with Austin's help check the enemy and save the bridge.

Joe Johnston comes, and Dalton's cantonments ring with joy. With spring, Sherman attempts the portals of the pass; and Rockyface and Buzzard's Roost repel him to Snake Gap. Resaca finds us in the thickest fray; and on that hill, from which we bore Simmons and Stuart, and in that pen, where Russell fell and found a grave beneath the cannon's trail, the Fifth company never showed more coolness, more valor, nor more fortitude. In quick succession come Calhoon, Adairsville, Kingston, and Cassville's lost opportunity. The Etowah is crossed. Dallas and New Hope Church claim more precious lives. 'Tis McGregor, 'tis Winston, 'tis Beggs, 'tis Mathis, 'tis Billy Sewell, with his last breath whispering into Slocomb's ear, "Captain, haven't I done my duty?" Can Pine Mountain and Kennesaw Ridge ever be forgotten? — those long days of constant fighting, those nights of sleepless vigilance and recurring labor, those works uncarried, where Barrail fell and Staub received his death wound.

At rest for once, since leaving Dalton, we find ourselves beyond the Chattahoochie; for Johnston waits to strike his crossing foe. But 'tis for us that comes the shock, and the Fifth company weep at the removal of Old Joe. Soon Peach Tree Creek recalls us to our work, and, in resisting its passage, we lose Legare, and Percy, and Ricketts. Legare, who begged " for one more shot at them," and fell with Percy, torn and mangled, before he could get it.

First on the right, then through the siege, the Fifth company battles for Atlanta, till Hood must leave, for Jonesboro is gone, and Hardee's heroic corps can stand the pressure no longer. Here Frazer, Vincent, Delery, find their death, and also that unrecorded priest who followed us into battle. And now 'tis on to Nashville. In snow we move from Florence to the task, ill clad, and badly shod. Columbia is taken, and Franklin's ditches are made level with Confederate dead. Bates's division is thrown toward Murfreesborough. At Overall Creek it is Leverich's canister saving us from destruction, and riderless horses sweep in line of battle through our intervals to the rear. Siebrecht is buried on the field. The morrow finds us attacking with Forrest, and yielding lines place the enemy in our rear. We lose two guns in running the gauntlet of their fire. On that sad day Bennett is laid beneath the snow.

Nashville follows, and after the defeat we spike our guns and cut down our carriages, no roads of escape being left. And now comes that terrible retreat, in the heart of winter, where snow-beaten paths are reddened by the blood of our soldiers' shoeless feet. We ford Shoal Creek on that bleak Christmas-day, and drop exhausted when the Tennessee is reached. The Fifth company lost no men by straggling, yet, on the banks of that river, of its numbers, there stood in ranks 45 barefooted and half-clad men.

Mobile is threatened, and we go to her defense, joining again our Louisiana brigade. They swear to capture the first enemy's battery met, that the Washington Artillery may be refitted. In Spanish Fort we stand a siege of fourteen days with Gibson, and are the last to spike our guns that night of evacuation. Rescued from out the sea marsh of Blakeley river the Fifth company is in Mobile again, where McIlhenny and Miller had preceded them to be buried. This siege has fitly crowned our military experience. The town is doomed. We march away, as light artillery, refitted and complete.

The end has come when Lee's surrender is announced. Our own soon follows. We furl our flag in tears, and Slocomb leads us home to weeping households, desolated firesides, and ruined estates.

Such is the hurried report of the services of the Fifth company. In their performance, soldiers never showed more courage, more endurance, more reliability, more cheerfulness, more discipline, more devotion, more fortitude. Ever ready, ever complete, in equipment and numbers, their horses superbly kept, ambitious of distinction, they were always at the front, on the breach, in active service; ever steady and resolute, however went the day, no danger could move, and no disaster could dismay them. In the annals of the Army of Tennessee they bear a proud name among the proudest.

To the battalion's fame they bring a harvest of laurels, won through the most trying and bloody campaigns of our great war. To the battalion flag they add the names of over forty battles, as desperate, as sanguinary, as ever fought. On our monumental shaft and roll of honor they have inscribed the names of fifty heroes, as pure, as gallant, as devoted, as ever died in a sacred cause. They have made the Washington Artillery the only organization, as legendary with the troops of the Army of Tennessee as it is with the troops of the Army of Northern Virginia. And the rivalry is not ended; they will push it in perpetuating the present organization, that our sons and latest descendants may belong to it, and proudly say, " Our fathers made the name of the Washington Artillery famous in the cause of the South on every battle-field of the Confederacy."

And, admonished by the untimely fate of so many of our comrades who survived our campaigns, and since have fallen in the battle of life, shall I not take advantage of this occasion to speak to you, representatives of the survivors of the Fifth company, here in the presence of your brothers of Virginia? Can I refrain from calling upon you, boys of the Fifth company, to rise that I may say to them, "Here stand the remnants of 380 men, who carried the banner of the Washington Artillery, in equal glory and devotion with you?" Can I refrain from thanking you for your unfailing confidence and devotion to your officers; from expressing to you their feelings of admiration and love; from telling you that they drew courage, energy, their reward, their pride, from your gallant acts, your heroic bearing, your friendly approbation? Boys of the Fifth company, the spirits of Slocomb, Vaught, and Blair at this moment marshal our brave " who roam enfranchised," and reécho my words, rejoicing at this first reunion of the Fifth and its brothers of Virginia !

May God bless you !

At the second reunion of the Battalion the same officer gave an idea of the spirit of the Fifth company, in his reply to the toast to them, in the following words : —

COMRADES, — Having responded at our first reunion for the Washington Artillery, Army of Tennessee, I did not expect to have bestowed upon me a like distinction on this occasion. The glorious company that is toasted could well have furnished from among its veterans many who would have better fulfilled the pleasing duty.

At your call, however, I take up the theme with a heart overflowing with proud recollections, and untiring in its admiration and love for the Fifth company.

And how shall I portray it to you? From its years of service, its life in camp, its record on the battle-field, what traits shall I select; what episodes shall I recount? Difficult is the choice, and I hope you will bear with me if my remarks are not merely postprandial, but bring you into more intimate acquaintance with your brothers of Tennessee, and fix in our common records facts and episodes that otherwise might pass away. Reunions like this are doubly useful, when from attending survivors aught has been drawn that illustrates the battalion's history or redounds to its fame.

And now, from memory's camping-ground, let me bring all my boys to the front.

Here they come, as of yore, youthful, gay, dashing, determined, daring, heroic; yielding to discipline, impatient of inaction, uncomplaining under trials and hardships, superior to fatigue, of unfailing cheerfulness, and unsurpassed in fortitude. I hear their jokes, their bragging about sections and detachments (the outgrowth of an *esprit de corps,* that made all vie to have their battery the best in the service, and their respective sections and detachments the best in the battery). I hear their camp songs — their glee club on the march, on that in Georgia especially — when, under the shades of night we stole away from uncarried and bloody works. Weary steps were quickened by the cadence of their voices (the only music allowed to break the stillness of the night) as the column moved to take another line of battle for the morrow.

I see them at Jackson gathered around the piano, saved, with chivalrous intent, from that stately mansion which war's necessities compelled us to destroy as Lauman's division charged upon our works.

'Tis. Andy Swain who holds the keys, and grouped about him stand the boys singing, in jolly chorus, " You shan't have any of my Peanuts." Our redoubt is on the Jackson Railroad looking toward New Orleans; the piano almost touches the guns; traverses of cotton bales protect our flank; some bales are on the parapet. The music has drawn officers and men of other commands, who hang outside the group. Gen. Adams lends his ear from his head-quarters established with us for the coming fray. Above all, the piano absorbs each mind. Far across the fields in front appears a heavy skirmish line; then comes the line of battle; another and another still. Briskly they move upon us, pressing in our skirmishers. Ned Austin, with his sharp-shooters, takes refuge behind our works and stands beside our battery as its support. Near and more near comes the foe. The order rings to man the guns; the piano's notes are hushed, that deeper and more thrilling ones may now be sounded. Our Maj. Graves is on the parapet, like some grand orchestral leader, and, when the lines are close enough, commands our fire to be opened. And there he stands until the end, with voice and gesture urging us to " Fire low, boys." Still, on they come, looming up through the dust our shrieking canister has raised, as it tears its way in ricochets across the field. Now, they are upon us almost; but our doubled charges hurl in their faces a storm of iron that nothing mortal can withstand. Down go their lines; we know the day is ours. " Cease firing " comes from Graves, as o'er the works our infantry spring to finish them. They yield; and those who marched so boldly up can now be seen breaking in flight to the rear. 'Tis over; with a rush the piano is sought again. Not twenty minutes have sped since its last notes have died away. A thousand men have lost life or limbs, or, writhing, have been made to lie around four stands of colors on that gory field, between its tuneful sounds; for now they rise above the din to the strain of "Oh, let us be joyful!" and every heart and every throat join in the chorus, — as grand a pæan as ever mounted to the throne of Heaven. Amid these sounds of exultation, prisoners and wounded of the foe are brought around us, awaiting Gen. Adams's interrogatories. In wonderment they look upon this spectacle of musical rejoicing, and ask what manner of men are they who thus glory in their terrible slaughter.

And now, with sadder notes and faces, but two months later, I see these boys grouped again around our loved Major. 'Tis Chickamauga's bloody field, the second day, and on the right. We've cleared the way, and Adams's brigade has charged beyond us, driving the enemy in the deep recesses of woods in front. We stand by smoking guns, planted across the Chattanooga road. Random shots from unseen batteries drop their shrapnel among us. Our troops in front prevent our firing in return. Slocomb and Graves stand mounted side by side. We see them clasp each other, and totter in their saddles. Devoted arms rush to receive them. Slocomb's horse is wounded, but Graves himself is pierced from side to side. We bear him to the hollow close in rear; and in the shade of its only tree, bend around him while the wound is sought. 'Tis mortal, and he feels it. Breckenridge arrives, and by his side kneels in touching lamentations. He orders him borne away, for the tide of battle seems to be driving back against us. All press around to take a last farewell, and tears are coursing down heroic cheeks besmeared with powder and with smoke, as Graves's hand is grasped. He gives to all, by pressure or by word, a last recognition.

And one among us takes his hand, whose face recalls to him some incident at Murfreesboro, where in the heat of battle Graves had misjudged the soldier's action, but since, had generously made amends; and now the recollection of this occurrence flashes upon his aching soul, and here again, before us all, he makes amends anew. "Boys," he tells us, as we part, "I know you think that I prefer my old battery to yours. It is not so. There is none that I admire and love more than yours. I wish a detail of your boys to carry me off, and to remain with me until I die." He's hurried off, for from those woods Adams is driven back. His horse and his adjutant's, dash riderless and madly out and past our guns.

They've fallen both, and both are left upon the field. We move across the hollow that its shelter may be used by our retreating infantry, and let us sooner sweep the field in front. We keep it clear with canister while numerous opposing guns cut us up with shot and shell. Liddell arrives at last; we pick up our dead and wounded, and move aside, in sorrow, to replenish and refit.

Thus you have seen them in joy and in sorrow. Their spirit was noble through every turn of fortune, and nobler still the nearer we reached the end. Of this let them speak themselves.

'Twas after Hood's defeat at Nashville, — that terrible retreat, — and after a no less trying ride of twenty-four hours in sleet and rain on open flat cars from Columbus to Mobile, in February. Seventy-five men per car; no platform rails, no seats, 'twas barely standing-room, and from the train many an exhausted soldier dropped upon the track that night. We reach Mobile and learn that Johnston again commands in North Carolina with our old army among his troops. We want to follow and thus apply : —

"HEAD–QUARTERS FIFTH COMPANY WASHINGTON ARTILLERY.

BATTERY C, MOBILE, March 4, 1865.

" GENERAL : — The announcement of your reinstatement to command in the field has filled us with new hope, and stimulated our desire to serve again under you. We therefore pray that you will use your influence to have the Fifth company Washington Artillery fitted up as a light battery, and ordered to report to you. We are at present manning heavy guns at this place, — an occupation very contrary to our wishes and to the active life we have always led in the front, since entering the service. Our spirits are chafed at lying here idle, whilst the army we have fought with from Shiloh to Nashville is encountering new dangers and facing its old foe.

" If, in the course of three years' hard and incessant service, we have deserved well of the Confederacy let our reward be a prominent position in the front of battle in the coming struggle. Strong in our faith of ultimate success, and anxious to do and to dare anything for its accomplishment, a compliance with our request, though it may not add to the respect, affection, and devotion we entertain for our General, will ever be remembered by us with pleasure and thankfulness.

" Most respectfully,

C. H. SLOCOMB, *Captain,*

J. A. CHALARON, *First Lieutenant,*

A. J. LEVERICH, *Second Lieutenant,*

CHARLES G. JOHNSEN, *Second Lieutenant,*

For the Company.

" To GEN. JOSEPH E. JOHNSTON, *Commanding Army of Tennessee.*"

The end came before this letter could reach him, and ten years after, when a copy of it was furnished him, listen how he appreciated the Fifth company. He wrote me : —

. . . . " I wish very much that the application for service with me, made by the Company March 4, 1865, had been received, for I should have had a great pleasure ten years sooner, — that of knowing that one of the truest and bravest bodies of Confederate troops, with which I served in trying times, gave me the confidence it inspired in all those who ever commanded it. Nothing that I have read in the last ten years has touched my heart like the copy of that application. Such proofs of favorable opinion and friendly feeling of the best class of our countrymen is rich compensation to an old man for the sacrifice of the results of the labors of a lifetime." . . . .

And now I see these boys at the surrender, in hours more trying even than those of the battle-field. Let the commander of the battalion they were attached to speak for them : —

" HEAD–QUARTERS SEMPLE'S BATTALION.

NEAR MERIDIAN, May 7, 1865.

" CAPTAIN : — Before we are dispersed and leave the service for our several homes, I desire to express to you my appreciation of the excellent company you have the honor to command. I served with it for several years in the Army of Tennessee, during which time its excellent discipline, the high character of its officers and men, as well as their conspicuous gallantry in every field, gained for it the distinction of being considered one of the very *best companies* of the famous artillery of that noble army.

"It has been under my command for only a few weeks, but it is not the least of its claims to distinction, in my opinion, that in a season of depression, and of almost universal demoralization, it has steadfastly preserved its discipline, and has been as honorably careful of the property agreed to be surrendered to the United States as if it were to be used by them for immediate action. Please say to your officers and men that I shall always remember them as highest exemplars of patriotic devotion and self-sacrifice, and that I pray they may enjoy the prosperity which their excellent character so richly merits.

"I am, Captain, with most affectionate regard, truly your friend,

"HENRY C. SEMPLE.

"To CAPT. C. H. SLOCOMB, *Commanding Fifth Company Washington Artillery.*"

And now let me dismiss my boys and theme, happy if I have saved from oblivion one episode, one fact that will make the Fifth company better known and the battalion feel more glorious. I thank you for your attention.

The loss of most of the Fifth company's official papers during the Tennessee campaign under Hood prevents a more extended notice of this company.

From its entrance into service, March 6, 1862, its activity was incessant in the shifting scenes of the war west of the Alleghanies; and it was often hurried through that vast territory from one field of battle to another, hundreds and hundreds of miles apart, ere the sounds of strife had fully died away on the last field it was called from.

The following data, compiled by its senior surviving officer, will give an idea of what it was, and of what it did : —

Members who left New Orleans with the company,
     March 8, 1862, or reinlisted 160
Members who joined after 167

Men temporarily assigned 9
Men temporarily assigned just previous to sur-
   render 39
                             — 48
Men who served with the company though not en-
   listed 6
Surgeons and assistants attached to company . . 7
                               388
Servants, white and black, if added . . . 30

Whole number of men with the Fifth company during the war 418

Tabular statement showing distribution of aggregate of 388 men who served with the Fifth Company Washington Artillery during the war : —

Killed in battle 31
Died of wounds 12
Died of disease or accident 7
Total killed or died during war 50
Discharged 59
Transferred and promoted 50
Deserted or absent without leave 36
Present with company at surrender . . . 132
Absent from company at surrender, sickness, fur-
   loughed or detailed 46
Prisoners or missing at surrender 15

   Total 388

Beside the killed and those who died of their wounds, over 100 men were wounded sufficiently to compel their quitting the field of battle.

The company was in service 1,165 days, during which time it was 121 days and 77 nights engaged in battle or under fire.

It was in the siege of Atlanta for 34 days and nights, and in the defence of Spanish Fort for 13 days and nights. It took part in 23 regular battles and in more than 15 engagements.

In the incessant fighting of Johnston's Georgia campaign its guns were several times knocked to pieces and replaced. Its losses there were, killed, 14 ; wounded, 29 ; prisoners, 6.

It lost six guns at Missionary Ridge, and four in Hood's Tennessee campaign, — the guns being abandoned only after the defection of the company's supports and the killing of its horses. 143 of the battery's horses were killed in action.

The company fired 5,906 rounds of ammunition during the war. It marched 3,285 miles, and travelled by railroad 2,939 miles more.

On the night of the evacuation of Spanish Fort, which was accomplished with great secrecy and silence, and in face of great danger of capture by the enemy of the whole command, Sergeant John Bartley took the guidon of the battery from its staff, wound it and sewed it around his body, and carried it safely to New Orleans and placed it in the hands of those who would keep it tenderly and sacredly.

CHAPTER XIX.

CONCLUSION.

The Washington Artillery after the War.

IN the years immediately following the war the Washington Artillery still retained its old autonomy as a relief and benevolent association, taking care of its sick and disabled men, and the families of the dead.

Partly owing to the orders of the military commander prohibiting reorganization of Confederate companies, batteries, etc., partly to a disinclination to bear arms under State governments whose policy was foreign to their sympathies, the reorganization into batteries and companies was not attempted until ten years after the close of the struggle.

In the month of July, 1875, the general aspiration for a better feeling at the various celebrations of the anniversary of American Independence, and the honorable part assigned Confederate soldiers at the centennial celebration of the battle of Bunker Hill, in Boston, awoke a responsive throb.

On the 22d July, a meeting of the surviving members of the companies of Washington Artillery who served in the Virginia and Western armies was called, and a formal organization at this and subsequent meetings, acted upon. The object set forth in the meetings was to take part as a battalion in the National Centennial of the following year. The battalion was divided into three batteries, and these, after according to the commanding officer who might be elected the privilege of appointing his staff, elected their field and company officers. The names given below represent the officers of the organization at that date.

Field Officers (elected).

J. B. Walton, Colonel.
W. J. Behan, Major.

Staff (appointed).

First Lieut. W. M. Owen, Adjutant and Chief of Staff.
"   J. N. Payne, Quartermaster.
"   John Holmes, Commissary.
"   W. B. Krumbhaar, Ordnance Officer.

Non-Commissioned Staff (appointed).

E. I. Kursheedt, Sergeant-Major.
W. H. Ellis, Quartermaster Sergeant.
M. W. Cloney, Commissary Sergeant.
O. F. Peck, Ordnance Sergeant.
Frank de P. Villasana, Chief Bugler.

Company A.

OFFICERS.

Captain. — M. Buck Miller.
Senior First Lieut. — Andrew Hero, Jr.
Junior First Lieut. — Frank McElroy.
Second Lieut. — George E. Apps.

Company B.

OFFICERS.

Captain. — Eugene May.
Senior First Lieut. — William Palfry.
Junior First Lieut. — W. T. Hardie.
Second Lieut. — M. J. Beebe.

Company C.

OFFICERS.

Captain. — John B. Richardson.
Senior First Lieut. — C. H. C. Brown.
Junior First Lieut. — George B. De Russy.
Second Lieut. — D. M. Kilpatrick.

The proposed visit to the Centennial at Philadelphia was not carried out, and on May 18, 1876, Col. J. B. Walton having resigned the colonelcy, Adj. W. Miller Owen was elected Colonel, and upon the expiration of one term of service, was unanimously reëlected for another, with John B. Richardson as Major, and E. I. Kursheedt as Adjutant.

On the 22d of February, 1880, the 40th anniversary of the Corps, the "Benevolent Association of the Washington Artillery" presented to the Battalion, through Col. Thomas L. Bayne, its president, the magnificent marble monument erected in Metarie Cemetery to its heroic dead, upon which were inscribed the names of those one hundred and thirty-six comrades killed or died in service, together with the sixty battles in which the Battalion was engaged.

After receiving the monument from the hands of the Association, and transferring it to the keeping of the command, Col. Owen resigned the colonelcy, and was immediately appointed by Louis A. Wiltz, then Governor of Louisiana, Inspector-General of the Louisiana State National Guard upon his staff, with the rank of Brigadier-General. He was succeeded in command by Maj. J. B. Richardson, who received the rank of Lieutenant-Colonel, and Capt. Andrew Hero, Jr., was commissioned Major. Up to this date the Battalion occupied an arsenal of very modest proportions, a one-story structure on Common street, and had equipped itself, with the assistance of its many friends, with a battery of four 10-pounder Parrott rifles; two 12-pounder howitzers; 100 artillery sabres; and 116 Springfield rifles, together with harness and ammunition. The uniform adopted was of gray cadet cloth. The command was several times called into active service during "reconstruction times" to preserve the peace in some of the turbulent parishes of the State, where their discipline and soldierly bearing soon quieted all disturbance.

Through a movement set on foot by Maj. Andrew Hero, ably seconded by Lieut.-Col. Richardson, the Battalion was fortunate enough to become the possessor of the fine piece of property on St. Charles street, known as the "Exposition Building," where it is now located, having the finest arsenal in the South, and excelled in the North only by the armory of the Seventh Regiment, N.Y.S.N.G., in New York city.

Here, on the 27th of May, 1882, the twenty-first anniversary of the departure of the Battalion from New Orleans to "take part in the late war between the States of the Union," a grand reunion of all the five batteries was held. At this time a company, composed of veterans only, was organized, having for its captain C. L. C. Dupuy.

On May 28, 1883, a second reunion was held, at which the battle-flag of General Beauregard, one of the three original flags made in 1861, by the Misses Carey, from their own dresses, was presented to the Battalion for safe-custody, in the name of Gen. Beauregard, by Judge Alfred Roman, and accepted by Col. J. B. Walton for the battalion. At this reunion the tattered battle-flags of the Fifth company were presented to the Battalion by Mrs. C. H. Slocomb, and were deposited among the relics of the command.

At this date the officers of the Battalion were as follows :—

Lieut.-Col., John B. Richardson, Commanding.
Andrew Hero, Jr., —— Major.

Staff.

Lieut. E. I. Kursheedt, Adjutant.
Capt. G. B. Underhill, Surgeon.
Capt. C. L. C. Dupuy, Ordnance Officer.
Lieut. J. H. Degrauge, Quartermaster.
Lieut. Horace J. Levi, Commissary.

Company A.

Captain. — C. M. Whitney.
Lieutenant. — E. M. Underhill.
Lieutenant. — Frank Fenner.

Company B.

Captain. — Eugene May.
Lieutenant. — J. S. Richards.
Lieutenant. — T. McC. Hyman.
Lieutenant. — George W. Booth.

Company C.

Captain. — H. M. Isaacson.
Lieutenant. — Dudley Selph.
Lieutenant. — Silas M. Oviatt.

Veteran Company.

Captain. — C. L. C. Dupuy.
Lieutenant. — Emile J. O'Brien.
Lieutenant. — Louis A. Adam.

Joseph H. Duggan, Treasurer.
Gus Leefe, Secretary.

Under its present organization the command is prosper-
ing, — the ranks being filled with the first young men of
New Orleans, — a large proportion of whom are the sons
of its veterans ; and the Battalion is proud of the fact that
from the year 1840 to the present time it has maintained
its distinct and continuous organization through peace and
war.

Under the care of its veteran armorer, Corp. Daniel
Kelly, the arsenal is kept with the neatness of the regular
barracks of the U.S. army.   At the end of the vast drill-

room hangs the celebrated picture by Julio, of the last meeting of Lee and Jackson before the battle of Chancellorsville. In the officers' quarters are shown the Battalion colors that accompanied the command to Mexico in 1846, upon which are inscribed, in letters of gold, its sixty battles and engagements from 1861 to 1865, and in a glass case lie "furled and folded," forever, the tattered, smoke-stained battle-guidons of the corps. That of Squires' and Owen's, First company ; of Rosser's and Richardson's, Second company ; of Miller's and Hero's, Third company ; of Eshleman's and Norcom's, Fourth company ; of Slocomb's and Chalaron's, Fifth company. There they rest, and, in the words of Father Ryan, we say : —

> " Furl the banner, true 'tis gory,
>   Yet 'tis wreathed around with glory,
>   And 'twill live in song and story,
>   Though its folds are in the dust :
> For its fame on brightest pages,
>   Penned by poets and by sages,
>   Shall go sounding down the ages, —
>   Furl its folds though now we must.
> Furl that banner, softly, slowly,
>   Treat it gently, — for 'tis holy, —
>   For it droops above the dead.
> Touch it not, — unfold it never,
>   Let it droop there *furled* forever,
>   For its people's *hopes* are dead ! "

Above the highest pinnacle of the arsenal, upon a lofty staff, there unfolds to the soft southern breeze *another flag*, — the flag of our reunited country, the " *Stars and Stripes.*"

Sons of Veterans, brave young hearts, greet it, and rally under it, and should our country ever become engaged in. foreign war and call to its aid the men of Louisiana, be assured the Washington Artillery will take the field at the first bugle blast, and again show the world of what stuff it was made in the days that are gone, when the brazen throats of its guns blazed forth on so many ensanguined battle-fields under the eyes of its beloved commanders, Lee, Johnston, Beauregard, and Longstreet.

ADDENDA.

POPULAR CAMP SONGS OF THE WASHINGTON ARTILLERY.

THE 'CANNONEER.

Air: "Happy Land of Canaan."

Words by A. G. KNIGHT, First Sergeant, Second Company.

We will sing of the boys who make the loudest noise,
And from fighting you can scarcely restrain them. *Aha!*
They have "guns," "howitzers," "rifles," and other sorts of trifles,
To send soldiers past the "Happy land of Canaan."

> *Chorus:*
> Oh! ho ho! Ah, ha ha!
> The good times, boys, are a coming,
> Oh, never mind the weather, but get over double trouble,
> When you're bound for the "Happy land of Canaan."

We will sing of number *one*, he comes first upon the gun,
And works like a horse without complaining. *Aha!*
He will let you know that he is not *too* slow,
In sending soldiers past the "Happy land of Canaan."

Next comes number *two*. He has as much as he can do
To make the enemy think 'tis iron raining. *Aha!*
He will let you know that he is not *too* slow,
At sending soldiers past the "Happy land of Canaan."

Then comes number *three*, who, as brisk as he can be,
His thumb upon the vent he's retaining. *Aha!*
He will let you know that he is not *too* slow,
At sending soldiers to the "Happy land of Canaan."

Next comes number *four*, who, to make the matter sure,
Pulls the lanyard with a steady sort of straining. *Aha!*
And then, with loud report, King Death cries out, "Come into court,"
If you're going to the "Happy land of Canaan."

Next comes number *five*, who, to keep the game alive,
Proves his legs must have the right sort of training. *Aha!*
For, with cartridge in his pouch, you can see he's no slouch,
At sending soldiers past the "Happy land of Canaan."

Then comes number *six*, who works hard his little tricks
For fear the others he'll be detaining. *Aha!*
And he knows — to help the fight — he must cut the fuses right,
So as to send them to the "Happy land of Canaan."

Next comes number *seven*, to whom important place is given;
Like five, his legs must have right sort of training. *Aha!*
For both of them must run 'tween the limber and the gun,
If they're going to the "Happy land of Canaan."

And here's to number *eight*, who with patience has to wait,
Though in this he's slightly given to complaining. *Aha!*
So he helps our number six, with all his little tricks,
At sending soldiers past the "Happy land of Canaan."

Now it never would be right, if the *Corporal* we should slight,
For he's the bully boy that does the aiming. *Aha!*
With his screw and with his trail, we hope he'll never fail,
At sending soldiers past the "Happy land of Canaan."

But what are we about? we have left the sergeant out;
No doubt of this slight he'll be complaining. *Aha!*
But he's a sort of *Boss*, you know, and we keep him more for show,
Than sending soldiers to the "Happy land of Canaan."

Note. — These words were first sung and composed by Sergt. Knight, at Camp
Taylor, near Orange C.H., Virginia, March, 1862.

"UPI–DE "

Is an old College Air, but some changes in and additions to the Chorus were made by Sergeant Knight, and his words were sung to this Air, for the first time, in winter quarters of 1862–63, Caroline County, Virginia.

With a good Chorus of many voices, either of these songs will generally meet with a hearty applause.

The shades of night were falling fast,
        Tra la la, tra la la.
The Bugler blew that well-known blast,
        Tra la la, la la.
No matter should it rain or snow,
That Bugler he was bound to blow.

Chorus.

        Upi, dei, dei, di, Upi de, Upi di,
        Upi, dei, dei, di, Upi dei, di.
        Wh'rrr, rrr, rrr, rrr,
        Yai! yai! yai! yai! yai! yai! yai!!!
        Upi, dei, dei, di, Upi de, Upi di,
        Upi, dei, dei, di, Upi dei, di.

In nice log huts he saw the light of cabin fires burning bright;
The sight afforded him no heat, and so he sounded the *retreat.*

He saw, as in their bunks they lay, how soldiers spend the dawning day ;
There's too much comfort there, said he, and then he sounded *Reveille.*

Upon the fire he saw a pot of savory viands smoking hot.
Says he, you shan't enjoy that stew, then *boots and saddles* loudly blew.

They scarce their half-cooked meal begin, ere orderly cries out *"Fall in !"*
Then off they march thro' mud and rain, only to march back again.

But, soldiers, you were made to fight, starve all day and march all night,
And, should you chance get bread and meat, that Bugler will not let you eat.

Oh! hasten, then, the glorious day, when Bugler shall no longer play ;
When we through peace shall be set free
        From " *Tattoo,*" " Taps," and " Reveille."

MUSTER–ROLL OF THE WASHINGTON ARTILLERY
OF THE ARMY OF NORTHERN VIRGINIA FROM
MAY 27, 1861, TO APRIL 8, 1865.

STAFF.

J. B. WALTON, Major; promoted to Colonel; made Chief of Artillery
Army of the Potomac, November, 1861; Chief of Artillery Longstreet's Corps; appointed by Secretary of War Inspector-General
of Field Artillery; recommended twice by Generals Beauregard
and Longstreet for promotion to Brigadier-General of Artillery;
resigned, July, 1864.

B. F. ESHLEMAN, Captain Fourth company, May, 1861; wounded at Bull
Run; promoted Major of Artillery, 1863; promoted Lieutenant-
Colonel of Artillery, *vice* Col. Walton, April, 1864.

W. M. OWEN, Adjutant, First Lieutenant; promoted Major of Artillery,
August, 1863; assigned Chief of Artillery Preston's Division, Army
of Tennessee; reassigned to Washington Artillery, April, 1864, as
second field officer; wounded at Petersburg, August, 1864; promoted
to Lieutenant-Colonel, 1865.

M. B. MILLER, Captain Third company, May, 1861; promoted to Major
of Artillery; assigned to Va. Battalion; reassigned to B.W.A.,
January, 1864.

E. I. KURSHEEDT, promoted from Corporal and Sergeant Major to
Adjutant, *vice* Owen, promoted; wounded at Fredericksburg.

E. S. DREW, Surgeon, present with the command in all its marches and
battles to the close of the war.

THOMAS Y. ABY, promoted Assistant Surgeon, February, 1863.

C. H. Slocomb, Q.M., May, 1861; resigned, November, 1861; Captain
commanding Fifth company W.A. of Western Army.

H. G. GEIGER, A.Q.M., May, 1861.

C. L. C. DUPUY, Sergeant Major, May, 1861; promoted to Lieutenant
of Artillery at Vicksburg.

W. A. RANDOLPH, promoted Sergeant Major, 1864.

B. L. BRASELMAN, Ordnance Officer, May, 1861.

ROLL OF FIRST COMPANY.

Isaacson, Harry M., Captain; resigned, August, 1861.

Squires, C. W., First Lieutenant; promoted to Captain, Sept., 1861; to Major of Artillery, C.S.A., Jan., 1864.

Richardson, John B., First Lieutenant; promoted to Captain; assigned to Second company, June, 1862.

Geiger, H. G., Second Lieutenant; detailed in Q.M. Dept.

Owen, Edward, First Sergeant; promoted to First Lieutenant, September, 1861; promoted to Captain, January, 1864.

Galbraith, John M., Sergeant; promoted to Second Lieutenant, November, 1861; promoted First Lieutenant, December, 1863; died of wound received at battle of Drewry's Bluff, May, 1864.

Brown, C. H. C., Sergeant; promoted to First Sergeant, October, 1861; to Second Lieutenant, May, 1864.

Dupuy, C. L. C., Sergeant; promoted Sergeant-Major, May, 1861.

Ruggles, Frank D., Corporal; killed at Fredericksburg, Dec., 1862.

Payne, E. C., Jr., Corporal; promoted Second Sergeant, October, 1861; discharged, February, 1862.

Fellowes, Wm., Jr., Corporal; returned to the ranks at his own request, August, 1861.

Case, F. F., Corporal; returned to the ranks at his own request, October, 1861; promoted to Corporal, April, 1863; to Sergeant, October, 1864.

PRIVATES.

Aby, Thomas Y., Promoted to Corporal, October, 1861; to Sergeant, October, 1861; to First Sergeant, July, 1862; to Assistant Surgeon, February, 1863.

Aby, Richard.

Aby, Samuel.

Alsobrook, R. H., Blown up on a caisson in Maryland, September, 1862, severely wounded.

Berthelot, Joseph H., Discharged, February, 1864.

Ball, R. J., Transferred to McGregor's Horse Artillery, November, 1864.

Baillio, S. A.,

Bayley, H. P.,

Blount, W. H., Promoted to Corporal, October, 1864.

Bozant, Jno.

Brown, L. L.

Bare, Jno.

Chambers, W.,   Kiiled at Rappahannock Station, August, 1862.

Chambers, H.,   Died at Camp Hollins, Va., December, 1861.

Chambers, C.,   Wounded at Sharpsburg, September, 1862; lost portion of his hand.

Chambers, George,   Killed at Drewry's Bluff, May, 1864.

Coste, A. F.,   Wounded at Fredericksburg; died, Dec., 1862.

Cowen, E. A.,   Promoted Captain Q.M., November, 1861; resigned, June, 1862.

Cleveland, J. B.,   Transferred to Second company, December, 1861.

Clark, S. M. D.

Clark, W. L.

Cummings, W. T.

Collins, E.

Carter, Thos.,   Captured at Petersburg, September, 1864.

Caylat, C. E.

DeRussy, Geo. B.,   Promoted to Sergeant, October, 1861; to Second Lieutenant, July, 1862; transferred to Second company.

Davis, R. N., Jr.,   Transferred to Fourth company.

Dupré, Geo.

Deacon, C. W.,   Transferred from Third company, April, 1862; promoted to Q.M. Sergeant, and captured June, 1864, at Petersburg.

Everett, C. A.,   Wounded at Fredericksburg, December, 1862; at Fredericksburg, May, 1863; at Drewry's Bluff, May, 1864.

Elfer, L. G.,   Transferred to Third company.

Falconer, W. R.,   Promoted to Corporal, April, 1862; transferred to Second Louisiana Cavalry, February, 1864.

Falconer, C. A.,   Transferred from Third company, June, 1861; killed December, 1862, at Fredericksburg.

Fazende, P. O.,   Transferred from Third company, June, 1861; promoted to Corporal, April, 1863; to Sergeant, July, 1863; captured at Drewry's Bluff, May, 1864; returned, having escaped, Nov., 1864.

Fell, John R.,   Wounded at Rappahannock, August, 1862; discharged.

Florence, H. C.

Florence, J. E.,   Killed at Fredericksburg, May, 1863.

Fowler, F. H.,   Wounded at Sharpsburg, September, 1862; detailed, Q.M. Dept.

Fisher, M.

Frolick, J., Jr.

Grima, Paul.

Genin, G. B.,   Promoted to Corporal, April, 1864.

Garland, D. H.

Hardie, Wm. T.,   Promoted to Corporal, October, 1861; to Sergeant, July, 1862; to First Sergeant, Sept., 1864.

Harrison, S.,   Promoted to Corporal, October, 1864.

Harby, J. R.

Hall, T. P.

Harris, Morgan E.,   Killed at Petersburg, July, 1864.

Horrock, J.

Judd, G. M.,   Promoted to Sergeant, October, 1861; killed at Sharpsburg, September, 1862.

Jarreau, J. E.,   Discharged, February, 1862.

Jarreau, J. U.

Janin, H. O.,   Wounded at Fredericksburg.

Jones, G. D. P.

Jones, Thos. P.

Kursheedt, E. I.,   Promoted to Corporal, October, 1861; to Sergeant-Major, April, 1863; to Adjutant, with rank of Lieutenant, 1864.

Kearny, J. W.,   Discharged, April, 1862.

Koss, Herman,   Killed at Rappahannock, August, 1862.

Keplinger, E. F.

Kilpatrick, D.,   Wounded at Petersburg, 1865.

Labarre, L.,   Transferred to Third Company.

Lobrano, Frank.

Lutman, T. J.,   Promoted to Corporal, April, 1863; killed at Fredericksburg, May, 1863.

Lappington, A. M.,   Detailed in Montgomery, Alabama.

Levy, E.

Leahy, P.

McGaughy, John R.,   Promoted to Sergeant, March, 1862; to First Sergeant, April, 1863; to Second Lieutenant, September, 1864.

Mount, M.,   Caisson ran over his leg, August, 1863; retired by Medical Executive Board, October, 1864.

Manico, J. P.,   Discharged, January, 1862.

Muntinger, J.,   Wounded at Sharpsburg, September, 1862; died, October, at Winchester.

Moore, A. M.

Marshall, R. T.,   Killed at Rappahannock, August, 1862, by explosion of his gun.

Maxent, George.

Muse, George W.,   Killed at Bull Run, July, 1861.

Moran, W.
Michel, P. A. J.,   Wounded at Sharpsburg.
McRobert, T. M.,   Discharged, August, 1862.
Mains, W.,   Killed, July, 1864.
Micou, A.,   Promoted to First Lieutenant on Gen. Fry's Staff,
                           May, 1864.
Marks, H. H.
Mathews, J. L.,   Detailed to Med. Dept. B.W.A.
Milhardo, N.,   Discharged, July, 1862.
Meyers, Joseph,   Detailed to Med. Dept. B.W.A.
McCormick, J.
McLean, W. J.
McCutcheon, J. B.,   Wounded at Sharpsburg, lost his arm.
McGehee, W. P.
McMillan, J. B.
McClellan, H. C.,   Died at Petersburg, November, 1864.
McCorkle, A. G.
McRae, W. A.,   Promoted to Corporal, October, 1864.
McIntire, C. M.
Norment, W. T.,   Promoted to Sergeant, April, 1863.
Ogden, E. S.,   Promoted Second Lieutenant First La. Artillery,
                           April, 1864.
Outlaw, J. W.,   Captured at Gettysburg, July, 1864.
Perry, W. F.,   Discharged by Medical Board, April, 1864.
Payne, J. N.,   Promoted to Sergeant, July, 1862; transferred to
                           Major Byrne's Batallion Artillery, March, 1864.

Parson, L.
Phelps, N. B.,   Detailed, November, 1864.
Pendegrass, D.
Pollard, R.,   Detailed, November, 1864.
Peychaud, E.,   Wounded at Drewry's Bluff, det. in Richmond.
Peychaud, H.,   Killed at Drewry's Bluff.
Peychaud, C.,   Detailed by Med. Board.
Rossiter, C.,   Wounded at Drewry's Bluff; retired by Medical
                           Board, October, 1864.
Rodd, J. E.,   Wounded at Fredericksburg; detailed.
Ranch, M.
Riviere, E.,   Captured at Gettysburg.
Richardson, John,   Detailed Q.M.D.
Reddington, James,   Killed at Rappahannock, August, 1862.
Spearing, R. McK.,   Promoted to Corporal, 1862; killed at Fredericks-
                           burg, December, 1862.
St. Amant, F. A.,   Discharged, July, 1861; disability.
Saul, W. T.

Street, C. N. B.,   Transferred to Moody's Battery, July, 1862.
Seibrecht, Ph.
Simmons, P. D.,   Killed at Drewry's Bluff, 1864.
Spencer, H. W.,   Died at Point Lookout, a prisoner.
Sagee, Frank.
Turner, T. S.,   Promoted Corporal, 1863.
Turner, S.,   Promoted Corporal, April, 1864; wounded at Drewry's Bluff.
Tarleton, John A.,   Discharged, July, 1862, special order Secretary War.
Turpin, J. M.
Fowles, W. E.,   Killed, railroad accident, March, 1863.
Villasana, F. de P.,   Chief Bugler of Battalion.
Vinson, Van,   Promoted to Corporal, July, 1863; to Sergeant, April, 1864.
Whitcomb, H.,   Killed, July, 1864.
Wiltz, E. V.,   Discharged.
Walden, C. R.,   Killed at Drewry's Bluff, May, 1864.
West, W. H.,   Promoted to Corporal, May, 1862; to Sergeant, April, 1863; killed at Fredericksburg, May, 1863.
Wayne, John A.
Webb, J. V.,   Discharged, May, 1862.
Wilson, T. J.
Woodward, B.
Woodward, J. P.
Wilkinson, H. S.
White, J. N.,   Detailed.
Zebal, H. L.,   Discharged by Med. Board, May, 1864.
Zebal, L. E.,   Discharged; furnished a substitute.
Allain, H. L.
Baehr, John.
Charlesworth, John.
Collins, H.
Earls, John,   Died in hospital.
Eshman, John.
Farrell, John.
Farrell, W.
Gallagher, E.
Hock, J. L.,   Promoted to Quartermaster Sergeant, Sept., 1864.
Hock, M.,   Detailed in Ord. Department.
Hammel, J.,   Discharged, June, 1862; Surgeon's certificate.
Jacobs, J.,   Detailed Medical Department.
Kinney, James,   Died from wound received at Fredericksburg, December, 1862.

Krafts, John,   Detailed to Ordnance Department.
Lehman, J. S.,   Transferred to Second company.
Lenon, J.,   Transferred to Second company.
Lester, F.
McCormick, J. A.
McKesson, B. D. F.
Norment, J. J.,   Promoted to Corporal, October, 1864; wounded
                             at Drewry's Bluff.
O'Neal, J. A.,   Discharged, April, 1864.
Oliver, William.
Rush, Charles,   Transferred to Second company.
Schmarbeck, F.
Scott, J.
Smith, E. W.
Smith, James.
Stewart, S. G.
Szar, A.

Names of Wounded omitted in above Roll.

Owen, E.,   Captain, at Sharpsburg and Drewry's Bluff.
Brown, C. H. C.,   Lieutenant, severely wounded, left on the field,
                             and captured at Gettysburg.
Falkner, W. R.,   At Rappahannock and Fredericksburg.
Fell, W. R.,   At Sharpsburg and Fredericksburg.
Hardie, W. T.,   At Fredericksburg.
Harby, J. R.,   At Fredericksburg.
Kursheedt, E. I.,   At Sharpsburg, 1862.
Micou, A.,   At Fredericksburg, 1862.
Myers, Jos.,   At Drewry's Bluff.
Phelps, N. B.,   At Drewry's Bluff.
Rossiter, C.,   At Fredericksburg and Drewry's Bluff.
Turner, T. S.,   At Rappahannock Station.
Vinson, Van,   At Gettysburg.
Wilson, T. J.,   At Drewry's Bluff.
Wilkinson, H. S.,   At Drewry's Bluff.
Zebal, H. L.,   At Bull Run and at Williamsport, Md.
Charlesworth, John,   At Fredericksburg, 1862.
Rush, C.,   At Fredericksburg, 1862.

The above statement has been taken from the Historical Record furnished to the War Department C.S., January 1, 1865, and is correct, and as full as can possibly be made from that Record.

LIEUT. C. H. C. BROWN,
Ranking Officer 1st Co. B. W. A.

NEW ORLEANS, Oct. 2, 1874.

ROLL OF SECOND COMPANY.

Lewis, C. C.,	Lieutenant commanding company, May, 1861; resigned, August, 1861.
Rosser, Thos. L.,	Captain; promoted to Lieutenant-Colonel of Artillery; wounded at Mechanicsville.
Richardson, J. B.,	Captain; assigned to company, June, 1862.
McPherson, Sam. J.,	First Lieutenant; resigned, August, 1861.
Slocomb, Cuthbert H.,	promoted to First Lieutenant; resigned, November, 1861.
Hawes, Samuel,	Second Lieutenant; promoted to First Lieutenant, December, 1861.
Britton, J. D.,	Second Lieutenant; wounded at Sharpsburg, September, 1862.
DeRussy, Geo. B.,	Second Lieutenant; promoted from Sergeant First company; wounded at Fredericksburg, May, 1863.
Wigfall, F. H.,	(Cadet); relieved from duty with company, June, 1862, by Order No. 137.
DeGrange, Jos. H.,	First Sergeant, 1861.
Brinsmade, A. A.,	First Sergeant; promoted to Second Lieutenant of Artillery.
Knight, A. G.,	First Sergeant, 1862.
Aime, Gustave,	Sergeant.
Wood, H. C.,	Sergeant; discharged, October, 1861, by order of Secretary of War.
Huchez, C.,	Sergeant.
Leverich, Charles E.,	Sergeant; appointed First Lieutenant P.A.C.S., July, 1863, by order of Secretary of War.
Emmett, J. W.,	Appointed First Lieutenant P.A.C.S., July, 1863, by Secretary of War.
Strawbridge, Geo. E.,	Appointed Second Lieutenant P.A.C.S., March, 1863, by Secretary of War.
Randolph, W. A.,	Sergeant; promoted to Sergeant-Major, September, 1863.
Hare, Walter J.,	Sergeant; wounded at Sharpsburg.
Fuqua, Thos. H.,	Sergeant.
Edwards, James D.,	Corporal; discharged, December, 1861.
Hutton, B. N. L.,	Discharged, July, 1861, by order of Gen. Beauregard.
Hawes, Samuel,	Promoted Second Lieutenant, November, 1861.
White, T. B.,	Corporal: discharged, November, 1862.

Hall, Ed. L.,	Promoted to Sergeant, August, 1863; wounded at Williamsport, July, 1863.
Parsons, Jno. W.,	Captured at Gettysburg, July 5; exchanged; promoted to Sergeant, November, 1863.
Meyers, S. Isaac,	Killed at Petersburg, August, 1864.
Jewell, E. J.,	Wounded at Williamsport, July 6, 1863; died at Williamsport, July 19, 1863.
Chalaron, Stephen,	Wounded at Gettysburg, July, 1863; captured; exchanged; promoted to First Lieutenant in Nit. & Min. Bureau, May, 1864.
Woodville, L. C.,	Wounded at Petersburg, June, 1864.
Goodwin, Jno. Howard,	Wounded at Drewry's Bluff, May, 1864; promoted to Ordnance Sergeant, June, 1864.
Twichell, C. C.	
Suter, Thos. H.	
Randolph, J. F.	
Patton, E. D.	
Clagett, Phil. A.	
Woodville, John C.	
Humphries, G? W.	
DeMeza, Jos.,	Q.M. Sergeant.
Craig, Leonard,	Artificer.
Keating, James,	Artificer.
Dempsey, Jno. W.,	Artificer, transferred to Third company, June, 1863.

PRIVATES.

Alewelt, Fred.,	Wounded at Sharpsburg; died at Shepardstown, September, 1862.
Axon, Randolph,	Detailed in Richmond, October, 1862.
Augustus, E. D.	
Alpin, Geo.	
Almundinger, Wm.,	Killed at Petersburg.
Buckner, F. P.,	Transferred to Fifth regiment, April, 1862.
Blakeley, A. R.,	Wounded Second Manassas, August 30, 1863; captured, August, 1863; exchanged, and detailed in Treasury Department.
Banister, R. J.,	Wounded at Williamsport, July, 1863; captured; exchanged; drowned while on furlough, in Mississippi river, February 8, 1864.
Brentford, J. T.	
Bee, E. M.	Discharged, October, 1862.
Brown, James.	

Byrnes, James.
Barr, Joe.
Brooks, Patrick,   Wounded at Sharpsburg, July, 1863.
Baker, Frank.
Bradley, John S.,   Promoted Q.M. Sergeant, April, 1861.
Bloom, John A.
Brooks, Henry.
Britton, Stephen W.
Cleveland, J. B.,   Transferred from First company, appointed Second Lieutenant P.A.C.S., March, 1863, by Secretary of War.
Curtis, W. P.,   Discharged.
Coleman, H. D.,   Captured at Chancellorsville, May, 1863; exchanged.
Clagett, Phil. A.,   Promoted to Corporal, October, 1863.
Carey, H. S.,   Detailed in Ordnance Department.
Coakley, John A.,   Wounded at Williamsport, July, 1863.
Cross, J. W.   Wounded at Williamsport, July, 1863; died August, 1863.
Cantzon, W. H.,   Detailed clerk, General Lee's Head-quarters, November, 1864.
Clark, N. J.
Duvall, C. A.,   Transferred from Fourth company, July, 1861; appointed Second Lieutenant P.A.C.S., March, 1863.
DeValcourt, A.
Davis, Wm.,   Honorable mention at Second Manassas, August, 1862; wounded at Williamsport, July, 1863.
Dyer, Theo. O.
Dougherty, Charles.
Driscoll, Dan. J.
Dyer, Thos. W.
Florance, W. E.
Forest, Wm.,   Wounded at Williamsport, July, 1863.
Fuqua, Thos. H.,   Transferred from Third company, July, 1861; promoted to Corporal, November, 1862.
Fallon, L. C.,   Wounded at Gettysburg, July, 1863.
Frierson, Geo. A.,   Wounded at Williamsport, July, 1863.
Freret, Armand,   Wounded at Sharpsburg, September, 1862; died at Winchester, September, 1862.
Freret, Jules,   Wounded at Gettysburg, July, 1863; died at same place.
Forshee, John H.
Francis, Wm. M.,   Transferred from Watson's Battery, July, 1864.

Giffen, Wm. C.,   Captured at Chancellorsville, May, 1863; exchanged.

Greenman, John M.,   Wounded at Bermuda Hundreds, May, 1864.

Giffen, John F.,   Wounded at Williamsport, July, 1863.

Gleason, D.

Gessner, Geo.,   Wounded at Drewry's Bluff, May, 1864.

Gillespie, F. M.

Gookin, Hugh S.

Gookin, E. E.

Hall, Jas. A.

Humphrey, Geo.,   Wounded at Williamsport, July, 1863; captured; exchanged, May, 1864.

Hartmann, S. C.,   Discharged, October, 1862.

Hefleigh, J.

Harris, Charles.

Hurley, Charles.

Anderson, Alex.

Harvey, C. M.

Ichstien, I.

Jewell, O.,   Died, February, 1863.

Jackson, J.,   Detailed, May, 1864.

Giggetts, D. E.,   Discharged, by order, May, 1864.

Jacques, B. C.

James, T. R.

Kelly, M.,   Discharged, May, 1862.

Kirk, B. F.,   Wounded at Chancellorsville, May, 1863.

Kirk, Wm.,   Transferred, June, 1864.

Knox, R. H.,   Appointed Cadet P.A.C.S., November, 1864.

Land, T. F.,   Discharged.

Little, Wm.

Lynch, B.,   Discharged, December, 1861.

Layman, W.,   Wounded at Gettysburg; died.

Lehman, L. S.

Lennon, James,   Transferred, February, 1864.

Lobdell, A. G.,   Retired, December, 1864.

Lapham, M. P.,   Wounded, and died at Drewry's Bluff, May, 1864.

Lynch, P. B.

Meyers, J. S.

McGowan, J. R.

Mills, W.,   Detailed, October, 1863.

Meux, John,   Transferred from Fourth company, July, 1861.

Maroney, W.

McCormack, J.

Moore, D. T.,   Died, August, 1884.

Madden, J.,   Detailed, February, 1865.
Miller, L.
McDonald, B. A.
Mallory, W. O.
Maynard, W. E.
McGill, H.
Payne, H. M.,   Retired, August, 1864.
Peale, A. H.,   Discharged, November, 1861, by order of General Beauregard.
Palfrey, William,   Promoted Second Lieutenant First Louisiana Artillery.
Purdy, J. C.,   Appointed Second Lieutenant P.A.C.S., March, 1863.
Perrin, W. A.
Peebles, J. H.
Randolph, I. H.,   Killed at Williamsport, July, 1863.
Roth, W.,   Discharged, August, 1861.
Rockwell, William,   Discharged, December, 1861.
Ridgill, J. W.
Ridgill, A. G.
Raoul, W. G.,   Appointed Captain and A.Q.M., March, 1864.
Richardson, J. L.
Summers, H. D.,   Captured at Chancellorsville, detailed with wounded; captured at Williamsport; exchanged, May, 1864.
Sayre, W. D.
Sutton, A. D. R.
Self, D.
Simpson, W. H.
Twichell, H. C.,   Discharged, October, 1861.
Twichell, C. C.,   Wounded at Williamsport, promoted Corporal, August, 1863.
Theineman, C. A. D.,   Discharged, August, 1862.
Thomas, G. J.
Urquhart, R.,   Wounded at Petersburg, June, 1864.
Von Colln, P.,   Wounded at Chancellorsville.
Woodville, L. C.,   Promoted to Corporal, April, 1863.
Wilkins, W. H.
Weber, J.
Wilson, F.
White, H. N.,   Killed at Second Manassas.
White, T. B.,   Promoted to Corporal, December, 1861.
Williams, F. M.,   Appointed Second Lieutenant P.A.C.S., April, 1863.

Ward, B.,   Wounded Second Manassas, captured; exchanged.
Watterston, G.,   Wounded at Williamsport, captured and died,
                          August, 1863.
Williams, T. E.,   Wounded at Gettysburg.
Webre, G. A.,
Waterson, Chas.
White, D. P.,   Wounded at Williamsport, July, 1863.
Winter, ——.
Walker, F. H. H.
Berthelot, H.
Sawyer, F. H.

The above statement has been taken from the Historical Record furnished to the War Department, C.S., January 1, 1865, and is correct, and as full as can possibly be made from that Record.

JOHN B. RICHARDSON,

Captain Commanding at surrender.

NEW ORLEANS, October 5, 1874.

ROLL OF THIRD COMPANY.

Miller, Merritt B.,   Captain, May, 1861; promoted to Major of Artillery, February, 1864.
Hero, Andrew, Jr.,   Second Sergeant, May, 1861; First Sergeant, November, 1861; Second Lieutenant, May, 1862; First Lieutenant, August, 1862; Captain, February, 1864; wounded at Sharpsburg, September, 1862; at Petersburg, April, 1865.
Whittington, Jos. B., First Lieutenant, resigned, 1861.
Adam, Louis A.,   Second Lieutenant, resigned, August, 1861; reenlisted as private, August, 1862.
Dearing, James,   Second Lieutenant; promoted to Captain of Artillery, April 8, 1862.
Garnet, J. J.,   First Lieutenant; assigned to Company, July, 1861; promoted Major of Artillery, 1862.
Brewer, Isaac W.,   First Lieutenant; killed at Rappahannock Station.
McElroy, Frank,   First Lieutenant.
McNeill, George,   Second Lieutenant.
Stocker, Charles H.,   Second Lieutenant; wounded at Petersburg, April, 1865.
Handy, John T.,   First Sergeant.
Prados, Louis,   Sergeant; promoted to Lieutenant La. Brigade.

Collins, W. A.,	Sergeant.
Maxwell, Robert,	Sergeant.
Ellis, W. H.,	Sergeant.
DeBlanc, O. N.,	Sergeant.
Coyle, W. G.,	Sergeant.
Kremelberg, F.,	Sergeant; killed at Petersburg.
Pettis, P. W.,	Sergeant.
Jewell, Ed. J.,	Corporal.
Peale, A. H.,	Corporal.
Fortier, C. E.,	Corporal; discharged.
Morgan, E. W.,	Corporal.
Many, R. P.,	Corporal; killed at Fredericksburg, May, 1863.
Leefe, W.,	Corporal; died in Louisiana Hospital.
Grimmer, A. E.,	Corporal.
Bartlett, N.,	Corporal.
Ballantine, T.,	Corporal.
Bland, Samuel,	Corporal.
Ballauf, R.,	Corporal.
Cantrelle, M. B.,	Corporal.
Dick, I. C.,	Corporal.
Porter, John R.,	Corporal.
Phelps, H. J.,	Corporal.
Collins, William A.,	Corporal; wounded at Second Manassas, August, 1863.

PRIVATES.

Avril, E.,	Corporal; wounded at Sharpsburg, September, 1862; discharged, December, 1862.
Anderson, John,	Transferred from First company, July, 1861.
Atkins, Henry J.,	Killed at Sharpsburg, September, 1862.
Andress, Frank M.	
Adde, J. A.	
Andress, S. S.	
Bruce, Robert,	Discharged, April, 1864.
Boush, Samuel C.,	On duty in Quartermaster's Department.
Blanchard, J. D.,	Died, March, 1864.
Bloomfield, James C.,	Promoted to Lieutenant in Magruder's army.
Becnel, Michel A.,	Discharged, December, 1861, by order of Secretary of War.
Bernard, George,	Detailed with ambulance.
Burke, M.	
Benton, J. P.,	Captured by enemy, June, 1864.
Bland, Samuel,	Wounded at Rappahannock, August, 1862.
Behan, James S.,	Died at Mobile, Ala.

Barton, Wm.

Bloom, Jos.

Ballauf, Rudolph,   Promoted to Corporal, April, 1864.

Brady, Geo.

Behan, Geo. B.,   Died at Culpeper, September, 1862.

Bush, C.,   Injured by falling of a tree, October, 1862. Detailed in Richmond.

Beyer, Ernest.

Brady, Charles.

Brooks, Henry G.

Benton, John H.,   Wounded at Petersburg, September, 1864; died, September, 1864.

Bryens, Geo. H.,   Killed at Gettysburg, July, 1863.

Berry, Lawrence.

Bryens, Richard.

Brewer, Wm. P.,   Promoted to Assistant Surgeon.

Bryan, B. F.

Ball, Robert J.,   Transferred to First company.

Burke, Steve.

Carl, F. A.,   Died, May 27, 1861.

Cloney, M. W.,   Wounded at Sharpsburg, September, 1862; captured at Gettysburg, July, 1863.

Colles, John H.,   Discharged, November, 1861, by order Secretary of War.

Charpieux, Ernest,   Wounded at Manassas, August, 1862; detailed Q.M. Dept., April, 1864.

Coyle, W. G.,   Promoted to Corporal, November, 1861; to Sergeant, October, 1863.

Casey, Wm.,   Transferred from Second company, July, 1861.

Crilly, James,   Transferred from Second company, wounded at Rappahannock Station, August, 1862.

Coyle, Frank E.,   Wounded at Gettysburg, July, 1863; killed at Petersburg, April, 1865.

Campbell, W.

Charlton, Geo. W.

Cressy, L. W.,   Killed by falling of a tree at Winchester.

Clark, Edward A.

Charlton, W. W.

Collins, T. S.

Clark, J. F.,   Killed at Gettysburg, July, 1863.

Deacon, C. W.,   Transferred to First company.

DeMeza, Jos. H.,   Transferred to Second company, July, 1861.

Duncan, Edward,   Captured at Petersburg and exchanged.

Douber, Fred.,   Killed at Sharpsburg.

Davis, J. F.

Dumas, A.

Dolan, James, Died from wound at Rappahannock.

DeBlanc, August.

Dick, Isaac C., Promoted to Corporal, October, 1864.

Dietz, H.

Dick, Benj. E., Captured at Fredericksburg and exchanged.

DeBlanc, Armand, Discharged, May, 1863.

Dennison, W.

DeLacy, Wm.

Doussan, Honoré.

Dupré, Adolph, Jr., Wounded and captured at Gettysburg.

Elfer, Louis G.

Evans, Edgar D.

Fazende, P. O.

Fortier, Charles E., Promoted to Corporal, July, 1861; discharged, September, 1861.

Fourshee, F. P., Wounded at Rappahannock.

Fuqua, T. H., Transferred to Second company.

Frank, Otto, Wounded at Fredericksburg.

Faisans, René.

Faisans, Auguste.

Guyot, Louis E.

Grimmer, A. E., Wounded at Fredericksburg; promoted to Corporal, November, 1863.

Gras, Fred. W.

Gore, Jno. W.

Gretter, J. B.

Gough, C. A., Wounded at Gettysburg, and died.

Givens, S. R., Discharged, January, 1863.

Gerard, Leon M.

Gerard, Philibert.

Grimes, G. A.

Guillote, Henry.

Hubbard, F. L., Right arm injured, and discharged, October, 1861.

Hart, C., Discharged, February, 1862.

Holmes, John, Jr., Wounded at Sharpsburg, and discharged, May, 1864.

Huisson, John.

Hottinger, John G.

Hubbell, Ed. D.

Jones, Wm.

Johnson, Wm. N.

Joubert, Eugene, Wounded at Rappahannock, and died.

Jagot, Jos. H.
Jourdan, F.
Jones, John,   Captured and escaped, July, 1864.
Kinslow, Joseph.   Bugler.
Kennedy, S.,   Transferred to Twenty-eighth Louisiana regi-
                          ment; resigned, 1864.

Kerwin, Thos.
Kobleur, Damas,   Wounded at Petersburg, October, 1864.
Kitchen, W. H.
Kitchen, R. H.
Kent, M.
Leefe, Wm.,   Promoted Corporal, April, 1863; died, October,
                          1864.
Loftus, Ed.,   Died, February, 1863.
Lynch, M. F.
Little, James,   Died, June, 1862.
Leytze, G.,   Missing after battle of Gettysburg.
Levy, S.,   Wounded at Rappahannock; discharged, Septem-
                          ber, 1862.

Luddy, J. T.
Land, John.
Land, Geo.
Leclere, Gustave.
Leclere, Eugene.
Lombard, Charles,   Transferred to Fourth company, June, 1863.
Lazarre, T.,   Died at Petersburg, December, 1864.
Labarre, Murville,   Died at Petersburg, December 31, 1864.
Labarre, E.,   Discharged, October, 1863.
Labarre, Lacestiere,   Transferred from First company, September,
                          1863.

Laresche, P. E.
Leefe, A.,   Wounded at Drewry's Bluff.
Lighthouse, N.
McFall, T. M.,   Promoted to Q.M. Sergeant, April, 1863.
McDonald, O.,   Killed at Rappahannock.
McCartney, J. H.,   Wounded at Sharpsburg.
Moore, J. H.,   Transferred to Seventh brigade.
Mills, W.,   Transferred to Second company.
Morgan, E. W.,   Discharged, July, 1861.
Maxwell, Robert,   Promoted to Sergeant, November, 1861; wounded
                          at Rappahannock, and discharged, 1863.

Martin, A. B.
Meek, G. H.,   Promoted to Ord. Serg., November, 1863.
Marmillon, C. B.,   Discharged, 1862, by Secretary of War.

Massy, G. W.,	Wounded at Sharpsburg; died, September, 1862.
Murphy, John C.	
Madden, Henry A.,	Killed at Drewry's Bluff, May, 1864.
Mahen, E. L.	
Noyes, S. W.	
Norcom, Albert,	Transferred to Fourth company.
Nesbitt, J. S.,	Discharged, May, 1862.
Noyes, L. T.	
Noble, W. P.	
Nulty, T.	
Ozanne, F.,	Captured and escaped at Hagerstown, 1863.
Pettis, Peyton W.,	Promoted Corporal, July, 1862; wounded at Rappahannock and Sharpsburg; promoted Sergeant, 1864.
Porter, Jno. R.,	Promoted, Corporal, August, 1864; wounded at Petersburg, October, 1864.
Phelps, H. J.,	Corporal, April, 1863; wounded at Fredericksburg, 1862.
Philips, Abraham B.	
Peirce, Geo. A.	
Patin, Paul T.	
Price, James W.	
Pinckard, Wm. F.,	Wounded at Petersburg, 1864.
Pinckard, Wm. M.	
Russell, C. P.	
Rousseau, Samuel,	Wounded at Petersburg.
Randolph, J. F.,	Transferred to Second company.
Raymond, Charles.	
Rideau, H.,	Killed at Gettysburg.
Ruleau, F.,	Wounded and died at Gettysburg.
Riviere, E.	
Rousseau, Jules A. A.	
Robinson, G. D.,	Severely wounded, July, 1863.
Shaw, Frank, Jr.,	Discharged by Secretary of War.
Stocker, Chas. H.,	Promoted Corporal, June, 1862; Sergeant, July, 1862; captured at Gettysburg, July, 1863; Second Lieutenant, March, 1864.
Saunders, S. G.,	Wounded at Sharpsburg.
Smith, Charles,	Captured at Petersburg, June, 1864.
Seicshnaydre, A.	
Seicshnaydre, Leon.	
Slade, S. B.	
Smelser, C. G.	
Smith, T. W.	

Smith, R.
Summers, H. D.,   Transferred to Second company.
Toledano, Wm. S.,   Discharged, September, 1861.
Toledano, E.,   Discharged, September, 1861.
Tully, Howard,   Wounded at Bull Run and Fredericksburg.
Turnell, Ralph,   Discharged, November, 1862.
Thompson, Hugh,   Killed at Rappahannock
Tully, James,   Wounded at Rappahannock.
Thomas, G. J.
Tew, Walter A.
Tisdale, Victor R.
Trémé, John.
Toledano, Oswald J.,   Killed at Petersburg, 1864.
Vidal, Ernest.
White, J. W.
Williamson, Thos. E.
Williamson, W.
Watson, W. J. B.,   Transferred to Fourth company.
White, J. N.,   Transferred to Fourth company.
Dempsey, J. W.,   Transferred to Second company.
Pielert, Geo.
Holmes, W. D.,   Transferred to Second company.
Nugent, Tom.
Keating, James,   Transferred to Second company.

The above roll is copied correctly from the historical records of the Third company of the Washington Artillery, and contains all details as to members of the company.

A. HERO, Jr.,
Late Capt. Commanding 3d Co. B. W.A.

ROLL OF FOURTH COMPANY.

Eshleman, B. F.,   Captain, 1861; wounded at Bull Run; Major, 1862.
Norcom, Jos.,   First Lieutenant, 1861; Captain, 1862; wounded at Gettysburg.
Battles, H. A.,   Second Lieutenant, 1861; First Lieutenant, 1862; wounded at Fredericksburg.
Apps, George E.,   Sergeant, 1861; Second Lieutenant, 1861; First Lieutenant, 1862.
Behan, W. J.,   First Sergeant, 1861; Second Lieutenant, 1863.
Reynolds, Joshua D.,   Sergeant, 1861; killed at Manassas, 1861.

Dearie, James W.,	Sergeant, 1861; discharged.
Fish, John S.,	Sergeant, 1861; first Sergeant, 1863.
Moore, Robt. F. F.,	Sergeant, 1861.
Gray, R. H.,	Sergeant, 1861.
Wood, John C.,	Corporal; Sergeant, 1861; wounded at Fredericksburg, 1862; discharged.
Banksmith, Ansel,	Sergeant; wounded at Fredericksburg, 1862.
Stewart, T. Jones,	Sergeant; First Lieutenant Cavalry, 1864.
Wilcox, John W.,	Sergeant.
Weidler, B. Frank,	Sergeant.
Valentine, Jno. B.,	Sergeant; wounded at Drewry's Bluff, 1864.
Haile, Sylvester T.,	Q.M. Sergeant.
Lescene, Joseph W.,	Corporal; wounded at Gettysburg, 1863; captured by enemy; appointed cadet, 1864.
Wood, George W.,	Corporal.
Brodie, Fred A.,	Corporal.
Hufft, Bernard,	Corporal; wounded at Gettysburg, 1863.
Babcock, O. S.,	Corporal.
Lilly, James F.,	Corporal.
Montgomery, George,	Corporal.
Ames, Fred W.,	Corporal.
McDonald, R. G.,	Corporal; killed at Drewry's Bluff, 1864.
Burke, R. S.,	Corporal.
Adams, Chas. L.,	Corporal; promoted and discharged, 1863.
Lewis, L. L.,	Corporal; mortally wounded at Chancellorville.

PRIVATES.

Adams, Joseph.	
Allen, J. S.	
Anderson, George,	Wounded at Chancellorsville, 1863.
Baker, H. H.,	Wounded at Bull Run, 1861.
Baker, Page M.,	Promoted; transferred to Navy.
Baker, J. McR.	Discharged by order of Secretary of War.
Baker, Lewis H.,	Wounded and captured at Gettysburg, 1863.
Bateman, Charles,	Transferred to Navy, 1863.
Beach, William,	Discharged.
Bee, Eugene M.,	Transferred to Second company.
Beck, George M.,	Discharged, 1861.
Behan, Frank A.	
Bier, C. C.	
Borland, James.	
Burke, Joseph W.	
Burke, R. S.,	Wounded at Manassas, 1862.
Boucher, Alexander,	Wounded at Gettysburg and captured.

Byrne, C. M.
Callahan, L. P.,   Artificer; wounded at Chancellorsville.
Cannon, John,   Deserted, July, 1862.
Carey, Thomas.
Carey, William.
Chastant, John B.,   Discharged, 1861.
Chapman, M. B.,   Promoted Chaplain Twenty-sixth Mississippi regiment, 1864.
Clayton, L. W.
Cook, Edwin O.
Cowand, Alfred S.
Cowand, Charles.
Cox, I. M.,   Captured at Gettysburg.
Conden, Edmund,   Killed at Drewry's Bluff.
Creecy, W. Pryor,   Wounded at Gettysburg.
Cronan, Dennis.
Caldwell, I.,   Transferred to First company.
Crutcher, George L.,   Wounded at Manassas; discharged.
Cummings, Thomas,   Discharged.
Curley, William.
Davis, Robert N.
Davidson, Robert.
Dennison, W.
Dirke, W. R.
Duval, C. A.
Edwards, James D.
Eckelberg, John.
Fagan, John.
Farrell, J. J.
Fell, William S.
Fish, John S.
Fowlkes, John,   Killed at Drewry's Bluff.
Gray, R. H.
Gregory, G. C.,   Died of fever.
Gubernator, E. F.,   Captured at Gettysburg.
Herbert, Thomas S.,   Discharged, insane, February, 1865.
Holt, Samuel E.,   Detailed Telegraph Operator.
Holmes, Wm. McC.,   Wounded at Drewry's Bluff.
Hood, I. G.
Humphreys, Geo. W.,   Transferred to Second company.
Jessup, Isaac,   Captured by enemy.
Jones, Wm. W.,   Captured by enemy.
Jones, W. C.,   Wounded at Fredericksburg and Petersburg.
Jordan, F.,   Transferred to Third company.

Joubert, E.
Keegan, M.
Knox, Samuel,   Discharged, sick.
Kinney, M. J.,   Taken prisoner while straggling.
Lazarre, T.
Lazarre, D.
Lake, Charles.
Laury, P. J.
Lauer, E.,   Discharged, sick.
Lescene, John F.,   Died at Petersburg, of dysentery, 1864.
Lund, J. R.
Marston, C. W.
Martin, William,   Wounded at Drewry's Bluff.
Marisole, Bernard.
McDonald, John,   Captured at Gettysburg, died of small-pox, Fort
                               Delaware.
McCulloch, J. B.,   Discharged, disability.
McGregor, C.
McGowan, Jno. R.,   Transferred to Second company
McManus, John,   Killed at Petersburg.
Mellard, E. A.,   Killed at Drewry's Bluff.
Meux, John,   Transferred to Second company.
Mooney, Pat,   Died of cholera, at Petersburg.
Myers, Henry.
Nicholas, R.,   Discharged, August, 1861.
Nolan, David,   Wounded at Manassas, 1862.
Norcom, Albert,   Wounded at Drewry's Bluff.
Norris, Thomas.
Nugent, Thomas,   Transferred to Third company.
O'Neill, W. T.,   Wounded, captured at Gettysburg.
Palfry, William,   Transferred to Second company; promoted Lieu-
                               tenant of Artillery.
Palfry, Charles,   Wounded at Orange Court-House; detailed in
                               Engineer's Department.
Peck, H. F.
Pheiffer, John G.,   Captured at Gettysburg.
Pipes, David W.
Purdy, I. C.
Plattsimer, A. L.,   Promoted; discharged by order of Secretary of
                               War.
Porter, J. N.
Redman, M. B.
Remy, P. Lewis.
Reynolds, George W.

Roesch, Louis.
Rohboch, J. M.,   Detailed hospital steward.
Ryan, I. M.
Seaman, H. D.,   Discharged, 1861.
Schmetzler, C. G.
Sheckler, J.
Shoe, Andrew.
Smith, J. H.
Smith, J.
Smith, Henry.
Shields, Leonard.
Sneed, W. T.
Soniat, A.
Stone, John H.
Stuart, Wilson N.,   Killed at Petersburg.
Sutton, Edward.
Terrebonne, U. D.
Vass, A. F.
Von Coln, Philip.
Walker, George.
Wall, James W.
Watson, W. J. B.
Webster, G. T.
White, T. B.
White, H. F.,   Killed at Second Manassas.
Wilson, H. F.
Wilson, John H.
Wilkinson, G. W.
Wood, P. N., Jr.

ROLL OF MEMBERS WHO JOINED THE FIFTH COMPANY, WASHINGTON ARTILLERY, ARMY OF TENNESSEE, AFTER ITS DEPARTURE FROM NEW ORLEANS.

Armant, A.
Anthony J. W.
Anderson, Jno. R.
Arroyo, Felix.
Arroyo, A.
Arroyo, Chas.
Adams, Jas.
Arnold, Thos.
Brown, Geo. E.

Boatner, H. J.
Butts, Jno. F.
Bein, Geo.
Bryan, Jesse A.
Bailey, C. P.
Baker, A. H.
Benson, C.
Belsom, D.
Belsom, F.

Belsom, Jos., Jr.
Boudreaux, J. J.
Brindly, L. D.
Brewerton, A. W.
Barrail, A.
Browning, Jas. L.
Berry, Jno.
Brevard, A. H.
Blackwell, Wm.
Barrow, A. D.
Barrow, C. J.
Burrows, F.
Clere, P.
Chalaron, A. J.
Chalaron, Henry.
Covey, D. H.
Collins, A.
Cottreaux, E. P.
Carpenter, J. D. F.
Commandeur, N.
Cotting, C. C.
Cotting, S. A. B.
Converse, F. M.
Crawford, G. W.
Capon, Phil.
Conrad, Paul.
Dapremont, L.
Daigle, L.
Dabney, J. W.
Daniels, Chas.
Delery, Armant.
Delery, Anatole.
Duggan, Martin.
Downing, J. B.
Doherty, L. M.
Eldridge, S. H.
Etter, G. D.
Elfer, J. A.
Engman, T. W., Jr.
Flood, P. H.
Freiler, Jno.
Feraud, Henry.
Frerett, G. J.
Fitzgerald, Jno.

Fitzwilliams, D. J.
Fox, Michael.
False, C. N.
Giffen, R. C.
Goodwyn, Fred.
Gollmer, Wm.
Gaines, A.
Gomez, J. F.
Gordon, Henry.
Giles, Geo.
Gillespie, Jno.
Greenwood, M.
Greenwood, P. P.
Galpin, S.
Galpin, F. H.
Hamilton, G. W.
Haney, J. H.
Hayward, W. B.
Hyde, F.
Hardy, Henry.
Henderson, V.
Hull, F. B.
Hazard, J. B.
Hayes, M.
Hopkins, Andy.
Hopkins, Octave.
Hall, W. H.
Harrison, Wm.
Kent, Jno. R.
Kénnett, L. M., Jr.
Keheo, Thos.
Keyes, Pat.
Lamare, J. M.
Levie, C. A.
Logan, Henry.
Law, Geo. H.
Legare, Oscar A.
Leverich, Henry.
McDonald, P. A.
Murray, Jno. R.
McDonald, Thos.
Marks, H. J.
Martin, W. P.
Mass, B. Van.

Miller, Jno.
Miller, Henry.
Meader, Herman.
McCormack, Jno.
Metzler, Jno.
Morel, Fred.
Mathes, Wm.
Miller, B. R.
McGregor, Wm.
McMillan, Robert.
McNair, H. M.
Marquette, L.
Murray, Robert.
Nish, Geo.
Newman, W. J.
Newman, S. B., Jr.
Ogden, H. V.
Ogden, Wallace.
Ponder, Jno.
Percy, C. R.
Philips, J.
Pugh, Geo. W.
Pugh, J. E.
Pugh, Robert L.
Robertson, Kenneth.
Rost, Alphonse.
Rice, D. A.
Richards, W. A.
Ryan, Pat.
Richards, H. M.

Ruffier, E.
Richardson, F. L.
Sevey, W. S. E.
Stephenson, P. D.
Sheridan, M.
Sebastian, Jno. B.
Scruggs, D. H.
Stakeman, Benj.
Swain, Andy.
Staub, C., Jr.
Turpin, E.
Tutt, W. F.
Thompson, F. M.
Vinson, R.
Vincent, Louis.
Virtue, E. J.
Vecque, J.
Webre, Jules.
Wild, Chris.
Wood, F. W.
Weingate, E. H.
White, T. J.
White, John G.
Woods, W. A.
Walker, Garry.
Watson, Robert J.
Wheatley, R. L.
Williams, Jas.
Williams, Morris.
Young, J. H.

ROLL OF FIFTH COMPANY (PRESENT AND ABSENT) AT THE SURRENDER.

Slocomb, C. H.,   Captain.
Vaught, W. C. D.,   Senior First Lieutenant.
Chalaron, J. A.,   Junior First Lieutenant.
Leverich, A. I.,   Senior Second Lieutenant; wounded and prisoner.
Johnsen, Chas. G.,   Junior Second Lieutenant.

SERGEANTS.

Bartley, Jno.,   Orderly Sergeant.
Gibson, Robert,   Quartermaster Sergeant.

Holmes, Curtis,	Commissary Sergeant.
Ogden, Wallace,	Ordnance Sergeant.
Allen, Thos. C.,	Sergeant of Piece.
Giffen, Jas. F.,	Sergeant of Piece; wounded and prisoner.
Smith, D. W.,	Sergeant of Piece; prisoner.
Smith, Jno. H.,	Sergeant of Piece.
Browning, Jas. L.,	Sergeant of Piece.
Rice, D. A.,	Sergeant of Piece.

CORPORALS.

Fox, Chas. W.
Allain, Alexander.
Scott, Jno. W.
Clarke, Jas.
Mather, H. J.
Meader, Herman.
Ruffier, E.
White, T. J.

ARTIFICERS.

False, C. N.
Richards, W. H.
Thompson, F. M.
Williams, Morris.

FARRIER.

Williams, Jas.

BUGLER.

Swain, Andy,	Absent, furloughed.

PRIVATES.

Abbott, Jno.	
Allain, V. F.,	Absent.
Adams, C. A.,	Absent.
Armant, A.,	Absent, on furlough.
Arroyo, F.	
Arroyo, A.,	Absent, sick.
Arroyo, C.	
Barstow, W. R.,	Detailed.
Bridge, Ben.	
Brown, Geo. E.,	Absent, sick furlough.
Boatner, H. J.	
Butts, J. F.,	Absent, detailed.
Baker, A. H.	
Belsom, D.	
Belsom, F.	

Boudreaux, J. J.
Brindley, L. D.
Brewerton, A. W.
Berry, Jno.,   Absent, wounded and prisoner.
Brevard, A. H.
Blackwell, Wm.,   Absent, sick.
Barrow, C. J.
Clere, P.
Chalaron, A. J.
Chalaron, Henry.
Covey, D. H.,   Absent, detailed.
Collins, A.
Cottreaux, E. P.
Carpenter, J. D. F.
Commandeur, N.,   Absent, detailed.
Cotting, C. C.
Cotting, S. A. B.
Converse, F. M.
Conrad, Paul.
Campbell, M.,   Absent, prisoner.
Dabney, J. W.
Delery, Anatole.
Davidson, Jno.,   Absent on furlough.
Davis, Sam. J.
Dooley, Wm.,   Absent, wounded and prisoner.
Eldridge, S. H.
Etter, G. D.
Elfer, J. A.,   Absent, sick.
Freiler, Jno.
Feraud, Henry,   Absent, wounded.
Frerett, G. J.,   Absent, sick.
Fitzgerald, Jno.,   "   "
Fitzwilliams, D. J.,   "   ".
Fox, Mike.
Feinour, E. C.
Fahnestock, A. M.,   Absent, sick.
Fraser, J. Y.,   Absent; said to have been promoted.
Giffen, R. C.,   Absent, detailed on account of wound.
Gollmer, Wm.
Gaines, A.,   Absent, detailed.
Gomez, J. F.   "   "
Gordon, Henry,   Absent, furloughed.
Giles, Geo.
Gillespie, Jno.,   Absent, missing in Tennessee.

Greenwood, P. P.	
Hayward, W. B.	
Hyde, F.,	Absent, prisoner.
Hardy, H.,	" "
Henderson, V.,	Absent, sick.
Hull, F. B.	
Hazard, J. B.	
Hall, Wm. H.	
Henderson, W. D.,	Absent, detailed.
Jamieson, J. J.	
Kelly, Patrick,	Absent, detailed.
Kent, Jno. R.	
Kennett, L. M., Jr.,	Absent, detailed.
Keheo, Thos.	
Lamare, J. M.,	Absent, sick furlough.
Levie, C. A.,	" "
Logan, Henry.	
Leverich, Henry.	
McDonald, P. A.	
Marks, H. J.,	Absent, paroled prisoner.
Martin, W. P.	
Mass, B. Van.	
Miller, Jno.,	Absent, prisoner.
Miller, Henry,	Absent, wounded, prisoner.
Metzler, Jno.,	
Mathes, William,	Absent, wounded.
McMillan, R.,	Absent, detailed.
Marquette, L.	
Mathis, Louis.	
Mussina, E.,	Absent, detailed.
Macready, L.,	" "
Miller, D. C.	
Newman, S. B., Jr.	
Ogden, H. V.	
Ponder, Jno.	
Pugh, G. W.	
Pugh, Robert.	
Palfrey, G. W.	
Robertson, K.,	Absent, prisoner.
Rost, Alphonse.	
Seevy, W. S. E.,	Absent, sick furlough.
Stephenson, P. D.	
Sheridan, M.,	Absent, prisoner.
Sebastian, Jno. B.,	Absent, detailed.

Scruggs, D. H.,   Absent, detailed.
Skidmore, D. W.,   "   "
Sambola, A.,   "   "
Stone, Warren, Jr.,   "   "
Turner, Geo. A.
Tynen, William.
Turpin, E.,   Absent, wounded.
Tutt, Wm. F.,   Absent, sick furlough.
Vecque, J.
Webre, Jules.
Wild, C.
Walker, Garry.
Wood, F. W.
Wingate, E. H.
Wheatley, R. L.
Watt, C. B.
Watson, Jno. W.,   Absent, detailed.
Wolfe, J. B.,   "   "
Withan, Chas.,   "   "

MEMORIES OF "TRY US."

Bull Run,
Manassas,
Munson's Hill,
Hall's Hill,
Lewinsville,
Shiloh,
Monterey,
Yorktown,
Corinth,
Williamsburg,
Farmington,
Seven Pines,
Mechanicsville,
Gaines's Mills,
Savage Station,
Frayser's Farm,
Malvern Hill,
Rappahannock Station,
Second Manassas,
Chantilly,
Boonsboro' Gap,
Sharpsburg,
Mumfordsville,
Perryville,
Fredericksburg,
Murfreesboro,
Stone's River,
Chancellorsville,
Gettysburg,
Williamsport,

Jackson,
Chickamauga,
Missionary Ridge,
Newbern,
Walthal Junction,
Resaca,
Drewry's Bluff,
Cassville,
Clay's Farm,
New Hope Church,
Dallas,
Chickahominy,
Pine Mountain,
Kenesaw Mountain,
Peach Tree Creek,
Right of Atlanta,
Atlanta,
Rough and Ready,
Jonesboro,
Lovejoy Station,
Mill Creek Gap,
Columbia,
Franklin,
Overall Creek,
Second Murfreesboro,
Nashville,
Spanish Fort,
Fort Gregg,
Petersburg,
Appomattox Court-House.

ROLL OF HONOR.

KILLED AND DIED IN SERVICE.

Fred Alewelt,
Henry J. Atkins,
J. W. Anthony,
William Almindinger,
J. R. Anderson,
R. J. Banister,
George B. Behan,
George H. Bryens,
Lieut. T. M. Blair,
James Bayle,
C. P. Bailey,
J. Belson, Jr.,
Lieut. I. W. Brewer,
J. D. Blanchard,
John H. Benton,
William Barton,
A. T. Bennett, Jr.,
John T. Beggs,
A. Barrail,
Lawrence Bery,
Leon Brocard,
W. Chambers,
H. Chambers,
George Chambers,
J. W. Cross,
Frank E. Coyle,
Joseph F. Clarke,
Phil Capon,
A. F. Coste,
F. A. Carl,
L. W. Cressy,
Edmund Conden,
James Dolan,
J. W. Demerritt,

Armand Delery,
Fred Douber,
L. Daigle,
M. F. Duggan,
John Earls,
P. W. Engman,
J. E. Florence,
W. E. Fowles,
C. A. Falconer,
Armand Freret,
Jules Freret,
John Fowlkes,
P. H. Flood,
Robert W. Frazer,
Lieut. J. M. Galbraith,
C. A. Gough,
B. H. Green, Jr.,
G. C. Gregory,
M. Greenwood,
W. B. Giffen,
Morgan E. Harris,
John Huission,
E. J. Hartnett,
William Harrison,
Stanford Higgins,
G. M. Judd,
E. J. Jewell,
O. Jewell,
Eugene Joubert,
James Rinney,
H. Koss,
F. Kremelberg,
T. J. Lutman,
T. Lazarre,

William Layman,
M. P. Laphan,
William Leefe,
Ed. Loftus,
James Little,
G. Leytze,
Murville Labarre,
John F. Lescene,
L. L. Lewis,
J. Leary,
O. A. Legare,
Patrick Long,
R. Taylor Marshall,
J. Muntinger,
George W. Muse,
W. Mains,
H. C. McClelland,
Isaac C. Meyers,
R. P. Many,
D. T. Moore,
G. W. Massey,
O. McDonald,
H. A. Madden,
R. G. McDonald,
John McManus,
E. A. Mellard,
J. P. Mooney,
John McDonald,
Martin Mathis,
E. S. McIlhenny,
Wm. McGregor,
B. R. Miller,
F. Morel,
W. J. Newman,
John O'Donnell,

H. Peychaud,
C. R. Percy,
J. Philips,
Joshua O. Reynolds,
Frank D. Ruggles,
Herman Ross,
James Reddington,
Isaac H. Randolph,
H. Rideau,
F. Ruleau,
James W. Read,
E. F. Reichert,
E. Ricketts,
Samuel Russell,
R. McK. Spearing,
W. B. Stuart,
Louis Seibrecht,
W. W. Sewell,
P. D. Simmons,
J. H. Simmons,
C. Staub,
Ben Stakeman,
W. B. Stewart,
Hugh Thompson,
O. J. Toledano,
Louis Vincent,
H. Whitcomb,
C. R. Walden,
W. H. West,
Henry N. White,
G. Watterston,
W. A. Woods,
T. B. Winston,
Thomas P. Jones,
John J. Norment,

H. W. Spencer.

THE END.

INDEX.

Abingdon, Va., 264–66, 273, 290, 295, 300–302

Aby, T. Y., 109n, 294–95, 309, 344n

Adairsville, Ga., 414

Adam, Louis A., 27, 33, 58, 97, 227, 430

Adams, Daniel W., 273, 413, 418–19

Adams, John I., 400

Adams, S. F., 267

Alabama, 337

Alabama troops: Jeff Davis Battery, 208; Hardaway-Hurt Battery, 209; Robertson's Battery, 409; Hilliard's Legion, 268; Confederate Guards, 203; 2d Infantry, 284–85; 3d Infantry, 94; 6th Infantry, 27; 41st Infantry, 268, 325; 43d Infantry, 268; 23d Infantry Battalion, 325n

Alburtis, Ephriam G., 36

Alexander, E. Porter, 186, 191–93, 209, 232, 232n, 233n, 236n, 238, 243–44, 247, 249n, 250, 262, 305, 308, 334–35, 339, 383, 389

Alexander's Bridge, 276, 282, 284

Allan, Willie, 64–65, 76

Alsobrook, R. H., 134, 227

Amelia Courthouse, 374, 389, 394

Amissville, Va., 110

Anderson, Edwin J., 100, 103–105, 106n, 116

Anderson, G. B., 145

Anderson, George T., 104, 111, 115, 152

Anderson, J., 227

Anderson, John R., 414

Anderson, J. Patton, 282, 405, 410

Anderson, Richard H., 119, 137n, 140n, 142, 147, 148n, 149n, 166, 180n, 184, 224, 254, 328–29

Andrews, R. Snowden, 84, 118, 120, 208

Anthony, John W., 413

Antietam, battle of, 136–67, 255

Antietam Creek, 137–39, 141, 141n, 142, 143–44, 151, 153,

155n, 158

Appomattox Courthouse, Va., iv, 373, 380–81, 383, 385, 387, 389n, 390–92

Appomattox River, 311–12, 331, 352, 371, 374, 376

Appomattox Station, Va., 389

Apps, George E., 77, 123, 138, 185, 216–17, 223, 233n, 262, 381, 390, 426

Archer, James J., 153–54

Archer, Lt., 109n

Arkansas troops: 3d Infantry, 145

Armistead, Lewis A., 251

Armstrong, Frank, 275

Army of Northern Virginia, 83n, 174, 207–10, 227, 264, 277, 340n, 346, 387, 389n, 416

Army of Tennessee, 338, 416–17, 421

Army of the James, 383

Army of the Mississippi (CSA), 411

Army of the Potomac (CSA), 54n, 339n

Army of the Potomac (USA), 199, 227

Ashby, Capt., 324

Ashby's Gap, 170, 238

Atkins, Capt., 36

Atlanta, battles for, 415, 424

Austin, John E. "Ned," 414, 418

Averell, William W., 301

Ayres, Romeyn B., 29

Bachman, William K., 116, 138, 141, 208, 261

Bahr, John, 20,

Bahr, Mrs. John, 21

Bailey, C. P., 414

Baker, Edward D., 61

Baker, Harry H., 26

Bakewell, A. Gordon, 402

Baldwin, Briscoe E., 118, 258n

Ball's Bluff, battle of, 61, 144

Baltimore, Md., 396

Banister, Rinaldo, 399

Banks's Ford, 213–14

Barksdale, Dr. Randolph, 81, 195, 306, 338, 379–80, 393

Barksdale, William, 61, 143, 176, 179, 211–12, 212n, 214–15, 215n, 217–21, 219n, 223, 245

Barnum's Hotel, Baltimore, 396

Barnum's Museum, New York City, 397

Bartley, John, 424

Barton, Capt., 178

Barton, Seth M., 315, 325n

Barton, T. S., 176, 178, 181

Bartow, Francis S., 34–35

Bate, William B., 415

Baton Rouge, La., 400

Battery Gregg, 351, 368, 371–73, 394

Battery Whitworth, 371–73

Battle House, Mobile, 203–94

Battle–flags, 60–61

Battles, H. A., 33, 57n, 76, 123, 138, 185, 198, 219, 368–69, 394

Bayle, James, 414

Bayne, Thomas L., 410–11, 427

Beard, Dr., 52

Beauregard, Pierre G. T., iii, 15,

29, 30, 32n, 33, 36, 38–42,
46–47n, 51–52, 53n, 54n, 55,
59–60, 60n, 61, 74, 206, 294,
313–14, 316, 318, 320–21,
339n, 342n, 385, 402, 408, 429
Beauregard, René, 55
Beck, Benjamin, 111
Beckham, Robert F., 39
Bee, Bernard E., 33–37
Beebe, M. J., 427
Beggs, John T., 414
Behan, William J., 262, 426
Belger, James, 317, 324, 326n
Bellanger, Alfred, 410–11
Bellfield, Va., 358
Belsom, Joseph, Jr., 414
Benevolent Association of the
Washington Artillery, 427
Benjamin, Judah P., 6–7, 129,
333, 339n
Benjamin, Samuel N., 29
Bennett, Archie, 415
Bennett, R. Tyler, 145
Benning, Henry L., 254, 288
Bermuda Hundred, Va., 310–11,
318–19
Berry, Hiram, 44–45
Berryville, Md., 239n
Berth, William G., 409
Berthelot, H. B., 227
Beverly Ford, 103, 106n, 107n,
234–35
Bier, C. C., 164
Big Black River, 413
Blackburn's Ford, 25–27, 32n, 33,
68
Blackburn's Ford, battle of, 25–32

Blackburn, Joseph C. S., 267, 271
Blair, Thomas McM., 414
Blake, William, 215, 222
Blakeley River, 415
Blakely, Andy, 397
Blakemore, William T., 323
Blakey's Mill Pond, 79–80
Blount, Joseph G., 208, 261
Blow's Mills, Va., 78
Bolling, Lt., 306
Bondurant, J. W., 208
Bonham, Milledge L., 30, 36
Boonesboro, Md., 134–36, 140n,
166
Booth, Capt., 5n, 6n
Booth, George W., 430
Boreman fuse, 56
Boston Club, 204
Bowles, James W., 268
Boyce, Robert, 100, 146, 148n,
149n
Boyd, Belle, 170, 239
Bozant, John, 437
Bradford, W. A., 267
Bradford, William D., 208
Bradley, John M., 213, 219n
Bragg, Braxton, 170, 266, 269,
272–73, 274, 278–79, 278n,
282, 285, 289–92, 301–302,
340n, 405, 411–14
Branch, Lawrence O'B., 153
Brander, T. O., 367n, 394
Brandy Station, 102
Brandy Station, battle of, 234–35
Brannan, John M., 284
Braxton, Carter M., 154, 208
Brazelman, B. L., 19, 165, 344n

Breckinridge, John C., 273–74, 282, 328, 408, 413–14, 419
Brewer, Isaac W. "Ike," 28, 76, 105, 106n, 107n, 201, 233n
Brinsmade, A. A., 222
Bristol, Tenn., 301–302, 306–307
Britton, John D., 56n, 123, 138, 154, 156, 162, 169
Brochard, Leon, 414
Brockenbrough, J. B., 142, 153
Brooks, James V., 209
Brother Jonathan, 135–36
Brown, C. H. C., 123, 138, 153, 185, 253, 322, 327, 344n, 389n, 427
Brown, J. Thompson, Jr., 209, 213, 228, 232n, 233n, 234n
Brown, James S., 100, 208
Brown, Robert, 215
Brown, T. Fred, 391
Brownlow, William G., 13
Bruce, W. L., 410–11
Buchanan, Franklin, 203
Buchanan, Robert C., 121n
Buckland Mills, Va., 112n
Buckner, Simon B., 203, 265–67, 276, 279, 293
Buell, Don Carlos, 170
Buhoup, I. W., 72n
Bull Run, 15, 24, 27, 29, 34, 41 (map), 42, 114, 121, 121n, 127
Bull Run, battle of, iii, 33–46, 68, 91, 385
Bullock, Robert, 268
Bunker Hill, Va., 239, 259
Burgess's Mill, 361–63
Burkesville, Va., 376

Burnham, Col., 220
Burnham, Hiram, 226
Burns, James, 129n
Burnside, Ambrose E., 137n, 154, 155n, 158, 172, 174, 176, 181, 194–96, 265, 288, 302
Burt, E. R., 61
Butler, Benjamin F., 78, 203, 310, 312, 318
Butler, Matthew C., 234
Buzzard's Roost, Ga., engagement at, 414
Byrne, Edward P., 408
Byrnes, James, 411

Cabell, Henry C., 208, 232n, 244, 249n, 261–62
Cabell, William L., 65, 70
Calhoun, Ga., 414
Callahan, J., 227
Cameron, Mr., 348
Cameron, Pvt., 311, 332
Cammack, Mr., 54
Camp Beauregard, 14
Camp Benjamin, 58
Camp Hollins, 59, 71
Camp Longstreet, 95, 99
Camp Louisiana, 50 (illus.)
Camp Orleans, 53
Campbell, James C., 222–23
Campbell, M., 411
"The Cannoneer," 433
Capitol Prison, 229
Carey, Constance, 60, 91, 295, 298
Carey, Hettie, 60, 295
Carey, Jennie, 60, 295
Carl, F. A., 11

Carlin, William P., 280n

Carlton, Caleb, 283

Carlton, Henry H., 261

Carpenter, Joseph, 142, 208

Carrington, James McD., 208

Carroll, Samuel S., 187

Carson, Mr., 169

Carson, Josie, 239

Carson, Julia, 169

Carter, Thomas H., 208, 232n

Casey, Silas, 82, 84

Cash, E. B. C., 39

Caskie, William H., 142, 208, 261

Cassville, Ga., 414

Caulfield, Ignatius, 401

Cedar Mountain, battle at, 99, 166

Cedar Run, engagement at, 172

Cemetery Hill, 244, 250, 253

Cenas, Hilary, 397

Centreville, Va., iii, 32n, 33, 41
(map), 42–44, 53, 56, 59–61,
66–67, 75, 125, 273, 334

Chalaron, J. Adolphe, 274, 401,
408, 413, 421, 431

Chamberlayne, John H., 347,
359–60, 378

Chambers, George, 317, 319

Chambers, Hubert, 18, 68

Chambers, W., 17, 109n

Chambersburg, Pa., 242, 248

Chancellorsville, battle of, 211–29

Chancellorsville, Va., 174, 211–12,
222

Chantilly, Va., 127

Chapman, George H., 121n

Chapman, W. H., 100, 103–104,
106n, 107n, 109n, 116

Charleston, S.C., 70, 293–94, 366

Charleston, Tenn., 269

Charlestown, Va., 170

Chattahoochie River, 415

Chattanooga, Tenn., 266, 269,
281, 288–89, 294, 302, 412,
414

Chase, Salmon P., 335

Chesnut, James, 52, 291

Chester Gap, 236

Chesterfield Courthouse, Va., 313

Chew, R. V., 367n

Chickahominy River, 79–80, 82,
84–85, 88, 327–28, 392

Chickamauga, battle of, 266–88,
292, 298, 301, 310, 323, 355,
414, 419

Chickamauga Creek, 271, 275–78,
285, 288

Chilton, Robert H., 156n, 207,
234n

Chinn House, 124

Chisholm, A. R., 38, 40, 52, 294,
407

Choppin, Samuel, 52

Christ Church, New Orleans, 8–9

Clark County, Va., 238

Clay, Mrs. Clement C., 298

Clayton, John, 411

Clayton, W. W., 411

Clear Creek, Miss., 411–12

Cleveland, J. B., 124

Clingman, Thomas L., 313,
315–16, 318

Clitz, Henry B., 97

Cloney, M. W., 426

Clopton, Lt., 316

Coalter's Battery, 208
Cobb, Howell, 143
Cobb, Robert, 414
Cobb, Thomas R. R., 179, 184–85, 188, 193
Cocke, Philip St. George, 36
Cohorn mortars, 343, 349, 352
Cold Harbor, battle of, 327–28
Coldstream Guards, 194, 303
Coleman, H. D., 227
Collins, William A., 105
Colquitt, Alfred H., 144, 313, 315
Colston, Fred M., v, 118
Columbia, S.C., 340
Columbia, Tenn., 415
Columbus, Miss., 420
Condon, Edward, 320
Connecticut troops: 7th Infantry, 324; 10th Infantry, 324
Connelly, John, 12
Cooke, John Esten, 249n
Cooke, John R., 146, 148n, 188
Cooper, Jennie, 299
Cooper, Samuel, 299
Coppens, G. A. G., 83
Corinth, Miss., 405, 411–12
Corley, James L., 377
Corpus Christi, Tex., 2
Corse, Montgomery D., 115, 312, 315–16
"Cosette," 296–97
Coste, A. F., 18
Couch, Darius N., 137n
Coward, A., 42
Cox, Capt., 229
Cox, Jacob D., 137n
Coyle, W. G., 108n, 389n

The Crater, battle of, 340–47
Crenshaw Mills, 54
Crenshaw, William G., 154, 208
Crilly, James, 108n, 320
Crisp, W. H., 72
Crittenden, Thomas L., 273, 285
Cross Keys, battle of, 363
Crump, G. W., 72n
Crutcher, George L., 35
Crutchfield, Edward, 267
Crutchfield, V., 234n
Cub Run, 43
Cullen, J. S. D., 31, 51, 76, 80, 95, 96, 195, 197, 256, 306, 328, 338, 379–80, 393
Culpeper Courthouse, Va., 170, 233, 235n, 236
Cumberland Courthouse, 393
Cumberland Gap, 413
Custer, George A., 384
Cutshaw, Wilfred E., 352n, 367n
Cutts, A. S., 209, 232n
Cutts, James M., 196

Daigle, Louis D. , 414
Dales, I. H., 72
Dallas, Ga., battle at, 414
Dalton, Ga., 414–15,
Dance, Willis J., 209, 367n
Danville, Va., 376
Davidson, Greenlee, 208, 347
Davidson, John M., 410–11
Davis, Jefferson, 14, 15n, 41, 59, 94–95, 229, 264, 291–92, 307, 314, 318, 329, 351, 365–66, 374, 389n, 396–97
Davis, Jefferson, Jr., 364

Davis, Jefferson C., 280n
Davis, Joseph R., 364
Davis, R. N., 389n
Davis, Samuel, 411
Davis, Varina H., 15n, 204
Davis, W. W., 124
Dearie, J. W., 31
Dearing, James, 16, 34, 37, 41, 73, 76, 83, 208, 232n, 249n, 261–62, 330, 376
Deas, George, 177, 183, 197
Deas, Zachariah C., 286
DeBlanc, O. N., 108n
Degrange, J. H., 429
Delery, Armant, 415
Del'Isle, V. G., 72n
Dement, William F., 208
Demeritt, John W., 410
Dempsey, James W., 164
DeRussey, George B., 123, 138, 154, 216–17, 227, 427
DeSaussure, William D., 153
Deslonde, E. A., 294
Dick, Benjamin, 227
Dickenson, Crispin, 347, 368
Dinwiddie Courthouse, 358, 392
Dooley, William, 411
Doswell, Temple, 176
Doubleday, Abner, 137n, 213, 220, 249n
Drainsville, Va., 68
Drayton, Thomas F., 103, 112, 115, 152–54
Drew, E. S., 18, 76, 158, 344n
Drewry's Bluff, battle of, 312–20, 323, 325n, 349, 355
Drewry's Bluff, Va., 80, 327

Dublin, Va., 302
Dug Gap, 272
Duggan, Joseph H., 430
Duggan, Martin F., 414
Duggan, Pvt., 311
Duncan, James H., 371
Dunn, Andrew, 332–33, 338, 355
Dunn, Mrs., 310
Dupuy, C. L. C., 18–19, 109n, 164, 309, 429–30
Dyer, Pvt., 289

Early, Jubal A., 27, 30, 34, 36, 39, 143, 157, 213, 213n, 219, 221–22, 224, 230, 237n, 335–38, 366
Eddins, John, 109n
Edward's Ferry, Va., 61
Egypt, 183n
Elliott, Stephen, Jr., 345
Ellis, W. H., 28, 108n, 147, 164, 241, 426
El Mahdi, 183n
El Mejid, battle of, 183n
Elzey, Arnold, 39
Eshleman, Benjamin F., 5, 13, 26–28, 57n, 71, 73, 76, 91, 100, 120, 123–24, 138, 151–54, 164, 168, 178, 185, 191, 198, 209, 232, 232n, 233n, 236n, 248, 256, 308–309, 311, 314–16, 328, 333, 344n, 348, 369, 431
Eshman, John, 227
Etowah River, 414
Eubank, John L., 209, 260
Eustis, Henry L., 220

Evans, Nathan G., 34–35, 51, 61,
    97, 104, 109n, 115, 118, 120
Everett, C. A., 190, 227–28, 320
Exchange Hotel, Richmond, Va.,
    14
Exposition Building, St. Charles
    Street, New Orleans, 428
Ewell, Richard S., iii, 25, 30, 33,
    43, 141, 143, 232n, 236–37,
    237n, 239, 243–45

Fairfax, John W., 61, 76, 113,
    148, 195, 246
Fairfax Courthouse, Va., 16, 24,
    25, 43, 55, 58–60, 127
Fair Oaks, battle of. *See* Seven
    Pines
Falconer, W. R., 109n, 190
Falmouth, Va., 176, 211, 215, 229
Farmville, Va., 376–77
Farnsworth, Elon J., 254
Faulkes, John, 320
Faulkner, Col., 163
Fayetteville, N.C., 366
Fazende, P. O., 18, 253, 320
Fearn, Walker, 295
Featherstone, Winfield S., 61,
    112, 115
Fell, John, 109n
Fellowes, William, Jr., 28, 227,
    382, 394
Fenner, Frank, 429
Ferguson, Samuel W., 40, 52
Ferrero, Edward, 347
Field, Charles W., 307
Fifth Corps, 161n, 192, 193n,
    252n

Finegan, Joseph, 359
Finley, Jesse J., 268
Fisher, Col., 68
Fizer, John C., 217, 219n, 301
Florence, Ala., 415
Florence, Henry, 177–78, 190
Florence, J. E., 226n, 228
Florida troops: 6th Infantry, 268;
    7th Infantry, 268
Flotte, Honoré, 397n
Flower, Sam, 29, 53, 94, 128
Flowerree, Charles C., 326n
Ford, Robert "Bob," 289, 298,
    300, 308
Forrest, William, 319
Forsythe, John, 203
Fort Clifton, 312
Fort Delaware, 229, 295
Fort Mahone, 330
Fort Niagara, 270
Fort Owen, 368
Fortress Monroe, 396
Fort Sedgwick, 330
Fort Stevens, 313, 316, 318–19
Fort Sumpter, 294
Fourshee, F. P., 108n
Franco–Prussian War, 183
François, 21, 22
Frank, Otto, 90, 227
Franklin, battle of, 415
Franklin, William B., 137n, 145
"Frank the Bugler," 333
Fraser, Jim, 303
Fraser, John C., 261
Frazer, Bob, 415
Frederick, Md., 133, 134n, 136,
    140, 140n

Fredericksburg, battle of, 174–99, 202, 212 (map)

Fredericksburg, Va., 77, 172, 174, 176, 179, 184, 195, 197, 198n, 200, 210–13, 223, 227, 230, 233–34, 237n

Fremantle, Arthur J. L., 244, 246, 256, 256n

French, William H., 137n, 144–45, 187

Friend, Mr., 322

Friend, Pvt., 311

Front Royal, Va., 237

Fry, Charles W., 208

Fulkerson, J. Abraham, 268

Gaines, Ned, 233

Gaines Mill, battle of, 140n

Gainesville, Va., 113–15, 119, 123

Galbraith, John M., 17, 28, 108n, 109n, 123, 138, 154, 185, 191, 227–28, 316–17, 319

Garber, Asher W., 208

Garden, H. R., 152–54, 163, 208, 261

Garland, Samuel, Jr., 136, 144

Garnett, Dr., 328

Garnett, John J., 16, 27, 28, 33, 43, 57n, 58–59, 76, 103–104, 105n, 207, 232n, 259

Garnett, Richard B., 153, 164, 251

Geiger, H. G., 57n, 161

Georgetown, Tenn., 269

Georgia troops: Leyden's Battery, 268, 271; Macon Battery, 315–16; Milledge's Battery,

209; Read's Battery, 208, 310, 329; A Battery, Sumpter Artillery, 209; B Battery, Sumpter Artillery, 209; C Battery, Sumpter Artillery, 209; 1st Infantry, 112; 2d Infantry, 152; 8th Infantry, 66–67; 9th Infantry, 111; 15th Infantry, 152, 156n; 17th Infantry, 152; 20th Infantry, 152, 156n; 65th Infantry, 268; Colquitt's Brigade, 313

Georgiana, 396

Germantown, Va., 55, 125, 127

Gessner, George, 73, 320

Gest's Hill, 219

Getty, George W., 189

Gettysburg, battle of, 243–62, 294, 301

Gettysburg, Pa., 242, 244

Gibbon, John, 214, 221, 373

Gibbes, Wade H., 345

Gibson, Randall L., 415

Giffen, Adam, 177, 181

Giffen, William, 227

Giffen, William B., 410

Gillmore, Quincy A., 313

Gilman Family, 396

Glass's Mill, battle of, 414

Glenn, Lt. Col., 283

Goochland County, Va., 361, 377, 394

Goodwyn, I. McGavock, 72n, 73, 83

Gordon, John B., 27, 27n, 237n, 361–62, 382–84, 393

Gordon, Mrs. John B., 27n

Gordonsville, Va., 99, 310
Goree, Thomas J., 76, 278
Gracie, Archibald, Jr., 266, 268,
    274, 276, 279, 283–84, 290–91,
    315, 319, 325n, 349, 355–56
Graham, Charles K., 246
Grand Junction, Tenn., 405
Grandy, Charles R., 207
Granger, Gordon, 284–85
Grant, Ulysses S., 20, 327–29,
    337–38, 346, 369, 375–76,
    384–86, 390, 392
Graves, Rice E., Jr., 414, 418–19
Green, B. Hildreth, Jr., 408, 410
Greencastle, Pa., 240
Greene, George S., 137n
Greenman, I. N., 320
Greenville, Tenn., 306–307
Greenwood, Milo, 414
Greenwood, Pa., 242
Gregg, David McM., 378–79
Gregg, Maxcey, 153
Griffin, Capt. Charles, 40, 54
Griffin, Gen. Charles, 161n, 189,
    193n
Griffin, Thomas M., 213, 215
Grigsby, Andrew J., 143
Grimes, Mr., 129
Groveton, Va., 115–16, 121n, 123,
    139
Guillotte, A., 320
Guillotte, G., 320
Gunn, Lt., 306
Guss, W., 72n

Habersham, Lt., 217
Hagerstown, Md., 135, 239n, 240,
    257, 258n
Hagood, Johnson, 313, 315–16,
    318, 331
Hale, John P., 44
Hall, Boling, Jr., 268
Hall, Chaplain William A., 333,
    344n
Halleck, Henry W., 395–96
Hamilton, S. P., 208
Hamilton's Crossing, 211, 213,
    215, 219
Hampton, Wade, 37, 335
Hampton's Legion, 36
Hancock, E. C., 60
Hancock, Winfield S., 147n, 187,
    249n
Handy, John T., 108n, 227
Harby, J. R., 227
Hardaway, Robert A., 209
Hardee, William J., 407–408, 413,
    415
Hardie, W. T., 18, 28, 227, 253,
    427
Hare, Pvt., 311, 332
Harper's Ferry, Va., 135–36, 139,
    140n, 153, 155n, 162, 166–67,
    170, 355
Harper, William P., 94
Harpeth River, 413
Harris, Morgan E., 227, 336–37
Harris, Nathaniel H., 371
Harrison, Julian, 66
Harrison, Tenn., 269
Harrison, Thomas, 280n
Harrison Landing, Va., 329
Harrodsburg, Ky., 413
Hartnett, C. J., 410

Haskell, John C., 343, 349, 367n, 380, 383, 389, 390

Haskin, Joseph A., 5

Hatch, John P., 120n, 137n

Hatcher's Run, 330, 356, 362–63, 367

Havana, Cuba, 60n

Hawes, Samuel, 123–24, 138, 154, 344n

Hawkins, Hiram, 267

Haymarket, Va., 112n, 114

Hays, Harry T., 39, 53, 143, 215–16, 219, 221, 237, 237n, 363

Hazard, John G., 391

Hazel River, 108

Heckman, Charles A., 315, 319, 326

Heg, Hans C., 280n

Helm, Benjamin H., 273

Henry, M. W., 232n, 244, 249, 254, 261–62

Henry House hill, 121, 121n

Hero, Andrew, 42, 108n, 123, 138, 146, 162, 164, 169, 215n, 216, 233n, 309–10, 313, 323, 344n, 369, 426, 428–29, 431

Heth, Henry, 243–44, 248, 250, 329, 347

Hewitt, Capt., 303, 305

Hews, Edson L., 400–401, 411

Heyward, Capt., 52

Hiatt, Sgt., 284–85, 291–92

Hicks Pasha, 183

Higgins, S., 410

Hill, A. P., 76, 86–87, 135–37, 137n, 139, 142, 152–55, 157,

161–64, 166–67, 184, 232n, 234, 243–44, 246, 333, 345, 347, 351, 352–53, 358, 360, 373

Hill, D. H., 87, 135–37, 137n, 138–39, 141–42, 144–45, 148, 157, 166, 273, 276, 278, 320, 322

Hilliard, Henry W., 268

Hindman, Thomas C., 271, 273, 279, 279n, 280, 282

Hinson's Mill, Va., 110

Hoch, John, 227

Hodgson, W. Irving, 274, 399, 401–403, 405–10, 412

Hoke, Robert F., 315–16, 322, 331

Holder, William D., 213, 219n

Holmes, Curtis, 411

Holmes, John, Jr., 156, 162, 169, 426

Holmes, Theophilus H., 36

Holt, John H., 268

Hood, J. S., 320

Hood, John B., 112, 115, 118, 120, 136, 137n, 141–43, 157, 232n, 239n, 243, 245, 254, 277–78, 279n, 280, 310, 338, 415, 420

Hooker, Joseph, 137n, 142, 148, 149, 155n, 193n, 211, 220, 222, 224, 224n, 227–28, 233–34

Hoop, Maj., 410

Hopewell Gap, Va., 112, 112n

Hopkins, Octave, 410

Horseshoe Ridge, 280, 282–85, 291

Howard, Oliver O., 187

Howe, Albion P., 214
Howlett Battery, 323–24, 327
Huger, Frank, 338, 346, 349, 367n
Hugo, Victor, 297
Humphreys, Andrew A., 192, 193n
Humphreys, Benjamin G., 213
Hunt, Henry J., 168
Hunton, Eppa, 61, 115
Hupp, Abraham, 209
Hurt, J. F., 367n
Hyman, T. McC., 430

Imboden, John D., 34, 256–57
Ingraham, Jim, 22
Inkerman, battle of, 305
Ira Smith and Co., 54
Isaacson, Harry M., 4, 15, 57n,
    58, 430
Ives, Mrs., 298

Jackson, John J., 405
Jackson, Miss., battle of, 413–14,
    418
Jackson, Thomas J., 33, 34,
    36–37, 41, 86, 94, 99, 101,
    110, 114–20, 120n, 122, 125,
    127, 129n, 131, 132, 135, 137,
    137n, 139, 140n, 141–42, 144,
    148–49, 155n, 157, 166, 170n,
    173, 175, 184, 210, 224, 229
Jacob, 348, 350, 355, 365
James, Theodore A., 399
James River, 77–78, 80, 89, 93–96,
    98, 310, 322–23, 328–29, 336,
    394
Janin, Eugene, 89, 128,
    128n–129n

Janin, Louis, 128n
Jasper, Sgt., 319
Jeffersonton, Va., 109
Jenifer, Walter H., 62
Jenkins, Micah, 115, 152–53
Johns, Thomas D., 220, 226
Johnsen, Charles G., 414, 421
Johnson, Andrew, 307
Johnson, Bushrod R., 276–78,
    279n, 280, 282, 315–16, 318,
    322–24, 342, 347, 384–85
Johnson, "Capt. Shabrack," 51
Johnson, Edward, 237n, 243
Johnson, Marmaduke, 209, 367n
Johnson, P. P., 367n
Johnson, T. K., 150
Johnston, Harris H., 267, 271,
    291
Johnston, Joseph E., 33, 36, 39,
    47n, 49, 53n, 60, 66, 74, 80,
    82–83, 83n, 305, 338, 375,
    390n, 413–15, 420–21
Johnston, Samuel R., 257
Johnston, William Preston, v,
    263–65, 291, 318, 389
Jones, Col., 156
Jones, David R., iii, 30, 33, 42,
    79, 101, 104, 105n, 112, 115,
    118n, 120, 124–25, 136, 138,
    151–53, 155n, 157–58, 164
Jones, Hilary P., 208, 232n, 237n
Jones, John R., 141–42
Jones, Sam, 66–67, 266, 302–303
Jonesboro, battle of, 415
Jordan, Thomas, 51, 71
Jordan, Tyler C., 192, 209, 260
Joubert, Eugene, 108n

Judd, G. M., 17,

Kearney, J. Watts, 17, 28, 407
Kearney, Philip, 128
Keedyville, Md., 138n
Kelly, Daniel, 430
Kelly, John H., 267–68, 275–76, 279, 283
Kemper, Del, 208
Kemper, James L., 27, 39, 115, 120, 126, 152–53, 251, 315, 325
Kennedy, James, 227
Kenner, Dick, 22
Kennesaw Mountain, battle of, 414
Kentucky Campaign, 413–14
Kentucky troops: Byrne's Battery, 408; 2d Cavalry (dismounted), 268; 5th Infantry, 267–68
Kershaw, Joseph B., 30, 39, 143, 188, 193, 278, 279n, 280, 282, 290, 306, 310
Kerwin, Thomas, 108n
Ketchum, Dr., 203
Kevan, Pvt., 311, 332
Kilpatrick, D. M., 427
Kilpatrick, H. Judson, 258n
Kimball, Capt., 229
King, J. Floyd, 302, 305, 328, 346, 368, 394
King, Rufus, 112n, 118n, 120n
Kingsbury, Henry W., 158
Kirk, Barton, 227
Kirkpatrick, Thomas J., 209, 367n
Knight, A. G., 433–34
Knight, John, 109n
Knoxville–East Tennessee, cam-

paign of, 288–301
Knoxville, Tenn., 265, 288, 413
Koss, H., 109n
Kremelberg, F., 108n, 345
Krumbhaar, W. B., 426
Kursheedt, E. I., 17, 130, 134, 189, 191, 308–309, 314, 316, 340, 344n, 361, 426–27

"Lady of Lyons," 177
Lafaye, John A., 397n
Lafayette, Ga., 272–73, 275
Laibold, Bernard, 280n
Lambert, Mr., 6
Lamothe, Alfred, 397
Landry, Ernest, 397n
Landry, Numa, 397n
Landry, R. Prosper, 104, 106n, 107n, 109n, 116, 191
Lane, James H., 371
Lane, John, 209, 367n
Lane, Mr., 236
Lane, P. C., 11
Langhorne, Lt., 306
Lanier, Mr., 54
Lapham, M. J., 320
Latham, J. Grey, 34, 51, 208, 261
Latimer, Joseph W., 208
Latrobe, Osmun, 190–91, 191n, 250, 278–79, 281–82, 289–90, 305, 338, 384, 393, 397
Lauman, Jacob G., 418
Laurel Brigade, 379
Lawley, Francis C., 244, 256, 289, 303
Lawton, Alexander R., 141–43
Lay, George, 320–21

Lazzare, T. J., 389n
Leacock, Dr., 9
Leake, Capt., 100, 110n
Leary, John, 410
Lee, Capt., 125
Lee, Fitzhugh, v, 66, 102, 136,
    229–30, 235, 327, 335, 382
Lee, George Washinton Custis
    "Custis," 329, 376, 396
Lee, Robert Edward, iv, 14,
    79–80, 80n, 84–87, 94, 98–99,
    110–11, 114, 117, 118n, 122,
    126–28, 130, 132–33,
    132n–33n, 136, 136n, 137,
    137n, 139–40, 140n, 141,
    149–52, 156–57, 158n, 166,
    169n, 170n, 172, 175, 180–81,
    189, 194–95, 199, 205, 210–11,
    222–24, 226–27, 234n, 240–41,
    241n, 242, 244, 246, 252n,
    256–58, 299, 308, 310, 327–28,
    335–36, 339n, 346–47, 356,
    366–67, 367n, 368–69, 373–76,
    379, 382–88, 391–93, 396
Lee's Hill, 212, 212n, 213, 215–16,
    215n, 219n, 220
Lee, Stephen D., 84, 95, 105,
    110n, 119
Lee, William H. F. "Rooney," 328,
    367
Lee and Gordon's Mill, 276–78
Leefe, Augustus "Gus," 320, 430
Leesburg, Va., 61, 62
LeFavour, Heber, 283
Leftwitch, Clark, 35
Légare, Oscar, 415
Legier, Octave, 397n

Letcher, John, 61
Leverich, Abram I., 274, 415, 421
Levi, Horace J., 429
Levy, S., 108n
Lewinsville, Va., 54, 55n
Lewis, C. C., 33, 57n, 58
Lewis, J. R. C., 209
Lewis, John W., 207
Lewis, L. L., 223, 227
Leyden, Maj., 302
Libby Prison, 78, 96
Liddell, St. John R., 414, 420
Lightfoot, Lt. Col., 315
Lilly, J. F., 389n
Lincoln, Abraham, 337, 366
Literary and Dramatic Associa-
    tion, Battalion Washington Ar-
    tillery, 171, 177
Little Falls, Va., 56
Logan, John, 394
Logan, Mr., 361, 377, 394
Long, Patrick, 410
Long Bridge, Va., 328
Longstreet, James, iii, 27, 30, 33,
    43, 61n, 66, 74, 78–79, 82, 85,
    85n, 86–89, 88n–89n, 90, 93,
    95, 99, 101–103, 105n, 112n,
    113–14, 116–19, 118n, 120,
    122–23, 126–28, 131, 136, 137,
    137n, 138–39, 140n, 141–42,
    146–48, 148n, 155n, 157–59,
    162, 165n, 166, 169–70, 172n,
    173, 173n, 175–76, 178n,
    179n, 180n, 182n, 184, 189,
    193–94, 197, 197n, 200, 205,
    212, 232–33, 232n, 238,
    244–51, 252n, 255–56, 260,

264, 277–79, 279n, 280–82, 284, 286, 288–90, 301–302, 305, 308, 310, 328–29, 332, 338, 339n–42n, 355, 375, 376–77, 382–85, 393

Lonsdale, H. H., 411

Lookout Mountain, 271, 290

Loudon, Tenn., 266, 269

Louisa Courthouse, 77

Louise, 62

Louisiana troops: Battalion Washington Artillery of New Orleans, iv, 1–3, 7, 12, 14n, 30, 90–93, 338n–44n, 370, 389; Louisiana Guard Battery, 208, 389n; Madison Battery, 152, 192, 209; Chasseurs à Pied, 3, 58, 60, 62, 69, 72, 72n, 82–83; Crescent Rifles, 3; Donaldsonville Artillery, 100, 104, 116, 186, 191, 193, 207, 389; 1st Zouave Battalion, 83; 2d Infantry Battalion (Louisiana Tigers), 34, 36, 42, 64; Louisiana Grays, 3; Louisiana Guards, 3; Orleans Cadets, 3; Sarsfield Rifles, 3; 6th Infantry, 27; 7th Infantry, 27, 29, 39, 42, 53, 94; 10th Infantry, 89, 94, 129n; 15th Infantry, 380; 17th Infantry; 20th Infantry, 406; Crescent Infantry Regiment, 407; Washington Regiment, 1–2; Louisiana Brigade, 362

Lovell, Joe, 204

Lovell, Mansfield, 403

Lovettsville, Md., 140n

Lusk, John A. M., 209

Lutman, T. J., 226, 228

Lynch, M. F., 108n

Lynchburg, Va., 12–13, 380, 390n, 393

Lytle, Bob, 287

Lytle, William H., 280, 280n, 286–87

McCarthy, Edward S., 208, 261

McCartney, J. H., 156

McClellan, George B., 55, 59, 63, 74–75, 77–78, 80–81, 85–88, 94–99, 136, 136n, 137n, 139–40, 140n, 155n, 158n, 166, 168, 170, 172

McCook, Alexander McD., 280n, 285

McCormack, James, 227

McCullough, Mr., 348

McDonald, O., 108n

McDonald, R. G., 320, 389n

McDowell, Irvin, iii, iv, 32n

McElroy, Frank, 108n, 123, 133, 138, 147, 154, 164, 185, 351, 368, 371–73, 426

McElroy, William, 347

McGaughey, John R., 17, 28, 317

McGregor, Capt., 367n

McGregor, William, 414

McGuire, Dr., 135

McIlhenny, Ned, 415

McIntosh, D. G., 152–53, 155n, 208, 209, 232n, 367n, 368, 378, 382, 388

McKnight, Milton, 411

McLaws, Lafayette, 137n, 140n, 142, 155n, 166, 179, 193, 199, 224, 232n, 239n, 243
McLean, Maj., 385
McLean's Ford, 24–25, 33, 42
McLemore's Cove, 271–72
McMahon, John J., 268
McMullan, J. B., 389
McNeil, George, 108n
Macoin, Edgard, 72n, 73, 83
Macon, Miles C., 208, 261, 313
McPherson, S. J., 57n
McRae, Duncan K., 144
McRay, W. A., 389n
Macready, L., 410
Madden, H., 320
Magruder, John B., 78, 89, 270
Mahone, William, 329, 331, 333, 337, 341, 344
Maine troops: 4th Infantry, 44; 6th Infantry, 226; 8th Infantry, 326n
Mains, W., 345
Mallard, E. A., 320
Malvern Hill, 97, 329
Malvern Hill, battle of, 89–93
Manassas, first battle of, 22, 33–46
Manassas, second battle of, 114–25, 116 (map)
Manassas, Va., 15, 22, 33, 33n, 41 (map), 44, 74, 110, 112n, 114, 118, 122, 125
Manassas Club, Mobile, 203–204
Manly, Basil C., 208, 261, 367n
Manning, John L., 52, 76, 278
Manning, P. T., 384
Mansfield, Joseph K. F., 137n, 142, 148–49
Many, R. P. "Bob," 73, 206, 223
Mardi Gras, 71
Marshall, Charles, 140n, 321–22, 382, 385–86
Marshall, R. T., 109n
Martin, Daniel, 109n
Martin, James G., 320
Martin, S. Taylor, 319
Martin, William, 320
Martinsburg, Md., 140n, 163, 168, 170n, 239–40, 336
Marye's Hill, 175, 177–81, 184–85, 188, 192–97, 196n, 203, 212–14, 213n, 216–18, 219n, 220–23, 220n, 226–29, 337
Maryland Club, Baltimore, 396
Maryland troops: 1st Artillery Company, 84, 208
Mason, Charles, 101–102
Massachusetts troops: 5th Infantry, 220; 7th Infantry, 220; 15th Infantry, 144n; 18th Infantry, 161n; 20th Infantry, 144n; 22d Infantry, 161n; 23d Infantry, 325n; 25th Infantry, 326; 27th Infantry, 325n
Massie, John L., 209
Mathis, Martin, 414
Maurin, Victor, 100, 106, 110n, 186, 191, 191n, 207
Maury, Thomas F., 51, 76, 81, 305–306
Maximilian, Emperor, 295, 391
Maxwell, J. Troup, 268
Maxwell, Robert, 108n

May, Eugene, 427, 430

Meade, George G., 137n, 252n, 255, 257–58, 391–92

Meagher, Thomas F., 187, 195

Mechanicsville, Va., 85

Meek, George, 171

Metarie Cemetery, New Orleans, 427

Mexico, 295

Michel, P. A. J., 156

Michigan troops: 4th Infantry, 161n; 22d Infantry, 283

Micon, A., 227

Middleburg, Md., 140n

Middleton, John J., Jr., 107n

Miles, William Porcher, 52

Milledge, John, Jr., 209

Miller, Benjamin R., 415

Miller, Capt., 83

Miller, Merritt B. "Buck," 5, 25, 33, 42, 57n, 73, 76–77, 80, 83, 91, 100, 103–105, 106n–108n, 116, 123, 138, 146–47, 148n, 149n, 154, 162, 164, 165n, 178, 185, 188, 198, 209, 212, 215, 215n, 217, 247, 255, 261, 309, 390n, 426, 431

Millwood, Va., 238

Milroy, Robert H., 237n

Mine Run, 173

Missionary Ridge, 289, 291, 293, 302

Missionary Ridge, battle of, 414, 424

Mississippi troops: Confederate Guards Battery (Bradford's), 208; Brown Rifles, 215; 6th In-
fantry, 410; 12th Infantry, 206, 371; 13th Infantry, 61, 213–14, 217, 219n, 220n, 221; 16th Infantry, 206, 371; 17th Infantry, 61, 213–14, 217, 219n, 220n, 221; 18th Infantry, 61, 84–85, 213–15, 217–18, 219n, 222, 226, 228–29; 19th Infantry, 371; 21st Infantry, 213–14, 217–18, 219n, 226, 231; 48th Infantry, 371

Mitchell, Mr., 181

Mitchell, Sam, 76

Mitchell's Ford, Va., 15, 33

Mobile, Ala., 203, 205, 296, 413, 415, 420

Model Farm, Va., 308–309

Monocacy Bridge, 337

Monocacy River, 131, 140n

Monterey, 397

Montgomery, Ala., 204

Montgomery, L. M. "Bliff'kins," 19–20, 26, 42, 73, 82–83, 109n, 117, 130, 165

Moody, George W., 152, 192, 209, 260

Moody, Young M., 268

Moore, Patrick T., 30, 64–65, 76, 81, 177

Moore, Robert H., 268

Moore, Thomas O., 400, 402

Morel, Fred, 414

Morell, George W., 120n, 137n, 161n, 162

Morgan, G. T., 53

Morgan, Peter K., 304

Morgan, Richard C. "Dick," 162
Morgan's Ford, 238
Morgan, Tom, 128
Morris, Orderly, 113
Morris Island, S.C., 294
Moseley, E. F., 353
Mount, M., 109n, 173
Morristown, Tenn., 13, 305
Munfordville, capture of, 413
Munson's Hill, Va., 54, 54n, 55
Muntinger, J., 162, 169
Murfreesboro, battle of, 413, 419
Muse, George W., 26, 28
Myers, Joseph, 227, 320, 330
Myers, Willie, 303

Nashville, battle of, 415, 420
Nassau, 183
Negley, James S., 271, 273
Negro cooks and servants, 21–22, 31
Negro troops, 345, 366
Nelson, William, 209, 232n, 367n
New, John, 53
New Hope Church, battle of, 414
New Jersey troops: 9th Infantry, 325n
New Market, Va., 41 (map), 305
New Orleans, La., 2–3, 5–6, 21, 51, 59, 60n, 71, 77, 202–203, 275, 302, 333, 395, 397, 400, 403, 418, 424, 430
New Orleans *Picayune*, 397
New Store, Va., 380
Newton, Frank, 213–14, 220–21
New York, 96
New York Hotel, 396

New York troops: 3d Artillery, 324; 5th Infantry (Zouaves), 120, 121n, 127; 11th Infantry (Fire Zouaves), 40; 12th Infantry, 32n; 14th Infantry, 40; 36th Infantry, 220; 79th Infantry (Highlanders), 40; 98th Infantry, 326n; 112th Infantry, 326n; Irish Brigade, 187, 196, 196n, 197n
Ninth Corps, 154, 155n
Noble, W. P., 227
Norcom, A., 320
Norcom, Joe, 33, 57n, 77, 123, 125, 138, 178, 185, 198, 216, 233, 247, 261–62, 310, 313, 323, 344, 381, 390, 431
Norment, W. T., 17, 320
North Carolina troops: Manley's Battery, 208; Rowan Battery, 116, 208; 5th Infantry, 144; 13th Infantry, 145; 14th Infantry, 145; 25th Infantry, 187–88; 27th Infantry, 145–46, 148n; 31st Infantry, 311; 58th Infantry, 268
Norvell, Lt., 306
Nottaway River, 358
Nugent, Robert, 196

O'Brien, Emile J., 430
O'Donnell, John, 410
O'Neill, M., 397
Observation balloon (Federal), 56
Occoquan Creek, Va., 17
Ohio troops: 21st Infantry, 283; 120th Infantry, 156

Okalona, Miss., 412
Opequan Creek, 163
Orange Courthouse, 75–76, 99,
    173, 260, 266
Ord, Edward O. C., 386
Oriental Saloon, Richmond,
    303–304
Otis, John L., 324
Overall's Creek, engagement at,
    415
Oviatt, Silas M., 430
Owen, Edward "Ned," 17, 28, 35,
    36, 57n, 76, 84–85, 109n, 116,
    123, 125, 138, 156, 162, 169,
    204, 223, 227–29, 295, 308–14,
    316, 317, 319, 324, 349, 361,
    390, 394, 431
Owen, William M., 107n, 126, 150,
    164, 198, 219n, 230, 255, 263,
    267, 270, 281, 290n, 291, 300,
    344n, 346, 367n, 390, 394,
    426–28

Page, B. C. M., 208
Page, T. Jefferson, 209
Palfrey, E. A., 7
Palfrey, F. W., 144
Palfrey, William, 427
Palmer, Dr. Benjamin M., 11
Palmer, John B., 268
Palmer, William T., 76
Parker, W. W., 209, 260
Parson, L., 183
Patrick, Marsena R., 229
Patterson, George M., 209
Patton, Capt., 112
Payne, E. C., 35

Payne, John N., 17, 28, 183, 192,
    426
Peachtree Creek, battle of, 415
Peavine Church, 271–72, 275
Peck, O. F., 426
Peck, William R., 362
Pegram, Hettie Carey, 362
Pegram, John, 362
Pegram, William J., 154, 208,
    330, 342, 367n
Pelham, John, 66, 95, 235, 235n
Pemberton, John C., 20,
Pence, Wesley, 109n
Pender, William Dorsey, 153, 164
Pendleton, D. D., 346
Pendleton, Edmund, 380, 390
Pendleton, William N., 36, 162,
    210–11, 215, 215n, 219,
    221–22, 233, 258n–59n
Penn, Davidson B., 53, 128
Pennsylvania troops: 66th In-
    fantry, 220; 118th Infantry,
    161n, 163n
Pensacola, Fla., 50
Percy, Charlie, 415
Perry, W. F., 17, 190
Perryville, battle of, 413
Petersburg, Va., 308–12, 320,
    322, 324, 329–330, 337, 354,
    358–59, 366, 372–73, 392, 394
Pettigrew, James J., 233n, 250, 259
Pettis, P. W., 108n
Peychaud, C., 227, 317, 319
Peychaud, Edward, 320
Peyton, H. E., 51
Phelps, N. B. "Byron," 227, 317,
    317n, 320

Phifer, Lt., 8
Philadelphia, Pa., 427
Phillips, Capt., 194, 256
Pickett, George E., 83, 115, 123–24, 179, 195, 197, 232n, 239n, 248, 250–52, 252n, 254, 310, 368–69, 384–85
Pierson, Jerry G., 400
Pigeon Mountain, 271–72
Pine Mountain, Ga., 414
Pizzini's ice cream, 48–49
Poague, William T., 141–142, 209
Polk, Leonidas, 272–273, 276, 278–79, 278n
Pond, Preston, Jr., 407–408
Poolsville, Md., 338
Pope, John, 99, 102, 108, 110, 114, 122, 127, 139, 172, 242
Porter, Fitz John, 118n, 120n, 137n, 161n
Potomac River, 134, 137, 141n, 149, 153, 157, 160–61n, 166, 170, 237n, 256, 258, 258n, 338
Potter, Robert B., 347
Potts, Pvt., 311
Powell, T. N., 129n
Prados, John B., 401
Prentiss, S. S., 129
Preston, Edward "Ned," 267, 271, 292
Preston, John S., 52
Preston, William, 263–71, 273–77, 279n, 280, 282–84, 286–87, 290n, 291–93, 295, 300–301, 307
Pryor, Roger A., 112, 115

"Quaker guns," 59, 75

Raccoon Ford, 232–33
Raine, Charles J., 142, 208
Ramsey, Douglas, 41
Randolph, William A., 173, 309, 316, 344n
Ransom, Robert, Jr., 179, 180n, 187, 193, 196n, 198n, 313, 315, 326n, 327–29
Rapidan River, 100, 173–74
Rappahannock River, 103, 106n, 107n, 108, 110, 166, 175, 211, 224–25, 224n, 227–28, 233–34
Rappahannock Station, artillery engagement at, 102–106, 202
"The Raven," 171
Read, Theodore, 376–77
Reams Station, battle of, 351
Reddington, J., 109n
Reid, John W., 413
Reilly, James, 116, 138, 141, 154, 160, 208, 261
René, Charles M., 72n
Resaca, battle of, 414
Reynolds, Joshua O., 38
Rhett, Thomas G., 49, 66, 70, 209, 260
Rhode Island troops: 2d Infantry, 84, 93, 162
Riceville, Tenn., 269
Richards, J. S., 430
Richardson, Charles, 207
Richardson, John B., 27, 28, 34–36, 57n, 91, 100, 120, 123–24, 126, 138, 151–53, 155n, 156n, 164, 179, 209,

211, 218, 219n, 261, 310, 323, 427, 431

Richardson, Israel B., 137n, 144–45, 147n

Richmond, Va., 13, 14, 16, 48, 50, 77–79, 84–85, 95, 97–99, 102, 135, 140n, 166, 168, 175, 178, 205, 229, 258, 264, 277, 290–91, 293–98, 300, 303, 308, 312–14, 318, 324, 327, 330, 351, 354, 356–57, 360, 363, 366, 368, 374–75, 377, 393, 395, 428–29

Richmond *Examiner,* 229

Rickarby, W. D., 29, 53

Ricketts, Evans, 415

Ricketts, James B., 40, 112n, 118n, 137n

Rierson, P., 227

Riley. *See* Reilly

Ringgold, Ga., 269

Ripley, Roswell S., 144

"The Rivals," 298

Riviere, E., 18

Robertson, Felix H., 409

Robertson, Jerome B., 254

Rock Spring, Ga., 273, 275

Rocky Run, Va., 380

Rodd, J. E., 17, 190

Rodes, Robert E., 145, 243

Rodman, Isaac P., 137n

Rogers, Arthur L., 100, 103–105, 106n

Roman, Alfred, 429

Rome, Ga., 414

Rosecrans, William S., 284, 288–89

"Rose Hill," 236

Roselius, Mr., 129n

Ross, A. M., 209

Ross, Fitzgerald, 244, 256, 289, 290n, 303

Ross, W. H., 367n

Rosser, Thomas L., 16, 25, 33, 43, 54, 55, 54n–57n, 58, 73, 76, 85, 120, 122, 125, 376–77, 431

Rossiter, C., 17, 28, 191, 317, 320

Ruggles, Daniel, 405–406, 409

Ruggles, Frank D., 17, 28, 134, 188–90, 194

Russell, Samuel F., 414

Rutherford, H., 267

Ryan, Abram J., 431

St. Charles Hotel, New Orleans, 397

St. James Church, 106, 236

St. Paul, Henry, 58, 62, 72n, 73, 171

Salem, Va., 110

Salem Church, 224

Saltville, Va., 263–64

Sanders, J. W., 72, 72n, 73

Sanford, John S., 267, 271, 302

Sanford, John W. A., 268

Sanford, Maj., 324

Savannah, Ga., 366

Scott, Winfield, 320

Second Corps (Army of the Potomac), 249, 351

Sedgwick, John, 137n, 143–44, 144n, 212–14, 220–22, 220n, 224, 228, 230

Seibels, John L., 26

Seibrecht, Louie, 415
Seignor Knighti, 206
Selph, Dudley, 430
Seminary Hill, 244, 246
Semmes, Paul J., 143
Semmes, Raphael, 337
Semple, Henry C., 422
Seven Days, battle of, 86–95
Seven Pines, battle of, 82–83, 83n, 91
Sewell, Billy, 414
Seymour, William J., 216
Shaler, Alexander, 220
Sharpsburg, battle of, 140, 166
Sharpsburg, Md., 136n, 137, 138, 138n, 146, 155n, 159, 168
Sharpsburg National Cemetery, 138n
Shenandoah River, 237–38
Shepherdstown, Md., 155n, 160, 162–63
Sheridan, Philip, 279n, 280n, 366, 375, 381–84, 386
"Sherman's Battery," 50
Sherman, William T., 366, 395, 413
Shiloh, battle of, 274, 405–11
Shoup, Francis A., 406
Shoup's Battery, 406
Siebrecht, P., 227
Siexas, James M., 411
Sillers, Maj., 145
Simmons, J. H., 414
Simmons, T. G., 319
Sixth Corps, 145, 148, 221, 337, 369
Slaten, C. W., 315–16

Slidell, John, 51
Slocomb, Cuthbert H., 17, 18, 21, 33, 56, 57n, 58, 273–74, 290, 401, 406, 408, 410, 412–14, 419, 421–22, 431
Slocomb, Mrs. C. H., 429
Slocum, Henry W., 137n
Smith, Benjamin H., Jr., 209
Smith, "Dignity," 67
Smith, E. W., 227
Smith, Edmund Kirby, 39
Smith, Gustavus W., 83
Smith, Marshall J., 408
Smith, Persifor F., 1
Smith, Pvt. (driver), 247
Smith, William "Extra Billy," 128
Smith, William F., 137n, 145, 148
Smithfield, Md., 239n
Soria, Capt., 2
Sorrel, G. Moxley, 76, 107, 113, 127, 148, 195, 200, 231, 236n, 243, 278, 302, 359, 362
South Carolina troops: Brooks' Battery, 209; Charleston German Battery, 116, 138, 208; McBeth Battery, 100, 146, 148n, 149n; Palmetto Battery, 152, 208; Pee Dee Battery, 152–53, 208; Hampton's Legion, 36; 2d Cavalry, 234; 2d Infantry, 39; 8th Infantry, 39; 15th Infantry, 153; 18th Infantry, 342; Hagood's Brigade, 313
South Mountain, Md., 137, 144
Spanish Fort, battle of, 415, 424
Spear, Col., 220, 226

Spearing, R. McK., 18, 171, 194
Spencer, S. W., 72n, 73
Sperryville, Va., 236
Spottswood House, Richmond,
    15n, 80. 290, 295, 298, 395
Spottsylvania Courthouse, 232
Squires, Charles W., 17, 25, 34,
    36, 55, 56, 57n, 73, 84, 91, 95,
    100, 103–104, 105n–10n, 116,
    123, 125, 138, 141, 150, 152,
    162–64, 178, 185, 190–91,
    193n, 198, 209, 214, 217, 223,
    227–28, 261, 309, 431
Stafford Heights, 175, 179, 182,
    195, 217, 233
Stakeman, Ben, 414
Stanhope, Philip W., 96–97
Stannard's Farm, 232
Stansel, Martin L., 268, 325n
Starke, William E., 143
Starr, Henry, 397n
Steven, William, 411
Stevensburg, Va., 101
Stewart, Alexander P., 271, 280
Stewart, Maj., 239
Stocker, Charles H., 108n, 177,
    313
Stone, John H., 344n
Strawberry Plains, Tenn., 305
Stribling, Robert M., 100,
    103–104, 106n, 107n, 108n,
    109n, 208, 261, 267n
Strong, Robert, 411
Stuart, James E. B., 30, 54n, 58,
    66–68, 75, 85, 95, 114, 117,
    120, 125, 137n, 139, 159–60,
    233–35, 235n, 242

Stuart, Oscar, 228
Stuart, William B., 414
Sturdevant, N. U., 311, 367n
Sturgis, Samuel D., 187, 189
Sudley Ford, Va., iv, 41 (map),
    114, 115, 127
Summers, H. D., 227
Summerville, Ga., 273
Sumner, Edwin V., 137n, 143–44,
    148
Swain, Andy, 418
Sweetwater, Tenn., 269
Sweitzer, N. B., 96–97
Sykes, George, 120n, 121n, 161n,
    162, 192, 193n

Tarleton, John A., 26, 28
Taylor, Tom, 45
Taylor, Walter H., 234n, 328, 356,
    382, 393
Taylor, Zachary, 2
Tel-el-Kebir, battle of, 183n
Tennessee Campaign, 1864, pp.
    420, 424
Tennessee River, 266, 271
Tennessee troops: Eldridge's Bat-
    tery, 268, 271; McClung's Bat-
    tery, 408; Williams's Battery,
    268, 271; 2d Infantry, 410;
    21st Infantry, 408; 63d In-
    fantry, 268
Terry, William R., 325n
Texas troops, 5th Infantry, 120,
    127
Thomas, E., 249n
Thomas, Edward L., 371
Thomas, Francis, 298

Thomas, George H., 284–85, 292–93

Thompson, Hugh, 108n

Thompson, J. A., 367n

Thompson, Thomas P., 144

Thorn Hill, Va., 77

Thoroughfare Gap, 111–13

Toledano, Oswald J., 345

Toombs, Robert A., 112, 115, 123–24, 139, 151–54, 164

Tracy, Elisha L., 2, 4, 401

Travers, William, 396

Trigg, Mrs., 301

Trigg, Robert C., 267–68, 273, 276–77, 279, 283

Trimble, Isaac R., 142, 143

Trudeau, James, 407

Tully, H., 26

Tully, James, 108n

Tupelo, Miss., 411–13

Turner's Gap, Md., 135–36

Turner, Sumpter, 227, 319

Turner, Thomas S., 17, 109n, 227

Tyler, Daniel, 32n, 33n

Tyler, Erastus B., 192

Tyner's Station, Tenn., 288

Underhill, E. M., 429

Underhill, G. B., 429

Union Hill, Va., 14

Union Mills, Va., 29, 41 (map), 43

Union Mills Ford, 25, 33

United States Army (regulars): Graham's Battery, 1st Artillery, 147n; Robertson's Horse Battery, 147n; 2d Artillery; Co. E, 3d Artillery; Co.

D, 5th Artillery, 54, 161n; Co. G, 5th Artillery United States Marines, 40

United States Arsenal, Baton Rouge, 4–5, 5n, 6n

Urquhart, David, 7

Urquhart, R., 331

Valentine, John B., 227, 320

Van Dorn, Earl, 60–61

Vaught, William C. D., 274, 401, 406, 408, 412

Venable, Charles S., 157

Vicksburg, Miss., 20

Victoria Cross, 305

Villasana, Frank de P., 426

Vincent, Louis, 415

Vinson, Van, 227

Virginia troops: Albemarle Battery, 233, 311; Alburtis'–Wise's Battery, 36, 100; Allegheny Battery, 142, 208; Amherst Battery, 209; Ashland Battery, 192, 209; Bath Battery, 209; Bedford Battery, 192, 209; Botetourt Artillery, 100, 103; Charlottesville Battery, 208; Danville Battery, 209; Davidson Battery, 302, 306; Dixie Artillery, 69, 72, 92, 100, 103, 109n, 116, 153; Fauquier Artillery, 100, 103–104, 106n, 107n, 108n, 109n, 208; Fluvanna Battery, 209; Fredericksburg Battery, 154, 208; Goochland Artillery, 100; Henrico (Courtney), 208;

Jackson's Flying Battery, 209;
Jeffress's Battery, 268, 276,
302; King William Battery,
208; Latham's–Blount's Battery, 34–35, 208; Lee Battery,
208; Lewis's Battery (Pittsyl-
vania), 207; Loudoun Battery,
100, 103; Lowrey Battery, 306;
Lynchburg Battery, 208, 302;
Martin's Battery, 319; Monroe
Artillery, 100; Morris (Louisa)
Battery, 208; Norfolk Battery,
207; Norfolk Blues Battery,
207; Otey Battery, 306, 347,
352, 360, 368; Parker's Battery, 209, 213, 220n, 228;
Peeples's Battery, 268, 273,
275–76; Powhatan Battery,
209; Purcell Battery, 154, 208;
Richmond Battery, 154, 208;
Richmond Fayette, 208, 316,
318; Richmond Hampden Battery, 142, 208; 1st Co. Richmond Howitzers, 208; 2d Co.
Richmond Howitzers, 209;
Richmond Letcher, 208; Richmond Orange Battery, 208;
Ringgold Battery, 306; Rockbridge Artillery No. 1, pp. 36,
141n, 209; Rockbridge Ar-
tillery No. 2, p. 209; Salem
Flying Battery, 209; Staunton
Artillery, 34–35, 208; Thirteenth Artillery Battalion, 305,
328, 346–47, 389; Thomas Artillery, 100, 116, 138; Warrenton Battery, 209; Wolihin's

Battery, 268, 275–76; 4th Cavalry, 234; 5th Cavalry, 86; 1st
Infantry, 31, 51, 64, 76, 81;
7th Infantry, 27, 39, 325n; 8th
Infantry, 61; 24th Infantry,
39, 179; 33d Infantry, 40; 54th
Infantry, 268; 63d Infantry,
268
Vizetelly, Frank, 183, 183n, 289,
303
Von Coln, Phil, 14, 227

Wade, John J., 268
Waggaman, Eugene, 94
Walke, Richard, 361
Walker, Alexander, 51
Walker, D. L., 306, 347
Walker, James A., 378
Walker, John G., 137n, 140n, 142,
146, 148n, 155n, 166
Walker, Joseph, 152–53
Walker, Leroy Pope, 7–8
Walker, Reuben L., 184, 208,
232n, 234n, 249n, 366–67,
367n, 380–81
Walker, Stephen W., 322
Walker, T. F., 4
Walker, William H. T., 276–78
Walsh, James, 220
Walsh, John A., 411
Walthal Junction, Va., 311–12
Walton, J. B., vi, 3, 5, 7–8, 12,
14, 14n, 18, 20, 22, 26, 29, 30,
34–35, 37, 38, 42, 52, 53, 53n,
57n, 59–60, 65, 69, 71, 73, 77,
80n, 84–85; 85, 85n, 86n,
90–93, 90n, 103, 105, 105n,

107, 107n, 113, 116–17,
122–26, 139, 150, 156, 165,
165n, 168, 177, 178n, 179n,
182–83, 185–86, 189, 198n,
199–200, 202, 209, 211–12,
215–16, 218, 227, 231, 232,
234n, 238, 239n, 243, 247–48,
249n, 256, 262, 269, 290n,
295, 308–10, 338 (resignation),
399, 426–27
Walton, Thomas, 148
"Waltonville," 69, 71, 74, 201
"Waltonville War-Cry," 73, 171
Walworth, Nathan, 280n
Ward, Bolivar, 63, 206
Ward, Frank, 298
Warren, Gouverneur K., 121n,
220
Warrenton, Va., 170
Washington, D. C., 55, 58, 64, 74,
122, 229, 335, 337, 395
Washington Artillery Varieties
Company, 205
Waterloo, battle of, 30–31
Watson, David, 209
Watson, John W., 411
Webster, G. T., 389n
Weldon Railroad, 330, 351, 358
West, Douglas, 286
West, W. H., 109n, 215, 226
West Point (U.S. Military Acad-
emy), 16
Wheat, Chatham Roberdeau, 34,
36, 42, 64–65
Wheaton, Frank, 213–14
Whitcomb, H., 345
White, Blake, 228–29

White, D. P., 72n
White, H. N., 126
"White Horse Battery" (Fifth
Company, W. A.), 413
White, Julius, 347
White Oak Swamp, 329
White Plains, Va., 110
Whitfield, Edwin, 267, 271
Whiting, William H. C., 112
Whitney, C. M., 429
Whittier, John G., 134
Whittington, J. B., 27, 28, 34,
57n, 58
Wigfall, Louis T., 14
Wilcox, Cadmus M., 112, 115–16,
118, 118n, 120, 169, 213–15,
219, 224, 248, 252, 329–30,
333, 371
Wilder, John T., 280n
Wilderness, battle of, 321
Wilderness Tavern, 233
Willcox, Orlando B., 137n
Williams, Alpheus S., 137n
Williams, Charles W., 107n
Williams, L. B., Jr., 76
Williamsburg, Va., 78
Williamsport, Md., 239n, 240,
256–58, 258n, 260
Willoughby Run, 246
Wilmington, N. C., 294–95
Wilson, Dan, 42
Wilson, James H., 335
Wilson, T. J., 320
Wiltz, Louis A., 428
Winchester, Va., 39, 162, 168–69,
169n, 236n, 237, 239
Wing, C. S., 411

Wingate, R. J. "Bob," 345
Winston, Tom B., 414
Winthrop, Capt., 301
Wisconsin troops: 2d Infantry, 41
Wise's Brigade, 320
Withers, John, 300
Wolseley, Sir Garnet, 169, 169n, 183n
Wood, John, 177, 183, 344n
Wood, Mr., 54
Wood, Thomas A., 284
Woodling, George W., 142, 209
Woods, Asa, 414

Woodruff, Capt., 194, 303
Woodville, Va., 236
Woolfolk, Picheqru, Jr., 192, 209, 260
Wright, Ambrose R., 344
Wright, S. T., 367n
Wyatt, James W., 233n
Wyndham, Percy, 235

Yorktown, Va., 77–78
Young, Pvt., 311

Zebal, H. L., 26, 28